New Visions for the Developmental Assessment of
Infants and Young Children

## Mission Statement

ZERO TO THREE's urgent mission is to advance the healthy development of America's babies and young children. We strengthen and support professionals, policymakers, and parents by: increasing public awareness; fostering professional excellence through training; inspiring tomorrow's leaders; promoting the discovery and application of new knowledge, model approaches, and "best practices"; stimulating effective service approaches and responsive policies; and educating parents and other caregivers about significant differences they can make in the lives of babies and young children.

Matthew E. Melmed, *Executive Director*
Carol P. Berman, *Associate Director*
Emily S. Fenichel, *Associate Director*
Haida S. McGovern, *Associate Director*

# New Visions for the Developmental Assessment of Infants and Young Children

SAMUEL J. MEISELS and

EMILY FENICHEL, Editors

ZERO
TO
THREE

National Center
for Infants,
Toddlers, and
Families

Cover Photo: Marilyn Nolt, Souderton, PA
Design: Susan Lehmann, Washington, D.C.
Copy Editor: Susan M. Spencer, Washington, D.C.
Printer: Corporate Press, Landover, MD

ISBN 0-943657-35-0
Library of Congress Catalog Card Number: 96-61078
Printed in the United States of America
First printing, August 1996
Second printing, March 1997
Third printing, March 1999

# Contents

# Preface

This book, like most worthwhile human creations, is a product of both passion and pain. It reflects adults' passion to understand the process and meaning of children's earliest development, as well as the commitment of families and professionals to nurture and enhance children's growth to the fullest extent possible. This book also reflects the pain that has been caused, or exacerbated, when lack of understanding or misguided practices and priorities have ignored, underestimated, or even undermined the developmental capacities of children and families.

Parents, clinicians, researchers, and policymakers from many backgrounds and disciplines have contributed to the "new vision for the developmental assessment of infants and young children" that this volume represents. This vision is most definitely a work in progress. It began taking shape in the summer of 1992, when ZERO TO THREE/National Center for Clinical Infant Programs (renamed ZERO TO THREE: National Center for Infants, Toddlers, and Families in 1996) convened a multidisciplinary parent/professional Work Group on Developmental Assessment. The task of the Work Group was to identify both problems and promising approaches in current assessment paradigms, policies, and practices. The vision grew from a preliminary list of principles scrawled on flip charts in a hotel conference room to a statement by the Work Group (which was distributed at ZERO TO THREE's National Training Institute in 1993 and was published in an article in the bulletin *Zero to Three* in 1994, which appears in this volume as chapter 1) to the

18 chapters you are about to read. Many of these chapters describe approaches to assessment and support of children's development that are currently being tested, as well as ideas that will guide research and practical innovations in years to come.

*New Visions for the Developmental Assessment of Infants and Young Children* is organized into five sections.

The two chapters of the first section, "New Visions of Assessment," define developmental assessment as a process designed to deepen our understanding of a child's competencies and resources, enhance our perspective on the caregiving and learning environments most likely to help a child make fullest use of his or her developmental potential, and describe the essential connections between assessment and intervention.

In the second section, "Parents' Perspectives," experienced parent advocates reflect on the complementary responsibilities of parents and professionals in the process of understanding and nurturing young children's capacities. They describe what it takes to achieve needed change in policy and practice.

The chapters comprising the third section, "Contextual Perspectives," remind us of how limited the "vision" of any one of us tends to be as we try, on our own, to understand the meaning of a baby's or toddler's behavior in the complex context of his or her family, community, and culture. These chapters suggest ways in which careful observation, listening, reflection, and trustworthy alliances with families and colleagues can expand our vision and make us more effective nurturers of young children's remarkable capacities for growth.

The fourth section of this volume, "New Approaches to Assessment," contains 10 chapters by researchers and clinicians whose pioneering efforts give practical meaning to a new vision for developmental assessment. Whether they are striving to help parents and practitioners create the fullest possible profile of a young child's development or are directing their attention to the nuances of a particular developmental period or domain, the contributors to this section maintain their focus on the critical issue—discovering the capacities and resources in the child and in the caregiving environment that can sustain and enhance developmental momentum.

The fifth and final section of this book, "Assessment and the Policy Context," reminds us that the values of the larger society—expressed, to a large extent, in its allocation of public resources—play a critical role in determining the opportunities available to children to achieve their fullest developmental potential. This country has taken important steps toward realizing a fair and equitable vision of support for the developmental capacities of all its infants and young children, but it still has a great distance to cover. ZERO TO THREE: National Center for Infants, Toddlers, and Families presents this volume in order to encourage continuing dialogue and debate, and the creation of ever more powerful and expanded visions of developmental assessment so that young children and their families can lead fuller and more satisfying lives.

The development and publication of this volume have been made possible through the generous support of the A. L. Mailman Family Foundation, whose board of directors and staff are steadfast in their passionate dedication to the well-being of this country's young children and families. We are grateful, as well, to the board, staff, and friends of ZERO TO THREE, who have made this extraordinary organization a true home for all who appreciate the importance of the earliest years of life.

Samuel J. Meisels and Emily Fenichel, *Editors*

# I. New Visions of Assessment

# 1. Toward a New Vision for the Developmental Assessment of Infants and Young Children

STANLEY I. GREENSPAN
and SAMUEL J. MEISELS,
with the ZERO TO THREE
Work Group on Developmental
Assessment*

Developmental assessment is a process designed to deepen understanding of a child's competencies and resources, and of the caregiving and learning environments most likely to help a child make fullest use of his or her developmental potential. Assessment should be an ongoing, collaborative process of systematic observation and analysis. This process involves formulating questions, gathering information, sharing observations, and making interpretations in order to form new questions.

The systematic assessment of various aspects of children's knowledge, skills, or personality involves some of the most difficult questions that early childhood researchers, practitioners, and policymakers must face. For example:

• Which features of a child's knowledge, skills, or personality can and should be measured?

---

* The ZERO TO THREE Work Group on Developmental Assessment was convened in July 1992 to discuss the state of the art of assessing the developmental status of infants and young children from the perspective of parents, professionals in a range of disciplines, and policymakers. The members of the group were Kathryn E. Barnard, R.N., Ph.D., Isaura Barrera, Ph.D., Carol Berman, Ph.D., Diane Bricker, Ph.D., Diana Cuthbertson, Stanley I. Greenspan, M.D., Asa G. Hilliard, III, Ed.D., Samuel J. Meisels, Ed.D., Lucy Jane Miller, Ph.D., O.T.R., Cordelia C. Robinson, Ph.D., Rebecca Shahmoon Shanok, M.S.W., Ph.D., Jack P. Shonkoff, M.D., Eleanor S. Szanton, Ph.D., Amy Wetherby, Ph.D., Serena Wieder, Ph.D., Mark Wolery, Ph.D., and Barry Zuckerman, M.D., F.A.A.P.

- Can the rapidly changing characteristics of infants, toddlers, and preschoolers be measured reliably?
- How can we enhance the accuracy of the measurements that are conducted in early childhood?
- Are assessment approaches in early childhood meaningful when conducted in isolation from the child's family and living conditions?
- Does information from early childhood assessments successfully predict long-term developmental status?

## ▤ Critical Issues in the Assessment of Infants ▪ and Young Children

Assessment is the process of obtaining information for the purpose of making evaluative decisions. The choice of a given assessment tool or approach depends on the type of decision that will be required as a result of the assessment. Assessments may be performed in order to:

1. Identify children who are likely to be members of groups at risk for health or developmental problems (screening);

2. Confirm the presence and extent of a disability (diagnosis);

3. Determine appropriate remediation (program planning);

4. Ascertain a child's relative knowledge of specific skills and information (readiness tests); or

5. Demonstrate the extent of a child's previous accomplishments (achievement tests).

Some assessment approaches are quite circumscribed in their goals. For example, assessing how long a child will look at a picture as part of a research study on preferential looking behavior has very limited goals and highly standardized parameters. Most assessment approaches, however, are part of a larger "clinical" decisionmaking process having to do with diagnosing emotional, cognitive, or other developmental problems, and/or planning and monitoring intervention. This discussion addresses developmental assessment in this broader context.

Any specific assessment approach is primarily a sampling process. It consists of a "snapshot," or series of snapshots, of a child's knowledge, skills, abilities, or personality characteristics taken at a particular point in time, from a particular vantage point, and with a particular instrument or recording device. A measurement or assessment approach that is not representative of a child's usual functioning will not be meaningful. This is a particularly important concern since the first three years of life constitute a period of such immense modification, growth, and development.

The constructs and phenomena that are assessed should be closely related to core processes of human growth and development. For assessment approaches to be meaningful, therefore, they must incorporate knowledge of how development transpires and how children's growth in the first few years of life is enhanced. One must recognize that development is a complex process. From the very beginning of life, multiple factors influence its course. Although areas of development can be addressed separately, they are not necessarily independent. Rather, they are interdependent.

Related to the interactivity among areas of development is the fact that both biological and environmental influences operate to support, facilitate, or impede the development of infants and young children. Thus, interpretations of data from assessments should consider both the child's biological status and the impact of environmental factors on the aspect of development assessed. For example, when one is assessing general cognitive functioning of a 2-year-old, one must look at observational or test data in the context of the child's experience. Is the child being assessed challenged by premature birth or a medical condition, living in poverty, and spending most of his or her waking hours in a poor-quality child care setting? Or is the child the product of a healthy, full-term delivery, and is he or she living in an economically secure, two-parent household that affords ample opportunity for play and discovery?

An understanding of protective and risk factors in the caregiving environment is essential to meaningful assessment. This is particularly the case for very young children and for children who are at risk developmentally. Longitudinal research by Sameroff and his colleagues makes this point very clearly (Sameroff, Seifer, Barocas, Zax, & Greenspan, 1987). Their study of 215 families in Rochester, New York, examined 10 variables thought likely to have a major impact on the development of children's competence at age four, including maternal mental health, parents' anxiety, education and occupation of the parents, family social support, and stressful life events.

Sameroff and his colleagues found that the higher the number of risk factors, the lower the competence of the child. More than 50 percent of the variance in 4-year-olds' verbal IQ could be explained by taking into account the environmental context of the child. Children with four or more risk factors were 20 times more likely to have marginal cognitive functioning than children who were subject to fewer than four risk factors. No *single* risk factor was always present or always absent among the children who were experiencing cognitive difficulties. Thus, an assessment approach which is intended to identify existing or potential developmental problems in young children and to suggest interventions that might eliminate or reduce risk factors needs to use a mixed measurement strategy that incorporates a wide range of data.

Knowledge and an understanding of the cultural context of a young child's caregiving environment is essential to understanding the meaning of the child's repertoire of skills, knowledge, and personality characteristics. Family and community culture influence, among other experiences, the child's access to multiple approaches to literacy; expectations regarding educational accomplishments; explicit and implicit connections to rite, ritual, and tradition; and overall sense of familial/communal interaction and support.

For measurement in early childhood to be faithful to the phenomena it seeks to document—for it to be meaningful—it must take into account how children are affected by the contexts in which they are reared. It is not necessary for each assessment approach to set the impossible task of taking all of this complexity into account at once. However, in order to give the data meaning, even assessments of relatively isolated aspects of functioning should be interpreted within a larger conceptual framework.

Assessment approaches that rely on structured tasks or questions in early childhood are marked by recurrent practical problems that contribute to error in determining early childhood capacities (Meisels, 1994):

- Young children have a restricted ability to comprehend assessment cues.

- Young children's verbal and perceptual-motor response capabilities are limited.

- Some types of questions require complex information-processing skills that young children do not possess.

- Young children may have difficulty understanding what is being asked of them in an assessment situation, and they may not be able to control their behavior to meet these demands.

It is no easy task to identify behaviors that represent the infant's or child's true range and depth of capacities; to understand the biological endowment, current health status, and caregiving environment that form the context for a young child's functioning; or to help a child represent his or her range of functioning, given immature perceptual and motor capacities. As we look at existing approaches to assessment in the first three years of life, we are struck by how much work is needed before the field adequately addresses these critical issues.

## ▤ Limitations of Current Assessment
## ▤ Approaches

Despite widespread awareness of the importance of a systematic, contextually based approach to the developmental assessment of infants and young children, demands for "immediate expertise" and the pressures associated with enormous service challenges present formidable barriers to best practice. Because professionals feel that they must act quickly, a fragmented, piecemeal, occasionally undermining approach to assessment has emerged, rather than one that reflects a comprehensive, integrated understanding of infants and young children and their relationships within their families and larger communities and cultures.

Under pressure to produce quick formulations or "scores," professionals have often called on their experiences with procedures and instruments developed for assessing selected competencies and skills in older children. These procedures and instruments can often yield misleading information. They are not built on a model of how the infant and young child develop within the family; they do not reflect an understanding of the specific types of difficulties and developmental challenges that children and families face in the first three years of life; and they do not represent the best ways to observe and assess the dynamic developmental process as it occurs in infancy and early childhood.

In addition, there has been a tendency to assess the functions of infants and young children for which there are tests or scales already in existence. We have generally put less emphasis on the aspects of development that are hard to measure and, as indicated earlier, have underemphasized the social and family contexts within which the infant or young child develops.

The most important factor is that we have not yet met the challenge of working with the infant's or young child's individual differences in the family context to elicit the best level of functioning. Indeed, it is commonplace for assessment approaches to overlook some of the capacities of the infant or young child, particularly those associated with social interactions. This seems to be the case especially when an infant or young child has severe relationship and communication difficulties that may interfere with his or her demonstration of seemingly hidden emotional or cognitive strengths.

Some assessment approaches may, inadvertently, be stressful for the infant or young child, and his or her family, or may undermine them. Not infrequently, for example, infants are expected to quickly perform for a stranger. More often than not, they are not adequately observed in interaction with parents or caregivers. At times, infants and young children are even separated from parents for the purposes of assessment.

## ▤ The Zero to Three Work Group on Developmental Assessment

The challenge before the field is to rethink our approach to the assessment of infants and young children and base it on our best state-of-the-art knowledge of infant and early childhood development. In recent years, there has been progress in assessing hard-to-measure areas of development, including children's individual differences, temperament, affective (emotional) development, interactive capacities, and coping capacities. We are learning more about the ways families can function to facilitate the development process.

In order to acknowledge this constructive movement and give its evolution encouragement and consolidation, ZERO TO THREE: National Center for Infants, Toddlers, and Families, with the support of the A. L. Mailman Foundation, convened a work group of clinicians, researchers, and parents representing the state-of-the-art knowledge base for assessing infants and young children. The work group took on the task of formulating the basic principles of assessment for infants and young children. It attempted to articulate:

1. Principles that clarify what constitutes an appropriate assessment; and

2. Current assessment practices that are at odds with state-of-the-art understanding of development in infancy and childhood and that should be avoided.

# Principles of an Appropriate Assessment

### Assessment must be based on an integrated developmental model.

Assessment of an infant or young child with developmental and emotional challenges must take into account the full complexity of the child's development. This includes the core functional areas of the child's development, as well as the factors that influence these areas. The functional areas include the child's functional emotional and social capacities; cognitive capacities; and language, motor, and sensory functioning. They also include the constitutional and maturational variations that influence the child's development, as well as the caregiver, family, community, and cultural patterns that influence it.

Most importantly, this approach to assessment represents an effort to understand infants and young children in the context of their families and their emergent developmental abilities to communicate with the world and relate to it. This approach recognizes that, in order to understand a child's capacities, we must find ways to see the child's *optimal* level of functioning. This means that parents or other familiar adults are *working* with the child, using what they know about his or her interests and abilities to discover more, through assessment approaches, about the child's capacities and the challenges he or she is facing. Parents and professionals must observe the range of the child's functioning in different contexts. We do not wish to test and grade a child, but to learn how best to be of help to that child.

### Assessment involves multiple sources of information and multiple components.

Assessment includes most prominently:

- The parents' description of the child's capacities in the different areas of development and discussions with the parents to determine their questions and concerns about the child's development;

- The parents' detailed description of the child's developmental history;

- Direct observation of the child, including interaction between the child and the caregiver(s);

- Observations of the family and discussions with them about ways they have found to support the child's development and about family patterns related to the child's development that are of concern to them; and

- Focused observations and/or assessments of specific areas of the child's functioning.

This approach builds on information from family members and adds sources of information—such as direct observation of the child's play and, if needed, assessment of a specific area of functioning—to help answer questions about the child's development. This approach is in marked contrast to some examples of current practice in which examiners use a series of structured assessment tools that look at specific areas of development, with only brief attempts to obtain a picture of the "whole" child from the family or other sources of information.

**An assessment should follow a certain sequence.**

1. Establishing an alliance with the parents, listening to their views of the child's strengths and challenges, and discussing the issues to be explored in the assessment;

2. Obtaining a developmental history of the child and an initial picture of the family's experience. While basic information may be readily available, some insights may only emerge over time, as part of an ongoing relationship and working alliance with the parents;

3. Observing the child in the context of unstructured play with the parent(s) or other familiar caregivers;

4. If appropriate, observing interaction between the child and a clinician;

5. Making specific assessments of individual functions in the child, as needed; and

6. Using a developmental model as a framework for integrating all the data obtained from parents' reports, direct observa-

tion, and other sources, and conveying and discussing assessment findings in the context of an alliance with the child's primary caregivers, with the potential for starting an intervention process if needed.

## The child's relationship and interactions with his or her most trusted caregiver should form the cornerstone of an assessment.

Emotional and social competencies, as well as cognitive, language, motor, and sensory patterns, should always be assessed in the context of spontaneous, motivated interactions between child and caregiver. This context provides an optimal setting for security and engagement (active interaction between the child and his or her environment), and is most likely to bring out the child's abilities. The clinician/assessor can build on these natural interactions, either through coaching the parent to try certain types of interactions in order to elicit a particular competency or through becoming part of the interaction pattern along with the caregiver.

Occasionally, when a caregiver has difficulty interacting with the child in a way that allows the child to evidence certain competencies, the clinician may need to use his or her own interactions with the child as the basis for observations of the child's competencies. Before the clinician interacts directly with an infant or young child, he or she must take time to get to know the child and must be sure that the child feels secure and comfortable in the interaction.

## An understanding of sequences and timetables in typical development is essential as a framework for the interpretation of developmental differences among infants and toddlers.

The period from birth to three is one of rapid physical growth and maturational change. While maturation generally proceeds in an orderly and predictable sequence, there may be considerable variation in both the characteristics of a particular skill and the timetable for the emergence of the skill. Therefore, there is considerable range in what can be regarded as normal or typical development.

There is more range in the expectable capacities of children in some areas of development than there is in others. For example, as long as an infant's social relating is increasing during the first few years of life, there is no significant concern, but if a child is only beginning to sit up without support as the end of the first year approaches, there is a clear need for a full assessment and potential intervention. To understand where a child is in his or her development, clinicians need to have in mind a broad sense of the *sequence* (what precedes what) and *timetable* (during what age range one can expect to see a capacity emerge) for different areas of development.

Understanding where a child is in his or her development in terms of sequence and expectable timetable allows the clinician to recognize what will come next in the child's development and to assess whether a particular capacity is emerging more slowly than expected. This kind of analysis is preferable to using a "score" or "quotient" to describe a child's developmental status. It allows the clinician to integrate many sources of information and formulate an intervention plan based on an understanding of the child's next steps in his or her developmental sequence.

The well-trained professional (or team) must have sufficient experience in observing a wide range of infants and toddlers, as well as their families, if he or she is to make judgments about (a) a child's mastery of certain developmental capacities in terms of the skills the child has acquired in relation to established or accepted norms; (b) the quality of the child's skills; and (c) the challenges that need to be met to help the child master new skills in the developmental sequence. The point is sometimes made that it is easier and less time-consuming to train professionals to conduct a standardized test than it is to train them in the skills of building alliances with parents, careful observation of children in spontaneous interaction, systematic organization of data from multiple sources, and clinical decisionmaking. This is true. However, we take the very strong position that only professionals with an excellent understanding of early development and demonstrated competence in the skills listed above should be given responsibility for assessments that will lead to a determination of a child's developmental status and/or a plan for intervention.

### Assessment should emphasize attention to the child's level and pattern of organizing experience and to functional capacities, which represent an integration of emotional and cognitive abilities.

The child's functional capacities involve such basic abilities as (a) paying attention; (b) relating and engaging; (c) entering into reciprocal, intentional interactions; (d) organizing, exhibiting, and recognizing patterns of behavior in terms of purpose and function; (c) constructing symbolic (representational) under- standing of the world, including affects (outward expressions of emotion), wishes, and intentions; and (f) learning to construct and observe relationships within this symbolic world (symbolic problem-solving).

These functional capacities can be described in detail. Each functional capacity, in addition to representing an integration of emotional and cognitive capacities, also builds on the child's lan- guage and on motor and sensory abilities (Greenspan, 1992, and this volume).

The child's level and pattern of organizing experience must be understood within the cultural context of the child and family. Most cultures support the child's development of the basic func- tional capacities of relating, interacting, and thinking. Yet spe- cific ways of relating and interacting, as well as the content of what is communicated with behavior or play and words, may vary considerably from culture to culture.

Specific areas of functioning should always be assessed and understood in the context of the child's broad functional capac- ities. For example, a desire to learn more about a young child's apparent difficulty in comprehending certain sequences of words may be addressed first through observation and then, if neces- sary, through use of specialized assessment tools and approach- es. It is essential to understand the impact of the specific diffi- culty on the child's core functional capacities. For example, one child with auditory-processing difficulties may use cues from adults' facial expressions and gestures, as well as observation of other children's behavior, to organize his or her behavior pur- posefully and thereby conform this behavior to group expecta- tions in a child care setting. Another child with similar auditory- processing difficulties may have less well-developed functional capacities and may be unable to organize his or her behavior and make it purposeful, thereby becoming impulsive and disorga- nized in a group care setting.

**The assessment process should identify the child's current competencies and strengths, as well as the competencies which will constitute developmental progression in a con- tinuous growth model of development.**

Many aspects of children's development proceed in a stepwise fashion; one capacity builds on another. Consider, for example, a 30-month-old child who relates to his or her caregiver but only with one or two simple gestures at a time. The child may be able to play peekaboo for 10 seconds but cannot yet sustain a long pattern of interaction or use words or pretend play. Our knowledge of developmental progression tells us that the child now needs to learn how to sustain a longer pattern of reciprocal interactions and then how to progress to complex, interactive social patterns, followed by pretend play and words.

Our knowledge of typical development tells us that most children develop the skills of this 30-month-old child by the age of 7 to 9 months. This is important and useful information. It can never be useful, however, to describe such a child as "21 months behind."

### Assessment is a collaborative process.

Assessment involves ongoing collaboration between clinicians and parents in understanding the child and family. Participation in the process of assessment should be open to everyone who is substantially involved in supporting the development of the child and family. Parents and other significant caregivers of the child, members of the family's informal and formal support networks, and professionals with special expertise all have important roles to play. The working alliances they create will vary in composition and assignment of responsibility, depending upon the purpose of the assessment, the questions to be explored, and the extent of involvement that the family chooses.

### The process of assessment should always be viewed as the first step in a potential intervention process.

Creating a working alliance with parents and reaching consensus on a shared view of the child's strengths, vulnerabilities, and new learning challenges are essential steps in identifying and planning ways to support the child's continuing development. Any assessment should contribute positively to this process.

### Reassessment of a child's developmental status should occur in the context of day-to-day family and/or early intervention activities.

The rapid changes in growth and development that typically occur in the first three years of life make ongoing monitoring and frequent reassessment of the child's capacities important.

Careful observation of the child's behavior in multiple but familiar contexts and on multiple occasions will provide a rich picture of the child's current strengths and challenges, as well as the steps to be taken next.

If the child is involved in early intervention, the team that is working with the child and the parents should come together regularly to have a discussion and compare observations. Once a child is involved in early intervention, the multiple sources of information available include the observations of the child, family, and early intervention staff regarding their individual and common day-to-day experiences. This discussion will also identify new developmental goals and the most promising ways of approaching them.

This approach avoids wasting scarce resources on a formal structured assessment conducted outside of the child's day-to-day context of family and community. For administrative purposes, periodic descriptions of the child's capacities in relation to age expectations will reflect the child's experience with intervention and provide a way of looking at the effectiveness of the intervention approach.

## Practices to Avoid in Assessment

Some current practices have no place in an assessment process that is conceptualized as an ongoing, collaborative effort to understand an infant's or young child's competencies and resources. We believe that the following "don'ts" are as important as the preceding positive guidelines for developmental assessment.

### Young children should never be challenged during assessment by separation from their parents or familiar caregivers.

A number of children have been diagnosed as having severe relationship disorders because they were extremely aloof and aimless in the context of assessment by relative strangers in new settings. In these situations, the examiners minimally observed interactions between children and parents and based their mistaken conclusions on their own interactions with the children, which occurred in only one meeting.

Observation of these children in interaction with their parents revealed that the children had extraordinarily intimate and warm ways of relating to their parents. These observations revealed the error of the earlier diagnoses and suggested more appropriate approaches to helping the children overcome the developmental challenges that they did face.

### Young children should never be assessed by a strange examiner.

Unfortunately, in many settings where assessments take place, very young children are introduced to examiners who are strangers. The children are expected, after only a brief "warm-up" period, to demonstrate their highest level of functioning to one or more of these examiners. This practice represents an unnecessary challenge to the child and is highly unlikely to yield meaningful information about the child's true capacities. Assessment by an unfamiliar examiner with the parent restricted to the role of passive observer also represents an unnecessary challenge to the child.

### Assessments that are limited to areas that are easily measurable, such as certain motor or cognitive skills, should not be considered complete.

Many assessments of infants and young children are conducted using tools that have been chosen simply because they are available or because available staff are trained to use them. Such assessments cannot be considered adequate since they do not provide an integrated understanding of the child's development, and they do not include information from caregivers or direct observation of the child's functional capacities as they are manifested in spontaneous interactions with caregivers.

### Formal tests or tools should not be the cornerstone of the assessment of an infant or young child.

Structured test approaches look at what an infant can and cannot do in relationship to a defined set of stimuli or test procedures. The data produced by formal tests tend, as discussed earlier, to be only approximations of real-world functional capacities and, in this sense, are less useful than observations of natural behavior.

Many widely available formal tests were developed and standardized with infants and young children who were not experiencing unusual developmental challenges or special needs. Consequently, these tests are not designed to bring out the unique abilities and potential of children with atypical or challenging developmental patterns. Yet it is the child with special needs who requires early, appropriate assessment and intervention.

In addition, many infants and young children have difficulty paying attention, relating, and conforming to the most basic expectations of formal tests. Skilled examiners who are aware of these factors may use the child's behavior around the test situation as a general, but not definitive, indicator of his or her abilities. The less experienced examiner, however, often mistakenly attempts to draw conclusions from whatever numerical score the child "achieves." In any case, a formal test situation is not the best context in which to observe the functional capacities of an infant or young child.

For too long, we have borrowed an assessment methodology devised for older children—a methodology that is highly limited in its usefulness for them as well—that views testing children in a totally standardized fashion as the psychometric ideal and, in some respects, seals them off from the "invasion" of the clinician. Reliability has taken precedence over validity. We have assumed that test scores represent meaningful information about children's capacities.

Conclusions drawn from misleading scores on standardized tests may lead to inappropriate recommendations for services and educational placements and programs. Compared to complete clinical assessments of infants and toddlers with disabilities or those at risk for developmental difficulties, test results frequently underestimate children's true capacities substantially. Unfortunately, as states and communities assess more and more infants and young children in need of appropriate special services and offer services to them, incorrect service recommendations based on inappropriate assessments may increase. Therefore, assessments of infants and young children that are intended to guide the planning of possible intervention approaches should use structured tests only as needed and only as one part of an integrated approach.

## Summary

The developmental assessment of infants and young children should build on our current understanding of young children's development. The cornerstone of assessment should be the observation of the child in interaction with trusted caregivers and the appreciation of the child's core functional capacities. Assessment involves multiple sources of information, organized and integrated in a continuous growth model of development. Incorporating these approaches into assessment should help parents and professionals to deepen their shared understanding of children's competencies and resources, as well as their understanding of the caregiving and learning environments most likely to help children make fullest use of their developmental potential.

 **References**

Greenspan, S. I. (1992). *Infancy and early childhood*. Madison, CT: International Universities Press.

Meisels, S. J. (1994). Designing meaningful measurements for early childhood. In B. L. Mallory & R. S. New (Eds.), *Diversity and developmentally appropriate practices: Challenges for early childhood education* (pp. 202-222). New York: Teachers College Press.

Sameroff, A. J., Seifer, R., Barocas, R., Zax, M., & Greenspan, S. (1987). IQ scores of 4-year-old children: Social-environmental risk factors. *Pediatrics*, *79*, 343-350.

# 2. Charting the Continuum of Assessment and Intervention

SAMUEL J. MEISELS

Assessment and intervention are critical tools for those who work with young children and their families. Although they are complementary processes, the relationship between assessment and intervention has historically been ill-defined. Early attempts at measuring mental functioning were based on the assumption that the gap separating assessment and intervention was nearly unbridgeable. Binet, in developing his original scale of intelligence, sought a separation between measuring intelligence and carrying out instruction: "It is the intelligence alone that we seek to measure. . . . It is a specially interesting feature of these tests that they permit us, when necessary, to free a beautiful native intelligence from the trammels of the school." (Binet quoted in Gould, 1981, p. 151)

In this chapter, I will discuss the implications of separating and integrating infant and early childhood assessment and intervention. As fully documented by the chapters in this volume, infant/toddler assessment today offers an alternative view to that of Binet, one that is in the process of refining the link between assessment and intervention. My primary task is to trace the evolution of this alternative view of assessment and to illustrate a continuum that leads to a reciprocal, or bidirectional, relationship between assessment and intervention.

# ▤ Conceptions of Assessment and ▩ Intervention

The reason for separating assessment and intervention is relatively simple. Assessment, as typically defined, consists of the measurement of several different aspects of children's knowledge, skill, ability, achievement, or personality. Assessments can be performed to identify children who are likely to be members of high-risk groups (screening), to confirm the presence or absence of a disability (diagnosis), to evaluate a child's intellectual or developmental functioning (IQ/DQ) or his or her socioemotional status (clinical interviews), to determine probable therapy or remediation strategies (program planning), to ascertain a child's relative knowledge of specific skills and information (readiness testing), or to demonstrate the extent of a child's previous accomplishments (achievement tests) (Meisels, 1994, contains a more complete discussion of these points). Commonly, assessments are expected to yield quantifiable representations of children's skills, abilities, or personality variables in relation to normative standards. Many of these measurements purport to reveal children's underlying abilities—the fundamental competence that is expressed or realized in specific performances and that intervention is expected to build upon.

The view that assessment uncovers the child's fundamental abilities is consistent with some perspectives regarding the measurement of IQ, DQ, and other general indexes of cognitive functioning, although it plays a much smaller role in the evaluation of socioemotional and adaptive behaviors. As the earlier quotation from Binet suggests, according to this perspective, measurement of intelligence is separated as much as possible from everyday experience—especially the experience of intervention. Only in this splendid isolation can "untrammeled intelligence" be evaluated.

In fact, intervention is an inseparable aspect of any assessment. When we evaluate a young child's functioning and render a diagnosis or draw a conclusion, we potentially have a major impact on the child—we *intervene* in the lives of this child and his or her family. This impact may result from a host of sources. For example, assessment can change the way the child is perceived by the parents, caregivers, or specialists working with the child and family, who subsequently adopt the judgment that the examiner puts forth, such as: "This is a child who is autistic,"

"This is a child who has nonspecific developmental delay," "This is a child with idiopathic brain damage," "This is an understimulated child whose environment must change before the child can recover," or "This is a child who has the potential to grow and develop normally." Any of these conclusions will potentially affect the family dynamic, even if the conclusion is ultimately rejected by the family (see chapters by Rocco and by Popper in this volume).

Another type of impact comes from a more functional assessment in which the parent is given relatively specific instructions about how to care for the child. For example, "Enroll the child in an early intervention program," "Try to interest the child in playing with toys that provide cognitive challenge and surprise," "Involve other children in the play sessions with your child," or "Keep doing things with your child that bring the two of you feelings of pleasure and effectance." These types of recommendations or conclusions can alter the experiences of the child and family, especially when they are presented as conclusions derived from an assessment.

However, these examples describe a linear, or unidirectional, view of the relationship between assessment and intervention. First, assessment takes place. Then, intervention is set in motion, whether through indirection, as in the first set of examples above, or through design, as in the second group of illustrations. But nowhere does assessment reflect either the impact of intervention or the information that can be acquired through sampling the changes brought about by intervention. The iterative possibility of assessing while intervening, or intervening while assessing, i.e., learning about the child and family in the process of intervention, is overlooked, if not intentionally avoided.

The chapters in this volume reflect a view that contrasts with the linear, or unidirectional, view of the relationship between assessment and intervention. They suggest that assessment without intervention is generally only part of the information that is needed to make decisions about how children can best be cared for, helped, and taught. From this perspective, assessment is not merely a quantification of a child's neurodevelopmental performance, nor is it strictly a sorting mechanism that ranks and compares children, or a way of making a decision about diagnosis, labeling, and placement, or a determination of success and failure. Rather, it is *a means of answering questions about children's knowledge, skill, achievement, or personality that relies on an analysis of children's behavior or performance in a variety of settings.* The type of assessment that will be carried out is intimately connected to our choice of questions—to what we want to know and do. But in no instance should a hermetic seal be erected between assessment and intervention. On the contrary, by opening up assessment to the potential insights acquired during intervention and by recognizing that intervention is, in part, an ongoing process of finding out about children and their families, more information is available to answer our questions, and the questions themselves are embedded in a process of continuous refinement.

## ▤ A Developmental Framework for Assessment

Research about young children's development provides us with several general observations that should be considered with care when designing assessments. These observations are more than simply a rationale for assessment activities; they can and should exert a prescriptive influence over what and how we assess. Described in some detail elsewhere (Meisels & Provence, 1989), the observations are neither novel nor revolutionary, although they tend to be overlooked by many conventional assessments. Used as a template, they provide shape to the types of assessments that will maximize the information needed in order to design meaningful interventions.

### Complexity of development

The child's development is complex and is determined by multiple factors from the very beginning of life. Assessments of development must take into account a child's status in a number of areas, including language, mobility, cognition, the organization of experience, and psychosocial and affective development. However, these areas of development are not independent or separate. Rather, they are interdependent, and they interact in many unexpected ways. This interactive character of human developmental abilities suggests that assessments must be complex and multidimensional in design, rather than focused on single aspects of growth. Following the enactment of mandates over the past generation for comprehensive, coordinated assessments, practitioners have begun to move away from normative assessments that are administered on a single occasion to assessments that rely on criterion-referenced or curriculum-based information, supplemented by clinical judgments and observations on multiple occasions by a team of observers or assessors (see chapters by Berman and Shaw and by Miller and McNulty, this volume).

## Impact of environment

Characteristics of the infant and young child are subject to environmental influences that operate to support, facilitate, or impede development. Among these environmentally sensitive characteristics are the infant's "shared, species-specific biological heritage, the infant's unique genetic makeup, the conditions of intrauterine life, the health of the mother, and events during and immediately following labor and delivery" (Meisels & Provence, 1989, p. 11). Also critical for the infant and young child, as well as for the older child, are the qualities of the child's culture and the nurturing environment overall. Indeed, research has demonstrated that the quality of the child's environment constitutes the most significant influence on development (Garbarino, 1990; Sameroff & Fiese, 1990). Assessments must encompass the child's environment or must, in some way, incorporate an evaluation of the impact of environmental factors on development (see Barrera, this volume). If environmental factors are excluded, assessments may overlook some of the most decisive information available, especially for designing interventions.

## Influence of parental figures

The influences of society and culture are, in the early years, mediated primarily by parental figures. Children's worlds are interpreted for them by their parents, and parents, of course, are influenced greatly by their own life experiences. Thus, the degree of family stress from any source—internal or external—that impinges on the young child will, in part, be a function of the adults' abilities to cope and make use of supports that can buffer this stress (Dunst & Trivette, 1990; Krauss, & Jacobs, 1990). Understanding risk and stress in children and intervening to mitigate them requires an understanding of these factors in their parents' lives as well.

## Role of context

Although assessment in early childhood shares many features with assessment of older children, it differs in its highly inferential character, its focus on the child from multiple perspectives, and its obligation to view the child within a broad context, rather than as an isolated source of information. For assessments in early childhood to be meaningful, they must abide by the principle of *contextualization*. This principle maintains that "the context in which a task is presented alters its very nature by virtue of constraining or facilitating factors inherent in the specific situation" (Messick, 1983, p. 479). Context plays a role in both the administration and the interpretation of early childhood assessments, and it highlights the importance of the link between assessment and intervention.

The four themes mentioned above play a role in the evaluation of the assessments that are presently available to us. They also provide critically important criteria for designing new assessments—especially those with strong links to intervention. As in moving from a topographical map to one replete with place names, destinations, roads, and other features, these themes provide a description of the general territory of early development. Now it is time to see how assessments do or do not take these features into account when providing us with information to help us reach our final goal—the optimal functioning of all children.

## ▤ Varieties of Early Childhood Assessments

Dramatic changes in the conceptualization of early childhood assessment have occurred over the years. Beginning as a downward extension of conventional standardized testing, early childhood assessment has gradually moved out of the tester's office into more familiar settings (e.g., homes, child care locations, early intervention programs) and has begun to use teams of assessors and many more innovative and contextually relevant techniques than ever before (see chapters by Bricker, Erikson, Samango-Sprouse, and Wetherby and Prizant, this volume). Recent modifications of conventional assessment procedures and the concomitant changes in expectations of caregivers and families, as well as changes in the information acquired from these assessments, can be described in terms of four different approaches: (a) norm-referenced measurement; (b) criterion-referenced tests; (c) curriculum-based evaluations; and (d) performance assessments.

These approaches will be described briefly below, and examples will be presented. Rather than attempting to report on the statistical characteristics of these tests or approaches to assessment, the focus will be on the potential connection between these assessments and intervention. Among the questions needing answers are the following: Do these assessments take into account contextual factors, family characteristics, and other salient ecological features of the child and family? Do these assessments tell us what children can actually do, what they know, or what they are experiencing? Can these assessments be used to design meaningful interventions? Do these assessments provide the information that intervenors need? Are these assessments open to feedback from both the intervenor and the intervention? In short, is the relationship between assessment and intervention bidirectional, one in which information acquired as part of assessment influences intervention and experience resulting from intervention is used in the process of assessment?

## Norm-referenced measurement

Norm-referenced instruments constitute a method of measurement that allows children to be ranked numerically and to be compared in relation to a set of external standards. Norms are statistics that describe the test performance of a specified group, such as children of various ages or those with handicapping conditions. Norm-referenced scores are interpreted on the basis of the standing of an individual child with respect to a larger population or group of children (i.e., the source of the norms). The average performance of children in a standardization sample thus becomes the basic reference point or norm against which individual scores or performances are compared.

The Bayley Scales of Infant Development II (BSID-II) (Bayley, 1993) is the most widely used norm-referenced test for infants and toddlers. Although its primary purpose is to rank the mental and motor performance of young children, the manual for the newly revised instrument claims that "the primary value of the test is in diagnosing developmental delay and planning intervention strategies" (p. 1). "Diagnosing developmental delay" is one of the outcomes of separating low-functioning from average- and high-functioning children, which is what all norm-referenced tests are intended to do. But the second purpose—planning intervention strategies—goes well beyond the data provided by the BSID-II and other assessments of this type. For example, the Bayley may tell us that a child can discriminate patterns, sort pegs by color, differentiate sizes, and complete a form board in 30 seconds or less. But this information does not constitute the basis for an "intervention strategy." For this goal to be fulfilled, one needs substantially more information about the functions that are tapped by each of the items on the Bayley. One also needs to take into account context, family factors, socio-emotional characteristics, and other qualitative information about children's preferences, approaches to learning, and styles of response.

Norm-referenced tests are best used for comparing children's performances to sets of norms or to the performances of other children of the same age. Hence, the meaning of a child's score on a test of this type is relative to that group, not to a curriculum or any other set of absolute criteria of development. Moreover, when information from the Bayley or similar instruments is used to design intervention strategies (cf. McCune, Kalmanson, Fleck, Glazewski, & Sillari, 1990), the transmission of information is one-way. That is, the performance of children on the test may provide the intervenor with some "hunches" about how to intervene, but the information acquired in intervention does not subsequently alter the classification decisions made on the basis of the test. Bidirectionality of assessment and intervention is not readily available in a norm-referenced context.

## Criterion-referenced tests

Whereas a norm-referenced instrument provides a score that is relative to other children, a score on a criterion-referenced test provides "absolute" information. A criterion-referenced score is indicative of a particular level of performance or a specific degree of mastery in relationship to an independent set of standards that reflect a domain or set of objectives. Thus, the score a child obtains on a scale measuring a domain-referenced criterion indicates the proportion of a specific domain or subject area that the child has mastered (e.g., language, gross motor ability, fine motor ability, cognition). The only "standards" that apply in this case are the standards of the domain of development or achievement that are being evaluated. The individual items on a criterion-referenced scale are inherently meaningful. They are intended to reflect the attainment of specific levels of competence in a developmental continuum.

The Learning Accomplishment Profile (LAP) (LeMay, Griffin, & Sanford, 1977) is an example of this type of instrument. Based on a task analysis model, the LAP "assumes that learning takes place in steps, with each step rooted in the mastery of lower-level prerequisite skills. These skills can be arranged in a normal developmental sequence moving upward from simple to complex learned behaviors" (Nehring, Nehring, Bruni, & Randolph, 1992, p. 1). Fundamental to this type of instrument is the validity of the developmental hierarchies on which the assessment of child progress is based. Without evidence of the accuracy of this ordinal view of development, such an instrument is difficult to evaluate. Unfortunately, scales such as this, known as "ordinal" scales because they assume that each step on the scale is arranged in a hierarchical manner in which later steps presume mastery of earlier steps, have not fared well when subjected to systematic research (Dunst & Gallagher, 1983).

Nevertheless, criterion-referenced instruments are much more sensitive to issues of intervention than are norm-referenced tests. They provide us with specific, rather than relative, information about what children can do in a number of developmental domains. Moreover, many of the tasks that are presented to children on such tests are derived from children's general everyday experience. But beyond this issue lies the question of whether criterion-referenced instruments are more bidirectional than norm-referenced tests. They are not. They inform the intervenor, but they are not informed by the intervention. They give parents and other family members useful information about their children's development, but they are not modified, in turn, by the specific context in which the child has been reared. They utilize generally familiar materials and interactions, but not necessarily ones that are familiar to a specific child and family. In short, they recognize the importance of intervention but maintain a critical distance from the intervention and interventionist.

## Curriculum-based evaluations

A related type of criterion-referenced assessment focuses less on hierarchies of development and more on specific objectives that are to be achieved by the child. The items in a curriculum-based assessment are drawn from a larger set of predetermined curriculum-related items. Curriculum-based measurement is defined as "ongoing observation of children's performance in preacademic, social, and other developmental areas [that] yields information needed to determine the conditions necessary for competent performance" (Barnett, Macmann, & Carey, 1992). Mastery is defined in a curriculum-based, objective-referenced test either by a perfect score on the selected items or by achieving a specified proportion of successes, for example, four successes on five trials for each of the selected items. Although the term "curriculum-based" suggests a very limited range of objectives (e.g., what is the "curriculum" of social competence?), this approach to assessment shares many characteristics with judgment-based assessment, a method that combines both quantitative information about child accomplishments and qualitative information collected from observation and interviews (Fleischer, Belgredan, Bagnato, & Ogonosky, 1990; Hayes, 1990).

The Vulpé Assessment Battery (Vulpé, 1979) exemplifies curriculum-based evaluation, although it can also be used as an assessment that is independent of the classroom or other everyday environment. As a curriculum-based evaluation, the Vulpé provides criteria for achieving specific objectives that are part of daily living, an intervention program, or an early childhood curriculum. The purpose of this instrument is to collect information that will enable the development of an individualized intervention program for a child. In the Vulpé, representative items consist of watching the child walk alone ("The child stoops to pick up toy or other object, assumes standing position, and continues walking"; p. 98); monitoring the child's vocal response to sound, speech, or smile ("Observe the child's response to the stimulation of various sounds, human speech, or adult's smile. The child responds occasionally with vocalization"; p. 152); or observing the level of self-assertion ("The child demonstrates confidence in self and the ability to do things independently, usually enjoying performing for others"; p. 269). However, the Vulpé and other instruments of this type treat this information in summary fashion. That is, they provide data for decisionmaking only at one time, in one place, and usually with one examiner. Once the intervention begins, the work of the assessment is completed, until a specified point is reached for reevaluation of overall progress. In short, although curriculum-based assessments are much more closely linked to the programs that are used by interventionists than are other forms of assessment, they still lack connection to intervention because they do not interact with it. They provide one-time-only information for use in intervention, rather than continuous observations that both modify intervention and are modified by it.

## Performance assessments

Performance assessments represent a significantly different approach to assessment. They present an alternative to norm-referenced assessments and to criterion-referenced and curriculum-based assessments. Performance assessments refer to methods that allow children to demonstrate their knowledge, skills, dispositions, and other aspects of development and expression through solving problems, acting on their environments, interacting with individuals in their settings, experimenting, talking, and moving. Although performance assessments are used primarily with children older than age three, they have great potential for use with infants and toddlers, and their families.

These assessments are formative: They provide information that can be used both to change the process of intervention and to keep track of children's progress and accomplishments. The major difference between performance assessments and the other approaches described above is that the former are ongoing. They are used to collect information about the child and his or her setting on a structured but continuing basis, and this information is then used both for the intervention and for the process of assessment. Because performance assessments are continuous rather than discontinuous, they can be used to monitor a child's progress longitudinally, instead of merely summarizing that progress on annual or semi-annual occasions.

Performance assessments thrive on context and on the evidence acquired from natural settings. They require multiple sources of information and multiple observations of the same or related phenomena before conclusions can be drawn. They rely on extensive sampling of behavior in order to derive meaningful conclusions about individual children. Moreover, they are highly sensitive to differences in the quality of children's performances. Two children may have highly comparable skills, but they may demonstrate these skills in very different ways. Of the forms of assessment discussed here, only performance assessments systematically provide information about qualitative differences between children, and only they can provide detailed information about change within a single child when that child is evaluated over time.

Later in this chapter, a design for a performance assessment for infants and toddlers, as well as their families, will be presented. Although performance assessment is rapidly becoming one of the most widely used approaches to assessment of preschool and elementary-age children (Darling-Hammond, Ancess, & Falk, 1995), its formal application in the first three years of life has not yet begun. Nevertheless, the fundamental principle of interactivity or bidirectionality between assessment and intervention that is embodied in performance assessment is assumed in many of the chapters in this volume and represents a common theme of the "new visions" presented here.

## Summary of assessment types

The four types of assessment described above clearly represent different approaches to assessment and the use of assessment data. Norm-referenced assessments principally discriminate among children on a linear scale, and each child's performance is judged in relation to the performance of the reference group on which the scale was normed. Criterion-referenced and curriculum-based assessments provide an "absolute" criterion against which children's performances can be evaluated. The primary use of these instruments is to ascertain the level of a child's functioning relative to well-defined standards that are implicit in a domain or area of development. The model that underlies criterion-referenced assessments suggests that the domains or areas being evaluated have homogeneous patterns or shapes. With curriculum-based assessments, we encounter still another set of purposes. These assessments are most relevant for program planning or intervention planning. They differ from most criterion-referenced assessments in their more frequent use of naturally occurring materials and experiences as the source of data for the assessments. Although they can be applied to the program-planning process, they usually reflect a single set of observations of a child, rather than a continuing process of multiple observations or assessments that goes beyond the planning stage.

Finally, performance assessments represent an alternative to conventional measurement models. They describe a child's current status within a domain or area of development by documenting within daily contexts the child's skills, knowledge, personality variables, and accomplishments in relation to specific developmental goals. Some of these goals are set by the child's family; some are the outcome of consultations with professionals; and some are derived from standards or milestones that have been articulated in practice and in the research literature. Unlike other types of assessments, performance assessments transform the historical model that separated assessment and intervention from each other into a model that fuses assessment and intervention into a common set of procedures. Performance assessment is based on the recognition that assessments depend on intervention data in order to obtain the most useful information possible for enhancing a child's development—information that accounts for the complexity of development, the impact of environment, the influence of parental figures, and the role of context.

When conducting performance assessments, we do not apply one set of assessment procedures to a child in order to use the information collected to prescribe another set of interventions, as is often done with the first three types of assessments described above. Rather, we assess during the process or within the context of intervention in order to learn how to intervene still more effectively. This change in outlook is a relatively recent innovation in the field of assessment, but it does have some precedents. The next section reviews several approaches to assessment and intervention that begin to illustrate the bidirectional perspective suggested in this paper. It will show how assessment and intervention can be connected or fused within a unified, systematic framework.

## ▤ A Continuum of Assessment and ▪ Intervention

Although assessment and intervention have historically followed separate paths, it is useful to recognize that they did not spring from separate sources. Rather, the origin, criterion, and fundamental purpose of assessment have always been intervention or instruction. Binet's original motivation for developing mental tests was to improve the functioning of children who were not performing well in school by identifying those who were likely to perform poorly. In order to accomplish this, he brought together a "hodgepodge of diverse activities" (Gould, 1981, p. 149) that he abstracted from everyday problems of life, as well as from common situations that called for reasoning and verbal skills. In other words, Binet's work had its origins in children's daily performances, i.e., their experiences in school, at play, and in the home. From these pragmatic situations, he extracted a series of short tasks that he believed would yield a single score reflecting a child's general potential.

Nevertheless, the gulf between the two activities has grown wide despite their commonalities. Below, I will describe three examples of how assessment and intervention have begun to fuse rather than move farther apart. The examples depict a continuum of assessment and intervention that relates both to the purpose of the assessment and to the types of questions being asked in the assessment. These examples do not include all of the possible illustrations of each type of assessment/intervention relationship. For example, play-based assessment, described so well by Segal and Webber (this volume) and by Wieder (this volume), is not included, nor is the general approach to assessing social and emotional functioning that has been devised by Greenspan (this volume). The three types of assessment/intervention processes that are described are (a) singular processes—intervention that occurs as a result of being part of an assessment administered on only one occasion; (b) periodic processes—intervention that occurs during the course of an assessment that may potentially recur; and (c) continuous processes—intervention that is part of, and in turn influences, an assessment, which occurs over time.

## Singular processes

Assessments that fall into this category provide a picture of an infant's or young child's functioning at a particular point in time. Such assessments may suggest implications for caregiving, monitoring, or intervention, but do not necessarily suggest a specific child or family plan. Examples of singular assessment processes are described in the chapters in this volume by Brazelton, Wetherby and Prizant, and Samango-Sprouse. One of the best illustrations of a singular process is Brazelton's Neonatal Behavioral Assessment Scale (NBAS) (Brazelton, 1973). Based on an analysis of neonates' early functioning, the NBAS evaluates infant neurobehavioral functioning. It focuses on interactive behaviors, self-regulatory abilities, physiologic status, and neurological integrity. When first devised, the NBAS was intended to provide a picture of the newborn's general status in these areas and, if administered on more than one occasion during the neonatal period, an indication of the baby's rate of recovery from the birth process. Another central purpose of the NBAS was to examine the infant's strategies for coping with the demands of his or her new environment.

Among the dramatic and innovative aspects of the NBAS is the instrument's attention to interactive behaviors (see Brazelton, this volume). The Scale includes such items as response to the examiner's voice and face, as well as the infant's cuddliness, consolability, irritability, and change of state of consciousness. Unlike most other assessments of children at any age, let alone infancy, the NBAS places a premium on evaluating the *quality* of a child's responses, not just the presence or absence of those responses or, in the case of newborns, reflexes.

Shortly after the formal introduction of the NBAS, Brazelton and other researchers began to explore its intervention potential. In his chapter in this volume, Brazelton calls this potential the Scale's "most important use" and mentions that nearly 40 studies have been published that demonstrate the NBAS's ability to facilitate greater sensitivity in parents with regard to their baby's cues. In one of the earliest of these studies, Widmayer & Field (1981) studied the impact of using the NBAS as an intervention for 30 black, teenage, low socioeconomic status (SES) mothers of healthy preterm infants. Their study employed procedures of random assignment to treatment and control groups. The mothers watched the administration of the NBAS to their newborns at birth and then completed a parent version of the NBAS three times in the next three weeks. When the infants in the experimental group were 1-month old, these infants demonstrated more optimal interactive skills when compared with the group that had received routine care but whose mothers had not witnessed the administration of the NBAS or completed the maternal adaptation of the NBAS. At age 4 months, the experimental group of infants had better fine motor and adaptive abilities, and they demonstrated more interactive behaviors that were in synchrony with their mothers. Finally, at 1 year of age, the infants in the experimental group had significantly higher Mental Development scores on the Bayley Scales of Infant Development than did the infants in the routine care group.

The authors of the study conclude that the NBAS may have enabled each mother to "become more sensitized to the unique abilities of her infant, more interested in observing his or her development, and more active in promoting and providing stimulation to facilitate this development" (Widmayer & Field, 1981, p. 713). In short, the NBAS represents an assessment that has intervention power, at least under certain circumstances (see the following for additional views of the impact of the NBAS on child and family development: Belsky, 1985; Britt & Myers, 1994; Cardone & Gilkerson, 1990; Liptak, Keller, Feldman, & Chamberlin, 1983; Myers, 1982; Worobey & Belsky, 1982). However, this assessment was not originally designed as an intervention, and the direction of effects is not bidirectional. The intervention itself is a byproduct of the structure and dynamics of the assessment, and the assessment's role in intervention is coincidental to its principal functions. This conclusion does not devalue the NBAS. Rather, it underscores the fact that the NBAS represents an early moment in the continuum of assessment and intervention.

## Periodic processes

Another point on the continuum is represented by periodic assessments. The aim of this type of process is "to influence the way in which parent and child interact in order to improve the child's development or behavior" (Seitz & Provence, 1990, p. 403). Hence, intervention takes place during the course of the assessment. Often called "developmental guidance," this approach revolves around the longstanding pediatric practice of giving advice to parents—how to keep their children healthy and how to care for them when they are ill—during the course of their child's health examination. Developmental guidance may be most effective when it is part of a continuing relationship between a parent and a clinician who is sensitive to what a parent is ready to hear and able to use (see Hirshberg, this volume, as well as chapters by Erikson, Bricker, and Miller & Robinson).

Periodic processes focus on educating the caregiver. Although they are "secondary effects" of assessments, since they do not represent the principal reason for the contact between clinician and parent and child, they often go beyond their limited objective by giving structure and purpose to an assessment. When the assessor is trying to learn something that can be useful to him or her and also to the caregiver, not only will the content of the assessment change, but the opportunity for modeling (demonstrating) interactions with the child will become possible as well.

These processes expose the potentially therapeutic aspects of the assessment process. As Parker and Zuckerman (1990) note:

> The assessment process itself should seek to enhance parents'
> understanding of their child, improve the fit between the parents'

caretaking style and the child's behaviors, empower and support the parents in their crucial role as the child's most significant caregivers, and model constructive ways to interact with the child. By addressing those aspects of the child's world that traditionally have been the province of separate disciplines, this model challenges all professionals to transcend the narrow focus of their particular specialty. The outcome of such an approach can provide immediate therapeutic benefits for families and more comprehensive information to assist the intervention team in planning integrated, coherent, and effective treatment plans. (pp. 365-366)

Such an approach should not be confused with the method of "opportunistic observation" or "surveillance" that can be found in the pediatric literature (see, for example, Dworkin, 1989; Houston & Davis, 1985). Opportunistic observations refer to methods in which developmental information can be obtained while another type of assessment is taking place, such as hearing or vision testing (Sturner, Funk, Barton, Sparrow, & Frothingham, 1980; Sturner, Funk, Barton, & Green, 1994). These types of assessments are "opportunistic" in that they are not designed with the primary goal of obtaining developmental information. They enable professionals to take advantage of "opportunities during ordinary consultations to identify problems and to offer advice" (Houson & Davis, 1985, p. 77). In short, they are methods of conserving time and resources during a pediatric visit with only a limited link to intervention.

Periodic processes are weighted in favor of assessment, whether they are "opportunistic surveillance" or "developmental guidance." Generally, their feedback loop for carrying information from the intervention back to the assessor is less well developed than the feedback from the assessor to the process of intervention. Their distinctive feature is that they are designed to support children, parents, and caregivers through normal processes of development, with all their variations and vicissitudes. From time to time, one may require more specific information from a singular process of assessment. In addition, one might need a more intensive, integrated process, such as the one described below.

## Continuous processes

The principal idea behind this integrative approach is that assessment is not a static phenomenon; it provides concurrent information that alters the actual target of assessment, thereby altering itself in the process. This dynamism is captured in two dimensions. First, in order to gain a thorough understanding of infant and toddler functioning, especially in interaction with parental figures, it is critical to engage in interactions or interventions with the child and the child's caregivers. This experience typically results in changes in assessment information, technique, and conclusions. Second, the process of assessment and intervention potentially has a long-term impact by influencing how those in the infant's environment will treat the child in the future. By witnessing the impact of the brief assessment or the way the assessor interacts with the child, and by being a participant in the intervention, the parent or other caregiver may alter his or her behavior toward the child, which in turn may alter the child's behavior. From this perspective, infant/toddler assessment is a moving target that changes as it is implemented. This dynamic model is reflected in many of the programs described in this book (see chapters by Greenspan, Miller & Robinson, Segal & Webber, Wieder, and Williamson). Another model, based on principles of performance assessment, is given below.

## ■ Performance Assessment for Children from ■ Birth to Age Three and Their Families

The Early Assessment System (Meisels, Dichtelmiller, & Marsden, in preparation) is a performance assessment that is under development for children in the first three years of life and their families. When completed, it will provide an interactive system of documentation, monitoring, and assessment for Early Head Start programs, early intervention programs, home-based and center-based infant and toddler child care, and programs for children at risk for special needs or those with disabilities. As a continuous progress assessment, the Early Assessment System will facilitate planning, curriculum design, and evaluation across the first three years of life for a range of typically developing children, as well as for children with special needs and children from multirisk families.

The Early Assessment System will serve several purposes, including documenting and evaluating child growth and development; providing a structure for family goal-setting and documentation; increasing family engagement in child development activities in order to enhance child outcomes; using assessment to organize intervention; and providing transitional information for preschools. Central to its design are the following features:

1. Providing an ongoing assessment of children's growth and development;

2. Creating a structure for families to chart their own personal goals for their children, as well as the factors that enhance or impede the realization of these goals; and

3. Enabling professional and community caregivers to document, monitor, and assess child growth and to learn from the family about their perceptions of their child's functioning.

## Elements of the Early Assessment System

The Early Assessment System consists of three elements, making it similar to the Work Sampling System for preschool, kindergarten, and elementary school, which is currently in use in preschool through Grade 5 classrooms nationally (Meisels, Jablon, Marsden, Dichtelmiller, & Dorfman, 1994). These elements are the Family Portfolio, Developmental Guidelines and Checklists, and Summary Reports. In the Early Assessment System, these Work Sampling System elements will be extensively revised and reconfigured. The Family Portfolio will be the pivotal element of the Early Assessment System.

### Family Portfolio

The Family Portfolio serves to keep track of family goals for the child, the family's perceptions of the child's strengths and areas in need of development, parent(s)' objectives for themselves and for their family in relation to specific goals for child services, and other interventions. Incorporating some of the features of a journal, scrapbook, and purposeful collection of children's work and accomplishments, the Family Portfolio contains both open-ended and structured opportunities for family members and program staff to record their goals, their accomplishments, and the child's challenges and achievements through the use of writing, photographs, or other means. After establishing goals with a program caregiver, early interventionist, or other professional—goals that are reviewed and revised periodically—the parent(s) will use the Family Portfolio to keep track of accomplishments and areas of difficulty. The Portfolio will also contain a number of developmental prompts that can apply to a range of families. These will help the family and caregivers keep track of various child, family, and program milestones. The Family Portfolio can be used, along with the other Early Assessment System elements, as part of an Individualized Family Service Plan (IFSP).

### Developmental Guidelines and Checklists

The Developmental Guidelines and Checklists provide a structure for organizing the early experiences of infants and toddlers. Performance indicators included in the Checklists are derived from ZERO TO THREE's *Caring for Infants and Toddlers in Groups: Developmentally Appropriate Practice* (Lally et al., 1995) and from child development and early intervention literature. They are described in detail in the Guidelines, which provide rationales, examples, and explanations for each Checklist indicator. The "Omnibus" version that allows indicators, rationales, and examples across the first three years of life to be shown next to one another emphasizes the continuous growth model of development that is implicit in the Checklists. This model extends the Checklists' appropriateness to infants and toddlers with diverse early experiences and to those with developmental delays. In other words, chronological expectations recede into the background as developmental progression assumes the focus of attention. Ongoing focused observations of a child's behavior and development are recorded in the Checklists several times per year. The Checklists reflect carefully researched indicators of developmental advance. Instead of a strictly norm-referenced or skills-oriented approach to early experiences, they provide a developmental structure or framework for organizing the child's experiences in home-based and center-based programs. Domains reflected in the Developmental Checklists will include Personal and Social Development (including Adaptive Behavior), Communication, Cognition, and Sensory and Motor Development.

### Summary Reports

Summary Reports provide an opportunity, under the guidance of the interventionist or other caregiver, to summarize and integrate child progress and performance, and keep track of family goals and accomplishments. Rather than being an "infant report card," or a record of achievement, per se, the Summary Report (which is completed three or four times per year) serves to evaluate both process and outcome. As a formative evaluation of the process of intervention, the initial Summary Report briefly documents how the family is reaching its self-defined goals for the child, to what extent the child is progressing in meeting the expectations set forth in the Family Portfolio and the Checklists, and what plan(s) of action are recommended. Once a year, a Summary Report is prepared that represents an overview of the child's and family's challenges, achievements, and accomplishments over the previous year. Written in nonjudgmental language and reflecting the evidence accumulated in the Family Portfolio and Developmental Checklists, this Summary Report helps all of those working with the child—family members, caregivers, program administrators, and other health and education professionals—to arrive at a common view of the progress of the child and family over the year and to establish objectives for future work.

### Summary: The Early Assessment System

The Early Assessment System is distinguished by multiple approaches to collecting information, structured methods of keeping track of children's accomplishments, and inclusion of family members in the assessment process. Extensive research during the past decade demonstrates that family engagement in young children's development is crucial for development to occur optimally. The Early Assessment System is a key organizational element in that engagement. Families using the Family Portfolio will not only describe their own goals and those of their child, but they will also have numerous opportunities to document, monitor, and evaluate both their own and their child's progress and accomplishments. The families' participation in the Family Portfolio process will be mentored by the child care provider or other program professional, and will be considered a crucial component of the intervention program's activities. In addition, the interventionist or other caregiver will brief the family on the correspondence between the child's performance in focused curriculum activities or tasks related to social and emotional growth and other functional domains, and the performance indicators on the Developmental Checklists. Finally, the information from the Family Portfolio and the Checklists will be combined three or four times per year into a Summary Report, which is intended to capture the accomplishments of the family and child, their areas of difficulty, and their approach to learning. It will also propose future goals toward which the family and caregivers can work.

The proposed Early Assessment System is a performance assessment that assists families and early interventionists on multiple levels. It helps families and caregivers set goals; it enables families and caregivers to work together to document accomplishments and identify areas in need of further development; and it provides a vehicle for family self-assessment and for broadly evaluating children's and families' growth. Above all, it links intervention with assessment, caregivers with families, and families with their young children's developing competence.

# New Visions of Assessment and Intervention

This chapter has traced the relationship between assessment and intervention over nearly a century of practice. Although the measurement model pioneered by Binet remains powerful to this day, various alternatives have emerged in recognition of the limitations of the original norm-referenced approach. Of great note to those in the field of infancy and early childhood is the emergence of bidirectional, performance-based approaches that meld the data from the assessment into intervention and the information acquired in the process of intervention into the conclusions drawn from the assessment.

The advent of a reciprocal, or bidirectional, relationship between assessment and intervention is closely connected to six significant changes in our outlook on assessment. These changes are seen first in the *target*, or object, of assessment. In the past, the child alone was evaluated; today, the child must be viewed in relationship to his or her family and caregivers. It is only in this way that accurate inferences about children's development can be obtained. A second area of change concerns *context*. Assessments previously occurred only in formal testing environments; today, they take place in naturalistic settings. No longer are we interested in creating a "gray room of assessment" that is free of stimulation and everyday experience. Our purpose is to maximize what we can learn about the child through evaluating that child in a context that is familiar and nonthreatening. Third, *methods* of assessment have changed. We have moved from highly specialized procedures to approaches making use of everyday experiences that more adequately enable children to show what they know, what they can do, and what they are experiencing. A fourth modification concerns the *personnel* involved in assessments. Formerly, assessments were performed by an assessor acting alone. Now, and for nearly the past quarter of a century, assessments have involved multidisciplinary teams of assessors who, in concert with parental input, engage in a process of assessment and intervention. A fifth change concerns the *uses* of assessment data. Previous practice was to use test information to label children; now, we have come to understand that this information is best used for hypothesis formation in order to devise potential interventions. These interventions, in turn, provide information that can alter both assessment strategies and conclusions. Finally, as noted throughout this chapter and the other chapters in this volume, assessment is more frequently characterized in terms of its *fusion* with intervention. We have moved from a firm policy of assessment in the absence of intervention to the development of methods of assessment that simply cannot exist apart from intervention.

Overall, these changes enable us to understand and capture the process of learning and growth, rather than just the "developmental status" of the child. In effect, we are saying that static portraits of children are to be replaced by dynamic processes that reflect the plasticity of child growth and development, as well as the interdependence of family and child processes. When assessment and intervention are conceived as two interconnected aspects of a complex phenomenon of acquiring information about children's knowledge, skills, achievement, or personality, we highlight the potential for asking and answering meaningful questions about those being assessed and those doing the assessment. In this way, each member of the assessment/intervention team—assessor/intervenor, child, and family member—becomes more open to the points of view of others, learns from the experience of others, and is altered by this bidirectional process.

**Acknowledgments:** I would like to thank Nick Anastasiow and Sally Atkins-Burnett for their helpful comments on an earlier version of this chapter. This work was supported in part by a grant from the John D. and Catherine T. MacArthur Foundation.

# References

Barnett, D. W., Macmann, G. M., & Carey, K. T. (1992). Early intervention and the assessment of developmental skills: Challenges and directions. *Topics in Early Childhood Special Education, 12* (1), 21-43.

Bayley, N. (1993). *Bayley Scales of Infant Development II* (2nd ed.). San Antonio: The Psychological Corporation.

Belsky, J. (1985). Experimenting with the family in the newborn period. *Child Development, 56*, 407-414.

Brazelton, T. B. (1973). *Neonatal Behavioral Assessment Scale*. National Spastics Society Monograph. Philadelphia: Lippincott.

Britt, G. C., & Myers, B. J. (1994). The effects of Brazelton intervention: A review. *Infant Mental Health Journal, 15*, 278-292.

Cardone, I. A., & Gilkerson, L. (1990). Family administered neonatal activities: An exploratory method for the integration of parental perceptions and newborn behavior. *Infant Mental Health Journal, 11*, 127-141.

Darling-Hammond, L., Ancess, J., & Falk, B. (1995). *Authentic assessment in action: Studies of schools and students at work*. New York: Teachers College Press.

Dunst, C. J., & Gallagher, J. L. (1983). Piagetian approaches to infant assessment. *Topics in Early Childhood Special Education, 3* (1), 44-62.

Dunst, C. J., & Trivette, C. M. (1990). Assessment of social support in early intervention programs. In S. J. Meisels & J. P. Shonkoff (Eds.), *Handbook of early childhood intervention* (pp. 326-349). New York: Cambridge University Press.

Dworkin, P. H. (1989). British and American recommendations for developmental monitoring: The role of surveillance. *Pediatrics, 84*, 1000-1005.

Fleischer, K. H., Belgredan, J. H., Bagnato, S. J., & Ogonosky, A. B. (1990). An overview of judgment-based assessment. *Topics in Early Childhood Special Education, 10* (3), 13-23.

Garbarino, J. (1990). The human ecology of early risk. In S. J. Meisels & J. P. Shonkoff (Eds.), *Handbook of early childhood intervention* (pp. 78-96). New York: Cambridge University Press.

Gould, S. J. (1981). *The mismeasure of man*. New York: W. W. Norton & Co.

Hayes, A. (1990). The context and future of judgment-based assessment. *Topics in Early Childhood Special Education, 10* (3), 1-12.

Houston, H., & Davis, R. H. (1985). Opportunistic surveillance of child development in primary care: Is it feasible? *Journal of the Royal College of General Practitioners, 35*, 77-79.

Krauss, M. W., & Jacobs, F. (1990). Family assessment: Purposes and techniques. In S. J. Meisels & J. P. Shonkoff (Eds.), *Handbook of early childhood intervention* (pp. 303-325). New York: Cambridge University Press.

Lally, R., Griffin, A., Fenichel, E. , Segal, M., Szanton, E., & Weissbourd, B. (1995). *Caring for infants and toddlers in groups: Developmentally appro-*

*priate practice.* Arlington, VA: ZERO TO THREE/National Center for Clinical Infant Programs.

LeMay, D. W., Griffin, P. M., & Sanford, A. R. (1977). *Learning Accomplishment Profile—Diagnostic edition manual.* Winston-Salem, NC: Kaplan Press.

Liptak, G., Keller, B., Feldman, A., & Chamberlin, R. (1983). Enhancing infant development and parent-practitioner interaction with the Brazelton Neonatal Assessment Scale. *Pediatrics, 72,* 71-78.

McCune, L., Kalmanson, B., Fleck, M. B., Glazewski, B., & Sillari, J. (1990). An interdisciplinary model of infant assessment. In S. J. Meisels & J. P. Shonkoff (Eds.), *Handbook of early childhood intervention* (pp. 219-245). New York: Cambridge University Press.

Meisels, S. J. (1994). Designing meaningful measurements for early childhood. In B. L. Mallory & R. S. New (Eds.), *Diversity in early childhood education: A call for more inclusive theory, practice, and policy* (pp. 205-225). New York: Teachers College Press.

Meisels, S. J., Dichtelmiller, M. L., & Marsden, D. B. (in preparation). *The Early Assessment System.* Ann Arbor, MI: The University of Michigan.

Meisels, S. J., Jablon, J. R., Marsden, D. B., Dichtelmiller, M. L., & Dorfman, A. B. (1994). *The Work Sampling System.* Ann Arbor, MI: Rebus Planning Associates, Inc.

Meisels, S. J., & Provence, S. (1989). *Screening and assessment: Guidelines for identifying young disabled and developmentally vulnerable children and their families.* Arlington, VA: ZERO TO THREE/National Center for Clinical Infant Programs.

Messick, S. (1983). Assessment of children. In W. Kessen (Ed.), *Handbook of child psychology* (Vol. 1) (pp. 477-526). New York: Wiley and Sons.

Myers, B. (1982). Early intervention using Brazelton training with middle-class mothers and fathers. *Child Development, 52,* 462-471.

Nehring, A. D., Nehring, E. F., Bruni, J. R., & Randolph, P. L. (1992). *LAP-D standardized assessment: Technical report.* Winston-Salem, NC: Kaplan Press.

Parker, S. J., & Zuckerman, B. S. (1990). Therapeutic aspects of the assessment process. In S. J. Meisels & J. P. Shonkoff (Eds.), *Handbook of early childhood intervention* (pp. 370-369). New York: Cambridge University Press.

Sameroff, A. J., & Fiese, B. H. (1990). Transactional regulation and early intervention. In S. J. Meisels & J. P. Shonkoff (Eds.), *Handbook of early childhood intervention* (pp. 119-149). New York: Cambridge University Press.

Seitz, V., & Provence, S. (1990). Caregiver-focused models of early intervention. In S. J. Meisels & J. P. Shonkoff (Eds.), *Handbook of early childhood intervention* (pp. 400-427). New York: Cambridge University Press.

Sturner, R. A., Funk, S. G., Barton, J., & Green, J. A. (1994). Simultaneous technique for acuity and readiness testing (START): Further concurrent validation of an aid for developmental surveillance. *Pediatrics, 93,* 82-88.

Sturner, R. A., Funk, S. G., Barton, J., Sparrow, S., & Frothingham, T. E.

(1980). Simultaneous screening for child health and development: A study of visual/developmental screening of preschool children. *Pediatrics, 65,* 614-621.

Vulpé, S. G. (1979). *Vulpé Assessment Battery*. Toronto: National Institute on Mental Retardation.

Widmayer, S., & Field, T. M. (1981). Effects of Brazelton demonstrations for mothers on the development of preterm infants. *Pediatrics, 67,* 711-714.

Worobey, J., & Belsky, J. (1982). Employing the Brazelton to influence mothering: An experimental comparison of three strategies. *Developmental Psychology, 18,* 736-743.

# II. Parents' Perspectives

# 3. Toward Shared Commitment and Shared Responsibility:

## A Parent's Vision of Developmental Assessment

SUSAN ROCCO

Assessments shape expectations. That is why they are so powerful. Assessments of infants and toddlers have a profound effect on how parents view their children's future and how they view their own competence as parents. Professionals who are involved in the assessment of very young children's development need to be aware of the power of the process and must be careful not to abuse it.

What can be offered to families as they come in the door so that they feel supported in the assessment process? Parents (especially first-time parents) look to family, friends, neighbors, pediatricians and other primary health care professionals, visiting nurses, and child care providers for guidance about what is coming. Parents also look to them for their sense of whether a child "fits the norm" of development. These are the people who may direct families toward a more refined assessment.

The next question to ask is: "Assessment of what?" To answer this question, early interventionists need to examine their own values and beliefs. Some cultures emphasize who a person is, valuing autonomy and dignity. Others may emphasize what a person has, valuing individualism and competition. Some people believe that a family's life is diminished by a child with a disability; others believe that disability is part of the diversity of life. I believe that the quality of life has everything to do with relationship and much less to do with "function." An assessment that focuses on identifying deficits devalues a child because of what he does not have. But we do not need to perpetuate a "functional" culture, in which people with disabilities will always be at the bottom of the barrel because they cannot compete. Instead, an assessment should reinforce a family's sense of their child as a child first (with the disability second). It should help a family look at their situation with different eyes, instilling hope rather than taking it away.

When assessments emphasize deficits and diminished expectations for future success, we parents generally begin to look for a way to thwart these negative prognostications. At the very best, we want a miracle cure. At the least, we want professionals to "fix" our children to the best of their ability. If a toddler is not walking, then how about physical therapy five times a week? We begin a frantic search for programs, treatments, and experts. We are putty in the hands of the traditional treatment-focused, top-down approach to intervention. We believe that professionals have all the answers and, therefore, all the power. We are powerless, except in our ability to manipulate the system.

In their efforts to be kind, some clinicians merely confuse. Often clinicians talk to families about "how far a child is behind" in meeting a developmental milestone. The term "developmental *delay*" was confusing to me. I took it to mean that my child was behind in many areas but had the potential to catch up and be "normal." I began to place inordinate attention on helping him "catch up." When the next evaluation showed him even further "behind," I took that as an indictment of my parenting skills. I figured that, if Jason was scoring the equivalent of "Ds" and "Fs" on his assessments, I was clearly flunking early intervention! After all, I was his main caregiver. There is an ancient Yogic saying: "What we focus on grows in our lives." When we parents focus totally on what is wrong with our children, that is all we see.

In my experience, the big question families bring to assessment (although it may not be asked directly) is: "Can we give our child what he or she needs?" When the needs described by professionals are great and parents are limited to being passive receivers of assessment findings, it is hard for families to remember that the disability is just one small piece of who the child is. The needs may seem to be not simply "special," but unique, and the child described in the assessment report may seem to come from a different mold. After this kind of experience, many families will feel that the resources to help their child must be sought somewhere else. *Other* people have the answers; *other* people are better than they are at helping their child.

When I talk about the assessment process, I do it as a battle-scarred veteran of twelve years. I have benefited from the struggles of parents before me, and I would like to make things easier for parents and children who come after me. I believe that the assessment process can be a wonderful opportunity for families to gain confidence in their own problem-solving skills, to learn what it is like to be on a team working on a child's behalf, and to gain confidence in their ability to contribute to the team. Blending information is the key. The people who are closest to the child—family members, caregivers, and front-line early interventionists—are rich in their experience of the whole child. Other professionals have expertise in a specific area. The assessment process balances what a parent knows about factors such as a child's mood and general health with what the specialist knows about a particular aspect of the child's development or his or her condition. People rely on one another to tune into *this* child and what he or she needs.

Brainstorming together is an energizing process. It can make assessment and planning look more like a celebration and less like a funeral: The focus of discussion becomes giving families normal life opportunities rather than creating "nearly normal" children. The team's job is identifying supports that will enhance the quality of life and the relationships of the child and family, rather than enumerating the child's deficits and how to fix them. This kind of assessment and planning builds people's confidence in their ability to work together. Including people on the team who will be significant to the child and family over time will help the family be successful in *rebuilding* teams beyond the context of early intervention.

None of us can take away the pain of a difference in the family. Our culture is not there yet. But, together, we can eliminate *extra* pain, negativity, waste, loss, and frustration over things we cannot control. We can work together and learn together. We can share commitment and responsibility.

# 4. Achieving Change in Assessment Practices:

## A Parent's Perspective

BARBARA K. POPPER

When my 2-year-old son, Lee, needed a hearing test, the audiologist invited me to wait outside the testing room. I explained that my son would be more cooperative if I remained in the room. The audiologist repeated "the policy." I made it clear that we were hoping to test Lee's hearing ability, not his readiness to leave his mother and follow a stranger into a cubicle. The audiologist told me, with a patronizing show of patience, that the results of the test might not be the same if I stayed in the room. I agreed with her wholeheartedly. I also wondered how—if I did not stay in the room—she expected to get any test results at all from a frightened, crying little boy. After completing the test—with me sitting in the room—the audiologist observed that Lee was unusually cooperative for a 2-year-old.

One of the basic principles of assessment for infants and young children formulated by the ZERO TO THREE Work Group on Developmental Assessment states in no uncertain terms that "young children should never be challenged during assessment by separation from their parents or familiar caregivers." This seems so obvious and such basic common sense when one is dealing with infants and toddlers. When I read this statement at the time of the initial publication of the principles in the bulletin, *Zero to Three*, the memory of my morning with Lee and the audiologist came flooding back.

I also remembered a much more terrifying experience. In

1970, professionals tried to separate me from my nursing infant, Nancy (Lee's older sister), as she was being admitted to the hospital on an emergency basis to be tested for what might have been a fatal neurological illness. My husband and I insisted on disregarding hospital policy regarding separation of child and parent during the three days of Nancy's hospitalization. I stayed with her for the entire period, during which many invasive procedures and a drug error of potentially serious proportions confirmed to me that I was right to follow my gut instinct. As a result of this experience, in 1972 a group of parents formed a nonprofit organization, Children in Hospitals, Inc. (CIH), with the goal of making 24-hour visitation an option available to all parents of hospitalized children in Massachusetts. CIH succeeded in achieving this goal and continues to help parents negotiate the health care system.

My twenty-plus years of work with CIH and more recent parent advocacy and training with colleagues at the Federation for Children with Special Needs have taught me some valuable lessons about what it takes to turn a "recommended guideline" into "accepted practice." As parents and professionals try, together, to make our new vision of developmental assessment a reality, the following lessons may be helpful:

### Change is painful.

When a newly hired head of pediatric nursing shared the insight that change is painful with me, I assumed that she was preparing to explain why she could not relax policies and remove barriers that hindered parents from continuing their parenting role when their children were hospitalized. To my surprise, this nurse, in fact, told me what she had learned about ways to pull people away from their tightly protected views and point them toward new ways of functioning that recognized the needs of families. While I had always focused on *what* I wanted changed, this professional showed me the importance of considering *how* to make change occur so that the people involved feel comfortable, not assaulted. This viewpoint is an essential ingredient of CIH's materials and advocacy.

### Any individual parent advocate can be written off as a crazy, overprotective mother or father.

When we defied hospital personnel so that I could stay with my baby daughter while she was hospitalized, my husband and I decided on a strategy within the first hour of our ordeal: I would not leave Nancy's side, and he would make sure that nobody insisted on enforcing the existing hospital policy of visiting hours for parents from 11 a.m. to 7 p.m. When we returned home three days later (with the finding that Nancy's alarming symptoms "must have been caused by a virus"), word of our victory spread rapidly through the community, as well as through the La Leche League and other childbirth and parenting education groups in the Boston area. Parents with children facing hospitalization called and asked, "How did you get to stay?" After CIH was formed, hospital officials took parents seriously. A committee always gets farther than an individual—and committee members have the support and enjoyment of one another's company.

### Find supporters.

In CIH's early years, the organization was discovered by an attorney, George Annas, who was interested in the new area of patient rights. He listened to our concerns and offered us legal arguments to match our parent instincts. (His book, *The Rights of Patients* (1989), discusses parents' rights.) Legal arguments opened some doors.

We also found that psychologists and psychiatrists (Edward Mason, M.D., for example) had done research in the 1960s demonstrating the benefits of having parents stay with their hospitalized children (Mason, 1965). In fact, as a result of research findings, Massachusetts General Hospital had begun suggesting at that time that parents bring sleeping bags to the hospital so that they could sleep in their child's room even if no beds were available. CIH did not need to set up a research project. We simply prepared a bibliography, disseminated key articles, and publicized examples that supported the research findings. We learned that peer pressure works on institutions as well as on children. In 1973, CIH published a *Survey of Hospital Policies* regarding this matter and has continued to do so every two years since then. The first edition attracted attention in the Boston newspapers, and, almost immediately, open visiting by parents became the policy at several hospitals.

Sometimes, supporters emerge from your own circle of contacts. In our case, Dr. T. Berry Brazelton told CIH that he needed consumer/parent support at a Boston hospital to accomplish changes within the hospital that some of his colleagues found strange at the time. With his leadership within the hospital and our pressure from the outside (including newspaper publicity), it became possible to bring parents into the Neonatal Intensive Care Unit of the hospital for the first time.

## Collaboration is powerful—among parents, and among parents and professionals together.

When CIH was established, few committees or task forces included parents as equal partners. The first task force I was invited to join was considering new pediatric hospital regulations, including a CIH request that parents be able to stay with their children as many hours a day as they felt necessary. This task force disbanded after I attended one meeting. Other members of the task force decided the group could not do its work with the participation of parents. Two years later, health department staff reconvened the task force. I was still a member (bringing along my newborn child, who was labeled "the consumer member"). Another CIH parent was included in the task force, along with physicians and hospital administrators who had been the only members of the first task force before I joined it. This second task force was successful because we all seemed ready to listen to one another. Perhaps the reason for this was that the health department staff who convened the group had carefully selected members who were open to change.

Consistent collaboration within CIH has been just as important as effective work with outside allies. We have needed one another as parents. We have also needed to demonstrate our capacity to follow through, commenting whenever our viewpoint has been invited and when we have thought an issue required parent attention, and then thanking people who helped improve conditions. CIH's newsletters and brochures have encouraged parents to be active and to express their views in telephone calls, meetings, letters, and articles. Sometimes, it has seemed as if most of the calls parents made were to us. Countless crying parents have called us from pay phones in hospital corridors. They have felt dismissed, denigrated, and disdained by hospital staff, and have badly needed to talk to someone who would understand what they were going through. Many have been fearful of going directly to hospital staff and have asked for our support so that they could remain anonymous within the hospital. Since we began to publish our consumer directory of Massachusetts hospital policies and gained access to newspaper publicity, things have changed. Some professionals have reported feeling "intimidated" by our publication.

Ongoing advocacy that may seem relentless (11 editions of the consumer directory have been published from 1973 to 1994) is sometimes necessary, but negotiation and collaboration are far more satisfying ways to achieve change. I have learned to enjoy the process of sharing ideas and working toward a common goal.

### Prepare parents as fully as possible for their roles as participants in the developmental assessment of an infant or toddler.

We need to recognize at the outset that the notion of an "assessment," whether it is the first examination of a newborn or a comprehensive developmental evaluation, triggers an impulse to take on one of two potentially conflicting parental roles—the child's "guardian angel," who protects the baby from all harm (including, perhaps, professional "pronouncements" about the child's condition) or the knowledgeable, cooperative "good parent" ally of the professional. The potential conflict between these roles becomes clear the first time a parent wants to ask what he thinks is a "dumb question." The parent wants an answer to a troubling concern but feels embarrassed at revealing limited knowledge or seeming "silly" or overprotective.

Well-trained, sensitive professionals—those who share a "new vision" of developmental assessment—are aware of parents' feelings and try to make every phase of an assessment an opportunity to share knowledge, observe a child together, and plan collaboratively. In these circumstances, professionals and parents see themselves as allies *on behalf of* the child.

Many parents continue to fight the same battles we in CIH thought we won conclusively 20 years ago, and, for years to come, many parents will be participating in developmental assessments in circumstances that are less than ideally supportive. The following guidelines for the parents' role in a developmental assessment may help parents be effective advocates for themselves and their children, and, therefore, reliable allies for each other and for dedicated professionals.

1. *Your role in an assessment is to be the parent.* As a parent, you know your child best and in ways that others cannot. That is your expertise. Your own gut feelings and personal observations over time are valuable in ways that go beyond

what any test measures will provide. You do not need to become any other kind of "expert." Continue to be your child's *parent*, and make use of other team members' expertise as it applies.

2. *No matter what your educational or occupational background is, you will not know all the technical terminology that might be used during an assessment, and you do not have to.* You can and should ask to have terms defined and explained so that you continue to understand the entire discussion. Your own familiar ways of describing your child are valid and will be understood by everyone.

3. *You do not need to agree with everyone at the assessment— or with anyone at all.* If you feel that the way your child is being described does not match what you see, say so. Accepting a picture of your child's situation as described by professionals and following the recommendations of these professionals will not be useful unless they fit what you believe is true for your child. If there is no match between what others see and what you see, ask for more discussion as soon as possible.

4. *Feeling "outnumbered" can be difficult.* It can be stressful when a group of people are discussing your child with you and a family member, or just with you. Professionals are more comfortable with colleagues present, even if their own opinions vary from those of their colleagues. As a parent, you can designate a person to bring to any meeting or appointment concerning your child, at which you want support. The support person can help take notes, keep track of information, and review the discussions with you later.

5. *As time passes, you may wish to be more or less involved in the process of assessment.* Your level of involvement at any given moment will depend on your child's needs, additional information you may have learned, and other life circumstances. Your decision will be accepted, not challenged. You should make it clear that you want to know if someone would like you to be more or less involved for a particular reason so that you can make a decision based on that information.

6. *The process of making decisions at each stage of assessment will increase your ability to advocate for your child.* Each assessment will give you new information that you can use as your child grows and will be a new opportunity to put infor-

mation to work when making decisions about your child's care and education.

7. *If you feel that an assessment is not adding to your under standing or helping you discover what you need to know, tell the team.* Spending time on a process that misses what you are concerned about delays your ability to help your child. Make your needs clear, even if this means finding others with whom to work.

8. *Find support for yourself over time, and find others who will benefit from what you have learned.* Each parent who has gained some expertise should be prepared to share it with others. Parents who are in the process of trying to learn what you have already discovered need your help. Every parent who has learned from another parent feels a continuing bond with his or her "parenting guide."

While each parent is concerned primarily with the experiences surrounding the situation of his or her own child, some parents have found that, as they continue to expand their knowledge, they become ready to participate in helping others in new ways, based on their experiences. They are eager to offer support to other parents, work collaboratively with professionals on committees, serve as speakers at conferences, and provide the parent viewpoint at every opportunity (as I am doing in this chapter). Even when not asked directly to participate, some parents have found ways to offer their involvement. This has led increasingly to new partnerships and a greater awareness on the part of professional groups and organizations of the fact that parents who are receiving services today are also potential partners in furthering an understanding of what families are seeking.

# References

Anderson, B. (1985). Parents of children with disabilities as collaborators in health care. *Coalition Quarterly.* Winter/Spring, 1985. Federation for Children with Special Needs, Boston.

Annas, G. (1989). *The rights of patients.* Carbondale, IL: Southern Illinois University Press.

Jeppson, E., & Thomas, J. (1995). *Essential allies: Families as advisors.* Bethesda, MD: Institute for Family-Centered Care.

Mason, E. (1965). Medical progress: The hospitalized child—his emotional needs. *New England Journal of Medicine, 272,* 406-413.

Popper, B. K. (1990). A parent's perspective: The changing role of parent involvement in the health care system. *Children's Health Care, 19,* 4.

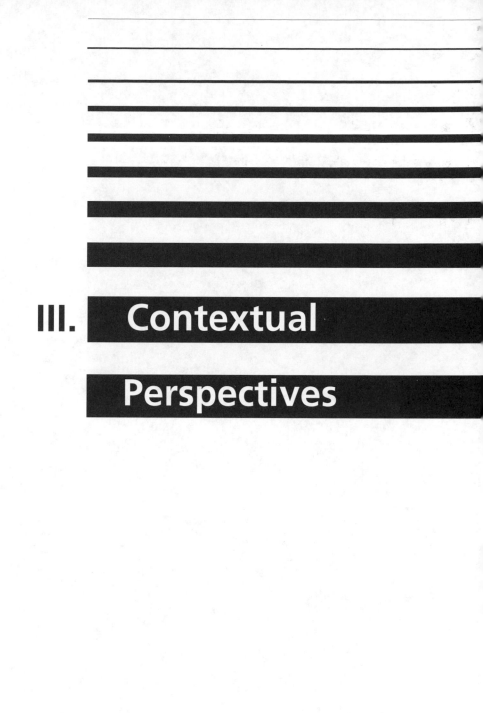

# III. Contextual Perspectives

# 5. Thoughts on the Assessment of Young Children whose Sociocultural Background is Unfamiliar to the Assessor

ISAURA BARRERA

Competent assessment of young children's development is a complex process. When assessors and families bring different world views, expectations, values, and behaviors to the assessment arena, that complexity is magnified (Anderson & Fenichel, 1989; Anderson & Goldberg, 1991; Baca & Cervantes, 1989; Lynch & Hanson, 1992). To conduct assessment competently, assessors must appreciate the complexity of their task and avoid the temptation of oversimplification. The "new vision" for the developmental assessment of infants and young children generated by ZERO TO THREE's Work Group on Developmental Assessment, of which I am a member, recognizes both the impact of culture on development and the importance of responsivity to that impact within a meaningful assessment process. This chapter elaborates on the "new vision" by exploring dimensions of sociocultural diversity, particularly as they relate to families with young children and to professionals who are responsible for assessing young children's development.

## Perceptions and Mindsets

The development of socioculturally competent assessment necessitates a shift from typical assessment paradigms. It is not sufficient simply to learn a new procedure or instrument; perceptions and mindsets must also be changed. Revised procedures without revised perceptions and perspectives will remain unresponsive to the complexities presented by individual families. The ways of thinking that often underlie nonresponsive assessment cannot be fully discussed in this article. However, a brief discussion of the most common issues that should be kept in mind when striving toward culturally responsive assessment will provide a foundation for examining the steps that are proposed for this type of assessment later in this chapter.

## Assumption of objectivity

Assessment, even when not norm-referenced, often carries an assumption of an "objective" and "valid" reality that can be observed and documented in a reliable fashion. Yet even "hard science" now recognizes that no such thing as objective observation exists. *All* observation changes what is being observed in some way. *Every observer has particular lenses (both personal and sociocultural) through which he or she views and evaluates what is observed.* This subjective aspect of observation is particularly relevant to socioculturally competent assessment. Only when the assessor acknowledges his or her own subjectivity (and that of his or her professional community) can the assessor recognize and respect the way a family's subjective world affects the behavior and development of a particular child.

## Ethnicity and race as primary determinants of "cultural diversity"

Culture is composed of the range of ways of perceiving, believing, evaluating, and behaving common to communities (Banks, 1994; King, Chipman, & Cruz-Janzen, 1994). Because every individual is a member of one or more communities, every individual's perceptions, beliefs, values, and behavior are to some extent influenced by the culture of those communities. It is important to remember, however, that some groups recognize and value their cultures more strongly than others, that some individuals identify more strongly with their community and its culture than others, and that every person internalizes culture uniquely (Ho, 1995).

While ethnic and racial affiliations have been considered the major markers of diversity, they are, in fact, only one way of identifying culture. And they are not always the best way because ethnic and racial affiliations do not always determine ways of perceiving, believing, evaluating, or behaving (i.e., being

Hispanic does not automatically determine how one behaves; one may be Hispanic and choose behaviors or beliefs not typically associated with that culture). *The perception that group membership is the primary or even sole determinant of culture often generates stereotypes.*

Diversity between an assessor and a child cannot, therefore, be judged solely on the basis of the child's apparent group membership. Rather, diversity must be judged reciprocally and relationally, through an examination of the backgrounds of the child, the family, and the assessor(s). When judged from this reciprocal relational perspective, *diversity is deemed to be present when there is the probability that the assessor, in interaction with a particular child or family, will attribute different meanings or values to behaviors or events than would the family or someone from that family's environment.* By this definition, diversity is present when the family and assessor are of different ethnicity. It can, however, also be an issue when the family and assessor share a common ethnicity but differ in other important group affiliations (for example, when the family are new immigrants from Mexico, with little or no schooling, and the assessor is Central American, with a professional education).

Culturally responsive assessment requires a sensitivity to the ways children and their families perceive, believe, evaluate, and behave, as well as to the ways assessors perceive, believe, evaluate, and behave. Group membership provides strong, but not absolute, clues to determining these ways of responding. Assessors need to go beyond the simple recognition of group membership to an examination of their own ways of perceiving, believing, evaluating, and behaving (whether or not these are linked to specific ethnic or racial affiliations) and to an examination of the interaction between these ways of responding and those of the individual children and families with whom they work. Ho (1995) observes: "At rock bottom, all interpersonal understanding, be it intracultural or intercultural, entails transcending egocentrism" (p. 15).

## Polarization of options

The ability to perceive, and consequently assess, reality in a multifaceted fashion is key to socioculturally competent assessment. Yet professional training in the United States has had a tendency to teach an approach to reality and problem-solving that encourages dualistic, either/or choices, rather than multifaceted perceptions. The conceptualization of a polarized reality leads to decisionmaking in which the selection of one choice means the automatic elimination of other possibilities. In supporting such singular choices, dualistic perceptions invariably limit the parameters of assessment across cultural environments. For example, once a child is identified as Hispanic, aspects of that child's culture that spring from association with an Asian grandparent or a strong English-speaking grandparent may be overlooked. Similarly limiting is a preoccupation with language "dominance" instead of the determination of relative language proficiency, a concept that includes the full assessment of proficiency in both English and the child's non-English home language(s). For example, parents are seldom asked, "What languages do you speak at home with your children?" Rather, they tend to be asked, "Is English spoken at home?"

The complexity of sociocultural reality cannot be captured by such polarized yes/no choices. Rather, rich "essay" questions must be posed—both explicitly, in interactions with families, and implicitly, through the assessment situations we structure. Many families in the United States are what Ho (1995) terms "bi-enculturated" or "multi-enculturated." They are people who are "not merely exposed to and knowledgeable of, but have in-depth experience and hence competence in, more than one culture. In short, the internalized culture of these persons embodies plurality of cultural influences of diverse origins" (p. 14). If assessment paradigms are to be appropriate to sociocultural reality, they must permit a similar embodiment of a "plurality of cultural influences of diverse origins."

## Polarization of "individuality" and group identity

One area in which polarized perceptions can be particularly troublesome is the area of identity. The behaviors, values, attitudes, and other aspects of identity developed by any particular child result from a unique synergy of both individual factors (e.g., personality, genetic endowment) and sociocultural factors (e.g., behaviors modeled and reinforced by the particular group(s) of people with which the child affiliates). To view a child's individuality without considering his or her group affiliation is to deny the reality of culture. On the other hand, to see only group membership is to deny the rich variability among human beings, that is, to stereotype. Socioculturally competent assessment requires the integration of *both* perspectives.

Some groups with which a child is affiliated may have names denoting their clusters of specific values, beliefs, and languages (e.g., Navajo, first-generation German-American); others may not (e.g., middle-class, suburbanite). In either case, the groups or communities of people in the life of every child influence and shape the ways in which that child learns to express his or her individual identity. In getting to know a child, the assessor must understand these communal or sociocultural influences, as well as the more individual factors typically built into assessment instruments and procedures. The assessor must also understand that communities themselves vary in the way they value group membership and identity in relation to "individuality." Some communities emphasize group membership and identity over "individuality"; others tend toward the reverse (Markus, 1994). Without an understanding of these basic factors, the assessor will have difficulty getting and interpreting information.

## Neglect of mediation as a planned part of the assessment process

Assessment has traditionally focused on the appropriate use of specific procedures or instruments. Yet the core of any assessment is communication—the transfer or distillation of information and meaning between two or more people. When these people do not share a common world view (that is, when they are likely to attribute different meanings or values to the same behaviors), a conscious bridging process must support the use of any procedure or instrument.

Mediation is such a process when it is applied as a *preconflict* strategy that involves the identification and development of optimal social, cognitive, and linguistic contexts for the purpose of maximizing the transfer of information between adult and child (Barrera, 1990; Jensen & Feuerstein, 1987; Tikunoff, 1987). An understanding of mediation in this sense is, ultimately, a better guide to the appropriate application and interpretation of assessment strategies than is recognition of membership in a particular group or knowledge of behaviors associated with such membership.

Mediation is needed, first of all, to bridge differences in communication across sociocultural contexts. A focus on children's proficiency in English or on the need for *language* translators or interpreters greatly oversimplifies this challenge. The *words* used in any situation are only a small part of the communication taking place. Our "real language," a language of values, beliefs, world views, perceptions, and feelings, lies underneath the words we speak. It is this deeper language that must be understood and mediated if interactions are to yield meaningful information.

Mediation is also required to bridge sociocultural and sensory-cognitive differences. Much of one's competent participation in a particular group comes from unconscious and intuitive (rather than conscious and explicit) knowledge. These dimensions of knowledge, springing from varied sociocultural affiliations, are less well explored than language.

# ▰ Steps in Culturally Responsive ▰ Assessment

The steps involved in carrying out culturally responsive assessment are not, in themselves, significantly different from those required by any assessment (see Table 1). The goal of all assessment is to capture a child's abilities and needs accurately, in order to plan appropriate intervention if necessary. There are aspects of each assessment step, however, that are especially critical when assessing young children from sociocultural backgrounds unfamiliar to the assessor(s). These key aspects are discussed below. Further information can be found in the references listed at the end of this chapter.

---

Table 1. **Steps in Culturally Responsive Assessment**
1. Gathering background information
2. Hypothesis formulation
3. Active assessment
4. Analysis and interpretation of information
5. Reporting findings
6. Program/intervention development

---

### Step 1: Gathering background information

Typical assessment items and procedures reflect assumptions that may be unwarranted when applied to children and families from diverse populations. In particular, some test items are assumed by their creators to apply to all children uniformly (i.e., they reveal children's "inherent" abilities, talents, dispositions, or personalities, regardless of social contexts). This assumption does not take into account the role of social groups in differen-tially reinforcing, valuing, and rewarding even the youngest chil-dren for some choices over others.

Gathering information on a child's individual and develop-mental context is fairly routine in all assessments. It is much less common, however, to also obtain information on the sociocul-tural context of the child and family (that is, features shared by the family with their community or group of affiliation). Yet it is this context that forms the environment within which individ-ual and developmental features acquire particular interpreta-tions and weights. It is, in fact, this context, as defined by the education and special education community, that has given assessment items their standardized interpretations and weights.

The child being assessed is only the "foreground" of a total picture. The background against which that foreground is framed—the child's sociocultural context(s)—must also be assessed. If it is a background similar to that which frames the assessor's reality, his or her perception and interpretation of the child's development and behavior will, in all likelihood, be con-sonant with the child's reality as it exists outside the assessment process. If, however, the child's background is different or even dissonant from the assessor's, the assessor must learn as much as possible about the components of the child's background *before* starting to observe and judge the child's behavior and develop-ment.

At least three dimensions of sociocultural context are of sig-nificance for service providers seeking to assess the needs and strengths of young children and their families. These dimensions typically require mediation to bridge differences:

1. *The personal-social dimension*: Rules and patterns for devel-oping and expressing one's identity and for interacting with others;

2. *The communicative-linguistic dimension*: Rules and patterns for appropriate and valued communication, including, but not limited to, the specific language used; and

3. *The sensory-cognitive dimension*: Preferred and valued ways of identifying and processing information about the world (for example, multiple intelligences, learning strategies).

The first step in a culturally responsive assessment involves gathering information about the way these three dimensions have been structured in the child's environment and the way the

Table 2. **Information Pertinent to Dimensions of Mediation**

*Personal-social dimension*

1. Child's and family's degree of acculturation: Information on the child's and family's degree of familiarity with and proficiency in the following aspects of the early childhood setting: communication roles/rules, behavioral expectations, values, beliefs, learning/play strategies, and teaching formats.

2. Child's personal-social knowledge and skills: Information on the child's knowledge and skills repertoire relative to social expectations and interactions, self-help strategies, and identity.

3. Child's and family's sense of identity and competence: Information on behaviors and characteristics valued by the child and family, including ethnic affiliations if these are present.

*Communicative-linguistic dimension*

1. Family/community communication environment(s): Information on the types of communication valued by the child's family and immediate community, and the language(s) spoken.

2. Child's relative language proficiency: Information on the level of proficiency in the non-English language as compared to the level of proficiency in English. This information should include identification of receptive and expressive levels of proficiency in English, as well as in the non-English language(s) used with the child at home and in the community.

3. Home-early childhood setting disparity in language usage: Information on the complexity of language(s), common topics of conversation, and use of verbal and nonverbal communication in child's home as compared with intervention setting.

4. Relationship between language use and sense of self of the child and family: Information on the role and value of English and non-English language(s). In which language, for example, does the mother feel more comfortable and better able to express affect? Which language is primary in the exchange of endearments between father and child? Does the child's affect or behavior differ depending on the language used?

*Sensory-cognitive dimension*

1. Child's comfort and familiarity with particular learning strategies: Information on preferred and valued ways of teaching in the home.

2. Home-early childhood setting disparity in funds of knowledge: Information on categories of knowledge valued and familiar in the child's home as compared to those valued and promoted in the intervention setting.

3. Family's beliefs about the value and role of intervention: Information on family's perceptions regarding the role of formal intervention. Are the early intervention providers, for example, expected to have primary responsibility for acculturating the child?

---

child has, in turn, learned to structure them for himself or herself (see Table 2). Without knowing about the child's experience concerning these dimensions, the assessor cannot understand whether observed behavior indicates a need or a strength. Much of the available information about identified diverse populations, though general in nature, can be helpful in identifying aspects of culture that may need to be explored further to understand a particular experience of a child and family (Lynch & Hanson, 1992). An assessor's best resource in an unfamiliar sociocultural environment, however, is someone who is familiar with both the environment of the child and family and the assessment environment. The term "culture-language mediator" has been developed to describe such a person (Barrera, 1990). The culture-language mediator has a dual responsibility: (a) to assist service providers in becoming aware of any unfamiliar values, behaviors, language, or rules that are part of the family's environment; and (b) to assist the family and child in becoming familiar with any unfamiliar values, beliefs, language, or rules that are part of the assessment and intervention environment.

Culture-language mediators must be bilingual, speaking and understanding the words used in the child's home and those used in the assessment setting. They must also be proficient in understanding and interpreting the contexts, values, and meanings underlying those words and the behaviors that accompany them. The culture-language mediator must, for example, be able to correctly interpret a missed appointment, recognizing that it may mean something other than lack of interest in a child's needs. The mediator must understand that a mother's statement that she cannot come to meet her child's teacher "because my husband won't let me" may reflect a preference for saying no indirectly, rather than directly, to a person in a position of authority. The culture-language mediator must also be able to understand the rationale for the protocol and behaviors peculiar to assessment interactions, and to interpret these to family members in ways that are meaningful in the context of the family's experiences and needs.

## Step 2: Hypothesis formulation

Once initial information—both individual and sociocultural—is gathered, the next step is to formulate hypotheses about the changes in typical assessment procedures and materials that may be necessary. Since preset assessment procedures and materials embody certain perspectives and reflect certain assumptions, the assessor should answer the following questions explicitly:

1. Given the child's individual and sociocultural characteristics, what are the optimum communicative-linguistic avenues that will elicit this child's strongest responses? (English? Spanish? Hmong? Close distance and touch, or greater distance and no touch? Questioning? Modeling, or demonstrating? Listening?)

2. Given the child's individual and sociocultural characteristics, what should the content of assessment include? (Manipulation of objects? Interpersonal behavior? Functional behavior?) What content will elicit the truest picture of the child's and family's strengths and needs? (For example, will this child's use of blocks give the truest picture of his or her hand-eye coordination?)

3. Given the child's individual and sociocultural characteristics, what environmental, situational, temporal, or relational features will be most appropriate for the assessment? (Timed? Indoors or outdoors? At home, with caregivers presenting tasks? Unfamiliar adults?)

Answers to these questions will vary depending on the purpose of the assessment. In general, if the purpose of the assessment is to determine basic abilities and developmental integrity, the assessor should select communicative-linguistic approaches most familiar to the child, and assessment content and context should also reflect familiar aspects of the child's environment. If the purpose of the assessment is to determine the child's readiness to function in an early childhood setting or his or her potential for learning in that setting, features from the child's early childhood setting should be incorporated into the assessment, and the child's responses to these features should be observed. When reporting assessment results, the assessor should always identify the purpose of the assessment, the specific adaptations made to procedures and materials, and the persons involved.

## Step 3: Active assessment

Following the formulation of initial hypotheses, more structured interactions with the child and family can be started. These interactions are primarily aimed at obtaining two types of information: (a) identifying what the child knows and can do within his or her current environment(s); and (b) identifying learning abilities, strengths, and needs vis-à-vis new sociocultural environments (e.g., an intervention setting). Typically, assessments tend to blur the distinction between these types of information, with the assumption that the child's current environment and the intervention setting closely resemble each other. This is not the case for many children, whose daily environment may call for and foster knowledge and skills that are quite different from those called for and fostered in the typical early childhood education or intervention setting.

When structured interactions are part of an assessment, the assessor must be especially careful to distinguish observations of behavior from *inferences* about the meaning of behavior. For example, an assessor may interpret a child's apparent reluctance to separate from his or her mother as inappropriate dependence. This interpretation may or may not be valid for the sociocultural context of the child and family.

Active assessment requires, in effect, a "clues and guesses" process. Observational data yield clues and lead to certain guesses about strengths and needs. The assessor then obtains additional information to confirm or deny the validity of the guesses. This new information yields more clues, and so on. While all assessment follows this clinical process to some extent, the need to recognize the tenuous nature of the process is especially important when diversity is present between assessor and family. The assessor should keep in mind several key questions throughout the active assessment:

1. Am I really communicating with this child and family in a way that will elicit desired responses?

2. Is my interpretation of the behavior of this child and family similar to the interpretation that a family member or other member of the child's community would make?

3. Do the child's and family's responses indicate their true abilities and potentials?

4. Do the child's responses suggest that he or she is unfamiliar

with the tasks presented or that, in the child's experience, little value is assigned to these tasks?

5. To what degree is the child's behavior being influenced by stress resulting from being in a situation where, because of unfamiliar norms and mores, the behavior of others is difficult or impossible to predict?

## Step 4: Analysis and interpretation of information

Interpreting the observational data gathered during Step 3 involves making informed judgments. Observations such as "the child, who was 2 years old, preferred to work with the mother and seldom initiated activities independently," or "the child, who was 3 years old, could not successfully complete a two-piece puzzle" can be interpreted in various ways, depending on sociocultural variables, expectations, and previous experiences. A typical inference (e.g., the child lacks independent exploration or problem-solving skills) may or may not be accurate, depending on these variables, expectations, and experiences. Only when such inferences are reviewed critically in light of the values, expectations, and experiences common to the child's most familiar environment can correct judgments be made about whether the child's behavior is appropriate within that environment. If this is the case, such behavior probably reflects intact learning abilities (that is, the child has successfully met the demands for functioning within his or her environment). If the demonstrated behavior is not appropriate within the child's most familiar environment, there is a stronger probability of limited abilities to learn or adapt. In the first case, the *content* of learning may need to be addressed. In the second, the *process* of learning would need to be more thoroughly assessed before content could be addressed.

Socioculturally responsive assessment requires going beyond noting the presence or absence of behaviors. It also requires specific attention to what such presence or absence may reflect. The following questions, related to those asked during the active assessment phase, must be addressed explicitly in this phase. Only when these questions have been asked and answered as accurately as possible can assessment data be interpreted in a nonbiased fashion:

1. Is the child's performance on a par with that of peers, although perhaps below the norms and expectations used by

the assessor? (That is, is the child exhibiting age-expected behaviors and skills for his or her community and peer group?)

2. If this is the case, to what degree are these behaviors and skills adaptive for the environments the child will be entering as he or she leaves home? How well will they serve the child in these new environments? To what degree can they be used as resources for developing the additional behaviors and skills needed for competent participation in the new settings? How does the child respond when presented with tasks calling for these new behaviors and skills?

3. If the child is not exhibiting behaviors and skills considered typical for children of his or her age in the community, has he or she had opportunities to learn these behaviors, or have circumstances—for example, chronic poverty or loss of a primary caregiver—interfered with those opportunities? Have the child and his or her peers had the same opportunities to learn, and has the child been unable to benefit from them? Does this inability indicate inherent learning impairment(s) or "temporary" impairment(s) resulting from chronic poverty or trauma?

4. Is the child exhibiting behaviors and skills that extend beyond what can be explained by sociocultural adaptation or limited opportunities to learn? When this appears to be the case, the possible presence of a disability or delay should be carefully assessed.

## Step 5: Reporting findings

How the results of the assessment are reported is as significant as how the assessment is conducted—and possibly more so. Many times, the greatest bias lies not in the actual assessment but in how the data are reported. For example, standardized scores may be reported without mention of correct responses obtained outside of the standardized procedure; or language levels may be reported with no indication that a translator was used, or without mention of the fact that the translator was an older sibling unfamiliar with the assessment process or with the tasks presented. Such errors of omission occur all too frequently. When they occur, the reader of the report lacks the information needed to judge the validity of the report's conclusions.

The assessor should report not only a child's performance, but also *how* that performance was elicited and measured (e.g., What items were presented? How familiar or unfamiliar were they to the child?). Information about community behavioral expectations—for both children and adults—is also important (e.g., Are children in this community expected to attempt responses in a trial and error format? Are adults expected to ask questions of children directly?). Only with this kind of information can the service provider make judgments about what represents a behavior that is typical for a particular group or community and what represents an individual difference that, even within the group or community, may be considered limited. In general, a child who is developmentally on a par with peers in his or her community has intact learning and language abilities, although he or she may need opportunities to learn and speak in ways that will be necessary to function well in other environments.

## Step 6: Program/intervention development

The cycle of assessment is completed with the identification of a child's strengths and the development of specific goals, objectives, and strategies to address the child's developmental needs. In thinking about the sociocultural diversity of young children, the goal is to help children learn to function in as many settings as their developmental capacities allow. Every effort should be made to give them the choice of competent participation in multiple settings. Both the child's relationships within home and community and his or her broader life options must be weighed (but not in a polarized fashion!). Are monolingual English-speaking settings or medical settings likely to be a major part of the child's future? If so, how can one prepare the child for these settings while maintaining and strengthening current connections to quite different home and community environments?

Early childhood assessment is an awesome task with life-changing implications for those assessed. As early childhood service providers, we literally step into and radically change lives. This aspect of assessment dictates that we be as competent as possible, especially in relation to children and families from social worlds different from our own.

# Conclusion

Assessment procedures, materials, instruments, and interactions are embedded in particular world views, expectations, values, and behavioral preferences. When these world views, expectations, values, and behaviors reflect those of both the assessor(s) and the families, the likelihood that valid information will be obtained and accurately interpreted is high. When they do not, the likelihood of inaccuracy is equally high. Careful thought must, therefore, be given to assessment procedures, materials, instruments, and interactions in the context of diversity. Children and families who are identified as culturally/linguistically diverse challenge a premise basic to much of today's assessment—that the behaviors of individual children can be meaningfully elicited out of context and then interpreted according to preset, group-referenced expectations and criteria. This challenge to current practice is a gift. May we all receive it with reverence and respond with our greatest competence and care.

# References

Anderson, P. P., & Fenichel, E. S. (1989). *Serving culturally diverse families of infants and toddlers with disabilities.* Arlington, VA: ZERO TO THREE/ National Center for Clinical Infant Programs.

Anderson, P. P., & Goldberg, P. F. (1991). *Cultural competence in screening and assessment.* Minneapolis, MN: Pacer Center.

Baca, L., & Cervantes, H. T. (1989). *The bilingual special education interface.* St. Louis, MO: Mosby.

Banks, J. A. (1994). *An introduction to multicultural education.* Boston, MA: Allyn & Bacon.

Barrera, I. (1990). *Honoring the differences: Six essential features of serving culturally/linguistically diverse children with special needs.* Unpublished monograph available from author: University of New Mexico; Special Education; MVH 3006; Albuquerque, NM 87131.

Figueroa, R. A., & Garcia, E. (1994). Issues in testing students from culturally and linguistically diverse backgrounds. *Multicultural Education, 2* (1), 10-23.

Ho, D. Y. F. (1995). Internalized culture, culturocentrism, and transcendence. *Counseling Psychologist, 23* (1), 4-24.

Jensen, M. R., & Feuerstein, R. (1987). The learning potential assessment device: From philosophy to practice. In C. Lidz (Ed.), *Dynamic assessment* (pp. 379-402). New York: Guilford.

King, E. W., Chipman, M., & Cruz-Janzen, M. (1994). *Educating children in a diverse society.* Boston, MA: Allyn & Bacon.

Lynch, E. W., & Hanson, M. (1992). *Developing cross-cultural competence.* Baltimore, MD: Paul H. Brookes Publishing Co.

Markus, H. R. (1994). A collective fear of the collective: Implications for selves and theories of selves. *Personality and Social Psychology Bulletin, 20* (5), 568-579.

Tikunoff, W. J. (1987). Mediation of instruction to obtain equality of effectiveness. In S. H. Fradd & J. Tikunoff (Eds)., *Bilingual education and bilingual special education* (pp. 99-132). Boston, MA: College-Hill.

# 6. History-Making, not History-Taking:

## Clinical Interviews with Infants and Their Families

LAURENCE M. HIRSHBERG

In a recent contribution to *Zero to Three*, Pawl (1995) address-es a basic element of human connection in simple and eloquent terms: "When a child is held in mind, the child feels it, and knows it. There is a sense of safety, of containment, and, most important, existence in that other, which has always seemed to me vital. . . . It seems to me that one of life's greatest privileges is just that—the experience of being held in someone's mind."

When an infant/family professional is conducting an interview with parents and a baby—perhaps in the home with the televi-sion blaring in the background, or with siblings running around tearing up the house, and probably with piles of forms to fill out—the interview process is likely to seem far removed from this basic act of human connectedness. And yet, by inviting par-ents to tell the story of their baby and their family carefully and thoughtfully, the professional is inviting them (and helping them) to connect in that way to their infant, to hold the baby in their minds. The professional is also promising the parents that he or she will engage in the same act of connection, offering to hold all of them (parents and baby) in his or her own mind. With all the things to consider in the interview process—the technical procedures and paperwork, the diagnostic and developmental considerations and complications, and the frantic scheduling and juggling of time and needs—it is easy to lose sight of this simple, basic fact. The professional should not lose sight of it.

*The most essential job of the person conducting the clinical interview with an infant and family is to be able to hold the baby and the family in his or her mind as fully and completely as possible.*

## Hindrances to the Clinical Interview

While consulting with early intervention programs, visiting nurse services, preschools, and day care centers concerning infant mental health, I have become familiar with some of the common hindrances to this holding process during the clinical interview. The most obvious and serious hindrance is time. Today, most clinical professionals feel enormously pressed to conform to time pressures dictated by fiscal limitations (due to managed care) and regulations governing public programs (such as the requirement to complete a comprehensive assessment within 45 days in early intervention). No clinical exhortations are likely to change these exigencies in the near future. One of the interviewer's basic jobs, therefore, is to contain these pressures and keep them from interfering with the family's telling of their story about themselves and their baby. Parents must have ample time to tell this story and must feel confident that those to whom they are telling it are genuinely listening. Just as it is critical for a parent to be able to physically hold a baby with care, patient attention, and calm readiness, it is also critical for the professional to hold the family in mind with these same qualities. Rushing to "get it done" in one home visit or "before the deadline" sends parents a message as surely as a parent sends a baby a message when he or she reads the newspaper or watches television while feeding the baby.

The second common hindrance to the clinical interview process is, oddly enough, knowledge. As a therapist and supervisor, I have found, over and over again, that what a professional knows, or thinks he or she knows, can easily get in the way of learning from a family. *The most helpful stance in conducting the clinical interview is one of principled, determined ignorance.* Assume that you do not completely understand a situation until you have listened fully and in great detail to what a parent is saying. For the same reason, it is critical to ask open-ended questions, ones which in no way imply, entail, or presuppose any part of the requested reply.

Feelings and wishes of the interviewer that can interfere with his or her willingness to listen and explore in an open, nonjudgmental fashion constitute a third common hindrance to the interview process. Competitive feelings or a sense of superiority on the part of the interviewer can hinder the development of an open exchange. In addition, if the interviewer has critical feelings about the way parents are responding to their child, these feelings will generally be sensed by the parents, creating an atmosphere that will not be conducive to an open exploration on their part. The interviewer can best deal with these critical feelings about the parents' behavior by asking the parents, in a respectful fashion, how they feel about that behavior. It is crucial to know, for purposes of treatment planning, to what extent parents may have regrets, misgivings, or other signs of conflict about their ways of parenting that might be detrimental to their child. If the interviewer helps the parents give voice to their own self-criticism and their parallel wishes to parent differently, they are far more likely to be helped than they would be if they sensed criticism coming from the interviewer. The objective, therefore, is to find access to the parents' own wishes to change their ways of parenting.

Perhaps less obvious—but, in my experience, not uncommon among early intervention professionals who do not have mental health backgrounds and training—is a fear of helplessness on the part of the interviewer. In consultations, innumerable professionals have commented to me: "I do not really want to know about that! I mean, what will I do then? What do I say if she says. . . . How will I handle that?"

Careful listening, in itself, is powerful help. It is a way, in and of itself, to "handle" many problems. In many cases, a solution will emerge in the course of a discussion, a solution which then comes from the parent rather than from the "expert advice" of the professional. Moreover, the important question is how *the parent* is going to handle the situation. What does he or she want to do, and what stands in his or her way? The interviewer's helpless feeling is connected to a sense of overresponsibility, as if it is the job of the professional to do something about the situation, rather than the job of the parent whom the professional is assisting. Finally, there is nothing wrong with not knowing what to do. A professional veneer of having all the answers is never helpful. Most parents sense that it is a veneer. All that is necessary is a genuine: "I do not know about that. We will have to see what we can come up with together." Dealing with uncertainty and ambiguity—not knowing the answer—is indeed one of the central tasks of being a parent. If the parent sees that the professional has a sense of calm and is confident in the face of this state of not knowing, it is the source of a very important, positive kind of learning on the part of the parent.

In general, if an interviewer has strong feelings about a family and a baby, that interviewer should consider the feelings to be a sign that he or she needs to reflect carefully on his or her own experience and history as well as the experience of the family. When a certain set of feelings repeatedly arises and interferes with the clinical process, it is likely that the professional's personal conflicts or painful experiences are imposing themselves on his or her professional work, and consultation and careful supervision are warranted.

## The Interview Process

### The goal of the interviews

In the view of the assessment process advocated in this chapter, the goal of clinical interviews is the mutual development (together with the parents) of a clear, focused understanding of the core of the problem that the baby and the family are experiencing.

This goal is fundamentally different from that which is often the purpose of the initial contacts between early intervention professionals and parents, that of determining eligibility for services for their child. Although it may be necessary to talk to parents in order to determine eligibility, this goal and the numerous technical requirements of determining eligibility should not be confused with the goal of the clinical interview assessment. In my experience with early intervention, the real understanding of the infant and family often develops *after* all the initial requirements of the formal assessment process have been completed as the family and professionals are trying to determine what to do about the issues and problems they face.

While gathering information is often an important adjunctive activity in the process of arriving at an understanding of the problem a baby and his or her family are experiencing, it *is* adjunctive. It is critical to gather the information as part of an active, ongoing effort, together with the parents, to construct an account of the family's experience and their experience with the baby. This account is then continuously modified or elaborated upon throughout the interviews and subsequent treatment.

When attempting to make sense of the central family problem, gathering a number of disjointed facts about the family is often much less productive than the careful analysis of a small detail or single experience which embodies the core of the problem. In his comments about the process of historiography, Walter Benjamin, a German social philosopher, made the same point more eloquently by quoting his favorite Jewish aphorism: "The Lord God dwells in detail." I take this aphorism to mean that the essence or spirit of the whole resides within the smallest parts and that the details of experience offer a sort of privileged access to a complete understanding of the essence or whole. I find this concept to be a useful guide in the clinical interview process. Any of the background "facts" may well be superfluous to a focused understanding of the core of the case. I believe Selma Fraiberg was referring to this phenomenon when she said that parents, when raising their infants, often repeat their own childhood traumas "in terrible and exacting detail" (Fraiberg, 1980). The repetition is frequently especially evident in the terrible and exacting detail.

## The clinical relational matrix

In the approach to the clinical interview with infants and families advanced here, it is assumed, as a basic principle, that when parents are talking to a professional about a problem with an infant, their responses to their infant, to each other, and to the professional are shaped by the nature of their relationship to the professional as it continuously unfolds in the interview process. As a result, the goal of the interview process is not to gather objective data, but *to form a personal relationship through which the assessor can elicit from the family and observe a range of psychological functioning on the basis of which the problem can be understood and a plan can be made cooperatively to resolve it* (Shevrin & Shechtman, 1973).

There are practical reasons why the professional must focus on his or her emerging relationship with the family. The most important one is that there are many families with which no in-depth evaluation can be conducted without steps to facilitate the establishment of a working alliance with the family. Unless the parents develop a degree of trust in the interviewer and experience empathic concern on his or her part, as well as a strong sense of respect for their wishes as parents and their needs as individuals, they are not likely to fully cooperate in the evaluation and disclose their painful experiences with their baby. Parental "characteristics," such as extreme emotional distance, coldness, or flatness in the interview; resolute failure to acknowledge any responsibility for the baby's problem; and insistence on blaming the baby for the problem, may be as much signs of distrust toward the interviewer (often seen as an agent of a program or social service agency) as they are products of a fixed character structure or psychopathology.

Mrs. M. described her 12-month-old daughter as impossible to soothe or regulate, constantly crying, and often tantrumming. Having been seen months earlier by another infant professional, she was wary in her initial appointments, expecting a repeat of what she had perceived as mistreatment at the hands of the previous professional. She reported that she had been told after one hour of observation that there was "nothing wrong" with the baby. She was furious about this outcome, feeling that it amounted to a dismissal of her concerns. She insisted heatedly that the child was really bad; in fact, she said, she frequently found herself calling this child, her second daughter, her "vile child."

Mrs. M. had recently been left by her husband, in part because he could not tolerate the baby's screaming. Initially, she was entirely unable to acknowledge any difficulties within herself in relation to the baby. Her denial persisted until we had talked about her frustration with the baby; her anguish, anger, and fear at being left by her husband; and her pride in her 4-year-old daughter and the pleasure that daughter gave her. In the context of these explorations, she began to describe her own history of extreme emotional and physical abuse. In this context, she mentioned that she had always been called "the problem child" and was the distinct and clear scapegoat, who was subject to frank and brutal abuse, in her family of origin.

Having developed some trust in the interviewer in the course of these sessions, Mrs. M. could then make use of a connection with her own troubled past when the phrases "vile child" and "problem child" were linked by the evaluator. Only then could she begin to describe the difficulties she had soothing and calming her distressed infant, her lack of tolerance for the infant's insistent demandingness, her extremely intense feelings of hatred when her baby so insistently signaled her own need, and her placing this baby in the all too familiar position of the family scapegoat.

Another practical reason for focusing on the nature of the relationship between the professional and the family in assessment relates to "treatment compliance." The likelihood that recommendations for treatment made as an outcome of the assessment will be favorably received and carried out by the parents depends in part on their relationship with the professional. If parents feel blamed or criticized, intruded upon, unheard or unappreciated, or even rejected, they will be much less likely to follow through on treatment than if they feel understood, accepted, respected, and appreciated.

But beyond these pragmatic grounds, there are theoretical reasons for the emphasis on the centrality of the relationship between parents and professional. Contemporary theories of knowledge call into question the long-held theory (and common-sense view) that "the facts" or data may properly be thought of as objective and external, existing in some sense apart from the "knowing" activity of the subject. According to this theory, which has been superseded, knowledge is attained by accurately uncovering or discovering "the facts" and their interrelationships. By contrast, contemporary theorists argue that all knowledge is a process by which the knower actively organizes, orders, or shapes what is given to perception or thought and thereby constructs or constitutes what is known (Hirshberg, 1989). Knowledge then represents an outcome of a dynamic interaction between knower and known, subject and object.

In the context of the clinical interview, the critical point is that *what is learned about the infant and family is a picture or account which is constructed in the course of an active dynamic exchange between family members and evaluator.* This means that the interviewer should carefully pay attention to how he is being experienced by the family, how he is experiencing them, and how the interpersonal or relational matrix in the clinical setting (including culture, class, race, and other factors) is shaping the interview as it unfolds and the story as it is emerging. As Fraiberg emphasizes (Fraiberg, 1980), this attention to the nature of the emerging relationship should begin, if possible, with the referral itself or the first phone contact.

## Transference

The view of the assessment process discussed above carries with it another implication. If the history one receives in an interview is necessarily a product of the current relational matrix, the diagnostic significance of that history recedes somewhat compared to the importance of a careful examination of the interview process, since the history itself is a product of that process. What counts most is how an account is being organized or construed during the interview and what is happening to the family and baby during the interview.

This view is in marked contrast to a history-taking or medical-model approach to the assessment interview, according to which the purpose of the interview is to obtain "the facts" about the course of the symptoms or problem over time, and about any other phenomena causally related to the symptoms or problem, in order to diagnose the problem and prescribe treatment. This view follows psychoanalytic clinical theory and practice in emphasizing the importance of transference phenomena.

In the history of psychoanalytic thinking, the concept of transference has been used to refer to the patient's imposition or transferring onto his experience with the therapist expectations, wishes, and fears derived not primarily from the context of the real patient-therapist relationship but from childhood relationships (Freud, 1912). Thus, transference represents the repetition of childhood relational experiences in the relationship between the patient and the therapist.

More recently, this construct has been generalized to explain how all experience in relationships is organized, structured, and interpreted (Greenberg & Mitchell, 1983; Mitchell, 1988; Stern, 1985). The notion is that we create mental images or representations of ourselves and emotionally-important others in interactions or relationships. These representations may vary across different types of experiences or interactions. Most theorists suggest that the emotional quality or tone of the interaction is a central feature of the representation.

These representations, schemas, internal working models, or object relational paradigms, as they are variously called, are based on our early experiences in relationships and are subject to modification and change as a result of our ongoing experience in interactions with others. It is on the basis of these organized sets of expectations about relationships that we perceive, structure, construe, and interpret all experience in interactions and relationships with others. According to this view, all social experience involves what psychoanalysts have called transference.

The implication of the concept of transference for the therapy process in psychoanalytic treatment has been that we pay as much—if not more—attention to what the patient is *doing* in saying something as we pay to the content of what he is saying. The idea is to pay attention to how the patient's responses are a reflection of his or her functioning in the relationship to the therapist. The same qualified recommendation holds true for the clinical interview with infants and their families: Pay as much, or more, attention to what the parents and infant are doing during the interview as you do to what they are saying. This includes not just how the parents and infant interact and relate to one another and to the professional during the interview, but also what the parents are doing interactively (with the interviewer and within the family) by saying what they are saying and how they are saying it. A parent's account of the infant's troubles may be organized for the purpose of persuading the interviewer that the infant is inherently bad, castigating and punishing a spouse for his or her perceived irresponsibility, or recruiting the interviewer as a nurturant caregiver for and ally of the parent as much as it is to convey "the facts" about the problem.

Clinical work with the infant in the context of the family is a setting that is, in many ways, ideally suited to the analysis of transference. However, in the context of the assessment of the infant and family, the patient-to-therapist transference is supplemented, or sometimes supplanted, as the primary arena for exploration and interpretation by the parent-to-infant and/or parent-to-parent transference. To translate this into contemporary terms, the area of focus in this context is on how each parent organizes and interprets his experience with the infant (and spouse) and, therefore, on the set of expectations, wishes, needs, fears, and fantasies which shape the parents' view of the baby (and spouse) and their view of themselves in relationship to the baby (and each other).

The organization of the parent-to-infant relationship has several advantages over the patient-to-therapist transference as a field for early exploration and interpretation. Most important is its affective intensity and availability. Very few things evoke as much intense emotion in people as troubles with a baby. Moreover, the emotion is often quite vivid and apparent during the interviews because the baby is present. If the parents impose expectations, needs, wishes, and fears on the baby that are inappropriate to the relationship between the parents and the baby, or are from the parents' own past, this situation can be more accessible to exploration. Often, you can see it happening before you. Through pointed, detailed exploration of some emotionally laden or particularly significant interactions or experiences during the interview, much that is significant in the organization of the parents' relationship to the baby can be revealed in the evaluation.

Another advantage of exploring the parent-to-infant relationship is the fact that, for most people, it is more sensible and seems more reasonable to expect parents to express important psychological conflicts in their interactions with their child than to expect them to reveal these conflicts to a therapist they have just met. Early exploration regarding the parent-to-infant relationship can often be approached more on the basis of common sense than can transference interpretations in psychoanalytic psychotherapy with adults. In addition, the motivation to change the disturbed way of relating is often much more intense when infants are involved than when psychotherapy of adults is the focus. As Fraiberg (1980) points out, most parents desperately want to do well by their babies and want to make a better life for them. Therefore, there is frequently ample ground on which to build an early working alliance between the parents and the professional that will be used to support an assessment style that is quite challenging.

## History-making rather than history-taking

It is important to learn basic background information, such as the history of the pregnancy, medical complications, and the parental marriage or relationship, as well as data on other influences in the life of the family, such as day care, work situations, extended family, and cultural contexts. However, information such as this is better learned as an integral part of the process of exploration carried out by the parents and the professional, that is, through the parents' account of the baby and the family, rather than as a result of a list of routine questions in different areas.

This is perhaps most important with regard to potentially sensitive and troubling information about the parents' own early childhood experiences and the effect of these experiences on them as parents. Many parents are, naturally, on the defensive when this line of inquiry comes up. Often, they are gritting their teeth in the expectation that they will be criticized and blamed for the baby's problem. Those who are most emphatic in their overt blame of the baby for the problem frequently blame themselves secretly and severely. The severity of their angry accusation about the bad baby reflects their own less overt but often quite intense self-criticism. And, after all, the parents are seeking help because the baby has a problem, not because they want to chat about their own childhoods. The goal, therefore, is to explore and discover, with the parents, *the past as it is active in the present.*

"Getting the history" through the parents' narrative has a

number of advantages. First, the evaluator's interest in this information is naturally linked to the parents' own concerns and motives. By learning the information in this way, he or she is more sensitive to these concerns and motives and is perhaps less threatening to the parents. Second, the history naturally becomes organized or focused around the problem as the parents interact during the interview. This often facilitates the recognition and emotional acknowledgment of dynamically important connections. It is also more likely that important determinants of the problem that become apparent in a baby-focused exploration such as this are more readily comprehensible to the parents and are perhaps more easily worked with because the disclosure of the information often indicates an ability and readiness to come to terms with it.

Mrs. M., the mother who referred to her daughter as the "vile child," illustrates this point. The evaluator asked about the phrase "vile child" when it was first used, but the mother was so angry and mistrustful that the question was not productive. Once she had formed an alliance with the evaluator and had explored some of the consequences of her own extremely troubled early experience, the significance of the phrase as an indicator of a "repetition of a childhood tragedy" (Fraiberg, 1980) could be understood and used. In this case, it led to a startling recognition by the mother that her experience with her baby reflected an unwanted, disavowed aspect of self. As she put it then, her baby was "her mirror image," giving loud voice to the angry neediness which she had always forcibly suppressed and had come to pride herself in not having.

Rarely can an important area of inquiry not be linked to the immediate account that the parents are giving. For instance, expressions of disappointment or frustration about difficulties with the baby can be used to explore the parents' expectations about the baby, about parenthood during the pregnancy, and, even before that, during childhood: "The way things have turned out is frustrating to you, maybe different from your image of what it is to be a parent (or to have a baby). How did you imagine it would be before he was born?" Similarly, questions about the parents' marital functioning can be asked in the context of accounts of the problem with the baby and how it is being handled within the family. Functioning in other areas of the marriage can similarly be linked: "So you have some serious conflicts about how to handle this problem with the baby. How do you get along otherwise?"

*Open-ended questions are key, as they allow the interviewer to understand how the parents put the complex picture of their baby and their family together, and how they construct the family experience.* I have found that this is another aspect of the interview process that is often foreign to early intervention professionals without mental health backgrounds and is difficult for them. Professionals from most other disciplines are trained to conduct a parent interview by asking a set of very specific questions and are accustomed to this approach. Without the structure and guidance of such a list, many professionals feel uncomfortably "at sea." They worry that they will not be able to get the facts, and they fear that they might not know how to respond to what they hear. Many, I think, are uncomfortable because they do not feel in control and in command of their professional procedures and language when the flow of the interview is guided by the concerns of the parents. I have found that, with practice and good supervision, most professionals can become comfortable with this process of working cooperatively with the story as it is told by the parents and with being able to observe how the parents organize and structure the story, which reflects how they organize and structure the life of the family.

After conducting one or two initial interviews in this open-ended manner, the professional is in a position to compile the information gained and to determine if any important areas of inquiry have been omitted. If so, direct inquiry can be made subsequently to fill in the complete picture.

## Experience in dynamic detail

In the assessment of the infant-parent relationship, it is perhaps most important to select some emotionally critical or nodal interactions which occur during the interview to explore in fine detail with the parents. Look for critical dynamic chains or sequences of responses by one partner to the other, in which an initial emotional response is subject to continuous influence and change due to the ongoing feedback from the partner. Such sequences can disclose important determinants of the infant's and parents' behavior which cannot be captured on the basis of general descriptive features of interactions or relationships, such as intrusiveness, noncontingency, or disengagement. This is illustrated in the relationship between S. and his mother, Mrs. A.:

S., an 18-month-old boy, was referred to assessment due to severe
headbanging. He is playing with a small wooden hammer, while his
mother, Mrs. A., talks with the interviewer. He is banging a variety of
objects, not with any particular aggressiveness or anger, but playfully,
experimentally, and with vigor and interest. S. approaches his mother
and gives her chair a rather gentle bang on the leg. Mrs. A. stiffens
immediately and, with noticeable suppressed anger but little forceful-
ness or assertiveness, asks him to stop it.  S., in turn, stiffens and paus-
es. He then bangs the chair repeatedly in a genuinely aggressive manner. Mrs. A. responds more angrily this time, but again somewhat inef-
fectually, by telling her son to stop. More angrily, he hits her chair
again, whereupon she gets out of the chair, grabs him by the arm, and
tells him he is being bad and has to cut it out. The toddler falls limp to
the ground so that he is hanging by his arm and begins to cry loudly.
His mother looks quite exasperated, hurt, and confused. She lets go of
his arm and returns to her seat, leaving him crying more loudly in a
heap on the floor. Then he begins to bang his head repeatedly on the
floor. While watching him, Mrs. A. yells at him several times to stop.
Then she stands up and grabs him by the arm again. She looks quite
withdrawn and cold; he appears absolutely forlorn, bereft of support
and contact, without any solution, and lost. At this point, the interviewer intervenes.

In the case of S. and Mrs. A., the initial emotional response of
each partner (mother and baby) was profoundly transformed by
that of the other. An initial experience of curious assertiveness
and interest in sharing was transformed into an angry, painful
interaction culminating in a distant, hopeless sense of impasse
and despair in both partners.

It is usually best to select such an interaction for assessment
after an overall sense of the problem and the functioning of the
relationships in the family have emerged. In this way, the interviewer will know which areas of difficulty are most important,
emotionally vivid and powerful, and likely to be fruitfully
explored, and he or she will have a sense of the parents' willingness and ability to explore their experiences in detail.

Having selected such an interaction, ask the parents to
describe what they were thinking and feeling at each point in the
interaction, what they felt like doing or saying, and what they
thought the infant was thinking, feeling, and trying to accomplish or communicate at each point in the interaction. Explore
how what occurred is similar to or different from interactions
occurring at home, the infant's interactions with other people,
and the parents' interactions with other children and adults. Ask
how the parents think others, including their spouses, parents,
and in-laws, perceive such interactions.

It may be necessary to be quite active in the process of this exploration. Parents may need to be provided with a slow pace by being walked through the interaction, especially if they initially produce a very simple or global account of the experience. It may be helpful to ask about the fine details of the interaction, beginning with its unthreatening aspects. Emphasize to the parents that people usually have numerous thoughts and feelings all at once, or in a very short time, and that you are interested in *all* of these thoughts and feelings, even if they might seem irrelevant or even silly. Initial attempts by the parents to disavow the significance or complexity of the interaction should be gently confronted by saying, for instance, that these are the kinds of things that parents often "do not pay much attention to" or that "seem unimportant," but they are often helpful in understanding how the troubles with the baby affect them. Much can be gained by resolutely "playing dumb."

During the interaction between S., the headbanging toddler, and his mother, Mrs. A., the interviewer proceeded by settling the toddler down to a snack and using this time to explore the interaction which had just occurred in detail with Mrs. A.

In a previous session, Mrs. A. had described her very intense, troubled relationship with her father in some detail. She was the oldest of two girls. Her father had desperately wanted a son and the youngest daughter's gender was a regular subject of heated argument between her parents. Mrs. A. filled in the gap after her sister's birth (which occurred when she was five) by becoming a tomboy and her father's "buddy." She spent her time fishing, hunting, target shooting, and working around the farm with him. She cherished the closeness with him that she had gained through her masculinization, and she delighted in her renown due to her success in boyish activities.

Her father was an extremely short-tempered, impatient, strict, proto-abusive man. He had a drinking problem which, according to her report, remained in control until the family moved to Florida. He could not find work there, so the family was supported by his wife. He began to drink heavily. He also lost his "buddy" at the same time, as his daughter had reached adolescence and discovered boys as objects of desire rather than competition. Her father reportedly became intensely preoccupied with her budding sexuality, extremely jealous of her dating, and regularly physically abusive. Due to the unabated physical abuse, Mrs. A. moved away to live with her grandparents at the age of fifteen.

In the course of the exploration, it quickly became clear that Mrs. A. had experienced S.'s banging as an aggressive attack on her. Almost instantly, she had become furiously angry, confused, paralyzed, and withdrawn—angry because she felt he was attacking her and confused because she could not understand why he was hitting her. He was supposed to love her, and she tried so hard to love him. She was paralyzed and withdrawn because she was afraid that, otherwise, she would hit him and hurt him. With detailed questioning, Mrs. A. was able to describe the sequence of these feelings in this interaction with her son. When the interviewer then asked the obvious question about what she had felt when her father attacked her, the identification of father and son was evident, palpable, and alive. She talked about wanting to kill her father at these times, aching to strike him back, but afraid that, if she did, his abuse would only grow more fierce. She also described her feelings of helplessness and despair, since she wanted so badly for him to cherish her again as he had when she was a child, and she could not understand his present dissatisfaction with her.

## Provoking anxiety

Of course, as in any clinical encounter, the interviewer must be aware of the effect of these interventions on the parents. If this type of encouragement of self-reflection meets with stiffened resistance or a negative response, it is important to note that, inquire about it, and take time to work with and respectfully challenge the resistance. Although it is critical not to alienate the parents with an intrusive style, many parents are able to use an empathic nudge from a professional to explore further.

Some professionals may worry about alienating parents with such a sustained and methodical focus on anxiety-provoking areas of their experience. The concern is that the anxiety will be so high that these parents might subsequently withdraw from the evaluation process or resist the recommendation for treatment. Although these considerations should certainly be borne in mind, the converse danger is the more serious and probably far more common one—that the parents may feel as if the interviewer "missed the boat" because he or she failed to explore, and hence failed to understand, the truly painful and worrisome experiences in their lives with the baby. In contrast to, and often together with, the expected anxiety at having painful conflicts disclosed and explored in this sort of focused interview, parents often feel a profound relief that finally someone else understands their problems, and, therefore, that help is possible. In this view, *it is the very anxiety that such exploration evokes that tells the interviewer he or she is on the right track and should move carefully ahead, and it signals to the parents that previously incomprehensible problems can be understood.*

Throughout the course of the interview, the professional should be alert to the signs of anxiety which betoken significant areas of conflict in the infant-parent relationship and should either make a mental note for later detailed exploration or zero in and explore the anxiety in fine-grained detail as it emerges. Problems with a baby almost invariably involve the most basic, intensely experienced emotions and conflicts in a parent's life. A clinical interview which does not explore these emotions and conflicts to the degree of depth that the parents can make use of and that will illuminate their significance for the parents and baby has, simply, failed in its dual task: It has failed to understand the infant's problems and has failed to form a therapeutic relationship on the basis of which the problems can be solved.

This aspect of the clinical interview process is another one that is commonly difficult for those without mental health backgrounds. The implicit social rule with which we all grew up holds that, when another person becomes anxious or uncomfortable, it should be taken as a signal to back off or talk about something else to relieve the other's distress. In the clinical interview process, the rule is largely reversed: If a topic is distressing or upsetting, it is important to look at it and understand it in depth.

In the case of infants with medical problems or developmental difficulties, it is often part of the job of the clinical interview to broaden the scope of the discourse to include a careful understanding of the meaning and significance of a baby's problem for the parents. Frequently, the interviewer's attempt to "open the door" to more private family and personal issues may not be immediately welcomed by parents. They may be reluctant to discuss these issues because they are focusing primarily on the baby's problem as the sole object of interest.

Several considerations should be borne in mind in these situations. First, it is best to pursue a shared understanding of these areas of the parents' experience by following up on signals from the parents themselves. These signals may take the form of verbalizations related to the baby and his or her difficulties, or they may be nonverbal signs of a parent's emotional response—a particularly sorrowful look, a way of touching or holding the baby, a sigh, or a gesture of gathering up one's strength. Frequently, parents will make very tentative initial forays into these painful areas of experience and wait for your response. These are careful trial balloons, and your acknowledgment of their significance and your respectful interest in their depth go a long way toward helping a parent feel safe enough to "open the door" more than just a crack. Highlight the signal and ask what thoughts or feelings go with it. If you are not getting these signals, begin with open-ended questions such as "What (is it like for you/are you thinking/goes through your mind/are you feeling) when. . . .?" Then follow up on the answer you get with a response that indicates your interest in all the complexities and details of the experience.

The mother of a child with autism was discussing the strains of having such a child: the incomprehension of relatives and friends; the well-meaning but infuriating advice; the odd looks in the grocery store; the trouble she was having understanding her child's behavior and responses; and the pain of recognizing the limitations in the child's relatedness to her. She was articulate and quite willing to speak of her feelings about her daughter. But there was a troubledness in her feelings that she could not put her finger on, a sense of unease or discomfort because of her daughter's disability. Almost as an aside in the course of this interview, she remarked that the quality of her daughter's cry bothered her a great deal. She could not really explain why; it just seemed weird to her and grated on her. She could tolerate well much of the stress of caring for her daughter, but this weird cry disturbed her greatly. The interviewer took this as one of those significant details and asked about her thoughts and feelings concerning this weird or odd thing her daughter did. The mother's train of associations led clearly to her feelings about her beloved father, who had a deformed arm. She was very close to her father, but there came a time in her development when she felt ashamed and embarrassed about his deformity and did not want to be seen in public with him; indeed, she did not want him to be seen in public at all. As ashamed as she was, she felt yet a greater sense of guilt for feeling this way about her father. In remembering these undeserved feelings of shame and the attendant guilt, this mother could recognize a similar sense of intense guilt about her feelings of embarrassment concerning her daughter's "weird" behavior and disability. Although more work clearly remained to be done in this area, this mother reported in the next interview that she no longer experienced that strong discomfort upon hearing her daughter's cry.

The parents' form of response to efforts during the evaluation to overcome anxieties and resistance and to explore personal experiences related to the problem with the baby is a crucial index for the assessment, especially when considering treatment recommendations. Does any initial wariness or defensiveness on the part of the parents give way to more open exchange as a consequence of the interviewer's respectful but active approach? How do the parents respond to careful challenges to defenses? Do the parents respond to the invitation to explore in detail their experience with the baby and what it means to them with deepened interest, richer, more revealing material, and a heightened level of relatedness to the interviewer, or do they respond with distance or hostility, as well as superficiality or vagueness?

If a parent or parents choose not to make use of this fairly assertive mode of help to achieve self-understanding, the interviewer will need to "back off" and take a somewhat less active and assertive stance. He or she will perhaps need to turn to other less threatening areas of the evaluation, noting this for the purpose of making a recommendation for treatment.

Having outlined an active, anxiety-provoking strategy for conducting the clinical interview with an infant and parents, it is important to emphasize that this kind of persistence in actively exploring areas of anxiety and dysfunction does not in any way mean that the interviewer is perceived or experienced by the parents as critical or blaming. Such *shared* recognition of the effect of inner conflict on the parents' behavior, which has emerged out of an emotionally-charged interaction and exchange with the interviewer, is quite different in the experience of the parents from being told by a distant expert that they are to blame for the child's problems. *The experience of being understood in a rich, complex, and deep way by another person, including being understood with respect to one's vulnerabilities and imperfections, is felt to be supportive, and it often elicits considerable energy and hope alongside the anxiety, and often supplants this anxiety.*

In this regard, it is important that the interviewer recognize, along with the parents, the areas of strength in the functioning of the infant and the parents and in the infant-parent relationship, as well as the areas of difficulty. It is particularly important to single out for comment the experiences with the infant during the interview that signal positive functioning and attachment, and to explore them with the parents. For many different reasons, parents may have trouble recognizing in themselves yearnings for closeness and love which they repudiated or suppressed in the past, and they may have trouble utilizing them in the service of the baby's development. Positive feelings and wishes may be expressed only in a tentative or restrained way, and exploration of the details of these experiences is as important as exploration of negative experiences.

A young mother had four children, three sons and a daughter. The two oldest boys (ages three and five) had been placed in foster care by child protective services and had had multiple psychiatric hospitalizations since then. The mother retained custody of her 2-year-old daughter and a newborn son, and was being interviewed while holding the new-born. Although she showed absolutely no tenderness or affection with the older boys and was describing their difficulties to the interviewer in a markedly flat and disengaged manner, she was observed at the same time to be gently stroking the newborn's head and rubbing his back and chest, without seeming to be aware of what she was doing. When asked how she felt while holding and stroking the baby that way, she replied in a distant or matter of fact tone that she felt nothing in par-ticular; she was just holding him. When the interviewer commented that her hands were communicating her loving feelings even as her voice and words denied them, she responded by reflecting on the dif-ferences in her feelings of closeness to her children and on her sense of alienation from the two children who had been taken from her. These explorations led her to memories of her own lifelong history of disrupt-ed and chaotic attachment and caregiving in her family of origin and in the numerous foster care arrangements which followed her removal from her mother's care in the first year of her life. She described these memories in a richer and more meaningful way in the context of this exchange than she had in an earlier interview.

Here, the positive affectionate feelings and yearnings were ver-bally repudiated or disavowed. However, through the interview-er's active encouragement and attention to the details of the pos-itive interaction as it unfolded, the mother was able to acknowl-edge her loving feelings, recognize important aspects of her rela-tionship with her children, and deepen her understanding of her troubles with her children and their relationship to her own prior experience. As a consequence, instead of experiencing the dominant view of herself as someone beset by bad or evil chil-dren, she could begin to perceive and experience herself as a mother who was striving to be a warm, affectionate parent despite psychological barriers within herself which had been erected over the course of her own development.

Apart from the importance of recognizing split off or dis-avowed positive feelings and wishes and working therapeutical-ly with them, it is also important to keep in mind that parental self-esteem and confidence can be given an important boost through the interviewer's recognition of the positive effects of the parents' efforts and care on the baby. Sustained and persis-tent focus on areas of difficulty should not be pursued at the cost of attention to and acknowledgment of parental strengths, and vice versa.

# Information Gathering

The goal of the information-gathering component of the clinical interview is to develop as complete and comprehensive a view as possible of *the infant in context*, in order to facilitate a shared understanding of the infant's problem and develop a plan for treatment. This includes information about individual characteristics of the infant; of the parents and other important people in the infant's life; and of the cultural and social world in which the infant is developing. It also includes information about the relationship between the infant and each of the significant figures in his or her life.

As emphasized above, it is preferable to learn as much as possible about all of these aspects of the case through observation during interviews and through the account given by the parents, rather than through responses to a fixed or routine series of questions to "get the history." However, what is learned through observation during interviews and through the parents' story often must be supplemented with some degree of direct inquiry. Again, it is best, when possible, to link this inquiry to experiences in the interviews. With regard to all the areas of evaluation mentioned below, it is also critical to explain their emotional or dynamic meaning to the parents in detail.

In some cases, it will be necessary to seek a specialized assessment, such as a cognitive, neurological, or speech and language evaluation, to supplement the interview process. If such a specialized assessment is warranted, it is important to prepare the parents for the referral by explaining clearly and carefully the concerns that led you to seek such an evaluation and the questions you want to have answered. You should also take time to answer any questions they may have and to probe for any concerns about the referral that they may have trouble expressing or acknowledging. It is also critical to formulate clear and specific referral questions for the professional to whom you are making the referral and to carefully integrate the findings of specialized assessments into the final formulation communicated to the parents.

## Parent-infant interaction and relationship

First, and most obviously, the family interview process presents an opportunity to pay careful attention to the samples of interaction between each parent and the baby. Be careful not to take the initiative to resume the interview too quickly after an inter-ruption by the parent to attend to the needs of the baby. It is important to allow the parent to pace the alternation of atten-tion to interviewer and baby and to manage the competing demands of the two as he or she sees fit. This is an important aspect of parental functioning which can be observed in the interview process, and precautions should be taken to see that the conduct of the interviewer interferes as little as possible with the unfolding of this process.

There are a number of important interdependent areas or domains of functioning to observe and assess in the infant-par-ent relationship. Although these are described and categorized by different theorists and professionals in varying ways (Clark, 1985; Emde, 1989; Greenspan, 1981; & Sander, 1975), there appears to be general agreement about the most important areas of observation. Emde (1989) proposes seven domains of func-tioning: (a) attachment and the organization of the experience related to emotional and physical closeness or contact, avail-ability, and separation, distance, and individuation; (b) vigilance and protection, or the organization of experience related to maintaining the safety of the infant; (c) physiological regulation of food intake, warmth, stimulation, and mental states (sleep, alertness); (d) play, symbolism, and communication of mean-ings; (e) teaching and learning; (f) power, control, and discipline; and (g) regulation of emotion or affect, including the expression and communication of emotion.

With regard to the functioning of the dyad (infant and parent) in each domain, it is important to assess relative strengths and weaknesses; the importance of stressors in the origin and main-tenance of any disturbance; the duration of any disturbance, its relative rigidity or responsiveness to change, and its impact on the development of infant and parent; and the level of perceived discomfort or distress experienced in relation to the disturbance. Looking across domains, it is important to assess the pervasive-ness or specificity of the strengths and weaknesses noted in each area.

### The attachment relationship

The assessment of the infant-parent attachment relationship requires careful observation of how the partners in each dyad organize their interactions and relationship to balance the need for a feeling of security or comfort through closeness with the need for exploration and mastery of the surroundings. (For a detailed description of normative and pathological development in the attachment relationship, see Zeanah, Mammen, & Lieberman in Zeanah, 1993.) It is very important to watch the infant's use of each parent as a secure base for supporting exploration of the room, including the toys available to him or her, and for supporting interaction with the interviewer (Ainsworth & Wittig, 1969). Does the infant use contact with or proximity to the parents, or distal communication and eye contact, in order to reassure himself or herself that the environment is safe and to facilitate moving away from the parents to explore? Does the infant do this initially upon entering the room, or upon being exposed to a new stimulus? Does the infant seek physical contact and proximity or visual contact in an ongoing way during exploration, and how does this work?

If and when the infant seeks comfort through physical contact with or proximity to his or her parents, is it effective in reassuring and comforting the infant? Is it pleasurable for the infant? Does it lead to the infant's return to exploration and play? How do the parents experience the infant's contact with them or his or her proximity-seeking? What do the parents communicate to the infant (overtly as well as implicitly) about the experience of closeness through their responses? What does the infant communicate to the parents about this experience? Perhaps most importantly, what does this communication and this experience mean to the parents and to the baby?

The quality of the infant's physical and social exploration is of interest in the assessment of the attachment relationship. Does the infant show pleasure, interest, or exuberance in the exploration, or is the infant cautious, wary, or sober, or listless, indifferent, or mechanical? Does the quality of the exploration evolve with the infant's familiarity with the situation? Does the quality of the infant's exploration differ on the basis of the parental response he is getting?

Looking at a process closely related to attachment, called social referencing in the developmental literature (Campos & Stenberg, 1981; Hirshberg & Svedja, 1990; Hirshberg, 1990; Sorce, Emde, Campos, & Klinnert, 1985), does the infant actively use the parents, through nonverbal communication, as a source of information concerning the unfamiliar situation, checking to see how they feel about the situation and making use of their response in regulating his or her exploratory or social behavior? Are the parents responsive to this referencing of them by their infant, providing feedback without unduly imposing themselves on the baby? How does the infant respond to the parental signals received?

Because the interview process rarely provides for a natural separation of infant and parents, it is usually necessary to inquire about how the infant and parents respond to routine separations. How does the baby respond to the immediate separation when left with other caregivers? How does the baby behave during the course of the separation? Does the baby adapt, settle down, and become comfortable, or does he or she remain overtly distressed or perhaps low-key (Mahler, Pine, & Bergmann, 1975)? Are these responses different when the baby is separated from the mother as compared to the father, and do they vary when the baby is left in the care of different people, say with relatives versus baby-sitters? How has the baby's response to separation changed over the course of his or her development?

Similarly, it is important to inquire in detail about all the thoughts and feelings each parent has when he or she separates from the infant. What do the parents think and feel if the baby clings to them to protest separation, or fails to do so? What do they want to do? What do they actually do? What do they imagine the baby is thinking and feeling? What do they believe to be developmentally appropriate? A related area of inquiry is how the parents respond now and how they responded in the past to the important developmental accomplishments of the baby, such as his or her first steps or weaning, which signify the infant's emerging autonomy and individuation. Are the parents able to foster the child's autonomy, or do they find it threatening and hence compromise or undermine it?

When assessing the quality of the infant-parent attachment, it is most important to note the interaction between the infant and the parent upon reunion from a separation. It is essential to develop a clear understanding of the details of this experience. Precisely what does the baby do upon reunion with each parent? Does the infant greet the parent or look briefly at him or her, and then does the infant avert his or her gaze? Does the infant fail to greet the parent and instead maintain his or her focus on toys or other objects? Does the infant approach the parent, signal to be picked up, and reach to be picked up? How does he or she respond upon being picked up? Does the baby settle down and become calm, continue to fuss, or alternate cuddling and fussing? Does the baby readily return to play, or continue to show distress and tension? Similarly, all the details of the parents' experience of returning to their baby are essential.

An 18-month-old boy was referred for treatment by a child development center after a comprehensive evaluation which detailed extremely intense aggressive and self-destructive behavior on the part of the toddler. The evaluation also noted an extremely high level of activity and protracted oppositional and defiant behavior by the toddler toward his adoptive parents. The evaluation team recommended to the parents that they seek professional help in order to develop strategies for managing the toddler's behavior problems. No careful assessment of the attachment between the child and his adoptive parents had been conducted.

In interacting with the toddler, both parents seemed somewhat remote from the child, but treated him with kindness. They expressed grave concern for his behavior problems and profound helplessness in the face of their inability, despite numerous strategies and great effort, to get him to behave. Both parents appeared to be worn down and exhausted by this child and quite pessimistic about their future together. Both were keenly skeptical about treatment.

Assessment of the attachment relationship revealed quite clearly that this toddler, who had come to them at 8 months of age, after being removed from the care of his mother, had been unable to make use of the availability of new and loving attachment figures and become attached to them. It became clear that his behavior problems were secondary to an attachment disorder. Moreover, it also became clear that his adoptive parents' demoralization and hopelessness resulted in large measure from their inability to feel needed by the baby and "attached to" him. They had not expressly presented this as a problem, and in fact had not been aware of it as a problem, but, when asked, both parents articulated great disappointment at feeling disconnected from the baby and unable to provide him with a sense of security and comfort when he needed it. Uncovering this most basic sense of failure and offering a plan to help resulted in the immediate improvement of the parents' morale and facilitated their mobilizing the necessary energy and enthusiasm to embark upon a treatment program. Three weeks after initiating treatment for the attachment disorder, the behavioral symptoms had virtually disappeared.

### Safety and protection

Another important aspect of the infant-parent relationship that should be observed is the parents' vigilance concerning protection of the infant's physical safety, as well as the infant's response to this input from the parents and his or her own self-regulation regarding physical safety. Is the parent continuously monitoring the infant's safety and taking action to protect him or her when necessary? Is the parent appropriately vigilant and protective, or overprotective and highly anxious about the baby's safety? Is the parent careless and lacking in awareness or concern? Does the infant or toddler show excessive caution and timidity, or reck-lessness?

Here again, observations regarding this area of parent-infant functioning should be combined with inquiry if there are indica-tions of difficulties. Consider, for example, a history of "accident proneness" on the part of the infant, or evidence of or com-plaints about a toddler's recklessness. Unless this area is part of the presenting problem as defined by the parents, it is best to link the inquiry regarding it to an observation. For example, one might note when the toddler climbs onto a table that he seems quite adventurous. Then one might wonder if this happens at home. It is usually best to begin with an open-ended and either neutrally- or positively-connoted question, rather than a series of specific questions, since the former allows the parents to reveal how they organize this area of experience—what seems important, relevant, and appropriate to them. The professional should couple the inquiry into the kinds of experiences a family may have had with an exploration of what these experiences mean and have meant to the parents. How do they experience the baby's physical strivings and adventurousness? How do they feel when the child hurts himself or herself, or is in a dangerous situation? What sorts of things do they imagine might happen? What are they afraid of if they are afraid, and how does that relate to their own history?

### Physiological regulation

A third domain of the functioning of the infant-parent relation-ship is the regulation of food intake, warmth, sensory stimula-tion, elimination, mental states such as sleep and alertness, and emotional states such as anger, sadness, and excitement. The developmental task of the infant-parent dyad is to facilitate, through reciprocal regulation, the emergence and consolidation of basic consistent rhythms of somatic experience so that orga-nized patterns of functioning are achieved, patterns which allow the infant to pursue developmentally facilitating activities in the wider world.

Likely areas of observation in the consulting room or clinic include the regulation of stimulation and of food intake. Note how aware the parents are of the infant's level of stimulation and arousal, and how willing and able they are to mediate this as necessary. Can the parents intervene to organize the infant or reduce stimulation if the infant becomes overstimulated or disorganized? Can the parents provide an interesting focus of activity for the infant if he or she becomes bored or restless? How does the infant respond to regulating input from the parents? Does the infant seem to seek this input and respond favorably to it, or does he or she shun and resist it?

Do the parents seem to keep track of the infant's hunger states and their likely effect on his affect and behavior? If the parents provide the baby with a meal or snack, this will afford an opportunity to observe how the family organizes the infant's eating experience and what the infant's eating may mean to the parents and is coming to mean to the infant.

Here again, inquiry will be necessary to supplement observation. Questions concerning the infant's physiological patterns are best posed initially in an open-ended fashion. If the response to this questioning is vague or nonspecific, it may be necessary to ask very detailed questions in order to construct a sense of how the dyad functions in this area. In order to obtain this information, it is often helpful to ask a parent to describe the previous day from moment to moment, starting at the baby's awakening and continuing until bedtime.

### Play

The clinical interview may also afford the professional an opportunity to observe the functioning of the infant-parent dyad at play. If this does not occur spontaneously as the interview unfolds, it may be advisable to tell the parents that you would like to take some time to see how the baby plays with them. Observe how relaxed or comfortable the parents are when playing with the infant.

Monitor, as well, the parents' ability to comprehend the infant's level of understanding or perspective, to follow the infant's lead when he or she is leading, and to provide organization, structure, or stimulation as necessary. Does the play seem pleasurable for the parents? Are they able, even in the context of a formal interview and in the presence of a stranger, to "loosen up," regress temporarily, and enjoy the "free space" of the play? Do they experience delight in the baby's play? Is the play pleasurable for the infant? Note with which parent the infant is more comfortable or joyful in play. Do the parents notice any differences in this regard? How do they understand these differences?

It is important to inquire how the parents' perception of the quality of their play during the interview compares to that of their usual play at home.

### Teaching and learning

Related to play is the area of teaching and learning. There may be spontaneous opportunities to observe the functioning of the dyad in this area, or it may be necessary to provide the parents with a simple task appropriate to the infant's developmental level and ask them to "help the baby learn" how to complete the task. Observe the parents' manner of introducing or explaining the task, the clarity of any cues or instructions, the timing of the cues, and the speed or pacing of the cues. Note the parents' level of flexibility in helping the child, as well as the parents' ability to keep the child focused on the task. Assess their ability to provide only the help necessary for the child to remain involved in the task and positively motivated to complete it.

Pay attention to the parents' ability to provide input which begins at the child's level and leads him or her to the next step, thus reflecting an understanding of the child's perspective on the task and what he or she is experiencing. Consider also their willingness and ability to support the child's own efforts at exploration mastery through responses such as verbal encouragement or physical support when necessary, expression of pleasure in success, and the general communication of positive involvement and interest in the child's experience while learning. Pay attention to the infant's response to parental "teaching" input. Does the activity appear to be familiar and comfortable? Is the infant responsive to the parents in this context? Does the infant seek and use parental help in learning?

### Power and control

Another dimension of relationship functioning to watch for in the assessment is the exercise of power and control. Do the parents present themselves to the infant as calm, confident, and in control of themselves, the infant, and the situation they are in? Or, by contrast, do they appear passive, overwhelmed, disorganized, confused, tense, or even potentially explosive? How do they manage the challenges the infant presents to them during the interview, such as a refusal to clean up, constant interruptions, aggressive acting out, or even the infant's mounting distress?

Does the infant basically acknowledge and appear confident

that his parents are organized and in control, or does the infant attempt to take charge through manipulative or controlling behavior? Such controlling behavior may be exhibited in a caregiving, solicitous fashion, or in an angry, critical, or provocative manner. Although current research is documenting the emergence of empathic responses in infants (Radke-Yarrow & Zahn-Waxler, 1984), a role-reversed relationship pattern in which the baby bears the emotional burden of the relationship with the parent betokens an attachment disorder which bears careful assessment in the clinical interview (Bowlby, 1973; Zeanah, Mammen, & Lieberman in Zeanah, 1993; Zeanah & Klitzke, 1991).

A mother was being interviewed while her toddler was busily involved in playing on the other side of the room. When the mother began to cry softly upon discussing her feelings about the death of her mother several years prior to the birth of the baby, her son immediately and abruptly interrupted his playing to rush over to his mother and pat her on the back consolingly. This same mother later described an occasion on which she put her son in his crib for a "time-out" and then sat in a rocker in his room to wait until it was over. Witnessing his intense distress over the confinement, she began to cry out of guilt and confusion, whereupon her toddler quickly ceased his crying, stood up in the crib, and called out to her, telling her not to cry.

Observe how the parents jointly manage the function of providing control over the infant. Do the parents subtly or overtly undermine each other, or does each parent use the child to provoke the other parent? Is there an alliance between the infant and one parent against the other parent?

### Regulation of emotion

Finally, carefully observe the functioning of the parent-infant relationship in the mutual regulation of emotion or affect, including the expression and communication of emotion. This is probably the most important area of relationship functioning since the emotions or affects experienced in any interaction are critical in determining the psychological significance or meaning of that interaction in the infant-parent relationship. For example, two feeding interactions, both of which might be similar in that they are quite competent from the point of view of the regulation of food intake, could, nevertheless, be quite disparate vis-à-vis their emotional significance to the infant and parent, and hence to the relationship. One interaction might be emotionally empty and mechanical, or tense and cold or distant, while the other, by contrast, is relaxed, joyful, and warm. However, the emotional quality of the feeding is the most salient characteristic of the organization of the infant-parent relationship.

More generally, a number of clinical theoreticians with varying points of view argue that it is the emotion experienced in an interaction that provides the core element around which the experience is organized psychologically, and, hence, it becomes effective in shaping later interactions and relationships (Kernberg, 1976; Emde, 1989; Horowitz, 1989; Mitchell, 1988).

There are a number of aspects of the emotional functioning of the infant-parent relationship that are worthy of note. What is the overall affective tone of the infant-parent interactions observed? Does the tone differ greatly from moment to moment, activity to activity, parent to parent, and session to session? For each partner in the infant-parent relationship, are affects expressed openly, or in a guarded, muted, or restrained way? For each partner, are they expressed congruently across different channels of expression, such as tone of voice, facial expression, gestures, and body language? Observe also whether a full range of emotion is experienced in the interactions and whether emotions are experienced at varying levels of intensity. Note that these are standard clinical dimensions for assessing affect in individuals. However, research and clinical experience suggest that many of these aspects of emotion regulation and functioning may show continuity within and variability across specific relationships, especially with respect to infants and younger children, but probably also to some degree with respect to adults.

Monitor the particular emotional responses each partner has in response to the emotions and behavior of the other partner. Look for the kinds of critical sequences in emotional exchanges described above, in which the emotional response of each partner continuously modifies that of the other and is modified by it.

It is important to recognize that infant-parent interaction can vary significantly in different relational contexts. For example, a mother and toddler may relate quite differently in the father's presence than when they are alone together. Consider also the place held by the infant's relationship with each parent in the network of relationships within the family, including the baby's siblings and grandparents.

## What the infant brings to relationships

Winnicott's dictum that "there is no such thing as a baby" may perfectly well be stood on its head. There is no such thing as a parent, but only parents of particular children. Particular characteristics of the infant—differences in regulatory capacity or style, developmental strengths or weaknesses, the infant's gender or appearance, or other dimensions along which individual infants differ—can cause parental functioning to be impeded or facilitated, conflicts to be smoothed out or powerfully elicited, and needs to be met or denied. The example of Mrs. M. cited above illustrates this point. Although she had a 12-month-old daughter who cried constantly, she also had a 4-year-old daughter with no significant behavioral problems. Her relationship with her first child was much less overtly conflicted, as the child had successfully adopted a role-reversed relationship with her mother, in which she adapted to the mother's intolerance or disavowal of neediness.

In the course of the interview, the professional will have the opportunity to make observations concerning the infant's individual characteristics and how they contribute to the presenting problem. Included are factors such as medical and developmental status and history, and a variety of aspects of appearance and temperament.

Note the baby's physical appearance. Is the baby particularly appealing or unattractive, thin or heavy, frail or robust, or small or large for his or her age? What do the parents make of this? Who do family members think the baby looks like in the family?

Also take into account the baby's medical history, including the course of the pregnancy and the infant's perinatal status, as well as his or her cognitive development and other important areas of development and maturation, such as the rapidity and vigor of the infant's motor development, the timeliness of the infant's development of social interest and social relatedness and of communicative and linguistic competence, and the infant's developmental level of play and symbolization. Any significant questions regarding these areas warrant a full-scale cognitive and developmental evaluation (Clark, 1985; Zeanah, 1993).

Another important area of observation involves the infant's capacities and patterns with respect to regulating physiological, sensory, attentional, motor, and affective processes, and organizing, maintaining, and shifting states of alertness and arousal

(Greenspan & Wieder in Zeanah, 1993). Observe and inquire about any signs of unusual responsiveness (underreactivity or overreactivity) to auditory, visual, vestibular, or tactile stimuli. In addition, observe and inquire about any unusual temporal patterns in self-regulation, such as an unusually rapid or slow rise-time in reactivity, or a low threshold of arousal. Is the process by which the infant attempts to modulate and regulate arousal smooth and integrated, or disorganized? Does the infant signal distress gradually or do overload and distress seem precipitous and unpredictable? Be aware of the infant's attempts at self-regulation and his elicitation of regulatory input from his caregivers. The way an infant adapts to changes in routine and transitions in activities is also significant. This can be observed in the course of the interview by seeing how the infant settles into the consultation or play room, how he or she responds to the end of the interview, and how the infant handles shifts, such as the interviewer's request that the parents play with him or her, or the beginning or end of play between the infant and the interviewer. Inquiry concerning the baby's coping with change and transitions should also be made.

Much can be observed about the infant's regulatory status in the course of the interviews. Questions concerning the infant's regulatory patterns are best posed *initially* in relation to an observation in the session and in an open-ended fashion. However, given the increasing recognition of the role of individual differences in regulatory style and capacity in the development of infants, it is essential to inquire carefully and systematically about the infant's regulatory patterns. Inquire as to how the infant responds to auditory stimulation, including various loud noises, and to auditory commotion, even if the level is not loud. Inquire as to how the baby responds to tactile stimulation, including light touch, firmer pressure, textures of clothes, labels, elastic, socks and shoes, hot and cold sensation, wetness, and sticky or messy tactile sensation. Ask how the baby responds when moved quickly or vigorously, and when positioned off the ground. Inquire also about the way the infant responds to swinging and spinning motion, and to riding in moving vehicles. Assess the infant's functioning with regard to visual stimulation. Does the baby seem to enjoy visual stimulation, or does he or she become overstimulated easily? Does he or she seem to prefer visually calm or visually exciting environments? Finally, ask whether the baby has shown a pattern of seeking out or avoiding great quantities of sensory stimulation—auditory, tactile, vestibular, and visual.

An 8-month-old boy was brought by his parents to an infant clinic for a consultation due to his inconsolable crying and inability to be soothed or calmed. His parents appeared extremely anxious and overwhelmed by this child. They expressed enormous confusion about their son and seemed to focus their attention to the extreme on his history of diarrhea and gastric distress. Their preoccupation with these symptoms had occasioned considerable doctor-shopping, which, in turn, had led them to acquire an intensely critical attitude toward medical help and an expectation that their concerns would not be taken seriously. One observer of the initial interview was struck by how the baby seemed to exist for them primarily as a collection of gastric symptoms. An extended evaluation was planned to further explore the nature of their anxious preoccupation with these physical symptoms. The recommended treatment of the parent-child relationship was briefly attempted, with little positive result

Two years later, this boy was referred to one of the clinicians who had observed the initial evaluation. The child was now capable of greater mobility, was more able to communicate his experiences, and was more able to regulate his sensory exposure on his own and hence reveal his sensory preferences. His parents were also much more familiar with his patterns of regulation. Thus, it was apparent that he suffered from a regulatory disorder. Undoubtedly, much of his distress as an infant was attributable to this regulatory deficit. Undoubtedly, also, this regulatory disorder was not appreciated due to an earlier emphasis on the anxiety apparent in the infant-parent relationship. This anxiety, in retrospect, seems to have been traceable in no small measure to the impact his problems concerning sensory processing and regulation had on his parents.

## What the parents bring to relationships

It is very important to assess how the parents perceive, experience, and interpret the infant's behavior. How have they organized or constructed their view or representation of the baby, as well as their perception of their relationship with him or her in relation to a variety of salient dimensions? How do they view the baby's personality? How is he or she like or unlike other children in the family? What had they imagined the baby would be like during the pregnancy, and how is the baby like or unlike that image? How is the baby like or unlike each parent, both with respect to the parent's personality now and to the kind of baby he or she was? This question usually opens up for exploration the parents' own early experiences and how they may be involved in the problems with the baby. Here again, it is crucial not to pass by or gloss over any areas of anxiety or conflict which may emerge, but instead to focus incisively on them in a persistent but respectful manner.

In a manner similar to what was described above with reference to the infant's individual characteristics, the interviewer should observe and inquire about characteristics of each parent which may play a role in the infant's problem. The goal is not, by any means, a complete psychological or psychiatric evaluation of the parents, but an assessment of how parental strengths and weaknesses are involved in the problem and may best be worked with to contribute to the solution. It is important to assess parental factors with regard to general aspects of parental personality and functioning, as well as with regard to specific aspects of the parenting of this baby.

One area of consideration is the degree of compatibility between the personalities of the parents and the infant. Observe the moods of the parents and their characteristic styles when expressing and regulating emotions such as anger, anxiety, sadness, love or affection, joy, and guilt, as well as their responses to these emotions in others, particularly the infant. Which emotions are easily tolerated or accepted in the self and in others, and which must be disavowed, suppressed, or otherwise defended against? Observe how the parents function with regard to control and self-control, and power and assertiveness or passivity in relationships. Note their level of defensiveness or openness. Are they able to acknowledge and tolerate emotional conflict, and accept weaknesses, imperfections, or failures in themselves and others? To what extent are they psychologically minded and empathic, and able to observe themselves and others, suspend judgment, take the other's perspective, and consider the other's needs, motives, and wishes? In which areas of experience can they do this, and in which are they unable to do it? To what extent do they have awareness or appreciation of their own psychological richness, complexity, and depth, and of that of others? Again, assess these areas of functioning with particular reference to the infant.

Pay attention to each parent's self-image. How do they perceive themselves? How do they wish to be perceived, feel they are perceived, and fear being perceived, both in a general sense and, more specifically, as parents? Also important is the question of how the parents are similar to and different from their own parents, both with regard to child-rearing attitudes and practices, and with regard to the kind of relationship they are developing with their child. Assess how the parents seem to be experiencing or perceiving other people as they interact with them, especially the infant. Observe each parent's defensive style and functioning, and other areas of ego functioning, taking note of strengths and weaknesses.

This information is especially important in developing a treatment plan. It is advisable to begin considering the various possible treatment options available and to take some time to actively assess the parents' ability to use the different treatment modalities successfully.

Inquire as to how the parents' view of the infant has changed over time as the baby has developed. It is often useful to inquire about the parents' experience with the baby at the common important periods of developmental transition. Assess whether the parent is flexible and open in his view of the infant, allowing it to alter as the baby changes, or, by contrast, closed and rigid.

Inquire about the parents' images or fantasies concerning the baby prior to and during the pregnancy—what they had been expecting, hoping for, fearing, or dreading—and about their experience with the baby at birth. It is often important to inquire whether the parents had wanted a boy or a girl, why, and how they responded initially and respond now to the baby if their wishes were unfulfilled. It is often useful to inquire about how the baby was named and why.

In general, a stance of principled ignorance is usually best, operating on the assumption that you only have a clear understanding of what the parents communicate fully and in detail. It is important to address any inconsistencies in the parents' account, or ways in which the baby as represented by the parents may diverge from the baby as observed in the interview. It can also be helpful to ask the parents whether a type of behavior or characteristic observed in the session is what they had in mind.

It is also useful to ask how the parents view the infant and themselves when in a variety of different affective states. What is the baby like when he or she is joyful, angry, sad, afraid, or frustrated? How do the parents feel when the baby is experiencing these emotions? How does the baby feel and respond when the parents are joyful, angry, sad, afraid, or frustrated?

The goal of this area of inquiry is to develop with the parents an understanding of how they have created or organized a way of experiencing the infant, how this is affected by their own history and inner experience—thoughts, feelings, wishes, dreams, and fears—and how their view of the baby affects their response to the baby and, hence, the baby's experience.

### Specific precipitant

One critical area for exploration which invariably emerges with the parents' first account of the problem is the specific precipitant for the appearance of the problem. The precipitant may be external events or developmental events. It is often important to be very detailed in this inquiry, as parents frequently overlook important precipitants to the baby's troubles. Inquire as well about the specific precipitant for the decision to seek help. Since the problem had been going on for some time, why did they decide to call on that particular day rather than any previous day?

### The wider context

It is critical to obtain information about the infant's wider life context—social, cultural, and economic. What other adults does the infant have significant contact with, and what are these relationships like? Is the infant in day care, and, if so, with whom, where, and for how long? Are there any salient cultural attitudes or practices regarding infants or infant-parent relationships which may have an effect on the problem? What is the family's financial and work situation, and what other stressors for the family might there be?

## Recommendations for Treatment

Ideally, the course of the interview carries with it its own conclusions. The experience of the parents and the professional is that *they have come to a new understanding together about the nature of the problem*. Thus, the diagnostic "formulation" is neither produced by the professional nor experienced by the parents as an abstract or arcane intellectual concoction. Instead, it is a summary of what has been cooperatively learned and should be communicated in terms that the parents can readily understand and will respond to emotionally.

It is best to avoid organizing such a formulation around higher-level or abstract clinical concepts, such as character dynamics, diagnostic entities, or psychodynamic speculations which have not been well verified by the experiential data of the interview. Instead, focus on material related to present life issues which are relatively close to experience, which have been disclosed in or revealed by the interview process, and which can be acknowledged on some level by the parents. In summarizing and communicating an understanding of the problem to the parents, it is useful to refer to experiences during the evaluation which have already been explored and at least partially understood.

It is crucial that the recommendations for treatment be experienced by the family as being developed cooperatively, just as the organized understanding of the baby, his or her problem, and the baby's family was. It is important to consider with the parents again at the end of the interview what they want help with and what kind of help they want. Consider also what kind of help the parents can make use of and what impediments to help there might be due to sociocultural, economic, and psychological factors.

It is often useful to consider available treatment modalities and to assess for the compatibility between family and modality prior to the final session in which results are communicated. The optimal way to assess which modality is appropriate is to make a trial intervention in the modality under consideration and observe how the family responds. One example has already been discussed, that of assessing the parents' response to the interventions from the interviewer which encourage exploration and understanding of the infant-parent relationship in psychological depth with regard to determining the appropriateness of focused infant-parent psychotherapy for the family. The interviewer will have made a number of trial interventions in accord with this model and will have noted the parents' response. An active, focused course of infant-parent psychotherapy may be appropriate if the parents were able to use the interviewer's help (a) to understand more fully the nature of their relationship to each other and to the baby and how it influences the baby's problems specifically and his or her development more generally; and/or (b) to develop a greater level of relatedness or closeness with the interviewer. The interviewer can then describe the treatment to the parents, making reference to the therapeutic work already begun in the evaluation.

If, by contrast, the parents were not able to use this kind of active, focused help in understanding the situation, infant-parent psychotherapy may still be the treatment of choice, but a somewhat slower-paced, less anxiety-provoking approach may be indicated (Lieberman & Pawl in Zeanah, 1993).

Another example of trial intervention might involve the possibility of interaction guidance or coaching (McDonough in Zeanah, 1993). The interviewer considering this as a treatment option might intervene in the course of an observed interaction to provide a representative intervention in this modality in order to observe the parents' response.

In formulating treatment recommendations, careful consideration should also be given to how parents have responded to interventions made by other professionals, such as pediatricians, or social caseworkers, before the evaluation. This is often a fruitful area for detailed exploration of how the parents experienced prior contacts with those aiming to help them and their families.

It is preferable for the assessing professional to provide treatment, although clearly this cannot always be the case. This is especially true when the kind of active anxiety-provoking techniques described above are successful in the interview and lead to a fruitful collaborative understanding of the problem. Despite the relatively small amount of contact, the parents may experience the interviewer as someone who has helped them in a very important way. When it is not possible for the assessing professional to provide treatment, the end of the evaluation represents a termination, as that process is understood in the literature on psychotherapy. Although it is generally not feasible to treat the end of the evaluation as a full-fledged termination, the interviewer should be attuned to these meanings of the situation. Some post-evaluation followup contact may be helpful to aid the family in the transition to a new professional.

# Conclusion

In concluding this chapter, I would like to return to the beginning (as often occurs in ending an evaluation or treatment). I have outlined many (perhaps too many) considerations to be borne in mind by the professional conducting clinical interviews with infants and their families. I want to conclude by recommending that you *strive to forget about them* when in the midst of the interview process. If, as I have suggested, the most basic job of the interview is to come to be able to hold the baby and the family in your mind as fully and completely as possible, it is clear that a large set of preoccupations about how the interview is to be done will be likely to impede rather than facilitate the process. As in riding a bike, swinging a golf club, or hitting a ball, thinking too much about what you are doing while you are doing it is inadvisable. Instead, *careful, regular, even leisurely supervision of you as the professional by a senior clinician is essential if you are to be able to forget about these features of the interview process while you are in the midst of it*. Under this supervision, you should have ample chance to replay interviews, consider options for responses and role-play alternatives, rephrase questions or comments, and see what was missed as well as what was not. This practice allows you to increasingly forget about these factors when with the baby and family.

In my clinical practice, when I feel that I am becoming confused or am having a welter of thoughts in my mind, I make use of this as a cue that I have become disengaged from the person I am sitting with. I ask myself this question: "What simple thing is this person trying to tell me?" In this way, I repeatedly return to the basic clinical task of holding the other person fully in mind. When I do so successfully, I am moved by the results. Indeed, in this way I am recurrently reminded that one of life's greatest privileges is just that—the experience of being able to hold someone else in mind.

**Acknowledgments:** I would like to express my appreciation to Guilford Press for permission to reprint portions of my previously published chapter, "Clinical Interviews with Infants and Their Families," from *Handbook of Infant Mental Health*, edited by C. H. Zeanah.

# References

Ainsworth, M. D. S., & Wittig, B. (1969). Attachment and exploratory behavior in one-year-olds in a strange situation. In B. M. Foss (Ed.), *Determinants of infant behavior* (Vol. 4) (pp. 111-136). New York: Wiley and Sons.

Bowlby, J. (1973). *Separation*. New York: Basic Books.

Campos, J. J., & Stenberg, C. (1981). Perception, appraisal, and emotion: The onset of social referencing. In M. Lamb & L. R. Sherrod (Eds.), *Infant social cognition* (pp. 273-314). Hillsdale, NJ: Lawrence Erlbaum.

Clark, R. (1985). *The parent-child early relational assessment*. Unpublished manuscript, University of Wisconsin.

Emde, R. N. (1989). The infant's relationship experience: Developmental and affective aspects. In A. J. Sameroff & R. N. Emde (Eds.), *Relationship disturbances in early childhood* (pp. 33-51). New York: Basic Books.

Fraiberg, S. (1980). *Clinical studies in infant mental health*. New York: Basic Books.

Freud, S. (1912). The dynamics of transference. *Standard Edition, 12*, 47-108.

Greenberg, J. R., & Mitchell, S. (1983). *Object relations in psychoanalytic theory*. Cambridge: Harvard University Press.

Greenspan, S. (1981). Developmental structuralist approach to the classification of adaptive and pathologic personality organizations: Infancy and early childhood. *American Journal of Psychiatry, 138*, 725-735.

Greenspan, S., & Wieder, S. (1993). Regulatory disorders. In C. H. Zeanah (Ed.), *Handbook of infant mental health* (pp. 280-290). New York: Guilford Press.

Hirshberg, L. (1989). Remembering: Reproduction or construction? *Psychoanalysis and Contemporary Thought, 12*, 343-381.

Hirshberg, L. (1990). When infants look to their parents, Part II: Twelve-month-olds' response to conflicting parental emotional signals. *Child Development, 61*, 1187-1191.

Hirshberg, L. (1993). Clinical interviews with infants and their families. In C. H. Zeanah (Ed.), *Handbook of infant mental health* (pp. 173-190). New York: Guilford Press.

Hirshberg, L., & Svejda, M. (1990). When infants look to their parents, Part I: Infants' emotional referencing of mothers and fathers: A comparative study. *Child Development, 61*, 1175-1186.

Horowitz, M. J. (1989). Relationship schema formation: Role relationship models and intrapsychic conflict. *Psychiatry, 52* (3). New York: Guilford Press.

Kernberg, O. (1976). *Object relations theory and clinical psychoanalysis*. New York: Jason Aronson.

Lieberman, A. F., & J. H. Pawl (1993). Infant-parent psychotherapy. In C. H. Zeanah (Ed.), *Handbook of infant mental health* (pp. 427-442). New York: Guilford Press.

Mahler, M. S., Pine, F., & Bergmann, A. (1975). *The psychological birth of the human infant: Symbiosis and individuation*. New York: Basic Books.

McDonough, S. C. (1993). Interaction Guidance: Understanding and Treating Early Infant-Caregiver Relationship Disturbances. In C. H. Zeanah (Ed.), *Handbook of infant mental health* (pp. 414-426). New York: Guilford Press.

Mitchell, S. A. (1988). *Relational concepts in psychoanalysis: An integration*. Cambridge: Harvard University Press.

Pawl, J. H. (1995). The therapeutic relationship as human connectedness: Being held in another's mind. *Zero to Three, 15* (4), 1-5.

Radke-Yarrow, M., & Zahn-Waxler, C. (1984). Roots, motives, and patterning in children's prosocial behavior. In E. Staub, D. Bar-Tal, J. Karylowski, & J. Reykowski (Eds.), *The development and maintenance of prosocial behavior: International perspectives on positive morality* (pp. 155-176). New York: Plenum Press.

Sander, L. (1975). Infant and caretaking environment: Investigation and conceptualization of adaptive behavior in a system of increasing complexity. In E. J. Anthony (Ed.), *Explorations in child psychiatry* (pp. 129-166). New York: Plenum.

Shevrin, H., & Shechtman, F. (1973). *Bulletin of the Menninger Clinic, 37,* 451-494.

Sorce, J. F., Emde, R. N., Campos, J. J., & Klinnert, M. D. (1985). Maternal emotional signaling: Its effect on the visual cliff behavior of one-year-olds. *Developmental Psychology, 21,* 195-200.

Stern, D. (1985). *The interpersonal world of the infant.* New York: Basic Books.

Zeanah, C. H. (Ed.) (1993). *Handbook of infant mental health.* New York: Guilford Press.

Zeanah, C. H., & Klitzke, M. (1991). Role reversal and the self-effacing solution: Observations from infant-parent psychotherapy. *Psychiatry, 54,* 346-357.

Zeanah, C. H., Mammen, O. K., & Lieberman, A. F. (1993). Disorders of attachment. In C. H. Zeanah (Ed.), *Handbook of infant mental health* (pp. 332-349). New York: Guilford Press.

# IV. New Approaches to Assessment

# 7. A Window on the Newborn's World:

## More than Two Decades of Experience with the Neonatal Behavioral Assessment Scale

T. BERRY BRAZELTON

It took about 18 years of waiting and clinical experimentation from the first time I saw Sally Provence play with a newborn until the publication of the Neonatal Behavioral Assessment Scale (NBAS) in 1973 (Brazelton, 1973). Now, in 1995, 22 years after publishing the scale, my colleagues and I are establishing the Brazelton Center for Infants and Parents in Boston. The Center will train professionals who work with infants and families in hospital, clinical, and educational settings on various applications of the NBAS, in order to meet the needs of families in today's society. This chapter describes the observations that led to the development of the NBAS and what we have learned, through its use, about babies' marvelous capacities for adaptation and about parents' passionate desire to understand and foster their babies' development.

## Observing the Capacities of Newborns

As I have said many times, three women contributed to the development of an assessment for newborns which went beyond the Apgar Scores. The first was Elsa Peterson, head nurse of the Neonatal Intensive Care Unit at Boston Lying-In Hospital. In the mid-1950s, she and I, a young pediatric resident, watched two 3-day-old, two-and-a-half-pound premature infants who were ill with respiratory disease. Both were pumping away, struggling for survival. Lying on their backs with arms akimbo, neither moved a muscle. Elsa said, "See that one on the left? He'll be better in three days. The other one will take longer." I asked, "Elsa, how do you know?" (She always did know.) "That one on the left has the leeway to stop his breathing when he looks up at the overhead light," she replied. "The one on the right can't afford to yet." To me, the babies had looked equally stressed, but now I could understand what Elsa was seeing. One had the physical balance and freedom to stop breathing briefly as he paid attention to the light. The other maintained only a fragile balance. For the first time, I recognized the vital interplay between a newborn's physiological homeostasis and the attentional system. Even more exciting was Elsa's observation that newborns could—and wanted to—*see*. In the 1950s, that came as a revelation. Newborn babies were not supposed to see or hear, or process information.

In 1956, Bettye Caldwell captured Judy Rosenblith and me in one swoop when she demonstrated the new Graham Scale for newborns (Graham, Matarazzo, & Caldwell, 1956), later designated the Graham Rosenblith (Rosenblith, 1961). Bettye showed us how she could increase a 2-day-old's ability to focus on and follow a red wool object. Looking at one baby, Bettye said, "This one's energy isn't up here. Let me get a pacifier. Now, she's sucking on it. Let's gradually withdraw it and bring her energy up to her eyes." The newborn began "magically" to fix on and follow the red wool object, as Bettye swung it back and forth in 180-degree arcs.

Sally Provence was like a ballet dancer with a newborn. She and the baby glided gracefully in a *pas de deux!* As they swayed to and fro, the 3-day-old baby began to concentrate on her face and voice, leaning slightly forward, suppressing other motor activity, and seeming to worship Sally in the process. I was captivated. "Sally, this response from a newborn would capture any new parent. How do you do it? It looks to me as if you get inside that baby, and he knows it. So he does anything you want him to do." Sally's quiet, gentle response changed my future. "Isn't there a baby inside each of us? Why can't we find our way inside each baby?"

Elsa Peterson, Bettye Caldwell, and Sally Provence taught me about the importance of respecting a baby's states of consciousness, about how the vital demands of autonomic and motor systems might determine when and whether an immature organism can respond to sensory cues, and about the concept of capturing the baby's interfering demands to reinforce his or her interest. In addition, I could see that newborns' other bodily systems could energize their marvelous capacity to maintain enough control so that they could pay attention to important stimuli from their world.

The concept of "best performance" came to me as a vital ingredient of an assessment, for it demonstrated the baby's ability to organize around an important learning experience. I could also see that newborns' efforts to get information from their environment were accompanied by behaviors that would signal to anxious parents: "Everything you do for me is important to me, and I want *you* to know it." The sight of a baby organizing for his or her best performance would abundantly reward observant parents.

I was stunned and exhilarated to recognize that, in order to pay attention and respond to social stimuli, a newborn—even under stress—would make massive attempts to control interfering motor activity and cardiorespiratory demands. As a newborn emerges from sleep and goes on to crying, he or she uses a series of maneuvers to maintain an alert state of consciousness. First, the baby turns his or her head to one side, setting off a tonic neck reflex. Second, the baby tries to overcome this by completing a hand-to-mouth maneuver. When this is accomplished, the infant will root and suck on the fingers that are next to his or her mouth. Then comes a sigh. Next, with a brightening look, the baby will survey the close environment with his or her eyes, paying attention to it with his or her ears. In other words, the newborn uses a series of reflex responses in an organized attempt to master motor activity, in order to listen and look. Anyone who witnesses such an attempt at self-mastery will realize that the newborn infant is an active, eager participant in the world and a contributor to interaction with the people in it.

## ■ Development of the Neonatal Behavioral
## ■ Assessment Scale

As my clinical colleagues, neurologist Mary Louise Scholl and pediatrician John S. Robey, and I worked to develop these observations into an assessment tool, we first rated newborns' performance as "good," "medium," or "poor." Our psychologist colleagues told us, however, that a 7-to-9-point scale, clearly defining each point from "good" to "poor," would be necessary to achieve reliability among observers. Fortunately, I had kept notes on the details of each baby's individual performance as I assessed him or her. These notes became the basis for the nine possible scores for each item on the NBAS. (Ever since, I have recommended that observers record individual differences in babies' performances that were not included in the 9-point scores. These qualitative observations can provide insights not only into individual differences among babies, but also into group differences among babies with varying ethnic and social backgrounds.) The Neonatal Behavioral Assessment Scale was first published in 1973, formulated with the help of anthropologist Daniel Friedman, pediatrician John S. Robey, and psychologists Frances Horowitz, Arnold Sameroff, Barbara Koslowski, and Edward Tronick.

My goal in developing the NBAS was not to "rank" babies. I wanted, first of all, to establish the newborn as a contributor to parent-infant interaction and, second, to share babies' successful performances with parents as a supportive intervention in the newborn period. I had been trained in the disciplines of pediatrics and child psychiatry, both of which, at that time, "blamed the victim [the mother]" for any failure in a child's development. It seemed obvious to me that this deficit approach did not reinforce parents or infants for their passionate attempts to succeed with each other. By identifying and labeling the parents' failures, professionals were likely to be playing into parents' insecurities. I had been so struck by the revelations that newborns had given me when I worked with them toward best performance that I already saw the Brazelton scale as a major tool for sharing babies' successes with parents. I was so passionate that my colleagues criticized me, arguing, "No one but you can produce the neonatal behavior you describe." I took this criticism as a challenge. We strove to achieve an assessment that many observers can use.

## ■ Newborn Behavior as a Reflection of ■ Intrauterine Experience

A newborn's behavior tells us a great deal about the baby's prenatal experience. Since developing the scale, I have become aware of how significantly intrauterine experience has already shaped a newborn's behavior. No longer can we conceptualize behavior at birth as a product of the baby's genetic inheritance alone. The infant's genetic potential has been shaped for nine months by the rhythms of the uterus and the metabolic, neuromotor, and neuroendocrine envelope in which the mother nurtured him or her in pregnancy. Prenatal experiences have been incorporated into a developing brain and have been fueling the development of this brain. We now know that nutrition, infection, drugs, and psychological experiences of the mother are indeed transmitted to her fetus and affect both the current behavior and developmental potential of the child. The fetus responds through the mother, but also responds directly, for he or she can and does see, hear, and respond to kinesthetic and vestibular experiences. In fact, the fetus responds differently to quantitatively different events and even shuts them out when he or she can no longer "afford" to respond. So the shaping of a baby's behavior has had a long and important history—both genetic and epigenetic in etiology—by the time of birth. The interaction between nature and nurture has already become intractably intertwined (see the figure below).

Looking at the neonate, we can make an assessment of intrauterine conditions and experience. In Guatemala, for exam-

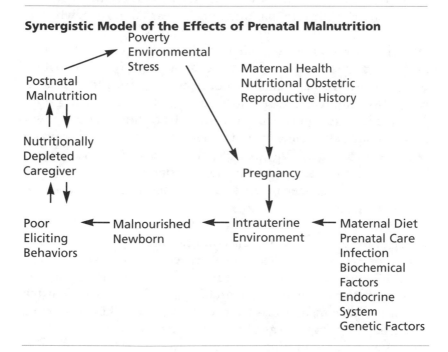

**Synergistic Model of the Effects of Prenatal Malnutrition**

ple, we studied newborns in a community whose inhabitants were chronically undernourished. Newborns' unresponsive social behavior (Brazelton, Tronick, Leghtig, Lasky, & Klein, 1977) correlated with the degree of maternal undernutrition and reduced maternal height, and with the mother's increased morbidity at the time of delivery. We felt that these correlations demonstrated a cross-generational effect of chronic undernutrition, which had affected the mother in her own mother's uterus. All of this was reflected in the neonate's behavioral responsiveness, and, of course, predicted his future outcome (Brazelton et al., 1977).

Unfortunately, the undernourished mother of a poorly responsive newborn is likely to respond to him in ways that will not help him recover from the stresses of birth. She is likely to feed him only "on demand" (in the community we studied, typically three times per day in the neonatal period) and to "leave him alone" when he provides her with inadequate feedback. The newborn cannot tell his mother that he needs more, not less, stimulation in order to recover. Within a group of severely undernourished Guatemalan newborns, we could predict with a very high degree of accuracy which babies would be likely to show signs of marasmus (a wasting of the body) in the first year or kwashiorkor (severe malnutrition) a year later. As newborns, these babies would show slow, too-quiet state changes, long latencies to responses, a poor quality of interactive behaviors, and autonomic instability. Since the mothers of these babies were themselves inadequately nourished and overloaded with too many children, they could feed and stimulate their babies only inadequately in the first few months of life. The stage was set for poor developmental outcomes. We need to find ways to reach out to underprivileged, overly stressed families *early*, so that intrauterine development can be optimized. We need to emphasize that proper nutrients and nontoxic environments in utero will lead to "smart babies."

Several specific behaviors of the newborn give us evidence of deprivation or insults experienced in the uterus, such as malnutrition or exposure to chemical substances. A baby who has suffered in utero may present negative responses to his or her new parents, such as gaze aversion, arching away from them, spitting up, or avoiding their efforts to reach him or her. These behaviors are a sign of a fragile, easily overwhelmed nervous system. The hypersensitivity is a result of a low threshold for taking in information and using it. Such a baby is easily overwhelmed, and his or her behavior reflects the baby's vulnerability. With sensitive handling, this vulnerability can be overcome over time.

## ▤ Changes in Behavior During the Neonatal ▨ Period

The dynamic model of the organization of neonatal behavior that underlies the conceptualization of the NBAS assumes that a baby's performance on the scale will change considerably during the first month after birth. We were initially criticized because there was no test-retest reliability on the NBAS from day to day. But since the newborn is recovering from powerful influences, such as labor and a new environment, I *expect* his behavior to change from day to day. Sampling problems related to time of day, feeding, circumcision, and handling by personnel make it unlikely that there will be stability to rely upon. Instead, I like to look at the baby's ability to adapt and to utilize extrauterine experiences as the best indicator of his capacity. His behavioral changes over time become, therefore, our best window into his ultimate individual personality and style of adaptation.

Many of the changes in the baby's behavior are due to the reciprocal feedback system between the infant and the caregiving environment. In fact, the NBAS examination itself is part of the infant-caregiver interactive system. This recognition of the importance of the effects of the caregiving environment came from accumulating evidence from longitudinal studies which showed little relation between early infant behaviors, specific events associated with early infancy, and later developmental outcome (Lester, 1979; Drillien, 1964). As a result, we now look to the infant-caregiver system as the context for continuities in development in the infant, rather than treating infant behavior as an isolated entity. We expect developmental prediction to come from the study of the processes of biobehavioral organization, based on a transactional view in which development proceeds as infant and caregiver continually modify their own and each other's behavior through reciprocal interaction.

We expect and value change in the baby's performance on the Brazelton scale during the neonatal period, seeing this change as evidence of the newborn's recovery from the stress of labor and delivery and of response to the new environment. The behaviors that are the most basic to the newborn's physiological organiza-

Table 1. **Neonatal Behavioral Assessment**

*Behavioral items*

Response decrement to repeated visual stimuli
Response decrement to rattle
Response decrement to bell
Response decrement to pinprick
Orienting response to inanimate visual stimuli
Orienting response to inanimate auditory stimuli
Orienting response to animate visual—examiner's face
Orienting response to animate auditory—examiner's voice
Orienting response to animate visual and auditory stimuli
Quality and duration of alert periods
General muscle tone in resting and in response to being handled
    (passive and active)
Motor maturity
Traction responses as he or she is pulled to sit
Cuddliness—response to being cuddled by the examiner
Defensive movements—reactions to a cloth over his or her face
Consolability with intervention by examiner
Peak of excitement and capacity to control himself or herself
Rapidity of buildup to crying state
Irritability during the exam
General assessment of kind and degree of activity
Tremulousness
Amount of startling
Lability of skin color (measuring autonomic lability)
Lability of states during entire exam
Self-quieting activity—attempts to console self and control state
Hand-to-mouth activity

*Elicited Responses*

| | |
|---|---|
| Plantar grasp | Rooting (intensity) |
| Hand grasp | Sucking (intensity) |
| Ankle clonus | Passive movement |
| Babinski | Right Arm |
| Standing | Left Arm |
| Automatic walking | Right Leg |
| Placing | Left Leg |
| Incurvation | |
| Crawling | |
| Glabella | |
| Tonic deviation of head and eyes | |
| Nystagmus | |
| Tonic neck reflex | |
| Moro | |

tion (e.g., habituation, autonomic regulation, and motor performance) may be least affected over time. On the other hand, the more interactive behaviors, such as orientation, use or range of states, and consolability, may change the most. (See Table 1 for a complete list of all behavioral and elicited items on the NBAS.) By plotting the neonate's patterns of performance over the course of a series of examinations, we can assess the baby's recovery from the immediate stress of labor and delivery and his or her adaptation to the postnatal caregiving environment.

Repeated assessments measure the baby's adaptive and coping strategies and capacities or his or her organizational adjustments to the demands of a new environment. These changing capacities in the neonate represent the vital interaction between inborn capacities of the baby and the important shaping influence of the environment.

Our goal is to study patterns of performance over repeated assessments in order to measure organizational shifts in underlying processes. Organizational process or recovery curves may predict the future coping capacities of the infant. Rather than predict from a single assessment, we expect to find the maximum predictive validity of the scale in the organizational processes captured by the descriptive parameters, such as the shape or function of these curves. From these features, we hope to identify patterns of individual differences—the infant's organizational "signature"—that will discriminate among normal infants and help identify the infant at risk (Lester, 1980).

We advise at least two, and preferably three, NBAS examinations of a newborn who is recovering from a difficult delivery or from intrauterine deficits. If one can see and evaluate such a baby soon after birth, then again at two weeks, and again at four to eight weeks, there will be three components in the summary scores. Some behaviors may change little over time and are not influenced by the environment. Other behaviors may recover completely and become optimal without intervention. The group of behaviors in the middle—behaviors that are changing, but quite slowly—may represent the areas which need to be targeted for early intervention.

## Using the NBAS

The most important use of the NBAS may be as a powerful demonstration to new parents of the baby's temperament and

---

Table 2. **Uses of Assessment in Infancy**

1. Developmental status
2. Communication between professionals and parents
3. Understanding the antecedents of current performance and predicting future behavior
4. Intervention

---

ability to adapt to nurturing. We have 38 published research papers demonstrating the NBAS's ability to help both mother and father to be more sensitive to their baby's cues. In this respect, the NBAS is as helpful to parents of newborns with disabilities as it is to parents of healthy newborns. Our experience suggests that parents are as aware as professionals are of disorganized behavior in a newborn with a disability. Grieving is to be expected, but professionals can use the baby's behavior as a shared language to convey to parents the nature of interventions which will optimize the baby's recovery. The immature central nervous system (CNS) is remarkably plastic; redundant pathways in the nervous system can be enlisted for use even in the face of CNS insults. But to enlist these pathways, an observer must be aware that hypersensitivity or hyposensitivity to outside stimuli is likely to be operating. From our work with newborns whose mothers were addicted to drugs or alcohol during pregnancy, we have learned that we could engage such babies by looking at *or* talking to *or* touching *or* handling them. But using more than one modality at a time overloads a disorganized central nervous system. And even a single stimulus must be carefully adapted to the baby's threshold. We can model this approach to new parents whose anxiety and grief would be likely to result in behavior that would overload a fragile baby (Als, Tronick, Lester & Brazelton, 1980).

The assessment of an infant might be used in several ways to enhance his or her development (see Table 2). First, a single assessment to determine the baby's performance and capabilities along the different lines of development might give a professional the necessary "window" into his or her level of development for work with the baby's family. How the infant performed, the quality of his or her performance, and how much work was necessary to obtain the infant's optimal level of performance could be scored and would be an asset to this understanding.

Second, an assessment might be used to provide a communication system between the professional and the family. As the baby performs in the course of the assessment, with the parents present, the examiner can describe the baby's behavioral responses (without labeling them) and can be sensitive to the parents' reactions. Parents and professional can then work out mutual goals, using the assessment as a shared frame of reference for communication about the baby. This kind of assessment would provide a window into the baby's performance and also open a window into the parents' feelings. Through the descriptive and visualized sharing of the infant's behavior, parents and professional could establish rapport, identify areas of concern, and, together, plan ways to foster the baby's future development.

Third, an assessment might help both parents and professional to visualize and elaborate upon the processes which the assessment suggests have led to the baby's current performance. In such an assessment, one would look for behaviors which point to the baby's past experience, represent a style of coping, and might also predict the baby's future use of the experiences and people in his or her environment.

These three uses of an assessment are different from one another. They achieve different goals, and, as such, they could and should be clearly delineated before a professional chooses a specific assessment approach.

The first type of approach might be labeled a "single-slice" technique and a stimulus-response kind of assessment. The examiner would use clinical acumen to obtain the baby's best performance and to assess his individuality or style in order to evaluate the baby's developmental status. The second and third types would require a more clinically oriented technique and an examiner who could not only sense and articulate the nuances and implications of how the baby performed, but could also uncover what that style meant to his parents. A single-slice technique and a stimulus-response model of evaluating a baby's performance might miss these clinical implications. To undertake the second and third types of assessment, an examiner must be trained in how to obtain a clear knowledge of the baby's maturation and the expectations of the parents. The examiner would hope to assess the forces from the past which provided the developmental base for the baby's current performance, which, in turn, constitutes the basis for a prediction of the baby's future development. In visualizing the baby's style of performance and his or her way of coping with the test situation, the examiner would see the forces for future coping and assimilation of environmental experiences. Clearly, an interpretation from this kind of assessment is ambitious and potentially dangerous, and must be carefully controlled.

An ideal assessment would embody elements of the past, present, and future. These antecedents of current performance and predictors of future behavior could become the base for an understanding of the infant. An assessment of an infant should be seen as an opportunity for interaction with the infant. By observing the infant's use of the examiner and the examining materials, one learns how this infant functions. By entering into the infant's world and responding to the infant, the examiner learns how the parents may react to the infant. The scoring of any assessment should record the subjective and clinical insights of the examiner, for these reactions will guide the examiner into a working relationship with both the infant and his or her parents to foster development.

We have learned the power of just such an assessment in our work with the Brazelton Neonatal Behavioral Assessment Scale. We work to reach and understand the newborn, and to envelop him or her in an adult's containing and facilitating interaction. In order to elicit the baby's best performance, we have realized the power of providing the baby with an opportunity to show us his or her processes of organization, to master his or her immature physiology and nervous system, and to achieve an optimal state of attention for interaction with his or her environment. As the baby shows us these processes, we can understand them through our identification with the baby. Our understanding helps us to predict fairly accurately the impact the baby will have on those caring adults around the baby who are also interested in helping him or her achieve best performance.

If we are ready to do so, we can share these observations and insights with the newborn's caretakers in order to join with them in setting goals for the newborn's best developmental outcome. An assessment of an infant is a multidimensional opportunity—for diagnosis, for prediction, and for entering into the parent-child interaction. The most exciting use of our own assessment techniques is that of communication and work with the parents of our research study subjects. We find that studying a group of infants in the presence of their parents automatically changes the study to an intervention study. Although we started out studying the dynamics of recovery and growth in a group of high-risk prematures and in a group of normal full-term infants, we found that we were soon studying babies' development within the envelope of devoted parents and caring researchers, who modeled for each other ways of eliciting the baby's best performance.

If we really mean to predict from behaviors at one age to another set of behaviors at a later age, we must improve upon the kinds of assessments which we are presently using. As a clinician who must attempt to assess the total child and the child's parents if I am to participate with them in illness, in problems, and in health, I must know how they will perform under stress, as well as in day-to-day living, and how their performance is likely to change with the discontinuities of daily life and of development. If I just assess the child for cardiac functioning or for cognitive or motor function within any single developmental line, I will not be able to predict from one time to another what I need to know to help the child.

I have found that I can use the NBAS most effectively for outreach to parents with a newborn with problems if I initially examine the baby by myself. I can then assess the baby for what he or she *can* do, as well as what he or she cannot do, and for demonstration of the areas which will need intervention. This is the fourth use of assessment. After interacting with the baby, I first share my observations of the baby's optimal behaviors with the parents. They will see that I am aware of and respect the baby's strengths. They feel that I am identifying with them as parents. Then, I can share the problem behaviors, communicating, "We can face these disorganized behaviors together. This is where he will need our intervention." Demonstrating the techniques I have learned to help the baby organize becomes a window for the parents into the baby's future organization and gives them the courage and hope necessary to seek early intervention.

I am making a plea for better, more comprehensive assessment techniques than we now have for children at *any* age, i.e., for wider, clearer windows on development. Assessments which include qualitative as well as quantitative information may find coping systems, the *way* the baby uses the examiner and the *way* the baby is brought to best performance, to be as significant as the infant's *level* of performance. Such instruments can add important new dimensions to our assessment capacities.

We have learned a great deal from the use of the NBAS over time, both about newborns' marvelous capacities for adaptation and about parents' passionate desire to understand and adapt to their babies. Using the NBAS as a window into other cultures, we have seen the power of genetically shaped behavior to influence a culture's early child-rearing practices. While cultural practices may shape behavior, babies also shape their culture, insuring their survival and promoting their own optimal development.

## Using the NBAS to Evaluate Infants at Risk

As the potential for early intervention increases, we need to evaluate at-risk infants as early as possible with an eye to more sophisticated preventive and therapeutic approaches. Early intervention may prevent the compounding of problems which occurs all too easily when the environment cannot adjust appropriately to the infant at risk. Premature and minimally brain-damaged infants seem to be less able to compensate in disorganized, depriving environments than well-equipped neonates, and their problems of organization in development are compounded early (Greenberg, 1971).

Learning to recognize the "cost" to the baby of receiving and organizing around stimuli has helped us understand much more about the baby's ability to adapt to his or her environment. Seven items added to the original NBAS cover three concepts related to "cost": (a) how much it costs the examiner to produce best performance; (b) how much it costs the baby to achieve best performance (autonomic motor, state, attention); and (c) the quality of the baby's performance when it is achieved. We have found that these items are somewhat linear in how they predict the test performance of 2- and 3-year-old children. As such, they give us insight into how the environment can best serve the baby's attempts at reorganization and recovery from intrauterine insults.

As noted above, quiet, nondemanding infants do not elicit the care they need from parents who are already overstressed. In poverty-stricken environments, such neonatal behavior may lead to serious malnutrition (Cravioto, Delcardie, & Birch, 1966; Klein, Habicht, & Yarbrough, 1971). In contrast, hyperkinetic, hypersensitive newborns may drive a mother and father to desperate child-rearing responses that reinforce the problems of the child, so that he grows up in an overreactive, hostile environment (Heider, 1966).

Parents of children who are admitted to Children's Hospital

in Boston for clinical syndromes, such as failure to thrive, repeated accidents and ingestions, and autism, often have other offspring without these problems. They feel, however, that they have "failed" with the hospitalized child. Parents often associate their feelings of failure with an inability to "understand" the child from birth onward, and they report that the child was different from their other children even in his or her earliest reactions to them. Assessment of risk in early infancy could mobilize preventive efforts and programs to support such children and their families. Babies with minimal brain damage, for example, make remarkable compensatory recoveries in a fostering environment. By understanding the baby and the problems he or she is likely to present to the parents, professionals may provide more support for the parents as they adjust to a difficult infant.

## Assessing Premature Infants

Although we are interested in developing a process-oriented assessment for high-risk and premature infants, we are aware that the NBAS, as presently conceptualized, is not appropriate for assessing a stressed or premature infant. The interaction between physiological demands on the full-term infant and the infant's capacity to gain control over these demands in order to interact with social stimuli is likely to be qualitatively different in the stressed or prematurely born infant. The amount and kind of examiner facilitation needed to produce the best performance in the infant at risk might also be quite different and might, indeed, be a measure of the baby's instability.

A system-oriented method for presenting and scoring the Brazelton scale must be applied to the assessment of premature infants. We feel that the premature infant's organization could best be assessed by separating it into five developmental lines: (a) physiological; (b) motor; (c) state; (d) attention/interaction; and (e) regulatory. To understand the premature infant's level of development, it is as critical to observe the amount and quality of the examiner's efforts as it is to observe the baby's capacity for managing his or her fragile, easily overwhelmed systems in order to respond. As we work with the infant, we are constantly recording the examiner's input—the latency, the pacing, and the controls that are necessary from him or her in order to produce the preemie's best performance.

We are coming closer to a "cost-effective" look at organization in the premature infant and to seeing how the different developmental lines interact to create a picture of organization in the fragile premature or sick infant. Through such a picture, the examiner can identify the organizational processes which are already relatively stable, as well as ones which are easily overloaded. The Assessment of Preterm Infant Behavior (APIB) (Als, Lester, Tronick, & Brazelton, 1980) is a process-oriented assessment. Using it, we feel we can more reliably identify the tasks for parents who must work with such babies toward optimal organization and function.

However, the APIB is complex, difficult to learn, and hard to score reliably. Consequently, we have been recommending that a set of 10 qualifiers be added to the Brazelton Neonatal Behavioral Assessment Scale to make it useful with at-risk and immature neonates. The NBAS can then be used as a clinical instrument for assessing these babies after they are out of danger and are in room air in an open crib (see Table 3).

---

Table 3. **Qualifiers for the NBAS**

Quality of Responsivity
Examiner Facilitation
Cost of Attention
Balance of Tone
Range and Flexibility of States
Regulatory Capacity
Robustness and Endurance
Control over Input
Need for Facilitation and Use of Stimulation
Attractiveness
(From Als et al., 1979; Als et al., 1980)

---

# Training Examiners

We have been able to train examiners to 90 percent reliability (missing no more than two out of 28 behavioral items by 2 points) and not more than two disagreements on the reflexes. Not only can reliability be achieved with examiners who are ready to shape their behaviors to the cues of the baby, but the reliability can be maintained for several years. We require reliability training for anyone who uses the Brazelton scale for research and have trained trainers carefully. There are now a number of centers at which people can be trained for reliability on the NBAS. There are six centers in the United States and five centers in Europe and Asia where reliable research using the NBAS is in progress. Over 120 papers involving use of the scale have been published in professional journals. A number of these studies (Field, 1980; Olson et al., 1981) have produced evidence demonstrating that a newborn's behavior toward his or her parents significantly affects their relationship to the baby.

Reliability testing is a vital step toward creating sensitive observers of babies. In our training model, a professional is tested for reliability after he or she has participated in a training program and has completed the required homework, studying the background of 20 to 25 babies and examining them using the Brazelton scale. When a trainee achieves reliability on the scale, we can see a positive change in his or her self-image as an examiner. The trainee now becomes absolutely certain of his or her own competence in bringing the baby to best performance and in being ready to share that performance with parents and other professionals.

We urge trained examiners to return to an NBAS training center every year, or at least every two or three years, for a "recheck" of reliability. Any "slippage" in reliable performance of the Brazelton scale is instructive since we have discovered that a sensitive observer unconsciously adapts to the subjects he or she is examining. For example, an examiner who has been trained to be reliable may begin to work with a group of babies who are different from the group seen in training. The babies may be from different cultures or may be different because of low birthweight or adverse intrauterine conditions. We have found that, if we observe such an examiner carefully for slippage in his or her performance of the Brazelton scale, we will be able to use the changes the examiner has made as adaptations to the group of babies he or she has seen. In other words, rather than interpreting these changes as slippage, we use them as a very subtle window into the adaptations which this group of babies has demanded. If one wants to guard against such slippage in reliability on the NBAS, we recommend that every fifth baby examined be one from a normative group or from a culture different from the special population one is studying.

# ▤ The Future of the NBAS

On April 1, 1995, Procter & Gamble, Pampers Division, provided the Brazelton Center for Infants and Parents with funding for training professionals who work with infants and families in hospital, clinical, and educational settings. The Center offers training on the different applications of the Brazelton scale and presents additional training on innovative service delivery models designed to reach out to and meet the needs of families in today's society. One early project will be using the NBAS to improve the outcome for newborns and parents who are being discharged from hospitals increasingly soon after delivery.

Underlying the work of the Center is the philosophy that support for infants and families from the beginning of life constitutes the most powerful form of preventive intervention for the high-risk infant and family. Courses and workshops for physicians, nurses, childbirth educators, physical and occupational therapists, psychologists, social workers, early intervention specialists, parent educators, and other allied health professionals are available. The Brazelton Center or regional satellite training centers in the United States will offer one- and two-day workshops as well as more intensive courses in assessment and intervention, including reliability training on the Brazelton scale. Training will also be available at European sites: Switzerland, Germany, Denmark, Portugal, Belgium, Ireland, United Kingdom, and Spain. Training centers have also been established in Japan, Israel, Brazil, and Canada.

The faculty of the Brazelton Center for Infants and Parents includes T. Berry Brazelton, M.D., Founder and Professor Emeritus; J. Kevin Nugent, Ph.D., Executive Director; Casey Schwartz, R.N., Administrative Director; Peter Gorski, M.D.; Constance Keefer, M.D.; Jean Cole, M.S.; and Donna Karl, R.N. Frances King Koch is Project Coordinator. The Brazelton Center will serve as a resource center and clearinghouse for newborn and infancy research, and will continue research on the Brazelton scale. The Center will attempt to promote quality control in research studies using the scale and hopes to facilitate the dissemination of research findings through its communication network.

Both existing and new NBAS-related programs will continue to be guided by a commitment to a brighter future for infants and their parents. By offering education and training programs that are based upon the principles of the NBAS—programs that support a "continuum of care" for families, beginning in pregnancy and continuing through the postpartum period—the Center can contribute to the building of a foundation of health and well-being for all families. In directing its programs toward health care practitioners who participate in a family's first days and weeks together, the Center has chosen to support those who will have the earliest and perhaps most critical impact upon the course of a new family's future.

# References

Als, H., Lester, B. M., & Brazelton, T. B. (1979). Dynamics of the behavioral organization of the premature infant. In T. M. Field, A. M. Sostek, S. Goldberg, & H. H. Shuman (Eds.), *Infants born at risk* (pp. 173-192). New York: Spectrum Publications.

Als, H., Lester B. M., Tronick, E., & Brazelton, T. B. (1980). Manual for the Assessment of Preterm Infant Behavior (APIB). In H. E. Fitzgerald, B. M. Lester, & M. W. Yogman (Eds.), *Theory and research in behavioral pediatrics* (Vol. 1). New York: Plenum.

Brazelton, T. B. (1973). Neonatal Behavioral Assessment Scale. *Clinics in Development Medicine, No. 50.* London: Henneman. Philadelphia: Lippincott.

Brazelton, T. B. (1984). Neonatal Behavioral Assessment Scale. *Clinics in Development Medicine, No. 88.* London: Spastics International Medical Publishers.

Brazelton, T. B., Tronick, E., Leghtig, A., Lasky, R., & Klein, R. (1977). The behavior of nutritionally deprived Guatemalan neonates. *Developmental Medicine & Child Neurology 19,* 364-377.

Cravioto, J., Delcardie, E., & Birch, H. G. (1966). Nutrition, growth and neurointegrative development. *Pediatrics Supplement, 38,* 319.

Drillien, C. M. (1964). *The growth and development of the prematurely born infant.* Baltimore: Williams and Wilkins.

Field, T. M. (1980). Interactions of preterm and term infants with their lower- and middle-class teenage and adult mothers. In T. M. Field, S. Goldberg, D. Stern, & A. M. Sostek (Eds.), *High risk infants and children.* New York: Academic Press.

Graham, F. K., Matarazzo, R. G., & Caldwell, B. M. (1956). Behavioral differences between normal and traumatized newborns. *Psychology Now, 70* (22), 17-23.

Greenberg, N. H. (1971). A comparison of infant-mother interactional behavior in infants with atypical behavior and normal infants. In J. Hellmuth (Ed.), *Exceptional Infants* (Vol. 2). New York: Bruner Mazel.

Heider, G. M. (1966). Vulnerability in infants and young children. *Genetic Psychology Monograph 73*, 1.

Klein, R. E., Habicht, J. P., & Yarbrough, C. (1971). *Effect of protein calorie malnutrition on mental development.* Washington, DC: Incap Publication No. I-571.

Lester, B. M. (1979). A synergistic process approach to the study of prenatal malnutrition. *International Journal of Behavioral Development, 2,* 377-393.

Lester, B. M. (1980). Behavioral assessment of the neonate. In E. Sell (Ed.), *Follow-up of the high-risk newborn: A practical approach.* Springfield, IL: Charles C. Thomas.

Olsen, R., Olsen, G., Pernice, J., Bloom, K., Zuckerman, B., & Brazelton, T. B. (April 1981). *Use of the Brazelton Neonatal Assessment Scale as an early intervention with adolescent parents in the newborn period.* Paper presented at the meeting of the Ambulatory Pediatric Society, San Francisco, CA.

Rosenblith, J. F. (1961). The modified Graham behavior test for newborns. *Biologia 3,* 174-192.

# 8. The Infant-Toddler Developmental Assessment (IDA):

## A Family-Centered Transdisciplinary Assessment Process

JOANNA ERIKSON

"Assessment is a pivotal point for families and children. The type and scope of the assessment often determine the type and scope of intervention. The child's development must be viewed in the context that includes a regard for multiple factors—biological, familial, and social." (Erikson, 1983, p. 1)

This statement was one of the major conclusions of a task force convened in Connecticut in the early 1980s. The mission of the task force was to review policies and practices statewide for the assessment of infants and toddlers, in order to make recommendations that would lead to higher standards and improved services in community agencies (Erikson, 1983). The IDA—the Infant-Toddler Developmental Assessment—grew out of this effort.

The IDA is a comprehensive, family-centered assessment for children from birth to 3 years of age. It has evolved through more than a decade of field-testing and evaluation in a community context. Professionals who practice in a wide range of health, mental health, social service, and educational settings have participated in the refinement and testing of the IDA.

The IDA approach addresses the complexity and interdependence of health, family, and social factors that influence a child's development. Parents and professionals are partners in all aspects of the assessment. Being an integrated clinical process, the IDA provides a framework for the review and integration of data from multiple sources, as well as guidelines for team process and decisionmaking. Based on a common core of knowledge for all practitioners, the IDA is designed to be conducted by a team of two or more professionals representing different disciplines. It includes an interview with parents or caregivers; a review of the child's history, health, and development; a profile of the child's competencies; consultation with the child's health care provider and other specialists as needed; and a conference with the parents to discuss findings and develop a plan.

The IDA's breadth sets it apart from "traditional" measures of early development. Its process for integrating complex information about a child and family is designed to assure comprehensiveness. The team approach, which is built into the process, lends reliability. The Provence Birth-to-Three Developmental Profile, the assessment tool which is a component of the IDA, devotes attention to affective domains as well as to more traditionally assessed developmental areas.

## The Development of the IDA

In 1982, a multidisciplinary task force was convened under the auspices of the Connecticut Department of Health Services Child Development Program to study the need for developmental assessment services for infants and toddlers in the state, particularly from an interdisciplinary and interagency perspective. Members of the task force—including state consultants, faculty from three universities, and community practitioners—represented pediatrics, special education, and child development. The task force was asked to make recommendations that would lead to improved services in community agencies (Erikson, 1983).

When the group reviewed policies and practices then current in Connecticut, they found that resources were inadequate, that many professionals lacked experience with very young children, and that no consensus existed on the appropriate standards for assessment. Typical assessment approaches in community-based settings were narrow in focus, lacked a comprehensive framework, and exhibited little awareness of the multiple lines of child development—particularly emotional development—and their interaction. Parents were seldom engaged appropriately in the assessment process.

From an interdisciplinary perspective, the task force found that, although clinicians from multiple disciplines were often involved in a child's assessment, professionals typically approached the assessment from their own perspectives and frequently presented their findings in ways that colleagues from other disciplines could not interpret easily. From an interagency perspective, the task force found that assessments and service recommendations tended to reflect the service focus of the agency where the assessment originated or was performed (for example, health, mental health, rehabilitation, social services, or education) rather than the more generalized needs of the child and family.

Reporting its findings in 1983, the task force concluded that a new approach was required, an approach built upon a process that could be used by *all* disciplines working with infants and toddlers within the mainstream of *all* agencies serving children. The task force recommended that every professional working with infants and young children and their families have a basic core of knowledge and skills related to early childhood and family development. This shared knowledge base would lead not only to improved assessment services, but also to improved communication among professionals from different disciplines and different types of service settings.

A subgroup of the task force continued to work on the major issues of the report. In particular, they identified the key components of a comprehensive assessment. (This group included Joanna Erikson, Consultant to the Child Development Program; Saro Palmeri, Chief of Health Services for Handicapped Children and Director of the Child Development Program; Sally Provence, Professor of Pediatrics at Yale University School of Medicine; and Susan Vater, Director of the Child Development Clinic, Hartford, Connecticut.) These efforts led to the development of the IDA model. The group reviewed best practices in both academic and community settings in light of evolving policy requirements, in order to identify exemplary clinical assessment practices and translate them into a format accessible to a wide range of practicing professionals.

Initially, the group looked at steps of the assessment process and prepared a manual of assessment procedures that would avoid a narrow "test-driven" focus. When the group recognized that a truly comprehensive process would require the use of a developmental profile, Sally Provence organized a profile of developmental domains and sequences that included attention to the child's feelings, social adaptation, and personality traits, as well as to more traditionally assessed skill areas. The domains and sequences of the IDA are now named the Provence Birth-to-Three Developmental Profile.

Formally titled the Connecticut Infant-Toddler Developmental Assessment, the group's draft manual of assessment procedures soon became known by its acronym, "IDA." The IDA's essential features, described below, remained constant during the years of field-testing, evaluation, modification, and refinement that led to formal publication in May 1995 (Provence, Erikson, Vater, & Palmeri, 1985, 1989, 1991, 1995).

## An Overview of the IDA

The IDA was designed to improve early identification of children who may be in need of intervention services. It is intended to bridge the gap between simple developmental screenings and complex multidisciplinary evaluations. The IDA can serve as an initial assessment for a child and family in order to determine the need for monitoring, consultation, intervention, or other services. Its framework can be used to organize and integrate information from a child's previous evaluations. The IDA can also be used to follow the development of vulnerable or at-risk children without obvious developmental problems.

The IDA approach is anchored in theoretical constructs and clinical perspectives which acknowledge the variety and interdependence of factors that influence the health and development of young children (Provence & Naylor, 1983). A child's development is complex. It involves biological endowment in interaction with environment and experience, an interweaving of nature and nurture.

Although putting such a model into practice is often difficult, Sally Provence frequently reminded her colleagues that the challenge is "to embrace the complexity." The IDA is designed to support practitioners as they accept the challenge; it acknowledges the complexity of development, and it offers practitioners a framework within which to organize their observations and formulate a meaningful synthesis and plan. Each phase of the assessment contributes important information and an essential perspective on the child's development. Additionally, the IDA stresses the importance of relationships, those between the parent and child, practitioner and child, and practitioner and parent, as well as the relationships between practitioners.

# Features of the IDA

The IDA includes an interview with parents about their concerns and the child's health and developmental history; a review of the child's health status; assessment of the child's developmental competencies along eight developmental domains (gross motor ability; fine motor ability; language/communication; relationship to inanimate objects; self-help; relationship to persons; emotions and feeling states; and coping) using the Provence Birth-to-Three Developmental Profile; consultation with the child's health care provider and others as needed; team integration and synthesis; a conference with the parents to discuss findings and develop a plan; and a written report.

Four characteristics are central to the IDA:

1. *The IDA is an integrated clinical process.* The IDA procedures provide a guide for gathering and organizing observations and information from multiple sources, and for team process and decisionmaking. They provide clinicians with a basis for informed clinical opinion. The various components—family, health, and development—are integrated via the forms and procedures used and the guidelines for team process.

2. *The IDA is family-centered.* Procedures are designed to include parents as partners in all phases of the assessment, and to help practitioners support the families and collaborate with them.

3. *The IDA is a transdisciplinary process.* It is designed to be conducted by a team of two or more professionals, each with credentials in one of the developmental disciplines (e.g., psychology, social work, medicine, nursing, speech/language pathology). Each IDA practitioner learns all of the components of the assessment and can then function as a developmental generalist. Typically, members of an IDA assessment team represent professional backgrounds that complement one another; each team member contributes his or her own professional expertise and experience to the process. Since the IDA process often clarifies concerns which require additional evaluation, the IDA assessment may, when indicated, be complemented by specialty evaluations provided by a team member or a consultant.

4. *The IDA process is flexible.* While each IDA assessment follows the same basic procedures, emphasis and timing may

vary, depending on the context of the assessment, the particular questions being raised, and the relationship of the practitioners to the child and family. The IDA has been used in settings such as primary health care centers, neonatal followup programs, early intervention programs, child guidance clinics, rehabilitation centers, schools, nursing agencies, and infant/toddler child care centers. An IDA assessment can take place in the home, at a center, or in an arena setting, in which several professionals observe the assessment.

The IDA yields a profile of the child's development that describes the areas and degree of concern regarding the child, a summary of health and family findings, and a description of the types of services a child and family may need. The IDA can be used to determine eligibility for services (for example, under Part H of IDEA, the Individuals with Disabilities Education Act) and can form the basis for an initial Individualized Family Service Plan (IFSP). When conducted by an interdisciplinary team, the IDA conforms to best practice guidelines of the field (Meisels & Provence, 1989).

## The IDA Phases

The IDA procedures include six phases, described briefly below (see also Table 1). Each phase, centered around a conceptual framework and common core of knowledge, develops from the preceding one. Each phase is considered complete only after discussion and review of information by the team. The published IDA manuals (Provence, Erikson, Vater, & Palmeri, 1995) include guides and materials for learning to conduct each phase; directions for conducting each step of the procedures; and forms to assist the team in gathering, organizing, and recording information.

### Phase One: Referral and preinterview data gathering

The first phase of the IDA procedures consists of gathering and assimilating preliminary information from the parents and the referral source in order to clarify the reasons for the referral. One team member makes initial contact with the child's parents or primary caregiver to determine their concerns and involve them in the assessment. Thus, a dialogue and a primary relationship begin that will continue throughout the evaluation.

The practitioner describes to the parents the nature of the

Table 1. **Overview of IDA Phases**

| Phase | Objectives | Forms |
|---|---|---|
| **1.** Referral and Preinterview Data Gathering | To confirm the referral; to gather and assimilate preliminary information regarding the family and child; to make initial contact with the family | IDA Record, Parent Report, Request for Health Information |
| **2.** Initial Parent Interview | To elicit parental concerns and engage the parents as partners during the assessment; to obtain information about the child's history, health, and current development status as they pertain to the referral concerns; to gather information about the family that has relevance to the child's development | Parent Report, Family Recording Guide, Health Recording Guide, IDA Record |
| **3.** Health Review | To gather and organize health information from parent(s), the health care provider, medical records, and other sources; to conduct the health review and complete the Health Recording Guide; to consider the role of health factors in the child's development | Request for Health Information, Health Recording Guide, IDA Record |
| **4.** Developmental Observation and Assessment | To create a profile of the child's development along multiple lines based on information obtained from parent(s) and other caregiver(s), the Provence Profile, natural and play-based observation, and a review of developmental and behavioral concerns | IDA Record |
| **5.** Integration and Synthesis | To review the information gathered from throughout the process; to consider the need for consultation; to integrate and summarize findings; to identify program options; to prepare for and schedule a conference with the parent(s) | Use summaries from Family and Health Recording Guides, IDA Record |
| **6.** Sharing Findings, Completion, and Report | To bring the assessment to completion, share findings, and develop a plan with the parent(s), and facilitate entry into services if needed | IDA Record |

assessment and aspects of the process, including the names of other team members who will be involved and the number, location, and purpose of the various visits. He or she inquires about any previous evaluations and the availability of other records that may be helpful in the assessment. The practitioner and parents schedule an interview for a time and place that will allow both parents to participate.

To prepare for the initial interview with the parents, team members review the information they have gathered from the referral source, the parents, and written records.

## Phase Two: Initial parent interview

This phase consists of an interview with the child's parents or other primary caregivers. The interviewer sets a tone so that the parents feel comfortable and supported as they tell their story. The interviewer engages them in the process of describing their concerns and priorities, reviewing pertinent information about the child's health and developmental history and their perceptions of the child's strengths, difficulties, and needs. Other information about the family that is relevant to the child's development is also obtained.

An important objective of the initial parent interview is forming an alliance with parents and engaging them as partners in the evaluation process, to which they will make a distinctive contribution. Because human relationships are central to how the child develops physically, cognitively, emotionally, and socially, the child's behavior and development cannot be understood apart from his or her relationships with the closest caregivers. Thus, although the child is the focus of the IDA assessment, parents' perceptions, concerns, priorities, and roles are also central. Practitioners must understand the child and family as part of a complex, interactive, functioning system. They must also be aware of the larger community in which the family lives and must recognize and respect the fact that cultures vary in their beliefs and traditions concerning family roles and relationships, child-rearing techniques, disability, communication, and styles of interaction, particularly in relation to members of the helping professions.

A successful interview with parents requires an interweaving of content and process. The IDA manuals and procedures provide strategies for organizing and conducting the interview, including guidelines for the content areas to be addressed and descriptions of the tasks of each stage of the interview process. The practitioner individualizes each interview depending on the particular situation, using a combination of open-ended explo ration and focused data gathering. Content areas to be explored include general themes regarding the child and family, as well as specific information concerning the child's current development, ability to use skills, and developing personality (areas that will be evaluated further through the domains and sequences of the Provence Profile). Another goal is to gain an understanding of the experience of the child and family together and of the risk and protective factors in the environment.

Team discussion completes this phase. Information gathered in the interview is recorded and reviewed in preparation for the next phase.

## Phase Three: Health review

In this phase, team members gather, organize, and record infor- mation about the child's health and health history. They obtain information from the parents (during the parent interview), from the health care provider (through requests for records and specific guided requests for information and consultation), from medical records, and from other sources. Team members review prenatal, perinatal, and general health factors in terms of risk and vulnerability. The focus is on identifying significant health concerns and their impact on the child's development, learning about parents' understanding and perceptions of health issues, and consulting with the child's primary health provider.

The health review is particularly important in the assessment of infants and toddlers because health problems may have an especially pervasive effect on the child's development during the first three years of life. During this period, the child's cognitive, emotional, and social development occurs in the context of rapid physical growth, particularly of the central nervous system and brain. Beginning at conception, early influences—both biologi- cal and environmental—can have a profound effect on the mat- uration process.

The concepts of risk and vulnerability create a dynamic model for considering health issues. *Vulnerability* is a state of physical or psychological fragility, or of inherent constitutional weakness. *Risk factors* are those elements in the physical and/or psychoso- cial environment which may influence development adversely. Some vulnerabilities remain latent and are never expressed fully.

In contrast, some children with seemingly minimal vulnerabilities experience poor developmental outcomes after exposure to risky physical and/or psychological environments. Generally, no single risk factor influences developmental outcomes directly; rather, it is the interaction of risks and vulnerabilities, and the absence of protective factors, that result in poor outcomes.

The IDA manuals and procedures provide directions for conducting the health review. They focus on strategies for gathering and organizing medical/health information and for identifying factors significant to the child's current status and needs. Practitioner preparation includes becoming familiar with key health concepts and terminology. Guidelines emphasize developing a partnership with the primary health care provider and respect for his or her role.

Team discussion completes this phase, and the information gathered is reviewed in preparation for the following phases.

## Phase Four: Developmental observation and assessment

In this phase, team members complete a profile of the child's development, using information obtained from the parents and other caregivers and from direct observation of the child's responses to structured tasks. The assessment is always conducted in the presence of the parents and incorporates naturalistic and play-based observations. Unless the child is very young, two sessions are recommended. One team member conducts a session, and the other team member observes and assists with recording. Items that cannot be administered successfully during the sessions can be credited if the parent or caregiver reports that the child has exhibited the behavior outside the assessment context. The profile provides a description of the child's current functioning, identifying competencies and areas of concern. Additionally, this phase includes a review of behavioral and developmental concerns to assist in identifying those that may not be apparent from the profile alone.

To interpret developmental differences among infants and toddlers at various ages and stages, an understanding of normal development is essential. Generally, development proceeds in an orderly and predictable sequence. However, each child is unique; there may be considerable variation in the timetable for the emergence of a particular skill and considerable range in what can be regarded as normal development. Development proceeds along multiple, interrelated lines. Because the infant's and young child's responses are less differentiated than those of older children, difficulty in any one area—motor, language, cognitive, or social-emotional—is likely to affect the other areas of development. Consequently, an assessment of a young child's development should not view one area independently of the others. Equally important are the child's sense of himself and the way the child relates to people and the world, which involve his temperament and evolving personality.

A developmental assessment should ask both "what" and "how" questions. First, what developmental competencies has the child acquired? How do these compare with those expected at a given age? What is the quality of these competencies? Second (and of equal importance), how does the child make use of these skills in his or her adaptation to and encounters with the human world? The Provence Birth-to-Three Developmental Profile reflects these issues. In developing the profile, Dr. Provence concentrated on selecting progressive sets of items in each domain that accurately identify a child's developmental level based on widely accepted normative expectations. The domains and sequences provide a breadth of observational opportunity. They invite practitioners to view the child along multiple lines and to "embrace the complexity" of the child's development. The Provence Profile is designed to assist practitioners in organizing and recording their observations and to help professionals from different disciplines achieve a high degree of inter-rater reliability. Because it is intended to contribute to an integrated whole, the Provence Profile is meant to be used only in the context of the full IDA process and should never be used alone.

The Provence Profile identifies the child's competencies and areas of concern in eight developmental domains, including emotional development, interpersonal relationships, and coping, as well as the more traditional areas of gross motor ability, fine motor ability, relationship to inanimate objects, language/communication, and self-help (see Table 2). Development in each of these domains is examined through sets of items typically accomplished by normally developing children ranging from 1 to 36 months of age. Cross-referenced items in the profile indicate interrelationships among the domains. These are the items that Sally Provence found to be most clinically significant during her 35 years of systematic observation and clinical work with infants and toddlers in both naturalistic and treatment settings.

---

### Table 2. **Provence Birth-to-Three Developmental Profile Domains**

#### Motor, Language, and Cognitive Competencies

*Gross Motor*
Includes skills and other characteristics of large muscle movement and control. These are familiar landmarks.

*Fine Motor*
Includes stages in the development of hand and finger skills and items of hand-eye coordination.

*Relationship to Inanimate Objects*
Reflects the child's interest in and insight into toys and other inanimate objects. Items include those that provide information about perception (visual and auditory), object permanence, and nonverbal problem-solving abilities. This domain includes competencies traditionally referred to as "cognitive."

*Language/Communication*
Includes well-recognized characteristics of the developmental line of language and its adaptive use, including steps in the differentiation and elaboration of expressive and receptive language. Progress in cognitive development also is reflected in many of the items.

*Self-Help*
Consists primarily of expectable behaviors in the young child's long road toward self-care and self-regulation of body functions.

#### Feelings, Social Adaptation, and Personality Traits

*Relationship to Persons*
Is composed primarily of behaviors observed in interaction with adults or behaviors that reflect developmental changes (e.g., separation anxiety, oppositional behavior) in the child's psychosocial development. In the third year, there are items that relate to experiences with other children.

*Emotions and Feeling States*
Includes the common forms of expression generally accepted as indicative of specific feelings and traces some steps in their differentiation and elaboration.

*Coping Behavior*
Includes behaviors that reflect the child's ability to use his or her capacities and skills in meeting the demands and opportunities of daily life. It focuses on what the child is *trying* to do and implies *effort*, not necessarily success.

---

The Provence Profile uses a standard set of procedures and materials for administering the items and for applying the scoring criteria to sets of items that identify a child's developmental level in each domain. The result provides information about the relationship between a child's chronological age and the specific developmental milestones he or she has reached.

The IDA manuals and procedures provide directions for planning and conducting the child observation and assessment; engaging the parent and child in the session; identifying issues that require further observation, consultation, or assessment from a specialist; and recording observations and findings. The practitioner's preparation includes learning the definitions and directions for the domains and sequences of the Provence Profile in order to achieve competence in the administration and scoring of the items.

Team members review and score the protocols and complete the profile, noting particularly the qualitative aspects of the child's performance, important interrelationships among the domains, and any developmental or behavioral concerns. The findings are discussed in preparation for Phase Five.

## Phase Five: Integration and synthesis

During this phase, team members systematically review and synthesize all the information they have obtained in the course of the evaluation, noting both strengths and concerns. This process of integration and synthesis requires experienced clinical judgment, close collaboration among team members, and effective team functioning.

The IDA manuals and procedures provide guidelines for team review of developmental, health, and family findings, as well as discussion of the next steps to be considered. The process results in a summary of the team's findings and a description of the *types* of services a child and family may need. Team members then identify resources or program options available to meet these needs. The IDA is *not* intended to be used in designing a specific therapy plan or instructional objectives. Typically, these will be determined in the context of an intervention program.

Completion of this phase results in a description of the child's developmental status and needs, which is based on the information gathered in response to the issues raised in the referral. Team members summarize and prioritize salient findings in preparation for sharing them with the child's parents or caregivers. The next step in the process will be the development, with parents, of recommendations and a plan of action.

### Phase Six: Sharing findings, completion, and report

The partnership that practitioners and parents have established during the first five phases of the IDA provides a foundation for the final phase, in which findings are reviewed and a plan consistent with the family's concerns and priorities is developed.

This phase begins with a conference in which team members and parents review the assessment process and discuss its findings in the context of parents' concerns, expectations, and understanding of the child's problems. If intervention or services are indicated, team members and parents review types of programs and services, discuss various options, and develop a plan of action.

The IDA manuals and procedures provide directions for conducting the conference with parents. The guidelines focus on the skills and strategies team members need to present assessment findings in a clear, unbiased, and supportive manner and to discuss findings with the family.

After the conference, team members share responsibility for completing the IDA Record and a written report that summarizes the assessment process, the findings, and the plan agreed upon. Parents review a draft of the report to assure that it is accurate and constructive. With parents' permission, the final report is sent to the referral source, the child's primary health care provider, and those who will be implementing the plan. Team members facilitate the family's entry into services and make a plan for followup. Finally, parents are asked to evaluate the assessment process.

## Experience with the IDA

The authors of the IDA wanted to investigate its validity and examine its usefulness in community-based services. Could professionals from many disciplines use the IDA? What role could it play in an interagency service delivery system?

From 1984 to 1988, the Federal Maternal and Child Health Bureau supported extensive review and evaluation of the IDA in the context of state-community collaboration (Erikson & Vater, 1988). During the four years of this demonstration project, more than 125 Connecticut professionals became IDA practitioners by participating in a professional development program that involved both didactic seminars and clinical supervision. Participants represented a wide variety of disciplines (special education/early intervention, social work, nursing, psychology/child development, pediatrics, family practice, occupational therapy, physical therapy, and speech and language pathology) and the spectrum of community agencies (early intervention, primary health care, nursing, public schools, child guidance/mental health, neonatal followup, and rehabilitation services).

## Evaluation studies

The evaluation of the IDA that began in 1984 examined both its content areas and procedures. Field-testing was done by an interdisciplinary, interagency group of professionals from health, education, and mental health settings who were selected for their expertise in early childhood development. Group members were asked to review all content areas, and teams of two clinicians assessed two or more children using the IDA process. Based on the group's recommendations, the IDA manuals were revised and expanded. This process resulted in a refined set of standard procedures for the assessment process and directions for conducting the Provence Birth-to-Three Developmental Profile. These efforts and subsequent revisions contributed to the content validity of the IDA. Additional studies of the IDA have presented data to support the validity and reliability not only of the Provence Profile as a standardized measure of development from birth to three, but also of the IDA Procedures as an assessment and decisionmaking process.

Anastasiow (1987) compared the items on the Provence Profile with items on three other widely used developmental assessments—the Bayley Scales of Infant Development (BSID) (Bayley, 1969), the Hawaii Early Learning Profile (HELP) (Furuno et al., 1979), and the Learning Accomplishment Profile (LAP) (Sanford & Zelman, 1981). In each case, high percentages of items were found in common, and agreement was high (84 to 96 percent) on the developmental age levels of those items. In a later study of 53 children, Salguero and Klin (1994) reported general agreement on the percentages of children falling below developmental age criteria on the IDA and the Vineland Adaptive Behavior Scales (Sparrow, Balla, & Cicchetti, 1984). Anastasiow (1987) reported high inter-rater agreement on the Provence Profiles, with 81 percent agreement in the language domain and 91 to 95 percent agreement in the seven other domains. Anastasiow (1991) also reported high inter-rater agreement on the full IDA process (78 to 97 percent for the family, health, and developmental findings and recommendations). Because the 35 practitioners who participated in the study had been trained over a six-year period, it also appears that inter-rater agreement remains high over time.

Anastasiow (1987) also reported a followup study of 57 children and families whom IDA practitioners had referred to 15 community agencies for services, based on IDA assessments. A questionnaire was sent to administrators of the agencies receiving the referrals, asking if they considered the referrals appropriate and if they found the IDA findings useful in understanding concerns about a child's development. Twelve of the 15 agencies responded to the questionnaire. Of these, 83 percent found the referrals appropriate to their agency and the case report helpful in understanding the developmental needs of the child.

Statistical analyses of Provence Profiles for 100 children reported in the IDA Administration Manual (Provence, Erikson, Vater, & Palmeri, 1995) examined several aspects of the reliability and validity of this assessment. High internal consistency reliability (computed using coefficient alpha) was observed for the eight domains, ranging from .90 to .96 for ages 1 to 18 months and from .77 to .96 for ages 19 to 36 months. The validity of each of the eight domains as a measure of development was assessed by examining the progression of mean scores across six-month age intervals from 1 to 36 months. The children's profiles showed higher scores in each domain at each successive age interval. The generally high intercorrelations among the eight domains reflected the reliability of these domains, and the predictable patterns of coefficients for younger and older groups added support to the construct validity of the Provence Profile.

To determine the efficacy of the IDA, a chart review of children assessed in one of the clinics of the Connecticut Child Development Program was conducted (Anastasiow, 1987). The multidisciplinary staff of this clinic conducted traditional multidisciplinary assessments and also began to use the IDA process. The charts of 43 children who had been assessed with the agency's traditional multidisciplinary approach were compared with 20 IDA assessments. The review examined (a) the time between the child's birth and the conclusion of the evaluation; (b) the time between referral and the conclusion of the evaluation; (c) the number of professionals involved in the assessment process; and (d) the completeness of the recommendations.

The review showed that the IDA assessments were completed in a shorter time period and involved fewer professionals for each assessment than the agency's traditional procedures. Nevertheless, IDA assessments were found to be comparable to the more extended assessment in comprehensiveness and accuracy. These findings suggest that the IDA may be more cost-effective than traditional multidisciplinary approaches. In addition, the review found that IDA teams were more selective in ordering specialty evaluations (e.g., speech and language, occupational therapy, physical therapy). The IDA assessments tended to take place earlier in a child's life, and, because of the more efficient process, IDA assessments were completed for significantly more infants below 1 year of age than was the case with traditional procedures. More families completed the IDA assessment, and the shorter time period required for the IDA allowed quicker referral for families for whom intervention was recommended.

## The experiences of practitioners

More than 300 professionals participated in evaluations of the IDA between 1985 and 1991. They completed self-evaluations before their experience with the IDA, evaluated the IDA coursework, and completed final evaluations that included a second self-evaluation and reflections on their experience with learning and conducting the IDA.

During the demonstration project (1985 to 1987), evaluations focused on the content and effectiveness of the IDA written materials and training program, the participants' ability to implement the IDA, and the practitioners' acquisition of new skills. Results were generally very positive, and findings contributed to further refinement of the materials and curriculum. Forty-six participants completed final evaluations, the majority of which were very positive (Anastasiow, 1987).

The evaluations conducted between 1988 and 1991 focused on participants' perceptions of the skills they had gained in assessing young children and their impressions of the IDA as an assessment tool. In their final evaluations, the majority of the practitioners again responded very positively concerning the improvement in their skills and the contribution the IDA experience had made to their professional growth. In 1990, practitioners who had completed the IDA program during the period from 1985 to 1989 were asked to evaluate their use of the IDA.

Eighty-seven percent of the respondents said that the IDA had been very helpful in their work. In response to open-ended questions concerning their experiences in implementing the IDA, practitioners have consistently emphasized three areas:

1. The comprehensiveness of the assessment content and process, which enables practitioners to organize a great deal of information and to "view the child as a whole";

2. The provision of opportunities for practitioners to expand their skills and increase their ability to apply knowledge effectively to the tasks of assessing across domains, working with families, and interacting with health care providers; and

3. The benefits of the IDA team approach, which provides perspectives from different disciplines, increased confidence in assessment findings, and added support for families.

Supervisors of practitioners trained in the IDA have been positive about the IDA's impact. In 1990, a questionnaire sent to supervisors of 34 IDA practitioners asked their opinion of the IDA and whether they felt participation in the IDA program had upgraded the skills of their staff. Almost all the supervisors responded to the questionnaire, and all the respondents reported improvement in staff skills, which resulted in improved agency services to young children. Responses indicated further that, when many professionals within a service delivery network used the IDA, communication among them improved, leading to improved child identification, interagency coordination, and continuity of care.

## Implementation and dissemination

IDA manuals have been used in the evaluation of thousands of children. In 1989, a national task force on screening and assessment convened by the National Early Childhood Technical Assistance System (NEC*TAS) cited the IDA as an assessment process consistent with best-practice guidelines (Meisels & Provence, 1989). After the completion of the federally funded demonstration project in 1988, dissemination of the IDA continued in the states of Georgia, Michigan, California, and New York. Experience suggests that the IDA is best learned and practiced in the context of mentorship, team discussion, and case review (Fenichel, 1991).

In 1995, the complete *Infant-Toddler Developmental Assessment* (Provence, Erikson, Vater, & Palmeri) was published. The set of IDA materials includes three manuals: the *IDA Foundations and Study Guide,* the *IDA Administration Manual,* and *Family-Centered Assessment of Young Children At Risk,* a book of readings. The *Foundations and Study Guide* provides the conceptual framework, a case illustration, and a study guide for each of the IDA phases. Materials are designed for courses, workshops, and seminars; clinical rotation for trainees in the health professions; in-service training; or self-study by groups, teams, or individuals. The *Administration Manual* summarizes the IDA phases and steps, provides directions for administering and scoring the Provence Birth-to-Three Developmental Profile, and includes IDA forms. For practitioners who have learned to conduct the IDA, the study guide and other materials serve as ongoing references.

## Summary

The IDA is an integrated, family-centered, clinical process. IDA procedures enable practitioners to organize complex information from multiple sources in order to develop a comprehensive plan for the child and family. The distinctive strengths of the IDA are:

- The breadth of the process, which addresses development in the context of health, family, and social factors;
- The Provence Birth-to-Three Developmental Profile, which, in addition to the assessment of the child's competencies, regards understanding of the child's emotional development and relationships as central to the evaluation process; and
- The team approach, a step-by-step collaboration which facilitates clinical decisionmaking and lends reliability.

From its beginnings, the IDA represented a partnership among public health administrators, policymakers, and clinicians, all of whom were committed to implementation of the highest standards of care for young children and their families. The IDA pre-dated and anticipated many of the guiding principles and requirements concerning services for infants and toddlers, and their families, of Part H of the Individuals with Disabilities Education Act (IDEA).

The IDA is intended to be a component within a continuum of care that extends from careful developmental monitoring of infants and young children to appropriate services. Assessment is the first step in intervention; it is an opportunity for the family to learn more about their child and his or her needs. When done sensitively, the assessment process has the potential to be a therapeutic experience (Parker & Zuckerman, 1990).

Ten years of experience with the IDA have demonstrated its effectiveness in identifying infants and toddlers who are at risk of developmental problems and in need of early intervention services. Professionals from all early childhood developmental disciplines can incorporate the IDA into their practice. The IDA enables them to expand their skills in working with families and in assessing children across developmental domains. Because the IDA provides a common frame of reference for practitioners from different disciplines and settings within a service delivery system, IDA practitioners report improved interdisciplinary and interagency communication, resulting in increased continuity of care for children and families.

**Acknowledgments:** From the outset, the IDA has been a team effort. Countless colleagues have made important contributions to its development—the original task force members, the first faculty who struggled with content and process, and the practitioners who lent support and tested the IDA in the "real world." All helped the IDA find its present form. Special thanks go to Lois Davis, Tom Hutchinson, Fran Stott, and Susan Vater for their careful review and helpful comments on this chapter.

Sally Provence, who was infinitely wise about young children and who powerfully influenced all her students and colleagues, died just as preparation was beginning for publication of the IDA. The IDA is an important part of the legacy she leaves.

# ■ References

Anastasiow, N. (1987, 1991). *IDA technical report.* Unpublished report.

Bayley, N. (1969). *Bayley Scales of Infant Development.* New York: Psychological Corporation.

Erikson, J. (1983). *Report of the task force on identification and assessment.* Unpublished report. Connecticut Department of Health Services, Child Development Program.

Erikson, J. (Ed.). (1995). *Family-centered assessment of young children at risk: The IDA readings.* Chicago: Riverside Publishing Company.

Erikson, J., & Vater, S. (1988). *A community-based approach to developmental assessment services: The Connecticut Infant-Toddler Developmental Assessment Program (IDA).* Report of a four-year demonstration project. Connecticut Department of Health Services.

Fenichel, E. (1991). Learning through supervision and mentorship to support the development of infants, toddlers, and their families. *Zero to Three, 12* (2), 1-9.

Furuno, S., O'Reilly, K. A., Hosaka, C. M., Inatsuka, T. T., Allman, T. L., & Zeisloft, B. (1979). *The Hawaii Early Learning Profile.* Palo Alto, CA: VORT.

Meisels, S., & Provence, S. (1989). *Screening and assessment: Guidelines for identifying young disabled and developmentally vulnerable children and their families.* Arlington, VA: ZERO TO THREE/National Center for Clinical Infant Programs.

Parker, S., & Zuckerman, B. (1990). Therapeutic aspects of the assessment process. In S. Meisels & J. Shonkoff (Eds.), *Handbook of early childhood intervention* (pp. 350-369). New York: Cambridge University Press.

Provence, S., & Naylor, A. (1983). *Working with disadvantaged parents and their children.* New Haven, CT: Yale University Press.

Provence, S., Erikson, J., Vater, S., & Palmeri, S. (1985, 1989, 1991). *IDA procedures manual and developmental profile.* Unpublished.

Provence, S., Erikson, J., Vater, S., & Palmeri, S. (1995). *Infant-Toddler Developmental Assessment: IDA.* Chicago, IL: Riverside Publishing Company.

Salguero, C., & Klin, A. (1994). *Disadvantaged children's eligibility for services.* Paper presented at the Annual Meeting of the American Academy of Child and Adolescent Psychiatry. New York.

Sanford, A. R., & Zelman, J. G. (1981). *The Learning Accomplishment Profile.* Winston-Salem, NC: Kaplan.

Sparrow, S. S., Balla, D. A., & Cicchetti, D. V. (1984). *Vineland Adaptive Behavior Scales.* Circle Pines, MN: AGS.

# 9. Assessment for IFSP Development and Intervention Planning

DIANE BRICKER

"Assessment should be an ongoing, collaborative process of systematic observation and analysis" (Greenspan & Meisels, 1994), not a process that yields a number, label, or little of substance to formulate sound intervention plans. Unfortunately, too often, assessment/evaluation processes for young children follow models and procedures in which hours of professional time are invested in activities designed to produce a diagnostic label and little else. The process is usually not collaborative in that professionals often conduct their assessments in isolation and rarely ask for meaningful input from caregivers. Rather than conducting systematic observation of children as they negotiate their day, professionals give children a set of standardized, often meaningless, tasks. Disregarding the child's unfamiliarity with the tester, setting, and tasks, professionals carefully record children's responses. While often contained in a thick file, the outcomes from this type of assessment process are of questionable validity and of little use in helping caregivers and interventionists formulate intervention plans. It is curious that so much of the effort directed toward the assessment of young children yields outcomes that are of so little value in the development of Individualized Family Service Plans (IFSPs) and subsequent intervention planning.

An alternative model, using what I believe is a more appropriate approach, designs an assessment process that yields information and insights on children and their families which accurately reflect their usual modes of behaving, accurately pinpoint their strengths, and accurately target areas in need of intervention. An appropriate assessment process should obtain information through collaboration between professionals and caregivers, and through careful and systematic observation of the child in a variety of settings and tasks. Information collected in this way yields outcomes that can be used directly to formulate and evaluate intervention efforts, making the process valid, efficient, and effective.

We are faced with an important challenge. The use of traditional assessment approaches will continue until appropriate alternatives become available. We must replace traditional assessment processes—which tend to produce outcomes that are designed to assign labels and tend to use insufficient and faulty findings to produce intervention recommendations—with assessment processes that are more appropriate, efficient, accurate, and useful.

The purpose of this chapter is to describe an assessment/evaluation process that differs significantly from more traditional approaches. This approach and associated tool:

- Use systematic observation to collect assessment information;
- Seek formal input from caregivers;
- Produce outcomes that are directly relevant to formulating IFSPs and intervention plans; and
- Can be used to effectively monitor child progress.

Specifically, the goals of this chapter are to describe a model that links the processes of assessment, intervention, and evaluation, and to describe the assessment/evaluation tool which fosters the linkage between these processes.

## The Model: A Linked Assessment Approach*

As indicated above, many approaches to assessment do not appear to appreciate the importance of the assessment outcome for intervention planning and subsequent evaluation. Rather,

---

* The remainder of this chapter is taken, in part, from Diane Bricker (Ed.). (1993). *Assessment, Evaluation, and Programming System for Infants and Children, Vol. 1: AEPS Measurement for Birth to Three Years.* Baltimore, MD: Paul H. Brookes Publishing Co.

procedures and tools are used which generate information that is useful for deriving numbers and labels, but they offer little assistance in the development of IFSP goals and subsequent intervention content. A logical analysis would suggest that such traditional approaches are costly, inefficient, and ineffective. An alternative is to use an assessment process which yields outcomes that are directly relevant to the development of IFSP goals and intervention plans. In other words, a direct relationship should exist between the processes of assessment, intervention and evaluation.

The proposed linked-systems approach is composed of three critical processes: assessment, intervention, and evaluation. *Assessment* refers to the process of establishing a baseline or entry-level measurement of the child's skills and desired family outcomes. The assessment process should produce the necessary information to select appropriate and relevant intervention goals and objectives. *Intervention* refers to the process of arranging the physical and social environment to produce the desired growth and development specified in the formulated intervention plan for the child and family. *Evaluation* refers to the process of comparing the child's performance on selected intervention goals and objectives, as well as the family's progress toward established family outcomes, before and after intervention.

Figure 1 provides an illustration of the linked assessment, intervention, and evaluation approach. The major processes are shown in the boxes which are linked by arrows to indicate the sequence in which the processes should occur. In addition, the vertical arrows indicate the desired participation of professionals and families in each of these three processes.

Figure 1. **A Schematic of a Linked Assessment-Intervention-Evaluation Approach to Early Intervention with Joint Professional and Family Participation**

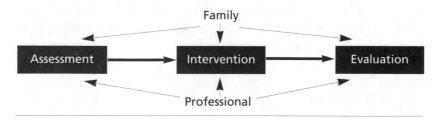

The assessment, intervention, and evaluation linked-systems approach can be divided into five phases:

**Phase One:** Initial assessment

**Phase Two:** Formulation of the Individualized Family Service Plan (IFSP)

**Phase Three:** Intervention

**Phase Four:** Ongoing monitoring for immediate feedback on individualized intervention procedures

**Phase Five:** Six-month and yearly evaluations of children and families.

As indicated in Figure 1, family input and participation should be encouraged throughout all these phases. The more families become involved in the assessment, intervention, and evaluation process, the greater the likelihood of improved outcomes for their children (Seitz & Provence, 1990).

## Phase One: Initial assessment

The link between assessment, intervention, and evaluation begins with the entry of children into a program. The major objective of the initial assessment is to formulate a realistic, appropriate IFSP that has an accompanying individualized evaluation plan.

The formulation of the IFSP is dependent upon an accurate assessment of the child's beginning skill level. On the basis of this assessment, an intervention plan can be developed toward improving areas in which the child has problems. In addition, the assessment strategies employed should yield information that precisely describes the child's behavior in the following ways: *First*, the assessment should include information about a child's performance of skills that are appropriate intervention targets. *Second*, the assessment should include a scoring system that is sensitive to how the child performed the skill and that indicates if the skill was performed independently, with different people, or in different settings. A standard binary scoring system only provides information on whether the child's response was "correct" or "incorrect." Because of this, important information for developing educational programs may be lost (Cole, Swisher, Thompson, & Fewell, 1985). *Third*, the assessment measure should be administered in the child's usual environment. Individuals working with the child should be able to use the test in the home or other environments in an unobtrusive manner. *Fourth*, the assessment should have a procedure for the formal inclusion of input from parents or caregivers. *Fifth*, and most important, the information generated by the test should be directly usable in the development of an IFSP.

An assessment that measures functional skills and is sensitive to the conditions under which a child is most likely to perform the skills will facilitate the development of appropriate and useful IFSPs. This will encourage child growth and development and will yield a sensitive measure of child progress throughout the intervention process.

Formulation of an IFSP requires specification of desired family outcomes as well as child goals. Family assessment should yield program-relevant information that will aid in developing functional outcome statements, but it should not be seen as intrusive by family members. We recommend the use of a parent-completed interest checklist followed by a structured interview to assist families in developing outcomes they see as relevant and important for the child and family.

## Phase Two: Formulation of the IFSP

The initial IFSP should be based primarily on information accumulated during the initial assessment period, although this assessment should be validated at the first quarterly evaluation or sooner. Relevant information should be obtained from parents' knowledge of their children as well as from professional observation and testing. The initial information should be used to develop a plan of action for the interventionists and family to identify the specific content areas that the IFSP will address. The child's portion of the IFSP should contain goals, objectives, strategies for reaching objectives, and a time frame for meeting selected goals. The IFSP should be straightforward so that it can be used as a working guide for interventionists and caregivers. The IFSP can also be used as a criterion for evaluating the success of the intervention.

The family portion of the IFSP should contain a statement of family strengths and needs related to enhancing the child's development. This statement is based on information obtained from the family's assessment of their interests and needs. Priorities can be collaboratively established during a structured interview for which the interventionist has developed a set of open-ended questions to which caregivers can respond, such as, "How can program staff be most useful to you and your child?" A set of outcome statements will evolve from these priorities, and activities and resources necessary for reaching outcomes, as well as a timeline, should be indicated.

### Phase Three: Intervention

Once the IFSP has been formulated by family members and interventionists, the actual intervention activities can be initiated. The child's performance on the program assessment indicates where teaching should begin. Items that the child is unable to perform become the goals and objectives, which often require prioritization. If the assessment tool is linked directly to the curriculum—that is, through the use of a curriculum-based assessment/evaluation tool—interventionists can easily locate the intervention activities that were developed to facilitate acquisition of specific goals and objectives. There is a direct correspondence between the assessment items (skills) identified as goals or objectives and the intervention content and strategies specified in the associated curriculum.

### Phase Four: Ongoing monitoring

A useful IFSP specifies both the tasks to be conducted and the manner in which the success of the intervention will be evaluated. A variety of strategies may be used for daily or weekly monitoring of child progress (e.g., trial-by-trial data, brief probes during or after intervention activities). The strategies selected should be determined by the specific goals or objectives, program resources, and the need for daily or weekly monitoring as a source of feedback to keep intervention efforts on track. Weekly monitoring may enhance the prospects of demonstrating individual improvement and program efficacy at quarterly and annual evaluations by providing ongoing feedback that will allow interventionists to detect and remedy ineffective program targets and strategies that impede child progress. Ongoing monitoring also allows timely identification of child progress (e.g., reaching the specified criteria) so that children can proceed with subsequent objectives in the most efficient manner.

The IFSP requires that specification of activities and an associated evaluation procedure be conducted for the family as well as the child. Parents and staff must arrive at a mutually agreeable procedure for monitoring progress toward selected family outcomes. Ongoing monitoring is important for these outcomes.

As is the case with child goals, family interests are dynamic and must be reviewed and updated to insure their appropriateness.

## Phase Five: Six-month and yearly evaluations

Six-month and yearly evaluations should complement the ongoing monitoring and should be used to compare the child's progress with some standard or expectation for progress. Without assigning expected dates of completion to objectives, it may not be possible to determine if the progress made by the child is acceptable or unacceptable. IFSP objectives should have accompanying timelines (for example, the child is expected to reach the designated criterion for specific objectives within six months).

By frequently plotting the child's progress toward the objectives, more realistic objectives can be established. In addition, comparisons between expected and attained outcomes will generate information that may eventually allow the establishment of relevant and useful norms for subgroups of children who are at risk and who have disabilities.

Six-month and yearly evaluations provide information for revising the IFSP program. If a child fails to reach his or her established objectives in the gross motor domain, program staff or caregivers may not be providing enough intervention time in this area, or the teaching may be ineffective. In either case, the evaluation may suggest that a modification of the program is in order. Information from six-month and yearly evaluations provides feedback about the child's progress and clarifies where modifications or revisions in the IFSP may be necessary.

Similar procedures can be used for monitoring family progress toward selected outcomes; however, quantifying change may present a significant challenge. Goal Attainment Scaling (GAS) has been suggested as one strategy to help families and professionals monitor progress (Bailey et al., 1986; Dunst, Trivette, & Deal, 1988). Using GAS or a modification of it, parents can regularly review progress toward an outcome (e.g., parental respite time) and can determine on a weekly, monthly, or quarterly basis that progress is better than expected (e.g., enables exceeding criterion of being away from the child for two nights per week), as expected or hoped for (e.g., enables being away from the child one night per week), or below expectations or criteria (e.g., does not enable leaving the child one night per week). Although they are relatively gross measures of progress toward selected outcomes, approaches such as GAS may be satisfactory for helping parents and professionals gauge the success of planned interventions.

## Summary

The five phases of the linked-systems approach to early intervention exemplify the need to directly relate the processes of assessment, intervention, and evaluation. Employing such a system allows for efficiency of effort and use of resources, accountability in terms of program impact over time, and individualization through the design of programs specific to the needs of children and their families. Fundamental to the operation of such a system is an assessment/evaluation tool that yields the information necessary to devise appropriate intervention plans. One such tool, the Assessment, Evaluation, and Programming System (AEPS), is described in the following section.

# ▄ The Assessment, Evaluation, and Program-
# ▄ ming System for Infants and Children

A linked assessment-intervention-evaluation approach is predicated upon having a measurement instrument that permits collecting program-related performance data on children that can be used to formulate IFSPs and guide intervention efforts. It is also important that the instrument be able to monitor subsequent child progress.

To be appropriate for infants and preschool children who are at risk and who have disabilities, and to provide useful programming and evaluation information, an assessment/evaluation instrument should meet certain criteria (Bricker, 1989b; DuBose, 1981). An assessment instrument for monitoring child progress and program evaluation should:

1. Be used by people who deal with the child on a regular basis (e.g., interventionists, aides, parents) in familiar settings (e.g., home, classroom);
2. Reflect curricular content of the intervention program;
3. Provide a logical developmental sequence of items or objectives that can be used as training guidelines;
4. Accommodate a range of disabilities;
5. Specify performance criteria that indicate if a child has a par-

ticular skill and if the skill is a functional part of the child's daily repertoire; and

6. Be a reliable and valid measure.

The Assessment, Evaluation, and Programming System for Infants and Children: Measurement for Birth to Three Years (Bricker, 1993) is a curriculum-based, criterion-referenced tool developed for use by direct service personnel (e.g., classroom interventionists, home visitors) and specialists (e.g., communication specialists, occupational therapists, physical therapists, psychologists) to assess and evaluate the skills and abilities of infants and young children who are at risk and who have disabilities. The Assessment, Evaluation, and Programming System (AEPS) Test was designed to yield appropriate information for the development of intervention programs and for program evaluation. The instrument was also developed to be used in conjunction with the AEPS Curriculum or other similar curricula (e.g., *The Carolina Curricula for Infants and Toddlers with Special Needs,* 2nd ed., Johnson-Martin, Jens, Attermeier, & Hacker, 1991).

Items on the AEPS Test cover the developmental period from 1 month to 3 years. Items are focused on determining a child's skill level across early critical processes. The AEPS Test is generally appropriate for children whose chronological age is from birth to 6 years. If the individual is functioning within a 1-month to 3-year developmental range, but is chronologically above 6 years of age, significant modifications may be necessary in the wording of items, criteria, and suggested testing procedures to make them appropriate for an older individual.*

In addition to having assessment/evaluation functions, accompanying materials are designed to enhance the AEPS Test. These materials include (a) a set of IFSP goals and objectives; (b) AEPS Test Data Recording Forms; (c) a curriculum composed of a comprehensive set of programming steps and suggested intervention activities (*AEPS Curriculum for Birth to Three Years,* Cripe, Slentz, & Bricker, 1993); (d) an assessment form designed to be completed by families (AEPS Family Report); (e) an assessment of family interests (AEPS Family Interest Survey); and (f) a child progress form (AEPS Child Progress Record).

---

*An AEPS Test for Three to Six Years is also available (Bricker & Pretti-Frontczak, 1996).

## Advantages of the AEPS Test

Personnel working with young children and infants who are at risk and who have disabilities are often frustrated in their attempt to use traditional instruments to assess and measure child progress. As discussed earlier, it is frequently the case that outcomes from direct-test, standardized measures are not reflective of a child's actual abilities or progress and are not helpful in selecting appropriate intervention goals and objectives. Furthermore, the progress made by children with disabilities may be slow and gradual, and the increments between items on traditional assessment instruments often do not reflect small changes in their behavior. Additionally, traditional standardized assessments often penalize children with communication, sensory, or motor disabilities by allowing only a single correct response. To counter these and other problems faced by personnel interested in assessing children who are at risk and who have disabilities, the AEPS Test diverges from other available instruments in a number of ways.

1. The AEPS Test measures functional skills and abilities thought to be essential for infants and young children to function independently and to cope with environmental demands. The focus on functional skills and abilities insures that each test item is potentially an appropriate intervention target.

2. The AEPS Test is comprehensive in nature. The content of the test covers the major domains of fine motor, gross motor, adaptive, cognitive, social-communication, and social development. The comprehensive nature of this instrument makes it valuable both as an initial assessment tool and as a tool for monitoring children's subsequent progress.

3. The primary and preferred method of obtaining assessment/evaluation information is through observation of the infant or child in familiar and usual environments. This feature of the AEPS Test provides the assessor with critical information about what responses the infant or child uses in a functional manner, and when and how they are used.

4. To avoid interfering with the child's performance, the AEPS Test allows the examiner to adapt or modify either the presentation format of items or the stated criteria for children with disabilities. In particular, examiners are encouraged to find and use adaptations for infants and children with senso-

ry or motor impairments. For example, the examiner is free to use sign language with children with hearing impairments and may allow children with motor impairments to use prosthetics to complete items such as "eats with a spoon." Freedom and flexibility in modifying the presentation or in the child's response are acceptable because the test results are not used for comparative purposes, but are, instead, intended to generate appropriate intervention targets for children.

5. The items on the AEPS Test are written to reflect conceptual or response classes rather than singular, specific responses. For example, an item asks about hand-eye coordination rather than the child's ability to insert pegs in a pegboard.

6. The AEPS Test has an associated curriculum (*AEPS Curriculum for Birth to Three Years,* Cripe, Slentz, & Bricker, 1993). Results from the assessment can be used to locate and select intervention content for children. There is a direct relationship between the items on the AEPS Test and the curriculum materials.

7. A parallel family assessment/evaluation form (AEPS IFSP Planning Guide, Bricker, 1993) is available for caregivers who want to assess their child to help promote involvement in the IFSP process. In addition, completion of a parallel family form (AEPS Family Report, Bricker, 1993) assists the family in preparing to contribute to the IFSP meeting. Asking caregivers to complete an assessment form on their child clearly indicates that the professional staff consider their knowledge of their child to be an important contribution to the assessment and IFSP process. In addition, there is a parallel form to assist families in monitoring their child's progress over time (AEPS Child Progress Record, Bricker, 1993).

8. An associated set of written IFSP goals and objectives that are keyed to individual assessment/evaluation items on the AEPS Test are available. This set of goals and objectives can be used to guide the development of IFSPs and intervention plans.

9. An associated assessment form to determine family interests (AEPS Family Interest Survey, Bricker, 1993) has also been developed. Using an unobtrusive format, parents or caregivers can indicate topics or areas of interest for the child, the family, and the community, and assign a priority to each selection.

These advantages make the AEPS Test an appealing choice for

interventionists and specialists who are interested in obtaining comprehensive information on children's behavioral repertoires. Perhaps the most appealing aspect of the test is the immediate, functional use of the information obtained to develop intervention goals and monitor progress.

## Assessment issues addressed by the AEPS Test

The AEPS Test does not provide norms for the test outcomes. Although this may seem to be a disadvantage, norms have been eliminated so that the focus of intervention is on assisting children to acquire functional skills and information in logical order, rather than on targeting items because they reflect the child's chronological age. For children with disabilities, the value of comparisons with developmental norms is, at best, questionable. Rather, it is more essential to determine the child's current level of functioning and work on the skills and information that will move the child forward toward selected developmental objectives. In addition, the lack of norms makes it impossible to calculate developmental quotients, mental ages, or IQs. The AEPS outcomes cannot be used to label children or assign numbers.

Assessment with the AEPS Test requires an initial time investment. Users of the AEPS Test have found that the administration time varies as a function of (a) familiarity with the test (e.g., the more familiar the assessor is with the AEPS Test, the more quickly assessments can be completed); (b) familiarity with the child (e.g., the more familiar the assessor is with the child's behavioral repertoire, the more quickly assessments can be completed); and (c) the child's level of functioning (e.g., an infant can be assessed more quickly than an older child). Such variations make it difficult to state precisely how rapidly the AEPS Test can be administered. However, interventionists familiar with the test and the children tested report that initial assessments require one to two hours, whereas subsequent assessments take one-quarter of that time. Users unfamiliar with the test can expect to take longer; however, as familiarity increases, administration time decreases.

Some interventionists indicate that an expenditure of one to two hours or more on assessment or evaluation per child is unrealistic, given their program's resources. We would argue that assessment/evaluation should not be viewed as a discrete activity that can be completed in a predetermined period of time. Rather, assessment/evaluation should be viewed as a continuous process that occurs across time and situations and allows for the development of a comprehensive developmental profile of the child. Hastily completed assessments or evaluations that do not include information about a child's performance across materials, people, and settings will yield results that are incomplete and often inaccurate. Comprehensive, detailed assessments are fundamental to the development of appropriate IFSPs and to the quality of subsequent intervention. If IFSPs are not based on comprehensive, accurate assessment data, they will be of questionable value and relevance to children.

Understanding general developmental patterns is fundamental to the appropriate use of the AEPS Test, unlike some assessment/evaluation instruments. For example, items that assess the child's understanding of means-end relationships probably will not be properly scored and interpreted if the assessor does not have an adequate grasp of the means-end concept and its importance to a child's overall development. Individuals who do not have an adequate background in early development should not administer the AEPS Test without careful supervision. Individuals who do have knowledge of early development will find that the AEPS Test has a structure that permits them to capitalize on their expertise and apply it to the creation of sound intervention programs.

In addition to being familiar with early development, users of the AEPS Test should be familiar with the organization and content of the instrument. The AEPS Test is not a simple checklist that can be examined briefly prior to its use. Before using it, the assessor should read each item, and study its associated criteria and indicated cautions. In addition, the user should be familiar with the Data Recording Forms, including the scoring procedures and the qualifying notes. Use of the AEPS Test without accurate preparation may yield inaccurate, misleading results.

The AEPS Test can be used by individual interventionists; however, the accuracy and quality of the outcomes will be enhanced if specialists (e.g., communication specialists, occupational therapists, physical therapists) participate in the assessment and subsequent evaluations. It is particularly important to involve motor specialists if the child has a motor disability, a sensory specialist if the child has a sensory disability (e.g., hearing or visual impairment), and a communication specialist if the child has a communication delay or disorder.

Formulation of appropriate IFSPs and subsequent intervention plans is fundamental to effective intervention. To accomplish this, the assessment process should generate accurate, reliable information on a child's behavioral repertoire in contexts that are typical for the child. Acquisition of such information requires an investment of time and effort, but it will yield accurate assessment data for developing appropriate IFSPs.

## Content and organization of the AEPS Test

Conducting assessment and evaluation with the AEPS Test allows interventionists and specialists to generate a comprehensive profile of the child's behavior in familiar environments, as opposed to a narrow description of one aspect of the child's behavior. The developmental range covered is 1 to 36 months. To collect comprehensive information on the child's developmental status, six broad curricular areas called domains are included: fine motor, gross motor, adaptive, cognitive, social-communication, and social. Each domain encompasses a particular set of skills, behaviors, or information that is traditionally considered to include related developmental phenomena. Each domain is divided into strands. Strands consist of related groups of behaviors organized under a common category. For example, behaviors relating to movement in a sitting position are grouped in the "balance in sitting" strand in the Gross Motor Domain. An overview of the six domains with their associated strands is provided in Table 1.

Items on the AEPS Test are sequenced to facilitate the assessment of a child's ability to perform a particular behavior within a developmental sequence of skills. Each strand contains a series of test items called goals and objectives. The goals were developed to be used as annual goals on a child's IFSP. The objectives represent more discrete skills and enable the examiner to accurately pinpoint a child's level within a specific skill sequence. These objectives can serve as short-term or quarterly objectives on the child's IFSP.

The number of strands varies by domain as shown in Table 1. Strands and goals are arranged from easier or developmentally earlier skills to more difficult or developmentally more advanced skills whenever possible. The objectives listed under each goal are arranged in a reverse sequence, i.e., the most difficult items occur first and the less difficult items follow sequentially. This was done to facilitate test administration. If a child performs a more advanced objective within a sequence of objectives (e.g., a superior pincer grasp within a developmental sequence of grasp-

Table 1. **Overview of the AEPS Test Domains and Strands for Birth to 3 Years of Age**

| Domains | Strands |
| --- | --- |
| Fine Motor | |
| | A. Reach, grasp, and release |
| | B. Functional use of fine motor skills |
| Gross Motor | |
| | A. Movement and locomotion in supine and prone position |
| | B. Balance in sitting |
| | C. Balance and mobility in standing and walking |
| | D. Play skills |
| Adaptive | |
| | A. Feeding |
| | B. Personal hygiene |
| | C. Undressing |
| Cognitive | |
| | A. Sensory stimuli |
| | B. Object permanence |
| | C. Causality |
| | D. Imitation |
| | E. Problem-solving |
| | F. Preacademic skills |
| | G. Interaction with objects |
| Social-Communication | |
| | A. Prelinguistic communicative interactions |
| | B. Transition to words |
| | C. Comprehension of words and sentences |
| | D. Production of social-communicative signals, words, and sentences |
| Social | |
| | A. Interaction with adults |
| | B. Interaction with environment |
| | C. Interaction with peers |

ing skills), the assessment of earlier objectives within the sequence (e.g., raking grasp) is generally unnecessary. This procedure makes assessment more efficient and is generally valid unless the child's behavioral repertoire appears to be uneven, that is, the child is inconsistent and performs a variety of splinter skills. In this case, assessment of a broader range of items is in order.

The identification system associated with the strands (e.g., A, B, C), goals (e.g., 1, 2, 3), and objectives (e.g., 1.1, 1.2., 1.3) reflects this sequential arrangement and has been included to assist the test user in locating items and referring to them.

### Interdisciplinary team assessments

Early intervention programs have a variety of staffing patterns. Many programs have more than one interdisciplinary team specialist who is regularly available to children and families. The participation of these specialists in the administration of programmatic assessments, such as the AEPS Test, is encouraged. Inclusion of specialists helps insure the efficient, comprehensive completion of the programmatic assessment for children. The team members may choose to participate in group, center-based assessments by observing and interacting with the children at a particular station. For example, the communication specialist might record a language sample on the Social-Communication Observation Form, while the physical or occupational therapist completes the fine motor and gross motor portions of the AEPS Test. Another alternative is for the specialists to observe and score the domains pertinent to their areas of expertise while the interventionist moves children through a series of assessment activities. To increase the awareness of the strengths and needs of the child across developmental domains, results should be compiled and shared among the team members. Such sharing also helps eliminate the redundancy and inconsistency that occur when professionals complete separate assessments. Incorporating the observations of the specialists and interventionists into one assessment protocol leads to more efficient and functional program planning.

### Summary

The use of curriculum-based assessment/evaluation tools such as the AEPS Test is fundamental to the creation of a new vision for developmental assessment, an assessment process that is child- and family-friendly and yields substantive information directly relevant to intervention.

## ▤ Family Participation in the Assessment/ ▰ Evaluation Process

Family input and participation should be encouraged in assessment, intervention, and evaluation. The greater the involvement of the families, the greater the likelihood of improved outcomes for the children and the families in general. To enhance and help insure family participation, the AEPS includes a set of materials that were developed to assist parents and caregivers in the assessment/evaluation of their child and to identify family interests. These family-centered materials can be used in conjunction with other AEPS materials. They include the AEPS Family Report, AEPS IFSP Planning Guide, AEPS Child Progress Record, and AEPS Family Interest Survey.

## AEPS Family Report

The AEPS Family Report (Bricker, 1993) is a set of assessment/evaluation items developed to obtain information from parents and caregivers about their infants' or children's skills and abilities across major areas of development. It was designed to be used in conjunction with the AEPS Test. Each item on the Family Report corresponds directly to a goal on the AEPS Test as shown in Table 2.

Table 2. **An Example of Corresponding Items from the AEPS Test and the AEPS Family Report**

|  | AEPS Test Item | AEPS Family Report Item |
|---|---|---|
| Domain | SOCIAL | SOCIAL |
| Strand | C: Interaction with peers | |
| Item | C1: Initiates and maintains interactions with peers | 6. Does your child start and continue playing with other children? |
| Domain | ADAPTIVE | ADAPTIVE |
| Strand | A: Feeding | |
| Item | A3: Drinks from cup and/or glass | 3. Without help, does your child drink from a cup by bringing the cup to his or her mouth and putting it down without spilling? |

Structured procedures to obtain assessment/evaluation information from parents and other caregivers are important for several reasons. First, caregivers often have more opportunity to observe their children's behavior than anyone else. This rich source of information should never be overlooked. Second, accurate assessment and evaluation are dependent upon gathering information from a variety of sources. Family perspectives about a child should always be included when gathering assessment and evaluation information. Third, caregiver and professional observations can be compared to determine points of agreement and disagreement. The points of agreement can serve as priorities for the development of IFSP outcomes. The points of disagreement indicate that additional information is needed. Fourth, asking caregivers to participate in the assessment/evaluation process conveys an important message: Program personnel believe caregivers can contribute to their child's intervention program. Finally, the use of formal procedures to involve parents and caregivers may assist in their increased participation in the IFSP process and subsequent monitoring of child progress.

The AEPS Family Report has several important features. First, it corresponds directly to the AEPS Test, which is used by professionals. The Family Report items are simple paraphrases of the goals on the AEPS Test. This feature permits a direct comparison between the caregivers' and professionals' assessments of the child.

Second, the Family Report measures skills that are functional for infants and young children; that is, only skills that may enhance the child's ability to cope with and adapt to the demands of the social and physical environment are included. This focus on functional skills insures that all of the items have the potential of being appropriate intervention targets. This feature of the Family Report makes the assessment outcome of direct relevance and use to the development of the child's IFSP. The assessment information can be used to assist in developing the child's IFSP and to formulate subsequent programming to be delivered by an intervention program.

A third feature of the AEPS Family Report that makes it valuable both as an initial assessment tool and as a tool for monitoring the child's subsequent progress is the comprehensive nature of the instrument. The major developmental areas of fine motor, gross motor, adaptive, cognitive, social-communication, and social behavior are included in the instrument.

Fourth, although caregivers may complete the Family Report on the basis of their knowledge of and experience with the child, they are encouraged to verify their knowledge through observation of the infant or child in familiar environments. This feature of the Family Report provides information about what responses the child uses in a functional manner, and when and how they are used.

Caregivers are asked to score each item on the AEPS Family Report by selecting one of three responses that most accurately describes their child's current level of functioning. The response categories are: "Yes," "Sometimes," and "Not Yet." Interventionists can translate caregivers' scores to 2, 1, and 0, respectively. Parents or caregivers are informed that their child is not expected to perform all the skills listed on the form. Before scoring each item, caregivers are encouraged to observe children in situations that are likely to elicit the skill, rather than to score items from memory.

## AEPS IFSP Planning Guide

The AEPS IFSP Planning Guide is a simple one-page form developed to assist families in preparing for their IFSP meeting. Parents or caregivers may or may not find completing this form to be useful. Whether or not to complete the Planning Guide should be the family's choice.

The Planning Guide is divided into three sections for recording information: IFSP logistics, strengths of the child and the family, and family priorities. The logistics section is used to enter the child's name and date of birth, the family name, and the date of the IFSP, the location, and the names of the people attending. The strengths section includes one column for listing the child's strengths and a second column for indicating the family's strengths. The final section—family priorities—provides space for writing the child's goals, those items that the parents noted as priorities on the AEPS Family Report. In addition, there is space to indicate the family interests that were noted on the AEPS Family Interest Survey (Bricker, 1993). A sample AEPS IFSP Planning Guide is shown in Figure 2.

Parents or caregivers can complete the Planning Guide independently or in conjunction with a professional. As indicated above, some families may find completing it to be a helpful step in preparing for the IFSP meeting.

## AEPS Child Progress Record

In addition to involving parents in the initial assessment of their child, it is useful to have parents and caregivers participate in the ongoing monitoring of their child's progress. The AEPS Child Progress Record (Bricker, 1993) was developed for this purpose.

---

Figure 2. **A Sample AEPS IFSP Planning Guide**

Child's Name _____ Birthdate _____ Family Name _____

Date of IFSP _____ Time _____ Location _____

Family Members/Professionals/Agency Representatives your family wishes to attend meeting

_____

_____

**Strengths**

| *Child Strengths* | *Family Strengths* |
|---|---|
| Include recent progress or changes, favorite activities, special qualities | Include available resources, special qualities, abilities, supports |

_____     _____

_____     _____

_____     _____

**Family Priorities**

| *Child Goals*<br>(Taken from AEPS Family Report) | *Family Interests*<br>(Taken from AEPS Family Interest Survey) |
|---|---|
| 1. _____ | 1. _____ |
| 2. _____ | 2. _____ |
| 3. _____ | 3. _____ |

---

As does the Family Report, the Child Progress Record parallels the AEPS Test. Each of the goals and objectives from the AEPS Test is listed hierarchically on the Child Progress Record by domain and by strand. As children meet the stated criteria for a goal or objective, that progress can be indicated by striking through or shading the particular goal or objective. This form provides parents and caregivers with a visual record of the child's accomplishments, current targets, and future goals and objectives. Figure 3 contains a completed strand from the Gross Motor Domain of the AEPS Child Progress Record.

The Child Progress Record should be updated semi-annually in conjunction with administration of the AEPS Test. For children with severe disabilities, interventionists may wish to add items to the Child Progress Record by scaling back the objectives to smaller, more discrete targets. Parents of children with severe disabilities may become discouraged if their child appears to be making no progress over time.

Figure 3. **A Sample Page from the AEPS Child Progress Record** (Bricker, 1993)

**Gross Motor Domain**

Strand A: Movement and locomotion in supine and prone position

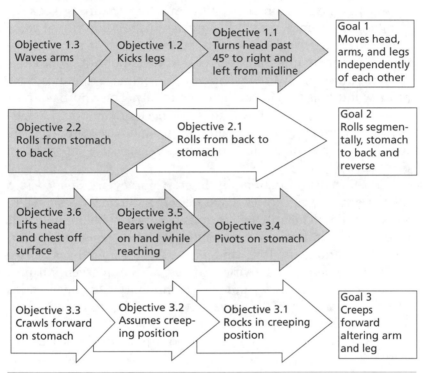

## AEPS Family Interest Survey

The AEPS Family Interest Survey (Bricker, 1993) is a self-assessment for families to identify their interests in the listed child and family activities. This measure has been developed to assist in the IFSP process as defined in Part H of the Individuals with Disabilities Education Act (IDEA). The Family Interest Survey is based on the philosophy that families should identify the outcomes they desire from their own and their child's participation in the program.

The Family Interest Survey is divided into three major categories: child, family, and community interests. These categories were derived from selected literature on family systems and ecologically based approaches to intervention (e.g., Peck, 1993;

Bricker, 1989a; Bronfenbrenner, 1979; Dunst, Trivette, & Deal, 1988; Turnbull & Turnbull, 1990). These approaches promote recognition of the child as a member of the family unit. In addition, they promote the understanding that what affects the child also affects other family members, and vice versa. In addition, these approaches emphasize the interconnectedness between families, communities, and the larger society. Adoption of these perspectives requires assessment and evaluation of the environmental factors that families perceive to be important. To accomplish this, the Family Interest Survey asks families to indicate the priority interests of the child and the family. This approach purposely avoids a problem, weakness, or need orientation that carries connotations of family pathology, which are inappropriate for the majority of families participating in early intervention programs.

The 30 items on the Family Interest Survey are divided into the three survey categories. Each item is a statement designed to assist families in identifying interests pertinent to their child. The statements help families define interests with respect to gathering information, support, and resources, and with respect to their participation in activities offered by the intervention program, related agencies, and the community. An open-ended question at the end of the survey allows families to list additional interests. Each item is written as a positive, action-oriented statement that can be transferred into a functional, measurable outcome.

Each item is followed by two sets of three boxes that parents or caregivers can use to indicate if the item is (a) a priority interest; (b) an interest, but not a current priority; or (c) not an interest at the present time. The first set of boxes is used for the initial IFSP development and the second set is used for semi-annual reviews.

## Summary

The importance of family participation in the assessment process has been repeatedly stressed by early intervention professionals, parents and caregivers, and legislatures. Leaving family participation to chance is no longer acceptable. Program personnel should have concrete strategies that insure family participation.

The AEPS provides a set of forms and procedures that promotes family participation. Use of forms such as the AEPS Family Report and AEPS Family Interest Survey not only promotes the participation of parents and caregivers, but it does so in ways that will yield useful and positive outcomes.

 **Conclusion**

New visions for developmental assessment require significant changes in the way repertoires of young children are currently measured and the way families participate in the assessment process. These changes include:

- Observation of children in their usual environments with an eye toward how they negotiate daily demands, problem-solve, and communicate with those around them; and

- Inclusion of family members in the process through a variety of mechanisms (e.g., providing history and current data, observing and noting child behaviors, providing family-relevant information, stating family desires and interests).

Outcomes from an assessment process that watches children at play and at work and that solicits and includes family input provide a rich, relevant source of information for selecting intervention goals and planning intervention strategies. Measures such as the AEPS Test and its associated family-involvement tools assist interventionists and specialists in the formulation of such outcomes.

Traditional approaches to assessment are well-entrenched and supported by state eligibility guidelines. It will not be easy to shift the assessment vision of professionals—who have been trained to administer standardized tests under standardized conditions—to assessment processes designed to yield a far different outcome; however, change will come. Fundamental to this change is the development of new approaches and new tools that lend themselves to a vision of developmental assessment designed to move us forward toward processes yielding relevant, practical information about children and families and, therefore, having direct relevance to the formulation of sound, appropriate, and effective intervention plans.

# References

Bailey, D., Simeonsson, R., Winton, P., Huntington, G., Comfort, M., Isbell, P., O'Donnell, K., & Helm, J. (1986). Family-focused intervention: A functional model for planning, implementing, and evaluating individualized family services in early intervention. *Journal of the Division for Early Childhood, 10* (2), 156-171.

Bricker, D. (1989a). *Early intervention for at-risk and handicapped infants, toddlers, and preschool children.* Palo Alto, CA: VORT Corporation.

Bricker, D. (1989b). *Psychometric and utility study of a comprehensive early assessment instrument for handicapped infants and children.* Final Report submitted to the U.S. Department of Education, Office of Special Education Programs, Washington, DC.

Bricker, D. (Ed.). (1993). *Assessment, Evaluation, and Programming System for infants and children, Vol. 1: AEPS measurement for birth to three years.* Baltimore, MD: Paul H. Brookes Publishing Co.

Bricker, D., & Pretti-Frontczak, K. (Eds). (1996). *AEPS Measurment for Three to Six Years.* Baltimore, MD: Paul H. Brookes Publishing Co.

Bronfenbrenner, U. (1979). *The ecology of human development: Experiments by nature and design.* Cambridge, MA: Harvard University Press.

Cole, K., Swisher, M., Thompson, M., & Fewell, R. (1985). Enhancing sensitivity of assessment instruments for children: Graded multidimensional scoring. *Journal of the Association for Persons with Severe Handicaps, 10* (4), 209-213.

Cripe, J., Slentz, K., & Bricker, D. (1993). *Assessment, Evaluation, and Programming System (AEPS) for infants and children, Vol. 2: AEPS curriculum for birth to three years.* Baltimore, MD: Paul H. Brookes Publishing Co.

DuBose, R. (1981). Assessment of severely impaired young children: Problems and recommendations. *Topics in Early Childhood Special Education, 1,* 9-21.

Dunst, C., Trivette, C., & Deal, A. (1988). *Enabling and empowering families: Principles and guidelines for practice.* Cambridge, MA: Brookline Books.

Greenspan, S., & Meisels, S. (June/July 1994). Toward a new vision for the developmental assessment of infants and young children. *Zero to Three, 14* (6), 1-8.

Johnson-Martin, N., Jens, K., Attermeier, S., & Hacker, B. (1991). *The Carolina curriculum for infants and toddlers with special needs* (2nd ed.). Baltimore, MD: Paul H. Brookes Publishing Co.

Peck, C. (1993). Ecological perspectives on the implementation of integrated early childhood programs. In C. Peck, S. Odom, & D. Bricker (Eds.), *Integrating young children with disabilities into community-based programs.* Baltimore, MD: Paul H. Brookes Publishing Co.

Seitz, V., & Provence, S. (1990). Caregiver-focused models of early intervention. In S. Meisels & J. Shonkoff (Eds.), *Handbook of early childhood intervention* (pp. 400-427). New York: Cambridge University Press.

Turnbull, A., & Turnbull, H. (1990). *Families, professionals, and exceptionality: A special partnership* (2nd ed.). Columbus, OH: Charles E. Merrill.

# 10.
# Assessment of Adaptive Competence*

## G. GORDON WILLIAMSON

Many clinicians ask: How do I collect and synthesize assessment information so that it results in a meaningful understanding of the child's daily functioning? And how does the assessment lead to relevant intervention practices? This article presents an assessment protocol that makes such connections, i.e., assessment based on the model of the coping process. Because the coping strategies of many infants and toddlers who are at risk, developmentally delayed, or disabled are erratic, rigidly repetitious, or restricted, an assessment process that focuses directly on coping facilitates intervention that promotes adaptive behavior and resilience in these young children.

Coping is the integration and application of developmental skills in the context of everyday living. It is the process of making adaptations in order to meet personal needs and to respond to the demands of the environment. An infant has to cope with the complexities of family life, changes related to physical growth, and innumerable novel experiences, such as learning to drink from a cup, excursions to a shopping mall, and enrollment in a child care center. The goal of coping is to increase feelings of well-being in situations interpreted as threatening or chal-

*This chapter was adapted from *Coping in Young Children: Early Intervention Practices to Enhance Adaptive Behavior and Resilience* (S. Zeitlin & G. G. Williamson, Paul H. Brookes Publishing Co., Baltimore, MD, 1994).

lenging. That is, children cope with situations in order to feel good about themselves and their place in the world.

In this frame of reference, coping is broadly defined and not restricted to the child dealing with adverse circumstances. Although stress interpreted as threat tends to have a negative inference, stress perceived as challenge is often associated with positive, energizing emotions.

The more effectively a child copes, the more effectively he or she learns. A child's adaptive competence is determined by the match between needs (demands) and the availability of resources to manage them. Successful coping reflects sufficient resources for handling the demands of daily life. Effective coping fosters the acquisition of developmental skills, a self-affirming identity, and the capacity for intimate social relationships. A four-step model of the coping process is the foundation for assessment and later intervention.

## The Coping Process

Although coping in young children is predominately emotionally driven and reflects rudimentary cognitive processing, it is useful to consider each interrelated step in the coping process: (a) determine the meaning of an event; (b) develop an action plan; (c) implement a coping effort; and (d) evaluate the outcome (see the figure below).

**Steps in the Coping Process**

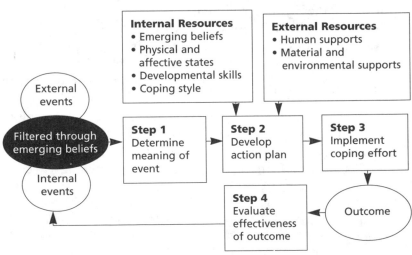

The coping process may be initiated by an event occurring in the environment (e.g., a demand by the caregiver, the approach of a rambunctious puppy) or within the child (e.g., a thought, emotion, physical sensation) The child gives meaning to the event based upon personal perceptions of whether it is threatening or challenging to his or her sense of well-being.

Based upon this interpretation, the child then decides what to do. The child's internal and external resources influence this decision. Key *internal resources* are the child's emerging beliefs, physical and affective states, developmental skills, and coping style. The essential *external resources* involve human supports and material and environmental supports. As a result of this decisionmaking, the child implements a coping effort (coping strategy) to deal with the situation. The result of this effort is then evaluated to determine whether it was successful or not.

In the assessment protocol, the clinician is concerned with identifying the demands (stressors) experienced by the child, the adequacy of the internal and external coping resources that determine the child's coping efforts, and the environmental feedback the child receives in response to these efforts. This information can be gathered through an interview with the parents, assessment of coping resources, and observation of the child's transactions. The following discussion highlights ways to assess a child's resources and coping transactions.

# Coping Resources

### Emerging beliefs

This coping resource influences the meaning a child gives to events (e.g., threat, harm, and/or challenge) and helps to determine the nature and type of coping efforts to be initiated. Beliefs are initially very primitive, global, and emotionally grounded. They are probably less of an influence in infancy than at later ages when they become more complex and focused as the child's experience and cognitive ability increase.

Emerging beliefs are intimately related to the development of a sense of self. They involve issues related to trust, security, expectation of success or failure, and predictability of events.

Information about emerging beliefs can be inferred through observation of the child's transactions in a variety of situations, including free play, social interaction, and goal-directed activities. Of particular relevance to coping is the child's evolving sense of efficacy—the perceived ability to produce an effect, control events, and trust that others will be responsive to his or her needs. These critical beliefs may be reflected in an "I can" or "I can't" orientation to the demands of daily living. That is, they influence the child's self-esteem, motivation, persistence, and autonomy. By observing these attributes, the practitioner can develop a better understanding of the child's beliefs and how they influence adaptive functioning.

Assessment of the following coping-related attributes are particularly useful in clarifying the nature of the child's emerging belief system: (a) willingness to engage in activities; (b) willingness to accept or create challenges; (c) the ability to manage feelings; and (d) the ability to demonstrate pleasure in successful accomplishments. In typical clinical practice, information regarding beliefs is acquired sequentially over time but begins in the initial assessment of the child's development and coping style.

Another indicator of beliefs is the quality of the child's attachment to caregivers. It suggests whether the child perceives the world as safe and secure, or threatening and dangerous. The assessor's observation of the infant-parent attachment helps to identify relevant beliefs that contribute to a child's coping performance. Clinical impressions of an infant's beliefs and their impact may be speculative or rather tentative. However, an understanding of the emerging belief system is integral to a comprehensive assessment of a child's adaptive competence.

## Physical and affective states

Relevant information regarding the child's physical and affective states can be gathered through a combination of sources, such as an interview with the parents, the child's medical records, contact with the primary health care providers, and direct assessment by the early intervention team. Particular issues related to the child's physical state include general health, physical appearance, endurance, alertness, past illnesses and hospitalizations, and pertinent medical conditions of the family.

Assessment of the child's affective state includes observation of moods, the range and expression of emotions, and responses to a variety of activities and demands. Particular attention needs to be paid to analyzing the coping transactions between the child and primary caregivers, especially the parents. Difficulty in regulation of affect may be noted by the following manifestations:

irritability, poor impulse control, marked mood swings, unhappy or depressed expression, hypo- or hyper-arousal, fussiness, and distractibility. These variations in affect undermine the child's ability to cope.

## Developmental skills

Another coping resource that needs to be assessed is the child's developmental status. The important issue from a coping perspective is to relate the developmental and coping assessments in such a way that the focus is not only on *what* the child can do, but also on *how* the child functionally applies skills as integrated coping efforts within situations.

The acquisition of developmental skills does not automatically lead to effective coping. A process-oriented approach to comprehensive assessment includes identification of the circumstances in which skills are demonstrated, the degree to which the child uses skills in a self-initiated manner, the approach to and organization of structured and unstructured tasks, and the ability to solve problems. The table below provides guidelines for behavioral observation that link assessment of developmental skills to their functional significance in daily living.

---

### Linking Developmental Skills to Adaptive Outcomes

- Under what conditions does the child demonstrate specific developmental skills?

- Does the child use the skills spontaneously or primarily in a reactive manner?

- What compensatory strategies does the child use to perform a requested task?

- Are there maladaptive behaviors which interfere with the acquisition of particular developmental skills?

- Is there a characteristic pattern for learning new skills?

- Is there a discrepancy in achievement among developmental domains that influences the child's adaptive functioning?

---

## Coping style

Coping style refers to the child's characteristic way of behaving in situations viewed as threatening or challenging to one's sense of well-being. It includes the repertoire of behavioral attributes that a child draws on to manage the opportunities, demands, and frustrations encountered in daily living. Coping style is most effectively assessed through observation of the child in a variety of situations. Observations can be conducted informally or through the use of an instrument.

The Early Coping Inventory, developed by the author and his colleagues (Zeitlin, Williamson, & Szczepanski, 1988), is useful for assessing the coping styles of young children. This observational instrument evaluates the behavioral characteristics of infants and toddlers that are most relevant for effective coping and therefore should be targeted for intervention. These attributes are clustered into three descriptive categories: *sensorimotor organization, reactive behaviors*, and *self-initiated behaviors*.

*Sensorimotor organization* refers to the child's regulation of psychophysiological functions and the ability to integrate the sensory and motor systems. These sensorimotor characteristics involve factors such as the child's ability to pay attention, to self-comfort, to control activity level, to manage the intensity and variety of sensory stimuli, and to adapt to physical handling.

*Reactive behaviors* are used to respond to external demands of the physical and social environment. They reflect the ability to accommodate oneself to daily routines, to accept warmth and support from familiar persons, to respond to vocal and gestural direction, and to adapt to changes in the environment.

*Self-initiated behaviors* are autonomously generated actions used to meet personal needs and to interact with objects and people. Whereas reactive coping behaviors are closely contingent on environmental cues, self-initiated behaviors are more spontaneous and intrinsically motivated. They include, for example, the ability to express a range of feelings, to anticipate events, to express likes and dislikes, to initiate action to communicate a need, to demonstrate persistence during activities, and to adapt, or generalize, learned behaviors to new situations.

The Early Coping Inventory provides a structured, systematic approach to assessing a child's unique coping style. Additional assessment information can be acquired through interviewing the parents. Questions to guide the discussion may include: Are there any situations that are particularly stressful for your child? What does your child do in these situations? How does your child respond to change? Does your child like to explore and try new things? How does your child play with adults and other children?

Whether assessment of the child's coping style is conducted formally or informally, several issues need to be considered:

1. To what extent does the child engage in self-initiated behaviors, and are these coping behaviors productive?
2. Is the child able to use coping strategies flexibly across a variety of situations?
3. Is there a difference between the ability of the child to cope with inner demands and his or her ability to cope with the environment?
4. How does the child seem to evaluate the effectiveness of coping efforts? The answer to this question often indicates the status of the child's self-esteem.

## Human supports

Most information about the child's human supports is learned by getting to know the family and their coping resources. This information is best generated through a continuing dialogue between the family and the assessment team. Such an exchange addresses the concerns and priorities of the family, their beliefs about their child and family members, their coping style, the demands they have to manage, and the availability of their personal resources. Parents and other caregivers are also observed in their interactions with the child. Such information contributes to understanding the human supports available to the child, as well as the caregivers' needs in relation to parenting. In addition, it is important for the practitioner to assess his or her relationship with the child and family since professionals also serve as human supports for them.

When a family is involved in an assessment process, it is important to gather enough information to facilitate intervention planning and a mutually supportive relationship between the family and the practitioners. Attempts to gather too much information too quickly can result in excessive demands on the parents and can generate unnecessary discomfort and wariness. Practitioners need to monitor their requests for information. They should ask themselves the following questions:

1. What information do I really need to know in order to collaborate with the family in designing a meaningful service plan?
2. When do I need to know it?
3. What is the best way to gather this information?

## Material and environmental supports

These supports can be identified through discussions with the parents or by offering an opportunity for them to complete a needs assessment survey. The practitioner can also visit the home and child care program to gain additional information. Of particular note in the area of material supports is the availability of sufficient financial resources, food, shelter, clothing, transportation, and developmentally appropriate toys for the child. Environmental supports are identified through observation of the physical surroundings that influence development, comfort, and safe exploration. Relevant characteristics include organization of space, levels of noise and light, and quality and temperature of the air.

A child's needs relative to material and environmental supports vary, based on age, developmental capability, and the presence of a disability. Clinical impressions are made as to whether the environment offers a variety of motivating toys, is organized, and is accessible to the child. Particularly when the child has a physical disability, the material supports required for the child to function optimally should be carefully examined. These supports may include mobility and positioning equipment, adapted toys, communication aids, and architectural modifications.

## Coping Transactions

In addition to assessing the availability and quality of coping resources, the clinician should appreciate the nature of the child's transactions. During the initial assessment phase and the ongoing participation in a program, there are numerous opportunities to observe the child coping with adults, other children, activities, and the physical environment. For instance, transactions can be observed during caregiving, free play, instructional and small group activities, periods of transition, and other typical daily encounters. Analysis of these transactions provides useful information for understanding family dynamics and for planning intervention services. It gives insights regarding stressors or demands on the child and family, the availability and use of resources, and the effectiveness of coping strategies, as well as guidance for establishing goals and activities for intervention. It also gives practitioners an opportunity to clarify the impact of their own behavior on reciprocal interactions.

Coping transactions have four components, all of which contribute to the outcome of the coping process: (a) an internal or external demand that initiates the transaction; (b) the coping effort the child uses to manage the demand; (c) the environment's response to that effort; and (d) the child's reaction to the response. This feedback influences the child's perception of the effectiveness of his or her coping effort. In other words, when observing and analyzing transactions, the practitioner needs to ask: What was the demand? What did the child do to manage the demand? How did the adult respond to the child's action? How did the child then react?

Events which are perceived as threatening, harmful, or challenging generate a demand for a coping effort. These events predominately stem from needs and expectations within the child, from expectations of the family and other caregivers, and from specific aspects of the child's physical environment. In assessing *demands*, the clinician must identify what these demands are and determine their relevance and developmental appropriateness.

Examples of inner demands include the child's physical and emotional needs for food, rest and comfort, personal preferences and desires, and expectations for success or failure. The internal needs and expectations of young children can only be inferred through observation of their actions; older children may be able to express internal demands verbally.

Adults' demands on the child stem from their expectations concerning the child's social behavior, performance, and management of daily activity, as well as from their own emotional needs. These expectations come from their personal and cultural backgrounds, their knowledge and experience as caregivers, and related factors. Awareness of these expectations and the demands they generate may be determined through interviewing the adults or through observing social transactions. Expectations generating demands that are particularly relevant for children with special needs include expectations of developmental achievement, independence in self-care, and participation in social and community activities.

The physical environment imposes a unique set of spatial and temporal demands that the child must negotiate, for example, ambulating in a crowded store, reacting to a thrown ball, and obtaining toys and materials in an often inaccessible setting. Physical demands are best identified through direct observation of the child in typical surroundings.

Assessment of the *child's coping efforts* in response to demands involves considering the repertoire of available coping strategies, flexibility in their use, the circumstances under which they are applied, and their success in managing specific stressors.

The next component of coping transactions is the *environment's response to the child's efforts.* This feedback, particularly from the primary caregivers, is critical for helping the child learn to cope and for the development of a personal identity. In assessing the nature of the feedback, one needs to determine how it is provided (e.g., physically, verbally), whether it gives accurate information regarding the child's performance, and whether it is offered in a timely, contingent, and emotionally supportive manner.

The last transactional component to be assessed is the *child's reaction to the feedback.* The practitioner observes the child's affect and subsequent actions to infer how the child interprets the effectiveness of his or her efforts. This process helps the practitioner to appreciate how the child internalized the meaning and quality of the transaction.

Analysis of numerous transactions enables the practitioner to describe the child's characteristic coping pattern as well as the coping of those who interact with the child. The following questions help the clinician to synthesize and integrate information gained from observing transactions. These questions are particularly relevant to understanding the reciprocal relationship between the child and the parents. They help the clinician to determine which components of the coping transactions may need to be addressed in intervention.

- *Are the expectations evidenced in the adult's demands appropriate for the child's developmental age?* If not, are they too high, too low, inconsistent, or unclear?
- *How do the child's resources influence his or her coping efforts?* (Consider emerging beliefs, physical and affective states, developmental skills, coping style, human supports, and material and environmental supports.)
- *What are the characteristic coping strategies that the child and adult tend to use?*
- *What are the quality and nature of the response of the adult or physical environment to the child's coping efforts?* Is the feedback timely, appropriate, and contingent?
- *Does the feedback contribute to the child's perception of per-*

*sonal adequacy and well-being?* (Consider positive and negative influences.)

* *What changes could enhance the effectiveness of the coping transactions for the child and adult?*

# Linking Assessment to Intervention

The assessment of the child's coping resources and transactions leads directly to intervention that targets promoting the effectiveness of the child's adaptive functioning. Children cope most successfully when there is a congruence between their coping resources and environmental demands and expectations. A goal of intervention is to encourage a "goodness-of-fit" between resources and demands so that the infant can manage daily living with a positive sense of self. In this process, the child modifies previously learned coping strategies and develops new ones.

There are three primary intervention options that address the components of the coping process. Each option is targeted toward establishing a better fit between the child and the environment. One can (a) modify demands so that they are congruent with the child's capabilities; (b) enhance the child's coping resources; or (c) provide appropriate, contingent feedback to the child's efforts. Due to the transactional nature of the coping process, all three intervention options are frequently used simultaneously.

## Modifying demands

The first intervention option, modifying demands, requires active collaboration of parents and practitioners to insure that they have an adequate understanding of the child. This knowledge enables them to set appropriate goals and expectations that match the child's ability to meet them. Over-expectation may lead to unrealistic demands being placed on the child and, therefore, to structured failure. Under-expectation may result in low demands that do not motivate the child for optimal learning. Inconsistent demands may foster feelings of confusion and insecurity. Children with a minimally effective coping style are in particular need of a consistent, focused approach.

Both the social and physical environments should be considered when modifying demands during intervention or parenting. The following examples illustrate a variety of ways to change demands so that they are developmentally appropriate:

1. Adapt the pace of intervention to the child's attention span and energy level.
2. Grade sensory experiences according to tolerance.
3. Use gestures and speech at the proper level of comprehension.
4. Provide specialized seating to decrease motoric demands.
5. Personalize teaching techniques based on the child's learning preferences (e.g., verbal cuing, physical prompting, and modeling, or demonstrating).

## Enhancing coping resources

The second intervention option involves enhancing the child's internal and external coping resources: emerging beliefs, physical and affective states, coping style, developmental skills, human supports, and material and environmental supports. For example, based upon an assessment of the strengths and vulnerabilities of a child's coping style, intervention can be targeted toward facilitating coping behaviors related to such attributes as flexibility, independent problem-solving, paying attention, generalization of learning, and self-initiation.

Intervention activities should help parents and professionals deal with common coping-related difficulties experienced by children with special needs, for example, low frustration tolerance and task persistence, hyper- or hypo-responsiveness to sensory stimulation, depressed or excessive activity level, inability to manage the range and expression of emotions, separation problems, and patterns of aggression or withdrawal. The emphasis is on ways to decrease maladaptive patterns and to increase the development and generalization of effective coping strategies. It is often necessary to teach the child specific strategies to manage concrete circumstances (e.g., coping with a baby-sitter, a car seat, bedtime, or new foods).

## Providing contingent feedback

The third intervention option is to support coping by providing contingent responses to the child's coping efforts. Appropriate feedback reinforces desired or newly acquired coping strategies, whereas inappropriate feedback perpetuates maladaptive behavior. When an effective coping effort receives positive, timely, accurate feedback, both the infant and adult feel successful, and they experience pleasure in the interaction. Such reinforcement leads to a sense of mastery that is usually reflected in subsequent coping efforts.

Some professionals may tend to implement intervention that is highly structured and adult-directed, with an emphasis on eliciting responses from the child which are then reinforced by the practitioner. In such cases, there is little opportunity for the young child to learn self-directed, purposeful behavior. This interactional pattern may unintentionally reinforce the tendency of many infants with disabilities to be passive and lack self-initiation. It is important to support child-initiated activity and provide feedback that invites the child to explore, problem-solve, and try new coping strategies.

## Conclusion

This assessment approach is designed to determine the component strengths and vulnerabilities of the child and the environment that influence daily functioning. It is particularly targeted toward children who have limited coping abilities or who live in high-stress environments. The transactional model of the coping process identifies the child's demands/stressors, coping resources, available coping strategies, and the responsiveness of the environment to the child's efforts. This information serves as a framework for the intervention options—modifying demands and expectations, enhancing coping resources, and providing contingent feedback. The goal is for assessment to lead to intervention that empowers young children to cope with self and the environment in ways that foster personal well-being.

# References

Garmezy, N., & Rutter, M. (Eds.). (1983). *Stress, coping, and development in children*. New York: McGraw-Hill.

Lazarus, R., & Folkman, S. (1984). *Stress, appraisal, and coping*. New York: Springer Publishing Company.

Murphy, L. B., & Moriarty, A. (1976). *Vulnerability, coping, and growth*. New Haven, CT: Yale University Press.

Werner, E. E. (1989). High risk children in young adulthood: A longitudinal study from birth to 32 years. *American Journal of Orthopsychiatry, 59,* 72-81.

Williamson, G. G., Szczepanski, M., & Zeitlin, S. (1993). Coping frame of reference. In P. Kramer & J. Hinojosa (Eds.), *Frames of reference in pediatric occupational therapy*. Philadelphia, PA: Williams & Wilkins.

Zeitlin, S., & Williamson, G. G. (1990). Coping characteristics of disabled and nondisabled young children. *American Journal of Orthopsychiatry, 60,* 404-411.

Zeitlin, S., & Williamson, G. G. (1994). *Coping in young children: Early intervention practices to enhance adaptive behavior and resilience*. Baltimore, MD: Paul H. Brookes Publishing Co.

Zeitlin, S., Williamson, G. G., & Szczepanski, M. (1988). *Early Coping Inventory*. Bensenville, IL: Scholastic Testing Service.

# 11.

# Nonstructured Play Observations: Guidelines, Benefits, and Caveats

MARILYN SEGAL

NOREEN T. WEBBER

With the new emphasis on early intervention, evaluation teams concerned with the identification of at-risk children have recognized the importance of including play assessments as part of a developmental evaluation. This policy is based on several premises. First, play for infants and toddlers is a natural behavioral expression providing a window into social, emotional, motor, and cognitive development. Second, the way parents and infants play together illuminates the quality of their relationship. Third, observing parents and child play provides an opportunity to identify family risks, strengths, and coping strategies. Fourth, when parents and professionals observe a child together, episodes from the play become a common language that enhances communication and facilitates the development of a parent-professional partnership.

Play observations are not a new idea. In writing up a developmental test report, it is standard practice to describe a child's behavior before, during, and after testing (Sattler, 1992). In recent years, however, play observations have been given a higher status because of an increased focus on the infant/toddler period and a recognition that the developmental status of an infant or toddler can be assessed most effectively through spontaneous play. As infants play alone or with a parent, clinicians can observe facets of development and can identify parent-infant interaction patterns that influence the course of development.

While play observations have gained new status in infant/toddler assessment, there is a lack of consensus among professionals as to how these observations should be conducted. A major distinction is made in the literature between structured and nonstructured play observations. Structured play observations are designed to measure a defined set of behaviors that can be observed through play. Behaviors displayed during the observation, even if they are relevant to the referral question, are not recorded if they fall outside the parameters of the defined set of behaviors (Comfort & Farran, 1994). In contrast, nonstructured play observations are designed to identify all behaviors that occur during a play period that may be relevant to the referral question and/or guide the intervention.

In addition to variations in the range of behaviors observed, structured and nonstructured observations differ from each other in several other significant ways. First, a fundamental difference between the two is that structured observations are characterized by specificity, and nonstructured observations are not. In a structured observation, a procedural protocol describes the conditions of the observation. These include the setting where it takes place (Gaensbauer & Harmon, 1981; Matheny, 1991), the toys that are used (Field, Vega-Lahr, Scifidi, & Goldstein, 1987), and the techniques for initiating the play sequence (Morgan, Maslin-Cole, Biringen, & Harmon, 1991). In a nonstructured observation, the infant is observed in spontaneous play that is initiated by the infant or caregiver, without restrictions in terms of toys, timing, and setting.

Second, structured and nonstructured observations call for different methodologies to record and describe observations. Structured observations are based on assessment tools (Greenspan & Lieberman, 1980) or rating scales (Field, 1980) with built-in coding systems. Nonstructured observations do not use assessment tools. Using a video camera, their own shorthand, or a tape recorder, the observers keep a running account of salient behaviors and report them in narrative form. Finally, and most significantly, structured observations use normed scales to rate a child's behavior or use behavioral observations of same-age children to derive a developmental scale. Nonstructured observations, on the other hand, do not yield a rating or a score. The nonstructured play observation is a clinical tool used by an assessment team as a key component of an assessment process.

# ▣ Guidelines for Nonstructured Play ▣ Observations

While a rich body of literature describes guidelines for structured play observations (Field et al., 1987; Gaensbauer & Harmon, 1981; Greenspan & Lieberman, 1980; Matheny, 1991; Morgan, Maslin-Cole, Biringen, & Harmon, 1991; Ruff & Lawson, 1991; Vendra & Belsky, 1991), the literature on nonstructured observations is relatively sparse. In this chapter, our purpose is threefold: (a) to present guidelines for conducting nonstructured play observations; (b) to identify their benefits; and (c) to describe their caveats. Suggested guidelines for nonstructured observations are described in four phases: preparing for the observation; setting up the observation; implementing the observation; and writing up the observation.

## Preparing for the play observation

Preparing for a play observation requires selecting the observer, gathering the background information, and identifying the focus of the observation.

### Selecting the observer

The selection of a play observer is likely to be based on the policy of the clinic staff or professional team responsible for the developmental assessment. Criteria for selection include areas of expertise, family preference for one observer over another, ethnicity or language of the observer, or availability. Depending on the policy of the agency, the observer may be the clinician who was responsible for the intake (initial) interview and/or the formal testing, or he or she may be a member of the assessment team with special expertise in the area of concern.

### Gathering the background information

The first step in gathering the background information is a review of the information that has already been collected on the child and family. This requires a review of the child's file, which may include background information on the child and family, results of formal testing, and reports from other sources, such as the pediatrician, neurologist, and/or child care center. In addition to reviewing the file, the observer may want to talk with the initial interviewer and/or other members of the team who have seen the family. The second step is a review of the literature relevant to the child and family. In some situations, it is useful to review observation scales describing developmental sequences in different domains of competency, age-related dimensions of temperament, and observation scales of parent-child interactions.

Antoinette, a 6-month-old Caucasian girl, is the product of a difficult pregnancy with intermittent bleeding beginning in the first trimester. She was born by Caesarean section at 8 months gestation, with a birthweight of 6 lbs., 2 ozs. She was placed in a Neonatal Intensive Care Unit because of breathing problems and was discharged from the hospital after 10 days. With the exception of postural asymmetry, no problems were noted at discharge. Antoinette developed at a slower than normal rate, and at age 5 months was referred by her pediatrician to the Family Center Developmental Clinic.

Following an interview with Antoinette's mother, Mrs. L., and a battery of formal tests, the team at the Clinic recommended a play observation. In preparation for the observation, the observer identified two developmental scales that could guide the observation process: the Uzgiris-Hunt Scales of Infant Development (1975) and a scale constructed by Mundy and colleagues (1992) on joint attention and imitation. Familiarity with these scales alerted the observer to the existence of subtle behaviors indicative of emerging skills that could be enhanced by mother-infant play. Later, the observer's narrative report of the nonstructured observation focused on such skills and was incorporated into the team recommendations.

### Identifying the focus of the observation

Once the observer has become familiar with the background information about the child, he or she is ready to identify the major focus of the observation. In almost every instance, the questions that parents ask about their child determine the observer's focus. If different or additional questions are asked by the referring source or the assessment team, these questions also must be taken into account in planning the observation.

Mia was a 9-month-old infant brought to the Family Center Developmental Clinic by her parents for a developmental evaluation. Although Mia appeared to be on target developmentally and showed no signs of hearing loss, her parents were concerned because she did very little babbling. Rather than scheduling a formal evaluation, the team recommended a play observation. The goal of the observation was to identify ways in which these motivated parents could encourage babbling. Knowing the referring question, the observer focused on the play style of both parents and on the techniques they used to encourage back-and-forth conversation.

When the referring question is straightforward, as it was with Mia, identifying the focus of an observation is not difficult. In most situations, however, there is more than one unknown or concern, and identifying the focus presents a greater challenge.

Mrs. T. lives with her husband, her 5-and-a-half-year-old son, Pedro, and her 2-year-old twins, Gabriel and Maria, in a small apartment on the third flood of an apartment complex. She brought Gabriel to the University Speech and Language Clinic because he was not talking. Mrs. T., who had recently immigrated from Brazil, also expressed some concern about Maria, who could follow simple directions but could say only four or five words.

Following a developmental and language evaluation, a home visit was scheduled. The team was seeking answers to several questions. Are we facing a generalized or pervasive developmental delay associated with prematurity and twin status? Are we looking at experiential deprivation associated with poverty and overstressed parents? Do the children, in a home situation, show behaviors consistent with a diagnosis of autism? What impact does the family's bilingualism have on the children's learning of language? Does Mrs. T. have difficulty with child management, and could it compromise a treatment plan?

Recognizing the complexity of the case, the team determined that two observers should go to Mrs. T.'s home. The observers were faced with an immediate problem. Which behaviors should they observe? Should they focus on the twins' use of language? Should they focus on the kind of play interactions that the three children engage in? Should they focus on the environment and the available toys and books to determine whether the living conditions are compromising the twins' learning? Should they focus on the interactions of the three children with one another and with their parents? Should they focus on Mrs. T.'s child-rearing practices?

As the observers entered the two-room apartment, the chaos of the situation was immediately apparent. The three children were running, climbing, and fussing back and forth with one another. Mrs. T. was trying desperately to calm the children, protect the cookies she had baked, and carry on a conversation with the observers. The observers immediately recognized how much there was to observe and how critical it was to focus their observations. Knowing that their observations could describe only a small part of what was taking place, the observers made a decision on the spot to focus on the kind of play the children were engaged in and the way Mrs. T. contributed to this.

In order to capture as much information as possible, the observers stationed themselves in different rooms. Although this decision facilitated the observation, the observers still had difficulty focusing on significant behaviors. Like professional photographers, following the actions of one of the children to identify antecedents and consequences of a particular behavior, they moved their camera from one scene to the next, zoomed in on a significant event, and panned the landscape to capture the speed, intensity, and frequency of the interactions.

Even in situations where the observer is quite clear about where to focus the "camera" and what kind of information to gather, the focus is likely to change in the course of the observation. This may occur because a skilled observer may see behaviors or parent-child interactions that appear to be significant, although they do not relate to the referring questions. Further, in the course of the observation, the parent may ask a significant question that he or she has not raised previously.

Although Mrs. T.'s initial concern was with language development, she asked questions pertaining to other behavioral elements during the course of the observation.

Should Maria have been screeching so loudly and so persistently when she did not get what she wanted? Did Pedro need to be in kindergarten, where he could learn to follow directions? Finally, at the very end of the observation, Mrs. T. asked her most pressing questions: "Am I doing something wrong? Am I a good mother?"

## Setting up the play observation

In a structured observation, particularly when it is part of a research study, a set of standard materials is used in a prescribed way. In a nonstructured, opened-ended play observation, the play materials that are used are selected by the parents. If the play observation is conducted in a clinic, the observer's task is to make sure that appropriate play materials are available to give the parents some options.

Although the observation of Antoinette was conducted at the Family Center Developmental Clinic and a wide selection of toys was lined up on the shelf, Antoinette's mother, Mrs. L., chose a toy that she had brought from home. Mrs. L. knew Antoinette was familiar with this toy and could make it work. The observer might not have had an opportunity to witness Antoinette's emerging competency if the parent had not had the opportunity to make the toy selection.

When an observation is made at home, it is appropriate in most instances to limit the selection of materials to toys that are in the home. A possible exception is when the observers are interested in a particular aspect of a child's behavior that may be elicited most easily by particular toys that are not available at home.

In the observation of Gabriel and Maria, the children played with the blocks and books given to them by their mother. Because these toys did not elicit symbolic play, the observers asked permission to share some toys with the children that they had brought with them. These toys included a doll, play food, a bottle, and a doll's chair. Given the opportunity to do so, both twins engaged in doll play, placing the doll in the chair, putting the bottle in its mouth, and wiping its mouth with a tissue. Mrs. T. was happy to see how well her children responded to these toys. Furthermore, with the observers engaging the children in play, Mrs. T. had the opportunity to talk to the observers about her most pressing concerns.

## Implementing the play observation

When conducting a nonstructured play observation, one of the most important decisions concerns how to record the data. Several options are available, including videotape, audiotape, paper and pencil, or reliance on memory. Videotaping an observation has many advantages. It maintains the sequence and events of an observation; it can be reviewed repeatedly by the observer, the parents, and the other members of the assessment team; and it gives the observer freedom to be responsive to parents' questions or to provide the parents with prompts in the course of the observation. Nevertheless, there are drawbacks to videotaping. Parents may either resist being videotaped or may act unnaturally during the videotaping (Field & Ignatoff, 1981). Evaluation programs may not have the appropriate video equipment, particularly for a home setting. More important, a single video camera may not be able to capture the interaction sequences between parent and child that are often the most critical components of a play observation.

Another question that arises during a play observation is the degree to which the observer should participate in the observation. In some situations, particularly in a clinic with an observation room, the contact between observer and family is minimized. This contrasts sharply with the situation in which the observer determines from the start that he or she will play an active role in the observation, prompting the play behavior, playing with the child, or using the play observation as an opportunity to elicit parents' questions and strengthen his or her relationship with the parents. In most situations, the role of the observer in a play observation is planned in advance in accordance with the objectives of the observation (Wilson, 1985). When, for example, an observation is designed to identify characteristics of parent-child play, the observer does not intervene. On the other hand, when an observation is designed to identify developmental strengths that are not apparent in spontaneous parent-child play, the observer plays a more active role. He or she may want to introduce materials or initiate a play idea that will demonstrate a child's capabilities. In the home observation of Gabriel and Maria, the introduction of representational toys demonstrated an unsuspected capacity to focus attention and play out a pretend scenario.

A final question associated with the implementation of observations is how to respond when parents ask difficult questions: "Is my child retarded or autistic?" "Is this something she will grow out of?" "What are her chances of attending regular school?" "Do you think she is bored with school and that is why she is acting up?" Avoiding these questions or talking around them is not helpful to the family. However, answering parents' questions without sufficient information can provide false hope or create premature despair.

An appropriate response to a difficult question may be: "I know how important it is for you to have an answer to that question. Unfortunately, at this point, I cannot provide an answer. When the evaluation is completed and you meet with the team, your questions will be addressed. We may not have the answers even then, but we will be honest with you and will respond to your questions to the best of our ability."

## Writing up the play observation

Following an observation, the observer is faced with the challenging task of producing the observation report. In some programs or agencies, there is a set format for writing up parent-child play observations. In other programs, the observer determines the format to be used in a particular instance, based on the nature of the observation. The three most commonly used formats are *sequential, categorical*, and *question-oriented*. The *sequential* report is a chronological description of the play exchanges that take place in the course of an observation. It describes ways in which parents and children initiate play overtures or respond to them, and it allows the reader to identify ways in which parents and children influence each other. The *categorical* report is organized according to domains of competency, such as physical, cognitive, social, emotional, and language. This format is useful when the play observations are compared to the outcome of standardized developmental instruments. The *question-oriented report* is organized around the major question or questions asked by the parents, referral source, and/or assessment team. It is especially useful when the play observation is expected to validate or clarify information already collected or to provide information that could not be gathered through other sources or methods.

Unquestionably, observations of parent-child play, when used appropriately and with discretion, make an important contribution to a comprehensive developmental assessment. Among other benefits, parent-child play observations provide a special opportunity for parents and clinicians to share expertise and to build a parent-professional partnership.

# Benefits of Play Observations

The benefits of play observations derive from both the information they provide and the opportunity they afford to create a parent-professional partnership. These benefits fall into eight categories.

*1. Play observations provide an opportunity to assess the functional behavior of a young child who either cannot or will not perform in a formal testing situation.*

Although a formal developmental assessment is a typical component of a comprehensive developmental assessment, young children are not always candidates for standardized assessments (Sattler, 1992). First, children under three do not understand the concept of being tested and are not motivated to do their best. Second, young children may be resistant to being tested. Perhaps they are wary of a new room, a strange person, or a closed suitcase, or perhaps they sense the anxiety on their parents' faces.

In other situations, a young child may fall below a scorable cut-off point on a standardized tool and yet have the capacity to perform tasks that the test is designed to measure. In a play observation, a well-trained clinician may be able to identify emerging skills and capacities in a very young child that could not be scored under standard conditions. Although the clinician's observations do not change a test score, they are useful both in terms of the interpretation of the developmental test and the design of an intervention plan.

Carmen was removed from her home at age two because of physical abuse and was placed with a foster family. During the day, she was enrolled in a therapeutic child care program for children in protective custody. Carmen made little apparent progress in the child care program. She spent most of her time wandering around the classroom or playroom throwing blocks, breaking toys, or rocking back and forth in a squat position. She seldom approached other children, but, when she did, she would approach them from the back, push them over, and then walk off without checking on the outcome of her push. The therapeutic team was unsure whether Carmen's behavior was associated only with psychological traumas or whether there was evidence of retardation and/or pervasive developmental disorder (PDD).

Attempts to test Carmen with the Bayley Scales of Infant Development (BSID) (Bayley, 1969) were of no avail. Carmen screamed in a high-pitched voice as soon as she entered the testing room and refused to perform on any of the items presented. Testing was discontinued, and Carmen was taken into the playroom by the guardian ad litem who had accompanied her to the testing. Because Carmen appeared to quiet down in the playroom and glanced at the toys on the shelf, it was decided that she would be brought back on the following day for a play observation. She was accompanied again by the guardian ad litem, with whom she had some rapport.

Carmen entered the playroom the next day without hesitation. Her guardian, as instructed by the team, stayed with her, and two observers watched from an observation booth. Carmen circled the room for several minutes, as if checking out the physical layout. She then lifted a baby doll out of the cradle, kicked its face, and appeared to glance briefly at the guardian, who remained quietly watchful. Next, Carmen walked over to the miniature kitchen, pulled some dishes and utensils out of the cabinet, and threw them around the room. The guardian picked up the baby doll, sat it in a high chair, and brought a bottle to its mouth. The guardian said simply, "Baby is hungry." Carmen watched for a couple of seconds, grabbed the bottle, put it in her own mouth, and then in the mouth of the doll. She then pulled the doll out of the high chair and threw it on the floor. "You bad," she told the doll, "bad, bad girl!"

In reviewing this play episode, the treatment team agreed that Carmen had been traumatized, but, based on her ability to engage in symbolic play and to use language appropriately, they felt that neither retardation nor PDD was an appropriate diagnosis. A recommendation was made for continued play therapy within the child care center. Over the course of the year, Carmen's play behavior became better organized and more sustained. At age 2 years, 11 months, she was tested on the Bayley (1969) and received a Mental Development Index (MDI) interpolated score of 86.

2. *Because of the flexibility and spontaneity of a play situation, infants and toddlers may achieve a level of object or symbolic play that they did not demonstrate on a standardized assessment.*

Even a child who is not actively resistant to formal testing may not perform at an optimum level during this kind of testing. While developmental tests for infants do allow for flexibility in the selection and presentation of items (Bayley, 1969, 1993; Mullen, 1984), the constraints of standardization make it difficult to identify partially attained or emerging skills through these tests. This is particularly true with infants who have a degree of motor involvement (Bayley, 1993). When designing an intervention program, it is more meaningful to base it on a play observation that identifies conditions under which a child can perform a task than on a developmental age (Wolery, 1994).

Antoinette, introduced earlier in the chapter, is a good example of an infant whose emerging capabilities could be captured in a play observation. The Family Center Developmental Clinic team interviewed Antoinette's mother, Mrs. L., and suggested an informal play observation. The goal of the observation was not to determine a developmental age, but to identify emerging skills that could be enhanced by mother-infant play. The interview with Mrs. L. suggested that Antoinette could anticipate when something good or bad was about to happen, but had difficulty focusing on a toy or engaging in back-and-forth conversation.

Prior to the testing, Mrs. L. supported Antoinette in a sitting position while she presented her with a toy she had brought from home. For approximately two minutes, Antoinette gazed at the toy without making any effort to reach for it. Mrs. L. then activated the toy by pushing a lever that released one of the blocks. Antoinette watched, but did not move her arms. Maintaining the same slow pace, Mrs. L. pushed the lever three more times. Each time a block fell, she spoke to Antoinette: "Look, the block fell down." When Mrs. L. pushed the lever the fourth time, Antoinette moved her arm toward the toy. Mrs. L. commented, "Yes, you can do it." Next, Antoinette swiped the toy with her hand. Immediately following the swipe, Antoinette's mother jerked the toy in order to release another block. Antoinette followed the block with her eyes as it fell to the ground. Apparently, she had made the connection between the swiping of the toy with her hand and the release of the block.

In writing up the evaluation, the examiner noted that Antoinette demonstrated an awareness of cause-and-effect relationships that exceeded her performance on the Bayley Scales of Infant Development II (BSID-II) (1993). This information was discussed by the treatment team, and a variety of cause-and-effect activities was included in the intervention plan.

3. *Play observations can provide important insights into temperamental variables.*

Unquestionably, play observations provide an opportunity to observe a child in a naturalistic situation and to identify capabilities that may not be recognized in a formal test. At the same time, play observations provide a wealth of information that cannot be gleaned in other ways. One of the critical factors that is often described in a play observation is temperament. Although child specialists recognize the importance of taking into account temperamental characteristics in designing intervention strategies, the literature on temperament provides more questions than answers (Garrison, 1990). Professionals do not agree on what aspects of an infant's behavior can be attributed to temperament, what aspects of temperament have long-term significance, or what methods should be used to measure temperament. At the same time, professionals do agree that individual differences in behavior that are not associated with developmental status can be identified in infancy and that these differences can be identified in a play observation. Of particular importance are behaviors related to engagement, persistence, attention span, and exploratory diversity. While further research is needed on the nature and persistence of temperamental characteristics, the information on temperament gleaned in a play observation may be useful both for making a diagnosis and for designing a treatment plan.

Constantine is a 2-and-a-half-year-old Hispanic boy who was brought to the Family Center Developmental Clinic by his parents at the suggestion of the director of the child care center. According to the director's report, Constantine was a withdrawn youngster who had not made a good adjustment to the group setting. He was described by his teachers as an unhappy child who would watch other children from a distance but would not join in their play. He was particularly frightened of trying new experiences and refused to taste new foods, pet the hamster, fingerpaint, or plant seeds in the garden. Because Constantine had never participated in any of the class activities, the teachers suspected emotional problems or cognitive delay.

Following an interview with the parents, Mr. and Mrs. F., Constantine was scheduled for developmental testing and a play observation. Because of Constantine's fear of new situations, a decision was made to begin with play assessment and postpone developmental assessment until Constantine was more familiar with the setting. When Mr. and Mrs. F. were asked to go into the playroom, Constantine positioned himself behind his father with his head under his father's jacket. Constantine did not come out from under the jacket until his father sat down on a play mat and showed Constantine a puzzle. Constantine slowly and cautiously took the pieces out of the puzzle while his parents talked with the examiner. Although both parents agreed that

Constantine was an unusually timid child, they did not share the concern of the teacher about either his emotional or his developmental status. "It is just the way he is," Mrs. F. explained. At the end of the interview, the examiner asked Mr. and Mrs. F. to play for a few minutes with Constantine while she watched from the observation booth.

At the suggestion of his mother, Constantine completed a six-piece inset puzzle and put it back on the shelf. Next, he followed his parents to the sand table. His mother announced that she was going to make a sand cake for Dad's birthday. Constantine stood back and watched as his mother filled a play cake tin with sand and placed some pegs in the sand. "Help Daddy blow out his candles," Mrs. F. suggested. After a few minutes of watching, Constantine joined the play and offered his father a plate of sand. "You want a hot dog?" Constantine asked his father.

Developmental testing was scheduled one week after the play observation. Constantine received an MDI score of 107 on the Bayley Scales of Infant Development (BSID) (Bayley, 1969), placing him in the average range. The parents were assured that Constantine's behavior at school should not be a concern at this point. Constantine appeared to be, by nature, a cautious or slow-to-warm-up child. The examiner agreed to talk with the teacher about ways to help Constantine adjust to the school situation.

4. *Play observations can reveal aspects of the parent-child relationship that help explain the behavior of the child.*

Play observations can contribute information about a child that guides the clinician in making recommendations. In certain situations, however, a play observation may be critical in helping a study team rethink their diagnosis and recommended course of treatment. This is particularly true when the parent-child play observation suggests a concern about the parent that had not been identified in the parent interview.

Daniel was referred to the Family Center Developmental Clinic by his pediatrician because of concerns about his general development and a suspected diagnosis of autism. Daniel is the product of a full-term pregnancy, birthweight 7 lbs., 11 ozs, with no pre- or post-natal complications. Motor development during the first year was on target, with sitting alone at six months and walking independently at ten months. Daniel was described by his mother, Mrs. S., as a difficult infant who had cried incessantly since the age of three weeks, was oversensitive to loud noises, and reacted with panic to new experiences and new people. Language development was relatively slow. Daniel could say three words when he was 2 years old, but they disappeared within weeks. At age two and a half, Daniel began both speech therapy and preschool. His teacher described him as a "loner" who was unable to follow directions without an individual prompt. At home, according to Mrs. S.'s report, Daniel had frequent tantrums and poor eating habits. He often engaged in repetitive behavior and was compulsively neat.

On the Bayley Scales of Infant Development II (BSID-II) (Bayley, 1993), Daniel received a score of less than 50 on the MDI (Mental Development Index) and a score of 51 on the PDI (Psychomotor Development Index). Orientation/engagement, emotional regulation, and motor quality were recorded by the examiner as nonoptimal. However, Daniel remained with the examiner during the testing and followed simple directions without showing resistance. On the Early Language Milestones Scale (Coplan, 1987), Daniel showed some rudimentary joint attention skills, turn-taking, and behavior regulation skills. Daniel did not demonstrate age-expected gestures such as pointing or showing objects.

Mrs. S. was asked to return to the clinic so that Daniel could be observed in the playroom during spontaneous play. Mrs. S. was instructed to play with Daniel and to encourage him to play with some of the toys. Mrs. S. picked up a toy truck and handed it to Daniel. "Here, take the truck and see if you can make it go." Mrs. S. then sat on the sofa and appeared to be staring into space. Daniel pushed the toy truck into his mother's shoe. She was startled, and then she scolded Daniel, "You are not supposed to run people over with the truck. Make your truck go over there." Daniel went over to the sand table and, using a ladle, began filling a container with sand. "Don't get sand on the floor," his mother warned. "The people won't like it." For the rest of the observation time, Mrs. S. remained on the sofa. Daniel continued to empty and fill the same container.

Although Daniel was certainly in need of intense intervention, the treatment team recognized that the behavioral differences observed in Daniel were related at least in part to Mrs. S.'s high level of stress and apparent depression. Counseling for Mrs. S. was included in the Individualized Family Service Plan (IFSP).

## 5. Play observations can provide insights into numerous domains of development.

Play is such an all-encompassing activity for young children that it offers a window into virtually all domains of development—cognitive, motor, social, emotional, and language. Accordingly, play observation is an appropriate technique regardless of the developmental focus of the referring question. Furthermore, even when the referring question relates to a particular domain of development, play observation provides a window into other developmental domains that may be significant in formulating a treatment plan. This is particularly true when a play observation points to an unexpected strength.

During play observation, for example, Constantine, the slow-to-warm-up child described above, revealed an unexpectedly strong ability to engage in symbolic play. While the referring question focused on social behavior, Constantine's ability to engage in pretend play demonstrated a cognitive strength that could, in time, compensate for his slow-to-warm-up temperament. The pinpointing of this strength supported the assessment team's "no treatment" recommendation.

6. *Play observations provide clinicians with special opportunities to learn effective play strategies from a child's parent.*

Play observations not only provide opportunities for clinicians to learn *about* their clients, but they also provide opportunities for clinicians to learn *from* their clients. In almost every instance, parents have a much greater capacity to read and respond to their baby's cues than even the most astute professional. Often parents become intuitively adept at providing their baby with the appropriate type and amount of stimulation. They know how long to continue with stimulation and when to let their infant disengage. By watching the "developmental dance" between parents and infants, professionals can help to craft an intervention program that incorporates successful strategies based on the experience of parents.

A speech and language clinic referred Roxanna to the Family Center Developmental Clinic at age 2 years, 3 months for developmental evaluation. Although the parents' initial concern was expressive language delay, the clinic recognized behavioral characteristics that could place Roxanna within the autistic spectrum. Roxanna, according to her parents' description, had been an easygoing baby with early milestones on target. When she was less than 1 year old, Roxanna was using expressive jargon and had acquired two or three meaningful words. Between 12 and 14 months, these early words were lost, and the parents noticed difficulty in establishing eye contact. At 2 and a half years, Roxanna had no expressive language, did not follow verbal instructions, and seldom responded to her name. Play skills were limited to mouthing, throwing, and spinning.

Prior to the administration of the Bayley Scales of Infant Development II (BSID-II) (Bayley, 1993), Roxanna was observed in a play session with her mother, Mrs. N. During the session, Mrs. N. sat on the floor beside Roxanna and attempted to engage her interest in a puppet. When Roxanna ignored the puppet, Mrs. N. began a finger-play game, accompanied by a repetitive song. Roxanna imitated her mother's hand movements and responded to the song with rhythmic rocking. Interactive play continued for over five minutes.

Mrs. N.'s success in using finger plays to initiate interactive play with her daughter provided a starting point for a home intervention program. Mrs. N. was encouraged to extend the interactive sequences within Roxanna's repertoire by introducing slight variations in the songs and finger/hand gestures. As Roxanna learned new movements and new songs, objects associated with the songs could be introduced. For example, if Roxanna and her mother were singing "Row Your Boat," Mrs. N. could show Roxanna a toy rowboat.

On a followup visit, Mrs. N. reported some success in getting Roxanna to respond to the words "ball" and "bunny," following a finger-play routine. Mrs. N.'s early success in finding a way to interact with her daughter was the starting point of a successful intervention plan.

### 7. Play observations suggest ways of helping parents modify play strategies that are not fully effective.

While parent-child play observations provide unique opportunities to identify effective intervention strategies developed by parents, they also provide opportunities to identify and modify strategies used by parents that are less effective. Frequently, observers will identify a well-intentioned parent who is trying so hard to achieve a result that his or her efforts are counterproductive. A play observation helps to identify effective play-style modifications that can help parents achieve the intervention goal (Field, 1983).

The observation of Mia, introduced earlier in this chapter to illustrate the process of identifying the focus of the observation, helped to identify intervention strategies.

Mia was a premature infant born at 7 months gestation, with a birthweight of three lbs., two ozs. Although both parents were convinced that Mia was developmentally on target or even ahead of target, they were concerned, given her prematurity, about the fact that she did not do as much babbling as other babies her age.

Prior to testing, Mia was observed in the playroom with her mother and father. Her mother, Mrs. G., assumed the role of player and followed Mia as she crept around the playroom. Mia was intrigued by three play mats that had been placed in layers in the corner of the room. For at least five minutes, she persisted in climbing up and down the mats. Mrs. G. stayed close by, keeping up a constant stream of chatter.

"You really like climbing up these mats. It looks like you are going to be standing up before long.

"I wish you would be a little more careful. Any minute now you are going to land smack on your nose. I bet you'd make a whole lot of fuss if that happened, wouldn't you?

"Mia, darling, you are having a problem getting off the mat. Would you like a little help?

"Mia, look at all the different colors on this ball. You like looking at different colors, don't you? See the red, yellow, green, blue, and orange?"

After a while, Mia noticed her father and crawled across the room to him. Mr. G. sat down on the floor behind her and pulled some toys off the shelf. Quietly, he stacked three blocks and knocked them down. Mia smiled. The next time her father stacked the blocks, Mia joined the game and knocked down the blocks.

As the treatment team reviewed the observation video, it was apparent that both parents had a good relationship with Mia and enjoyed playing with her. Interestingly enough, although Mr. and Mrs. G. played with Mia in different ways, neither parent was encouraging language development. Mrs. G.'s constant stream of conversation did not invite interactive babbling, while Mr. G. tended not to talk at all. The team assured Mr. and Mrs. G. that Mia's development was on target and provided them with simple techniques to encourage language development.

8. *Play observations implemented within a home can identify strengths, coping skills, and risk factors that impact on a diagnosis and may be useful for designing a treatment plan.*

The play observations we have described in this chapter, with the exception of those involving Mrs. T. and her three children, were carried out in a clinic playroom. Play observations in a clinic are relatively easy to arrange and are not very costly in terms of equipment and personnel time. This is not true of home observations. Play observations that take place in a home are often difficult to arrange and unquestionably costly. Nevertheless, home observations provide an ecologically valid picture of everyday interactions between parents and children, and they reveal risk and protective factors that can play a significant role in the design of an intervention plan. Home observations can also provide special opportunities to build rapport with parents, engage in meaningful communication, and build a trusting relationship. This is well illustrated in work with the "T." family.

When the observers arrived, Mrs. T. was waiting for them. The apartment was sparsely furnished but very clean. The observers explained that they wanted to watch the twins, Gabriel and Maria, play together at home in order to observe how they communicated in a home setting. Almost immediately, Gabriel ran across the living room and out to a small porch, and began to climb on the banister. Mrs. T. chased after him, explaining that he loved to climb, but it was dangerous. While Mrs. T. was carrying Gabriel back into the house, Pedro, the 5-and-a-half-year-old, took a tin of cookies off the kitchen table. Mrs. T. reminded him that he was not supposed to open the tin. Pedro opened it and stuffed a cookie in his mouth, and Mrs. T. told him that he could not watch his favorite television show for two days. Next, Mrs. T. put Gabriel on the floor and took down two books, one for him and one for his twin sister, Maria. Maria snatched the book from Gabriel and screamed loudly when Mrs. T. returned the book to her brother. "No matter they have the same toy, she wants what he got," Mrs. T.

explained. Seconds later, the house became chaotic. Maria snatched the book back from Gabriel. He burst into tears, and Pedro took advantage of the moment to climb back on the kitchen table to retrieve the tin of cookies. Despite Mrs. T.'s efforts to maintain control, the activity of the children continued to escalate, and the noise level increased. Gabriel and Pedro hassled over a slinky toy. Maria continued to take toys from both her siblings. Mrs. T. appeared increasingly overwhelmed and exhausted.

The home visit with Mrs. T. was a critical component of the developmental evaluation for several reasons. First, watching Mrs. T.'s courageous efforts to manage her challenging young family forced the treatment team to rethink their plans for an intervention program within the home. Second, although the parents' concern had centered on Gabriel, the home visit suggested that all three siblings were in need of services. Pedro was not registered for kindergarten. Maria was exhibiting behaviors suggestive of an emotional disorder, as well as language delay. Third, the home visit provided Mrs. T. with an opportunity to share her concerns and frustrations and to reach out for help. "My Pedro, better he go to school, but how he can get there? How I go walk with him to school? Gabriel, he run; I got to hold him. Maria, she don't answer what I say. Just all the time she screaming. Maybe I do something wrong. So much I want to be a good mother." As a result of this home visit, a comprehensive IFSP was developed with Mrs. T. that included all three children and that enabled Mrs. T. to access services outside the home, including an early intervention preschool program for the twins and a kindergarten program for Pedro.

### 9. *Play observations can enhance the parent-professional partnership.*

A major benefit of a play observation is the opportunity it offers to parents and professionals to develop a common language, based on concrete examples derived from the observation. Play observations, whether they are carried out in a clinic or at home, provide opportunities for professionals and parents to enhance their communication and establish a meaningful partnership.

During the IFSP conference with Mrs. T., the team referred to how upset Maria was when Pedro was given a turn to play with a top. Mrs. T. explained that Maria was always like that. Once she began to cry about something, it was impossible to get her to stop, even when she was given the very thing that she had been crying about in the first place. This kind of behavior made her worry about Maria's health. She was relieved that the team was not just telling her to forget about the behavior, expecting that it would go away.

## Caveats about Play Observations

Although the addition of play observations to a developmental evaluation makes good clinical sense, it is a difficult task to undertake for many reasons.

*1. Play observations are expensive.*

Even when play observations are conducted in a clinic, it can be an expensive undertaking to find a time when both parents and clinician are available, a room that can be set up in advance where interruptions are likely to be limited for a reasonable span of time, and a playroom that is appropriate for recording. This is particularly true when video cameras are used to record the play. The frequent need for more than one observer is a further expense of play observations.

*2. Some families may consider play observations intrusive.*

Play observations, particularly when they are carried out in the home, may be considered intrusive by the family. In some cultures and in some families, bringing a stranger into your home may be considered improper or even dangerous. In other situations, parents may be embarrassed about some aspect of their home. For example, the home is being shared with other people, the lights have been turned off, the house is sparsely furnished, or a spouse has a drinking problem.

Mrs. T. appeared very anxious about being visited at home. The fact that she provided a very precise time for the visit suggested that she had some concerns. At first, the observers attributed this precise time to her need to have the house in order, but this did not seem to be the case. The real reason was revealed soon enough. After the observers had been in the house only a few minutes, Mrs. T.'s husband arrived for a very brief visit. After meeting the visitors, he left the house abruptly, without an explanation. The observers recognized that, in accordance with his responsibilities as defined by his culture, Mr. T. was checking out his unknown visitors.

*3. Play observations, whether at home or in a clinic, take a great deal of time and are not always fruitful.*

Although this chapter includes several vignettes that illustrate the benefits of play observations, in many situations they do not provide new information. Child play is likely to be repetitive: The block tower is built, knocked down, and built again; the parent is served glass after glass of sand lemonade; and peeka-boo becomes an endless game. When parent-child play is repetitive, it may not be possible to continue an observation long enough to collect new or significant data.

Although the observation of Gabriel and Maria was described briefly on one page, the actual home visit required two and a half hours. Gabriel became intrigued with a simple slinky toy, and, for almost 40 minutes, he manipulated the toy in a variety of ways. During this time, the observer stood by and took brief notes. Although she was not obtaining new information, she could not interfere with the repetitive activity without destroying the spontaneity of the play.

*4. The logistics of a play observation may be difficult to arrange.*

Setting up a play observation, whether at home or in a clinic, requires an appropriate room as well as sufficient time. In an ideal situation, videotaping is available so that the observer does not have to take notes and the tape can be shared with the treatment team. At the least, a play observation requires a room where there will be no interruptions and where there is sufficient space for the observer to watch without interfering with the play. These conditions are difficult to meet, particularly in a home situation. The observation of Gabriel and Maria's play was interrupted not only by the father's visit, but also by a telephone call, a package delivery, and a neighbor returning some sugar.

*5. A play observation is dependent on the knowledge and skill of the observer.*

Because a play observation is open-ended and nonstandardized, the validity of a play assessment is dependent on the skills of the observer. As we list the attributes of a competent play observer, we recognize that he or she must be a competent clinician in every sense. On the basis of knowledge, experience, and acumen, the observer must be able to interpret very subtle play interactions, recognizing the contributions of both child and parent to the play exchange. In some situations, the observer is also called upon to relate and respond to the parents' questions and concerns.

The expertise required of play observers includes (a) an awareness of the development of infants and toddlers; (b) an awareness of and sensitivity to temperamental variables; (c) an understanding of the developmental stages of parenthood and the subtle transactions that take place between parent and child in the early years; (d) an awareness of the early indicators that may place a child at risk; and (e) familiarity with the culture, neighborhood, and language of the families.

In the observation of Daniel, described above, the play observation provided little information about his level of play or his capacity to interact with other people. Indeed, the play observer spent little of the observation time recording the nature or quality of Daniel's play. From the beginning of the observation, the observer recognized that the flat affect of the parent and her noninvolvement in Daniel's play limited the amount of information that could be derived from watching Daniel play. At the same time, the observation yielded critical information on the nature of the dynamics between parent and child, which guided the development of a treatment plan.

## 6. In order to obtain useful information, it is often necessary to set up more than one play observation.

Although a major advantage of a play observation is that it can be repeated several times without destroying its validity, few programs or clients have the resources for repeat observations. Particularly when observations are conducted in a home setting, it is difficult to capture a "typical" moment on a "typical" day. The baby awakens tired from a nap and just wants to cling to mother; a neighbor arrives unexpectedly with two active children; or the light for the video camera blows the fuses in the house. Every developmental team that depends on home visits can add sad tales to this list.

## 7. Ethical concerns may arise during an observation that are difficult to resolve.

A major concern of clinicians who make home visits for the purpose of play observations is that they will encounter child abuse or neglect, which has to be reported. While this kind of situation can arise, a more common ethical problem relates to the withholding of information. Quite naturally, parents who have invited a clinician to observe in their home want to ask questions about their child. For many reasons, including incomplete or noncorroborated findings, the ambiguity of findings, the absence of a parent, or the presence of an older sibling, the clinician may not be able to provide answers. Even when careful explanations and apologies are given, the family may feel let down or even betrayed.

After the observation of Antoinette and her mother, Mrs. L., described above, Mrs. L. asked the observer if she felt that Antoinette would be able to go to a regular school. The observer acknowledged the question without providing an answer. "I know what you are going through. When a child has a problem, whether big or small, every parent has a desperate need to know when and whether the child will be like other children. Unfortunately, in most situations we do not know the answer to this. Babies are so different from one another and babies like Antoinette are so full of surprises that it wouldn't be fair to talk about the far future. I can tell you that Antoinette has already shown us some exciting emerging abilities, and this is certainly encouraging. When the evaluation is completed, we will have a conference with the team, and you will have an opportunity to ask your questions. Together, we will design an intervention plan that will work for your family." Mrs. L. was obviously dissatisfied and frustrated by the clinician's equivocal answer.

*8. With even the most skilled clinician, play observations are difficult to execute.*

A play observation, whether at home or in a clinic, requires the full concentration of the observer. The classic role of observer assumes no interaction with the child or the family. In a real situation, this is impossible to achieve. The mother asks a question; the baby hands the observer a toy; a sibling is about to jump off a table and needs to be rescued. But even if these contingencies do not occur, the play observer may identify an opportunity to gather critical information that requires an entrance into the play.

The goals of the visit to Mrs. T.'s home to observe the twins and their older sibling could not have been accomplished without two observers who were willing to enter into the play. With three children, a small house, and few toys, the play could easily have remained at the level of jumping, chasing, and play fighting. While an observation of this active type of play would have provided some information about Mrs. T.'s daily routines, the presence of two observers allowed one observer to talk with the parent while the second one introduced play ideas to the children. Obviously, few programs have the luxury of sending two trained, experienced observers to a home observation in an area that is far away from the program office.

## Summary

Unquestionably, nonstructured play observations in which the observer focuses on the spontaneous play behaviors of the parent and child, or child alone, add an important dimension to a clinical assessment. Although standardized tests and structured observations allow for peer comparisons, a nonstructured play observation is a snapshot of a child and family that identifies their uniqueness and may be useful for making a diagnosis and designing a treatment plan.

A nonstructured play observation presents behavior through the lens of a clinician. The image that is recorded is shaped or tinted by the characteristics of the lens. The behaviors that are salient to the observer reflect his or her degree of intimacy with developmental norms and expectations, knowledge of the client and the questions the client is asking, and the ability to recognize and record a sequence of significant behaviors.

A nonstructured play observation can confirm or surprise; it can validate the outcomes of a developmental evaluation; it can generate a new hypothesis; or it can suggest a new mode of treatment. A nonstructured play observation does not replace other forms of assessment, but, in the hands of a good clinician, it provides a way of knowing a child's and family's strengths, coping strategies, and creativity. It allows us to glimpse at what a child or a dyad (parent and child) are really like when they are watched and not compared. Portraits of a child and parent in spontaneous play, repeated at regular intervals as part of a collaborative assessment, can help answer questions raised by a team and can generate new questions.

# References

Bayley, N. (1969). *Manual for Bayley Scales of Infant Development.* San Antonio, TX: Psychological Corporation.

Bayley, N. (1993). *Manual for Bayley Scales of Infant Development* (2nd ed). San Antonio, TX: Psychological Corporation.

Comfort, M., & Farran, D. C. (1994). Parent-child interaction assessment in family-centered intervention. *Infants and Young Children,* 6 (4), 33-45.

Coplan, J. (June 1987). *Early Language Milestones Scale.* Austin, TX: PRO-ED, Inc.

Field, T. (1980). Interactions of pre-term infants born to lower-class teenage mothers. In T. Field, S. Goldberg, D. Stern, & A. Sostek (Eds.), *Interactions of high-risk infants and children.* New York: Academic Press.

Field, T. (1983). Early interactions and interaction coaching of high-risk infants and parents. In M. Perlmutter (Ed.), *Development and policy concerning children with special needs.* The Minnesota Symposia on Child Psychology. Hillsdale, NJ: Erlbaum.

Field, T., & Ignatoff, E. (1981). Videotaping effects on play and interaction behaviors of low-income mothers and their infants. *Journal of Applied Developmental Psychology, 2,* 227-236.

Field, T., Vega-Lahr, N., Scifidi, F., & Goldstein, S. (1987). Working mother-infant interactions across the second year of life. *Infant Mental Health Journal, 8,* 19-27.

Gaensbauer, T., & Harmon, R. (1981). Clinical assessment in infancy utilizing structured playroom situations. *Journal of the American Academy of Child Psychiatry, 20,* 264-180.

Garrison, W. T. (1990). Assessment of temperament and behavioral style. In J. H. Johnson & J. Goldman (Eds.), *Developmental assessment in clinical psychology: A handbook* (pp. 197-218). New York: Pergamon Press.

Greenspan, S. I., & Lieberman, A. (1980). Infants, mothers, and their interactions: A quantitative clinical approach to developmental assessment. In S. I. Greenspan & G. H. Pollock (Eds.), *The course of life: Psychoanalytic contributions toward understanding personality development. Vol. 1. Infancy and early childhood* (pp. 271-312). (DHHS Publication No. ADM 80-786). Washington, DC: U.S. Government Printing Office.

Matheny, A. P. (1991). Play assessment of infant temperament. In C. E. Schaefer, K. Gitlin, & A. Sandgrund (Eds.), *Play diagnosis and assessment* (pp. 39-63). New York: Wiley.

Morgan, G. A., Maslin-Cole, C. A., Biringen, Z., & Harmon, R. P. (1991). Play assessment of mastery motivation in infants and young children. In C. E. Schaefer, K. Gitlin, & A. Sandgrund (Eds.), *Play diagnosis and assessment* (pp. 65-86). New York: Wiley.

Mullen, E. M. (1984). *Mullen Scales of Early Learning manual.* Warwick, RI: T.O.T.A.L. Child, Inc.

Mundy, P., Kasari, C., & Sigman, M. (1992). Nonverbal communication, affective sharing, and intersubjectivity. *Infant Behavior and Development, 15,* 377-381.

Ruff, H. A., & Lawson, K. R. (1991). Assessment of infants' attention during play with objects. In C. E. Schaefer, K. Gitlin, & A. Sandgrund (Eds.). *Play diagnosis and assessment* (pp. 115-129). New York: Wiley.

Sattler, J. M. (1992). *Assessment of children* (3rd ed.). San Diego, CA: Author.

Uzgiris, I., & Hunt, J. M. (1975). *Assessment in infancy: Ordinal scales of psychological development.* Urbana, IL: University of Illinois.

Vendra, J., & Belsky, J. (1991). Infant play as a window on competence and motivation. In C. E. Schaefer, K. Gitlin, & A. Sandgrund (Eds). *Play diagnosis and assessment* (pp. 13-38). New York: Wiley.

Wilson, J. M. (1985). Play in the hospital. In C. C. Brown & A. W. Gottfried (Eds.), *Play interactions: The role of toys and parental involvement in children's development.* Skillman, NJ: Johnson & Johnson.

Wolery, M. (1994). Assessing children with special needs. In M. Wolery & J. Wilbers (Eds.), *Including children with special needs in early childhood programs.* Washington, DC: National Association for the Education of Young Children.

# 12. Assessing the Emotional and Social Functioning of Infants and Young Children*

STANLEY I. GREENSPAN

Traditional approaches to assessing children's development have tended to focus on one component or another of development, rather than producing a profile of an integrated, functioning, whole child. For example, we have tended to assess separately a child's language functioning, motor functioning, sensory functioning, different aspects of cognition, and various domains of adaptive, social, and emotional functioning. Moreover, to measure these components of development, we have used structured tests that bear little relation to the child's everyday, functional world and that, as a result, fail to reveal most children's highest capacities. Not surprisingly, the intervention recommendations that flow from such fragmented, piecemeal assessments are also fragmented and do not suggest specific, individualized types of developmental experiences, involving both children and their caregivers, that will foster further growth.

In contrast to structured, piecemeal assessment approaches, this chapter suggests a functional developmental approach that assesses the whole child's core functional capacities in his or her most important everyday interactions with key caregivers. The Functional Emotional Assessment Scale (FEAS) assesses the

---

*This chapter is an adaptation of material in *Infancy and Early Childhood: The Practice of Clinical Assessment and Intervention with Emotional and Developmental Challenges* (Stanley I. Greenspan, International Universities Press, Madison, CT, 1992).

child's social, emotional, cognitive, and communicative capacities in the context of interactions with key caregivers. It is derived from an integrated understanding of the social, emotional, and cognitive development of infants and young children (Greenspan, 1979, 1989). This approach looks at such core capacities as the child's capacity for self-regulation, engagement, intentional communication, forming a complex sense of self, elaborating symbols and representations, and creating logical bridges or differentiations within his or her emerging symbolic world ("emotional thinking"). It postulates a number of levels of development. For each level, the scale describes expected primary emotional capacities; the range of sensorimotor capacities; and related motor, sensory, language, and cognitive capacities. The scale also addresses infants' constitutionally- and maturationally-based capacities, as well as patterns of caregiving that may facilitate or undermine the child's development.

FEAS recognizes that the world of the infant or young child is a world of feelings and relationships. It is in the context of relationships with important caregivers that babies and toddlers develop—and demonstrate—their cognitive, motor, and language skills, as well as intentionality and motivation. Spontaneous interactions between young children and their familiar caregivers reveal core functional interactive capacities (as well as cognitive, motor, and language skills). These capacities are the glue that holds the child's development together.

The assessment of an infant's or young child's core emotional and social capacities provides families and clinicians with a rich, nuanced profile of how a very young child experiences his or her physical and human environment, the ways in which the child uses his or her own resources and the support of caregivers to engage with the world, and the challenges that confront the child. Perhaps most importantly, insights from this assessment approach suggest specific, individualized intervention approaches that will reinforce a child's and family's unique strengths and will help them work effectively to overcome developmental challenges.

## ▰ Functional Assessments and Structured ▰ Testing

The assessment of a young child's emotional and social functioning through observation of unstructured interactions with all the child's important caregivers and with the clinician takes time, care, and skill. My colleagues and I are constantly asked to compare the results of our approach to the results achieved through use of formal, structured assessment instruments. Three issues seem central to this discussion: (a) accuracy; (b) the consequences of error; and (c) cost.

## Accuracy

A formal test approach looks at what an infant can and cannot do in relationship to a defined set of stimuli or test procedures, which, at best, can only be approximations of a child's ordinary experience. Currently available formal tests of young children's development were, for the most part, developed and standardized with infants and young children who were not evidencing atypical or challenging developmental patterns. Formal tests are not designed to elicit a child's (especially a challenging child's) unique abilities and potential. Yet it is precisely the child with special needs who requires early assessment and intervention. And it is precisely the young child with special needs who may have the most difficulty paying attention, relating, and conforming to the most basic expectations of formal tests. Skilled examiners who are aware of these issues may use the challenging infant's general behavior in the formal assessment situation as an indicator of his or her abilities, substituting an informed clinical opinion for a formal score or profile. The less experienced examiner, however, may simply score the challenging child's performance on the test items in their standard presentation (leading, often, to what one parent described as "Johnny's 'can't do' reports") and attempt to derive conclusions from the numerical score. In either case, the formal testing situation is not the best context within which to observe the true functional capacities of any infant or young child.

## The consequences of error

Misleading and incorrectly interpreted formal test data often lead to inappropriate recommendations for intervention. The wrong placement can lead to actual deterioration in the development of some children with delays or atypical patterns, hardly a desirable outcome for initiatives designed to offer early identification of these delays or patterns and appropriate intervention. Unfortunately, as states and communities are attempting to assess more and more infants and young children in need of appropriate special services and offer services to them, the number of incorrect service recommendations may be increasing. Recently, more and more parents of toddlers and preschoolers have been coming to me for consultation after being offered inappropriate services and educational placements based on misdiagnoses derived from misleading standardized test scores. A complete clinical, relationship-focused functional evaluation of such children often reveals abilities six or seven months ahead, developmentally, of those reflected in standardized test results. Since many of these children are below 2 years of age, the difference is quite significant.

## Cost

Often, time can be saved and resources conserved by using formal structured assessments very selectively to explore questions about specific areas of functioning that have not been answered by the clinical functional assessment. More importantly, an assessment approach that builds on a foundation of careful observation of the infant or young child with his or her family and other important caregivers is likely to avoid errors in educational placement and service recommendations, which waste community resources and unconscionably deplete children's and families' strength, energy, and developmental potential.

## ▰ Goals of the Functional Emotional ▰ Assessment Scale

The Functional Emotional Assessment Scale offers a method of systematizing the clinical functional assessment of the infant and young child. It focuses on the infant's core emotional and social capacities at each stage in his or her development. It also outlines the related motor, sensory, language, and cognitive capacities that go along with each of the core emotional and social capacities. While it is always tempting to use rating scales to simplify complex clinical judgments, it should be clear that the goal of the FEAS is to assist clinicians in systematizing and fine-tuning clinical judgments, and in incorporating judgments about functional emotional capacities into research protocols. The scale points out critical areas for further clinical inquiry.

The scale is designed to help clinicians organize and interpret their observations of free, unstructured interactions between the infant or young child and his caregiver(s), as well as interactions between the child and the clinician. These unstructured interactions are invited when the clinician simply asks the caregiver to interact or play with the infant or child as he or she might at home. If further suggestions are needed, phrases such as "Just the way you like to interact with each other," "The way you like to enjoy each other," "The way you like to be together," and so on may be useful. If necessary, the clinician offers a series of semistructured interactive opportunities to the infant or child to help elicit his or her core competencies. (Examples of such interactive opportunities will be described later in this chapter.) These free, unstructured, and, if necessary, semistructured interactions are close to the infant's natural way of interacting with his or her world. They can be observed both in the office and at home and can be repeated as many times as necessary in order to gain a true picture of the child's and caregiver's capacities. It is often very helpful to see the infant or young child and his caregiver(s) interacting on at least two or more separate occasions. In reaching an overall clinical judgment, one must also take into account historical data and caregivers' reports of the child's current functioning.

The Functional Emotional Assessment Scale addresses six areas:

1. *Primary emotional capacities.* Evidence of the child's attainment of the primary emotional capacities characteristic of the developmental level corresponding to his or her chronological age suggests whether or not a child has progressed to his or her age-expected functional emotional developmental capacity.

2. *Emotional range—sensorimotor (including speech).* This area focuses on the range of sensory and motor equipment, including motor gestures, touch, and speech, that the infant or child is able to employ in mastering his or her primary functional emotional capacities. Older children will need sensory, motor, and speech capacities to support higher-level functional and conceptual abilities.

3. *Emotional range—affective.* This area focuses on the different affective themes (e.g., dependency, aggression) that the child can organize at his or her age-expected developmental level (e.g., one child can use words and pretend play in relationship to the theme of dependency, while another child can only use play and words to express aggression).

4. *Associated motor, sensory, language, and cognitive capacities.* This area comprises selected developmental items not already covered in the primary emotional capacities. (However, many capacities that would traditionally be assessed within the cognitive domain are addressed in the assessment of functional emotional capacity.)

5. *General infant tendencies.* These are constitutionally- and maturationally-based capacities.

6. *Overall caregiver tendencies.* These are caregiving patterns that facilitate or undermine the child's development.

Each of these capacities can be rated as "not present," "fleetingly present," "intermittently present," "present most of the time," or "present consistently under all circumstances."

When using the Functional Emotional Assessment Scale, the clinician should first assess the age-expected primary emotional capacities of the infant or young child. He or she should then assess all the prior primary emotional capacities which, one hopes, were mastered at earlier ages but continue as part of the child's basic capacities. The clinician should then assess sensorimotor emotional range and affective emotional range. If, in both categories, the infant or young child evidences an optimal emotional range for his age level, the clinician need not assess developmentally earlier categories of emotional range. On the other hand, if the infant or young child evidences constrictions in his or her emotional range, the clinician should keep assessing the developmentally earlier categories of emotional range (either sensorimotor or affective, or both) to see if the infant or young child was ever able to establish a broad, flexible emotional range in the sensorimotor or affective areas. The clinician should next observe how the child functions in terms of motor, sensory, language, and cognitive capacities to see if these are consistent with, behind, or advanced for the child's functional emotional capacities. Next, the clinician should assess the infant's constitutional tendencies and the caregivers' capacities.

The clinician arrives at a number of judgments regarding the infant's capacities, including (a) the developmental level, in terms of primary functional emotional capacities; (b) the sensorimotor range; and (c) the affective range. He or she gains an understanding of contributions from the infant's constitutional and maturational tendencies and the caregiving patterns. The clinician will determine if a child is at or below the age-expected functional emotional development, as well as how well earlier functional emotional capacities have been mastered. The clinician will also gain an impression of the infant's emotional range.

The clinical interpretation of the child's profile must be a clinical judgment based on the child's overall adaptation. A child who is at a developmental level lower than expected with regard to functional emotional capacities but has an optimal emotional range at that level is not necessarily at greater risk than a child who is at his or her age-expected functional emotional developmental level but has a constricted sensorimotor and affective range. For example, a child whose developmental momentum was temporarily delayed by a medical illness but who is now developing at an appropriate rate in all areas may be at less risk than a child who is already chronically constricted in his or her emotional range. In other words, a 2-and-a-half-year-old who operates in all areas like a well-functioning 2-year-old may be at less risk than a 2-and-a-half-year-old who talks and engages in some pretend play, but avoids pleasure and only deals with dependency through physical touch and impulsive behavior.

In general, one first determines the child's developmental level in terms of primary functional emotional capacities. This provides a sense of where the child is developmentally. Then one determines how flexible or wide-ranging his or her adaptive and coping capacities are at that level (i.e., sensorimotor and affective emotional range). If one wants to see how stable the child's capacities are, one looks at the ratings themselves. Lots of "fleetingly present" or "intermittently present" ratings suggest unstable capacities. "Present most of the time" or "present consistently under all circumstances" ratings suggest stable capacities.

The clinician may then look at the associated sensory, motor, language, and cognitive items to see which areas are ahead, at, or behind the functional emotional capacities. For example, a child's fine motor and motor planning capacities may be behind, while receptive language and cognition are advanced. If this child is also constricted in his or her emotional range, especially in dealing with aggression, one may wonder if the lag in fine motor and motor planning is contributing to this constriction (i.e., a lack of security in the fine control of the motor system). Another child may evidence lags in primary functional emotional capacities and the affective emotional range but be advanced in the motor, sensory, language, and cognitive areas. Here, one may wonder whether the child's interactive opportunities with caregivers are fully supporting his or her development.

After one gains a sense of the child's developmental levels in different areas, one should look at the infant's constitutional and maturational patterns (e.g., oversensitivity or undersensitivity to touch or sound) and caregiving patterns.

The goal of the Functional Emotional Assessment Scale is to describe functional emotional capacities as systematically as motor, sensory, language, and cognitive capacities have been described. The scale is designed to help clinicians organize their observations in order to arrive at appropriate clinical judgments and, most importantly, to use their understanding to recognize the types of experiences an infant and his caregivers require. The FEAS enables the clinician to (a) foster further growth at each stage of the child's emotional development; (b) work with the child's unique constitutional and maturational patterns; (c) help family members and caregivers understand their own responses and patterns of interaction with the child; and (d) address and overcome lags, constrictions, and deficits in the child's emotional development, as well as associated symptoms.

# The Functional Emotional Assessment Scale

This section presents the Functional Emotional Assessment Scale, to be used with infants and young children from 3 months to 48 months of age. The capacities to be observed (or elicited) are listed in terms of the six stages of emotional development. Each set of capacities, while usually first in evidence at a certain period in infancy or early childhood, continues as the child grows. The child's current level, as well as the levels he or she may have already mastered, should be observed.

## Regulation and interest in the world

By 3 months, the infant can be calm; recovers from crying with comforting; is able to be alert; looks at one when talked to; and brightens up when provided with appropriate visual, auditory, and/or tactile experiences.

*Primary emotional capacities*

1. Shows an interest in the world by looking (brightening) at sights or listening to (turning toward) sounds. Can pay attention to a visual or auditory stimulus for three or more seconds.

2. Can remain calm and focused for two or more minutes at a time, as evidenced by looking around, sucking, cooperating in cuddling (e.g., molding with caregiver), or other age-appropriate activities.

*Emotional range—sensorimotor*

1. Looks at interesting sights for three or more seconds (brightens or turns toward sights).

2. Listens to interesting sounds for three or more seconds (brightens or turns toward interesting sounds).

3. In response to touch (light or firm), relaxes, smiles, vocalizes, or looks.

4. In response to caregiver's moving of infant's arms and/or legs, relaxes, smiles, vocalizes, or looks at caregiver or own limbs.

5. Tolerates and/or shows pleasure (e.g., smiles) in gentle horizontal and vertical movement in space (e.g., caregiver moving infant up and down and from side to side).

6. Tolerates or evidences pleasure in routine smells (e.g., a fruit odor such as lemon, an after-shave lotion, or perfume).

7. When held firmly, relaxes or evidences pleasure.

8. When rhythmically rocked, relaxes or evidences pleasure.

9. Recovers from distress with help from caregiver (e.g., holding, rocking) within twenty minutes.

*Emotional range—affective*

1. Shows an interest in caregiver by looking, listening, or evidencing curiosity and pleasure (as compared to being interested only in inanimate objects or in nothing).

2. Shows interest through looking, listening, or signs of pleasure when caregiver makes happy, joyful facial expressions, or laughs.

3. Shows interest when caregiver is assertive and reaches out by means of his or her facial expressions and vocal tones (caregiver saying, in a regular tone of voice, "What a wonderful nose and mouth and little chin you have!"; "Will you hold this rattle? You can do it! You can do it!").

*Selected associated motor, sensory, language, and cognitive capacities not included above*

1. *Motor:* (a) holds head upright on own; (b) lifts head by leaning on elbows while on stomach; (c) keeps hands open 75 per-

cent of the time; (d) rolls from side to back or stomach to back; (e) reaches for rattle or other toy; (f) and manipulates rattle or other toy.

2. *Sensory:* (a) follows objects in horizontal plane (e.g., light); (b) follows objects in vertical plane; (c) responds to a variety of sounds; and (d) tolerates deep pressure-type touch.

3. *Language:* (a) watches lips and mouth of speaker; and (b) vocalizes with at least one type of sound.

4. *Cognitive:* (same as sensory and language).

## Forming relationships (attachments)

By 5 months, the infant evidences positive loving affect toward the primary caregiver and other key caregivers, and looks and/or smiles spontaneously and responds to their facial expressions, voices, or touch with signs of pleasure, such as smiling, relaxing, and "cooing."

*Primary emotional capacities*

1. Responds to social overtures with an emotional response, such as a smile or other indication of pleasure, a frown or other facial expression, vocalizations, arm or leg movements, or postural shifts.

2. Responds to social overtures with an emotional response of pleasure (e.g., smile, joyful vocalizations).

*Emotional range—sensorimotor*

Shows emotional interest or pleasure in caregiver's:

1. Vocalizations (indicate which type works best—high or low pitch; loud, medium, or soft tone).

2. Facial expressions.

3. Touch (indicate part of body—back, abdomen, face, arms, or legs—and type of touch—light or firm—that works best).

4. Gentle moving of the infant's arms or legs.

5. Moving of infant horizontally or vertically in space (indicate rhythm that works best, e.g., fast, slow).

*Emotional range—affective*

1. Evidences a relaxed sense of security and/or comfort when held or rocked.

2. Evidences signs of pleasure (e.g., smiles, happy sounds) when either talked to, held, looked at, moved around, touched, or all of the above.

3. Evidences a curious, assertive interest in caregiver (e.g., looks at and studies caregiver's face).

4. Anticipates with curiosity or excitement the presentation of an interesting object that has been presented a moment earlier (e.g., a smiling, vocalizing caregiver making interesting sounds leads to anticipatory looks and facial expressions).

5. Evidences signs of discomfort, lack of pleasure, or sadness when, during interactive play, caregiver is unresponsive for 30 to 60 seconds (e.g., while playing, caregiver stops interacting and is silent and still-faced).

6. Evidences anger or protest when frustrated (e.g., angry cry or facial expression).

7. Within 15 minutes, can recover from distress assisted by caregiver's social overtures, such as vocalizing and making interesting facial expressions.

*Selected associated motor, sensory, language, and cognitive capacities not included above*

1. *Motor:* (a) pushes up on extended arms; (b) shifts weight on hands and knees; (c) readies body for lifting while being picked up; (d) can reach for a toy; (e) can roll from back to front; (f) sits with support; (g) can cooperate in being pulled to a sitting position; (h) can bring hands together; (i) can grasp objects voluntarily; and (j) can hold rattle.

2. *Sensory:* (a) reacts to paper on face; (b) looks toward sound; and (c) tolerates roughhouse play.

3. *Language:* (a) regularly localizes source of voice with accuracy; (b) vocalizes two different sounds; and (c) vocalizes to caregiver's facial expressions and sounds.

4. *Cognitive:* (a) can focus or pay attention for 30 seconds or longer; (b) looks and scans for objects and faces; (c) smiles at face in mirror; (d) looks toward object that goes out of visual range; (e) looks at own hand; and (f) manipulates toys, such as a rattle or ring, and plays with them.

## Intentional two-way communication

By 9 months, the infant is able to interact in a purposeful (i.e., intentional, reciprocal, cause-and-effect) manner, and is able to initiate signals and respond purposefully to another person's signals. The infant uses multiple sensory modalities, the motor system, and a range of emotions in these intentional interactions.

*Primary emotional capacities*

1. Responds to caregiver's gestures with intentional gestures of his or her own (when caregiver reaches out to pick up infant, infant may reach up with his or her own arms; a flirtatious caregiver vocalization may beget a playful look and a series of vocalizations).

2. Initiates intentional interactions (e.g., spontaneously reaches for caregiver's nose, hair, or mouth; uses hand movements to indicate wish for a certain toy or to be picked up).

*Emotional range—sensorimotor*

Responds intentionally to caregiver's:

1. Vocalizations.

2. Facial expressions.

3. Touch (e.g., holds caregiver's hand when being touched or tickled).

4. Moving of infant around in space.

*Emotional range—affective*

Uses gestures to initiate:

1. Closeness. The infant reaches out to be picked up or hugs back when hugged.

2. Pleasure and excitement. The infant can be playful and can smile and vocalize joyfully while putting finger in caregiver's mouth or taking rattle out of caregiver's mouth and putting it in own mouth.

3. Assertive exploratory behavior. The infant touches and explores caregiver's hair.

4. Protest or anger. The infant pushes undesired food off table with an angry look and screams intentionally when desired toy is not brought to him or her.

5. Fearful behavior. Infant turns away and looks scared or cries when a stranger approaches too quickly.

6. Infant can recover from distress within 10 minutes by being involved in social interactions.

*Selected associated motor, sensory, language, and cognitive capacities not included above*

1. *Motor:* (a) can sit with good balance; (b) can hold toes while sitting; (c) while sitting, can reach up in air for objects; (d) can go from lying on back to sitting; (e) can go from sitting to

stomach position; (f) creeps or crawls on stomach or hands; (g) holds block or toy using thumb and finger; (h) can scoop a Cheerio or small object into palm; (i) bangs hands or toy while playing; and (j) transfers objects from hand to hand.

2. *Sensory:* (a) will feel textures and explore them; (b) notices when toy or object is put on different parts of body (stomach or foot) (e.g., looks at or touches textured toy); (c) not sensitive to loud noises (e.g., vacuum cleaner, toilet flushing, or dog barking); (d) not sensitive to bright lights; and (e) enjoys movement in space.

3. *Language:* (a) responds to name and/or some simple directions (e.g., "No"); (b) vocalizes different sounds from front of mouth (e.g., "Ba" or "Ma" or "Da") and causes sounds to convey intentions or emotions, such as pleasure or satisfaction; (c) responds to different sounds with different vocalizations of own or with selective behaviors; and (d) can imitate a few sounds (e.g., a "raspberry" or tongue click).

4. *Cognitive:* (a) can focus on toy or person for one minute or longer; (b) explores and examines new toy; (c) makes sounds or creates visual or tactile sensations with toy (e.g., cause-and-effect playing); (d) can discriminate between different people as evidenced by different responses; (e) looks for toy that has fallen to floor; and (f) can pull on part of an object (e.g., a corner of a piece of cloth) to get the object closer.

## Complex sense of self I: Behavioral organization

By 13 months, the infant begins to develop a complex sense of self by organizing behavior and emotion. The toddler sequences a number of gestures together and responds consistently to a caregiver's gestures, thereby forming chains of interaction (i.e., opens and closes a number of sequential circles of communication). The toddler also manifests a wide range of organized, socially meaningful behaviors and feelings dealing with warmth, pleasure, assertion, exploration, protest, and anger.

*Primary emotional capacities*

The infant strings together three or more circles of communication (interaction) as part of a complex pattern of communication. Each circle or unit of communication begins with an infant behavior and ends with the infant building on and responding to the caregiver's response. For example, an infant looks at a toy and reaches for it, opening a circle of communication; the caregiver points to the toy, gestures, and vocalizes, "This one?" The infant then nods, makes a purposeful sound, and reaches further for the toy, closing the circle of communication. As the infant explores the toy and exchanges vocalizations, motor gestures, or facial expressions with the caregiver, additional circles of communication are opened and closed.

*Emotional range—sensorimotor*

The infant can organize three or more circles of communication (with a responsive caregiver):

1. Using vocalization.

2. Using facial expressions.

3. Involving reciprocal touching.

4. Involving movement in space (e.g., rough-and-tumble play).

5. Using motor patterns (e.g., chase games, searching for objects, handing objects back and forth).

*Emotional range—affective*

With caregiver support (i.e., responsive empathetic reading of infant's types of communication and responding to them), the infant can organize three or more circles of communication around:

1. Negotiating closeness. Gives caregiver a hug and, as caregiver hugs back in response, nuzzles and relaxes.

2. Pleasure and excitement. Infant and caregiver play together with an exciting toy or with caregiver's hair or toes, or infant's toes.

3. Assertive explorations. Infant and caregiver examine new toys and explore the house.

4. Cautious or fearful behavior. Infant hides behind caregiver when in a new setting; negotiates degrees of protection needed with caregiver.

5. Angry behavior. Infant can gesture angrily back and forth.

6. Infant can recover from distress and remain organized while distressed by entering into complex gestural negotiation for what he or she wants (e.g., banging on door to go outside and play).

*Selected associated motor, sensory, language, and cognitive capacities not included above*

1. *Motor:* (a) walks on own or by holding onto furniture; (b) can squat while playing; (c) can throw a ball forward; (d) can feed self finger foods; (e) can stack two cubes; and (f) can organize one-step motor planning, such as pushing, catching, or throwing a ball.

2. *Sensory:* (a) infant explores and tolerates different textures with hands and mouth (e.g., willing to explore different foods); (b) infant is comfortable climbing and exploring off of the floor (e.g., on couch, table top); (c) infant is not sensitive to bright lights; and (d) infant is not sensitive to loud noises (e.g., vacuum cleaner).

3. *Language:* (a) understands simple words like "shoe" or "kiss!"; (b) uses sounds or a few words for specific objects; and (c) jabbers.

4. *Cognitive:* (a) can focus and pay attention while playing on own for five or more minutes; (b) copies simple gestures like "Bye-bye" or "No"; (c) can find toy under caregiver's hand; (d) will try to imitate a scribble; and (e) explores how toy works and figures out simple relationships, such as pulling a string to make a sound.

## Complex sense of self II: Behavioral elaboration

By 18 months, the infant elaborates sequences of interaction which convey basic emotional themes.

*Primary emotional capacities*

1. Comprehends and communicates, via gestures, basic emotional themes as evidenced by the ability, with a responsive caregiver, to open and close 10 or more consecutive circles of communication (e.g., taking caregiver's hand and walking toward refrigerator, vocalizing, pointing, responding to caregiver's questioning gestures with more vocalizing and pointing, finally getting caregiver to refrigerator, getting caregiver to open door, pointing to desired food).

2. Imitates or copies another person's behavior and then uses this newly learned behavior intentionally to convey an emotional theme (e.g., putting on Daddy's hat and walking around the house with a big smile, clearly waiting for an admiring laugh).

*Emotional range—sensorimotor*

Elaborates complex interactions (i.e., 10 or more consecutive circles of communication) using:

1. Vocalizations and/or words.
2. Facial expressions.
3. Reciprocal touching and/or holding.
4. Movement in space (rough-and-tumble play).
5. Large motor activity (e.g., chase games, climbing games).
6. Communication across space (e.g., while playing with pots, infant vocalizes to caregiver from across room; caregiver vocalizes back; infant continues playing and vocalizing without needing to come over and touch caregiver).

*Emotional range—affective*

1. Elaborates complex interactions (10 consecutive circles of communication) dealing with the emotional themes of:

    a. Closeness and dependency. Uses facial expressions, motor gestures, and vocalizations to reach out for a hug, kiss, or cuddle. Can be coy and charming, or even provocative, if necessary, in order to be close. Can also use imitation to feel close (e.g., talks on play telephone while Mom talks on telephone with a friend).

    b. Pleasure and excitement. Can share a joke with another toddler, or with an adult. For example, when the toddler drops some food accidentally and it makes a funny sound ("Splat!") or a mark on the floor, the toddler may giggle and look toward the other person to share in the pleasure. Making funny faces or sounds, or imitating the behavior of adults or other toddlers may be a basis for giggles and pleasure.

    c. Assertiveness and exploration, including relative independence. Can now explore more independently and can balance dependence with independence. Uses ability to communicate across space to feel close to caregiver while playing on own (e.g., may go into another room, or to a far corner of the same room, to look for a toy while periodically looking at or vocalizing to the caregiver). May also come over to touch base with caregiver and venture out again.

    d. Cautious or fearful behavior. Can now, via vocalizations, motor gestures, or a few words, tell caregiver exactly how to be protective in a new situation (e.g., hides behind caregiver but pushes caregiver toward a toy or toward new people as though to run interference), or says, "No," and hides behind caregiver.

e. Anger. Can hit, pinch, yell, bang, scream, or lie on the floor as part of an organized pattern well under toddler's control. Can also give the angry cold shoulder to a wayward caregiver. Can sometimes use an angry gesture, look, or vocalization instead of hitting, screaming, or pinching.

f. Limit setting. Can respond to caregiver limits communicated through gradually louder vocal gestures, serious-looking facial expressions, and body postures, as well as to simple phrases such as "No, stop that!" "Leave it alone!" and "Come here!" For example, with the above type of limit setting, the toddler puts telephone down and returns to caregiver.

2. Can use imitation to deal with and recover from distress (e.g., toddler may bang hands on floor and yell after being yelled at).

*Selected associated motor, sensory, language, and cognitive capacities not included above*

1. *Motor:* (a) can plan motor pattern involving two or more steps (e.g., can bounce balloon and try to catch it); (b) tries to imitate scribble or scribbles on own; (c) holds crayon or pencil adaptively; (d) puts items in cup or toys in box; (c) builds tower with two or three blocks; (f) can put pegs in pegboard; (g) can put round block in round opening on board; and (h) can take off socks.

2. *Sensory:* (a) enjoys or tolerates various types of touch (e.g., cuddling, roughhousing, touching different types of clothing, brushing teeth or hair); (b) is comfortable with loud sounds; (c) is comfortable with bright lights; and (d) is comfortable with movement in space.

3. *Language:* (a) comprehends some simple questions, and carries out directions (e.g., with a ball); (b) imitates simple words; and (c) uses words to make needs known.

4. *Cognitive:* (a) uses objects functionally (e.g., vocalizes on toy telephone, combs hair with toy comb); (b) searches for desired toy or hidden object in more than one place; (c) can play on own in focused manner for 15 or more minutes; (d) imitates behaviors just seen or seen a few minutes earlier; (e) recog-

nizes family pictures; and (f) can use stick or other object to get another object.

## Emotional ideas I: Representational capacity

By 24 months, the child creates mental representations of feelings and ideas which can be expressed symbolically (e.g., through pretend play and words).

*Primary emotional capacities*

1. Can construct, in collaboration with caregiver, simple pretend play patterns of at least one "idea" (e.g., dolls hugging or feeding the doll).
2. Can use words or other symbolic means (e.g., selecting or drawing a series of pictures, creating a sequence of motor gestures) to communicate a need, wish, intention, or feeling (e.g., "Want that." "Me toy." "Hungry!" "Mad!").

*Emotional range—sensorimotor*

Can communicate symbolically about intentions, wishes, needs, or feelings with:

1. Words.
2. Complex gestures and facial expressions (e.g., making angry facial expressions in an exaggerated manner).
3. Touching (e.g., lots of hugging or roughhousing as part of pretend drama where child is the "daddy").
4. Motor movement (e.g., showing caregiver what to do).

*Emotional range—affective*

Can use pretend play or words employing at least one idea to communicate themes dealing with:

1. Closeness or dependency (e.g., as dolls are feeding each other, child says, "Want Mommy").
2. Pleasure and excitement (e.g., child makes funny faces like clown on television and laughs).
3. Assertiveness and exploration (e.g., cars are racing, child looks at a real car in wonderment and asks, "Car?").
4. Cautious or fearful behavior (e.g., says, "Scared").
5. Anger (e.g., as dolls are fighting or hitting, says, "Me mad").
6. Limit setting (e.g., child says to self, "No hit").
7. Can use pretend play and/or words to recover from and deal

with tantrum or distress (e.g., after a few minutes, tantrum-ming child uses words and sounds to argue with caregiver).

*Selected associated motor, sensory, language, and cognitive capacities not included above*

1. *Motor:* (a) catches large ball from a few feet away using arms and hands; (b) jumps with both feet off ground; (c) balances momentarily on one foot; (d) walks up stairs, two feet on each step at a time; (e) can run; (f) can stack more than four blocks; and (g) can both scribble and make a single stroke with a crayon or pencil.

2. *Sensory:* (a) enjoys or tolerates various types of touch (e.g., cuddling, roughhousing, touching different types of clothing, brushing teeth or hair); (b) is comfortable with loud sounds; (c) is comfortable with bright lights; and (d) is comfortable with movement in space.

3. *Language:* (a) understands simple questions ("Is Mommy home?"); (b) uses simple two-word sentences ("More milk," "Go bye-bye"); (c) can name some objects in a picture; and (d) begins to use some pronouns.

4. *Cognitive:* (a) can focus or pay attention for 30 minutes or more; (b) can do pretend play on own; (c) can search for favorite toy in place where it was the day before; (d) can do simple shape puzzles (two to three shapes); (e) can line up objects in a design (e.g., a train of blocks); (f) can point to body parts of doll; and (g) can put round and square blocks in correct places on board.

## Emotional ideas II: Representational elaboration

By 30 months, the child, in both make-believe play and symbolic communication, can elaborate on a number of ideas that go beyond basic needs (e.g., "Want juice") and can deal with more complex intentions, wishes, or feelings (e.g., themes of closeness or dependency, separation, exploration, assertiveness, anger, self pride, showing off).

*Primary emotional capacities*

1. Creates pretend drama with two or more ideas (trucks are crashing and then they pick up loads of rocks, or dolls are hugging and then have a tea party). Ideas need not be related or logically connected to one another.

2. Uses symbolic communication (e.g., words, pictures, motor

patterns) to convey two or more ideas at a time that express complex intentions, wishes, or feelings (e.g., "Daddy play with car," "No sleep, play"). Ideas need not be logically connected to one another.

*Emotional range—sensorimotor*

Can communicate symbolically about intentions, wishes, or feelings with:

1. Words.
2. Complex gestures and facial expressions (e.g., acting tired and needy).
3. Touch (e.g., lots of hugging or roughhousing as seen on television).
4. Can participate in simple spatial and motor games with rules (e.g., taking turns throwing a ball).

*Emotional range—affective*

Can use pretend play or other symbolic communication (e.g., words) to communicate themes containing two or more ideas dealing with:

1. Closeness or dependency (e.g., dolls say "Hug me," child says, "Give you kiss").
2. Pleasure and excitement (e.g., making funny words and laughing).
3. Assertiveness and exploration (e.g., pretend airplane zooms around room).
4. Cautious or fearful behavior (e.g., pretend drama where baby doll is scared of loud noise).
5. Anger (e.g., soldiers shoot pretend guns at one another).
6. Limit setting (e.g., dolls follow rules at tea party, "Must sit").
7. Use of pretend play to recover from and deal with distress (e.g., plays out eating the cookie he could not get in reality).

*Selected associated motor, sensory, language, and cognitive capacities not included above*

1. *Motor:* (a) walks up and down stairs; (b) throws ball; (c) stands on one foot; (d) can walk on tiptoe; (e) draws line with crayon or pencil; (f) can turn knob; (g) can remove cap; (h) can fold paper; and (i) can make a tower of eight or more blocks.
2. *Sensory:* (a) enjoys or tolerates various types of touch (e.g.,

cuddling, roughhousing, touching different types of clothing, brushing teeth or hair); (b) is comfortable with loud sounds; (c) is comfortable with bright lights; and (d) is comfortable with movement in space.

3. *Language:* (a) understands sentences with two or more ideas (e.g., "You can have a cookie when we get home."); (b) understands directions with two or more ideas; (c) organizes sentences with two or more ideas (e.g., "Want apple and banana"); and (d) refers to self using a pronoun.

4. *Cognitive:* (a) can point to some pictures from a verbal description; (b) can name objects in a picture; (c) can make a train of blocks after seeing one in a picture; and (d) can repeat two or more numbers.

## Emotional thinking

By 36 months, ideas dealing with complex intentions, wishes, and feelings in pretend play or other types of symbolic communication are logically tied to one another. The child can differentiate between what is real and what is not, and switches back and forth between fantasy and reality with little difficulty.

*Primary emotional capacities*

1. Pretend play, however unrealistic, involves two or more ideas that are logically tied to one another (e.g., "The car is visiting the moon [and gets there] by flying fast."). In addition, the child can build on an adult's pretend play idea (i.e., close a circle of communication). For example, the child is cooking soup and when an adult asks, "What is in it?" the child says, "Rocks and dirt" or "Ants and spiders."

2. Symbolic communication involves two or more ideas that are logically connected and grounded in reality: "No go to sleep." "Want to watch television." "Why?" asks the adult. "Because not tired." The child can close symbolic circles of communication (e.g., child says, "Want to go outside." Adult asks, "What will you do?" Child replies, "Play.").

*Emotional range—sensorimotor*

Logically connecting two or more ideas, can communicate symbolically concerning intentions, wishes, needs, or feelings using the following:

1. Words.

2. Complex gestures and facial expressions (e.g., pretending to be an angry dog or cat).

3. Touch (e.g., lots of hugging or roughhousing as part of pretend drama where child is the "daddy").

4. Spatial and motor games with rules that child can organize (e.g., takes turns going up small incline, or holds hands with others and goes around in a circle).

*Emotional range—affective*

Can use pretend play or words to communicate themes containing two or more logically connected ideas dealing with the following:

1. Closeness or dependency (e.g., doll gets hurt and mommy doll fixes it).

2. Pleasure and excitement (e.g., says "bathroom words" like "doody" and laughs).

3. Assertiveness and exploration (e.g., good soldiers search for missing princess).

4. Cautious or fearful behavior (e.g., scary monster scares baby doll).

5. Anger (e.g., good soldiers fight bad ones).

6. Limit setting (e.g., soldiers can only hit bad guys because of the "rules").

7. Use of pretend play to recover from anger (e.g., plays out eating the cookie he could not get in reality).

*Selected associated motor, sensory, language, and cognitive capacities not included above*

1. *Motor:* (a) walks upstairs alternating feet; (b) catches big ball; (c) kicks big ball; (d) jumps forward; (e) hops; (f) copies circle; (g) cuts paper; and (h) can unbutton buttons.

2. *Sensory:* (a) enjoys or tolerates various types of touch (e.g., cuddling, roughhousing, touching different types of clothing, brushing teeth or hair); (b) is comfortable with loud sounds; (c) is comfortable with bright lights; and (d) is comfortable with movement in space.

3. *Language:* (a) understands and constructs logical bridges between ideas with full sentences; (b) uses "but" and "because"; (c) answers "what," "who," "where," and "what are you doing" questions; (d) comprehends actions/verbs; (e) uses plurals; and (f) uses two prepositions.

4. *Cognitive:* (a) engages in pretend play that has logical structure (i.e., pretend ideas are connected); (b) perceives spatial designs as complex and interrelated (i.e., a house made of blocks has connected rooms); (c) identifies "big" and "little" as part of developing a quantitative perspective; and (d) can identify objects by their function as part of developing abstract groupings.

## Forty-two to 48 months

By 42 to 48 months, the child is capable of elaborate, complex, pretend play and symbolic types of communication dealing with complex intentions, wishes, or feelings. The play or direct communication is characterized by three or more ideas that are logically connected and that reflect an understanding of causality, time, and space.

*Primary emotional capacities*

1. Elaborates on complex, partially planned pretend play with three or more logically connected ideas dealing with intentions, wishes, or feelings. The planned quality (e.g., a special car is used) and "how," "why," or "when" elaborations give depth to the drama (e.g., child sets up castle with an evil queen who captured the princess. "Why did she capture the princess?" "Because the princess was more beautiful." "When did she capture her?" "Yesterday." "How will the princess get out?" "You ask too many questions.").

2. Participates in reality-based, circle-closing symbolic conversation using three or more ideas dealing with intentions, wishes, or feelings. In a reality-based dialogue, the child can deal with causality. ("Why did you hit your brother?" "Because he took my toy." "Any other reason?" "He took my cookie.")

3. Distinguishes reality from fantasy (e.g., "That's only pretend." "That's a dream. It's not real.").

4. Uses concepts of time and space to deal with intentions, wishes, or feelings. Caregiver: "Where should we look for the toy you can't find?" Child: "Let's look in my room. I was playing with it there." Caregiver: "When do you want the cookies?" Child: "Now." Caregiver: "Not now; maybe in five minutes." Child: "No. Want it now!" Caregiver: "You can have the cookie in one, two, or five minutes." Child: "Okay. One minute."

*Emotional range—sensorimotor*

The child is able to use elaborate, complex, logically connected ideas (three or more) and communicate using:

1. Words.

2. Complex gestures and facial expressions (e.g., giving someone a dirty look, observing to see if they react, and giving them an even angrier look if they haven't apologized, and soon!).

3. Touch (e.g., giving caregiver a back rub, looking longingly into her eyes and smiling, and then asking for a new toy).

4. Spatial and motor games with rules that child can organize (e.g., can partially play baseball or basketball).

*Emotional range—affective*

The child is able to use elaborate, complex, logically connected ideas (three or more) when dealing with:

1. Closeness or dependency (e.g., doll gets hurt and mommy doll fixes it, and doll goes to party and meets prince).

2. Pleasure and excitement (e.g., says "bathroom words" like "doody" and laughs, and then goes and says words to caregiver, looking for her to laugh or get mad).

3. Assertiveness and exploration (e.g., good soldiers search for missing princess and find her, but have to battle with evil soldiers to save her).

4. Cautious or fearful behavior (e.g., scary monster scares baby doll, who hides under covers and then gets up and hits monster).

5. Anger (e.g., good soldiers fight bad ones and use secret bombs and rockets to defeat enemy).

6. Limit setting. Child can now set limits for himself or herself by reasoning about consequences (e.g., using ideas causally and in time framework: "If I am bad now, I will be punished later."). Even though he or she does not always follow them, child now is able to understand rules in terms of limits. Child can also form abstract principles. "You shouldn't be mean to them."

7. Separation and loss. Child can now picture Mom at home while he or she is at school, or in waiting room while he or she is in office, and can relate some feelings of sadness and loss (e.g., "She is in the waiting room. I miss her a little, but I am having fun.").

*Selected associated motor, sensory, language, and cognitive capacities not included above*

1. *Motor:* (a) skips; (b) hops; (c) rides tricycle; (d) catches ball; (e) bounces ball; (f) shows hand preference; (g) copies cross; (h) strings beads; and (i) cuts across a line.

2. *Sensory:* (a) enjoys or tolerates various types of touch (e.g., cuddling, roughhousing, touching different types of clothing, brushing teeth or hair); (b) is comfortable with loud sounds; (c) is comfortable with bright lights; and (d) is comfortable with movement in space.

3. *Language:* (a) comprehends complex "why" questions, such as "Why do we need a house?"; (b) can express ideas reflecting an understanding of relative degrees of feeling expressing wish or intention: "I am only a little mad."; (c) can repeat a five- to ten-word sentence; and (d) can repeat four to seven numbers.

4. *Cognitive:* (a) can point to pictures that show an object with attributes that are first described verbally (e.g., "What do you eat with?" "What makes food?"); (b) can deal with concepts of quantity (e.g., "Which is biggest?" "Which box has more marbles in it?"); (c) can identify similarities and differences among shapes and verbal concepts (e.g., triangle and rectangle, or people and animals); and (d) can recall and comprehend experiences from recent past.

## General tendencies (regulatory patterns): All ages

1. The infant is able to be calm and/or calm down, and not be excessively irritable, clinging, active, or panicked.

2. The infant is able to calm down and take an interest in sights, sounds, and people, and is not excessively withdrawn, apathetic, or unresponsive.

3. The infant is able to focus his or her attention and not be excessively distractible.

4. The infant enjoys a range of sounds—high and low pitched, loud and soft—and different rhythms, and is not upset or confused by sounds.

5. The infant enjoys various sights, including reasonably bright lights, visual designs, facial gestures, and moving objects, and is not upset or confused by various sights.

6. The infant enjoys being touched (on face, arms, legs, stomach, trunk, and back), as well as bathed and clothed, and is not bothered by things touching his or her skin.

7. The infant enjoys movement in space (being held and moved up and down and from side to side), does not get upset with movement, and does not crave excessive movement.

8. The infant is able to maintain motor tone and carry out age-appropriate motor planning sequences (e.g., put fist in mouth, reach for object).

9. The infant enjoys a range of age-appropriate foods and is not bothered (e.g., with abdominal pains, skin rashes, irritability, or other symptoms) by any age-appropriate, healthy food as part of a balanced diet.

10. The infant is comfortable and asymptomatic around household odors and materials, and is not bothered by ordinary levels of household odors, such as cleaning materials, paint, oil or gas fumes, pesticides, plastics, composite woods (e.g., plywood), or synthetic fabrics (e.g., polyester).

If the rating is less than "present at all times under all circumstances" for any of the above, also rate the items below.

1. Infant tends to be hypersensitive or overly sensitive to:

    a. Touch (light or heavy).

    b. Sound (high pitch, low pitch, or loud).

    c. Sights (bright lights).

    d. His own movement in space (e.g., being moved horizontally or vertically).

    e. Smells (e.g., ordinary household odors, perfumes).

2. Infant tends to be hyposensitive, or undersensitive (i.e., does not respond to sensations and may crave them) to:

    a. Touch.

    b. Sound.

    c. Sights.

    d. Movement in space.

    e. Smells.

(Note that an infant may have a mixture of hypersensitivities and hyposensitivities.)

3. Infant tends to have difficulty processing, organizing (making sense of), or sequencing:

a. Sounds (e.g., 3-year-old having difficulty following two simple directions, such as "Take the glass, and put it in the sink.").

b. Sights (e.g., 3-year-old having difficulty identifying or copying a design like a circle).

c. His or her own motor pattern (e.g., tying shoes).

## General caregiver patterns (obtained through history and/or direct observation)

An infant or young child may have several important caregivers, including parents, other family members, and regular child care providers. If possible, the clinician should talk with each important caregiver and observe him or her in interaction with the child, noting the amount of time the caregiver spends with the child (e.g., father, three hours a day; primary child care provider, eight hours a day weekdays).

The following patterns tend to facilitate development:

1. *Caregiver tends to comfort the infant,* especially when he or she is upset, by methods such as relaxed, gentle, or firm holding, or rhythmic vocal or visual contact.

2. *Caregiver tends to find appropriate levels of stimulation to interest the infant in the world* by being interesting, alert, and responsive, including offering appropriate levels of sound, sights, and touch (including the caregiver's face) and appropriate items such as games and toys.

3. *Caregiver tends to pleasurably engage the infant in a relationship* through actions such as looking, vocalizing, and gentle touching.

4. *Caregiver tends to read and respond to the infant's emotional signals and needs in most emotional areas* (e.g., responds to desire for closeness as well as child's need to be assertive, explorative, and independent).

5. *Caregiver tends to encourage the infant to move forward in development:*

a. The caregiver helps the baby to crawl, vocalize, and gesture by actively responding to the infant's initiative and encouragement (rather than overanticipating the infant's needs and doing everything for him or her).

b. The caregiver helps the toddler make the shift from proximal, physical dependency (e.g., being held) to feeling more secure while being independent (e.g., keeps in verbal and visual contact with the toddler as he or she builds a tower on the other side of the room).

c. The caregiver helps the 2- to 3-year-old child shift from motor discharge and gestural ways of relating to the use of ideas through encouraging pretend play (imagination) and language around emotional themes (e.g., gets down on the floor and plays out dolls hugging each other, dolls separating from each other, or soldiers fighting with each other).

d. The caregiver helps the 3- to 4-year-old take responsibility for behavior and deal with reality, rather than "giving in all the time," infantilizing, or being overly punitive.

The caregiver characteristics described above cover a number of developmentally based adaptive patterns. If, in considering these patterns, the clinician observes that they are not observable most of the time, it may be useful to observe interaction to determine if, and under what circumstances, the caregiver tends to be:

1. Overly stimulating.

2. Withdrawn or unavailable.

3. Lacking pleasure, enthusiasm, or zest.

4. Random or chaotic in reading or responding to signals (e.g., vocalizes and interacts, but without regard for infant's signals, by pinching, poking, or "revving baby up").

5. Fragmented and/or insensitive to context (e.g., responds to one part of infant's communication but misses the "bigger pattern," as when caregiver gets excessively upset and hugs active toddler who accidentally banged his or her leg while trying to run and obviously wants to keep exploring the room).

6. Overly rigid and controlling. Tries to get the child to conform to rigid agenda (e.g., insists that toddler only play with a toy one way).

7. Concrete in reading or responding to communication (e.g., unable to tune into symbolic level in pretend play or in dialogue, and, instead, keeps communication at behavioral and gestural levels. For example, a child is pretending with a toy telephone that he will not talk to his mother. The mother perceives this as a literal sign of rejection and refuses to "play any more.").

8. Illogical in reading or responding to infant's communication (e.g., caregiver is so flooded with emotion that he or she misreads what is communicated. A 3-and-a-half-year-old says, "I am scared of the monster, but I know it is just make believe." The caregiver explains, "Monsters will never get into the room because the door has a big lock on it, and monsters can be nice, too. You know you shouldn't play with these toys anyhow, and how did you get that scratch on your hand?").

9. Avoidant of selected emotional area(s) (e.g., in pretend play, parent ignores child's interest in aggression and always ignores separation themes). The clinician should consider which of the following emotional areas seem to be troublesome: (a) security and safety; (b) dependency; (c) pleasure and excitement; (d) assertiveness and exploration; (e) aggression; (f) love; (g) empathy; and (h) limit setting.

10. Unstable in the face of intense emotion (e.g., caregiver can facilitate development only if emotions are not too intense. If strong emotions are expressed, the caregiver's behavior tends to become chaotic, unpredictable, withdrawn, or overly rigid).

## Suggestions for eliciting the infant's emotional and developmental capacities

To learn about the infant's emotional and developmental capacities, observe 15 to 20 minutes or more of free interaction between the infant and caregiver, followed, as needed, by free interaction between the infant and clinician. If the infant or child does not evidence age-expected patterns, the clinician or caregiver may attempt to elicit age-appropriate developmental capacities using some of the suggestions described below. These suggestions are intended only to help get things going. Follow the child's lead to keep the interactions "cooking."

The capacities to be elicited are listed in terms of the six stages of emotional development. Each set of capacities, while usually first in evidence at a certain period in infancy or early childhood, continues as the child grows. The child's current level, as well as the levels he or she may have already mastered, should be observed. When the suggestions below refer only to the age at which a child first masters a particular capacity, the clinician should improvise a way to support that capacity in an older child (e.g., wooing an older child into a relationship with smiles and play rather than with smiles and sounds).

*Capacities related to regulation and interest in the world*

1. Paying attention.

2. Being calm.

3. Experiencing sensation through each sensory modality without being hypersensitive or hyposensitive.

4. Organizing motor movements.

To elicit these capacities, hold baby or put baby in infant seat with mother or father near. Offer baby opportunity to look at caregiver or clinician as one of them offers different types of sensations:

1. *Sights:* Beginning with a six- to eight-foot distance, make funny faces and gradually move closer (no closer than two to three feet). Hold your position for 30 seconds or more, at what appears to be optimal distance, moving slowly a little to the left, and then a little to the right. Then gradually move away. If baby does not clearly look at you for five seconds or more, repeat exercise while shining a light (use a flashlight) on your face. If there is still no response, try again, putting a colorful toy in your mouth (e.g., a rattle).

2. *Sounds:* Experiment with different sounds, beginning with a soft, medium pitch and going higher and lower in pitch (while still soft). Increase loudness two times. Vary pitch at each higher sound level and note if and when baby looks at you for five or more seconds. To be sure baby is looking at you, move a little to the left or right and see if baby follows your voice with his or her eyes.

3. *Touch:* Stroke baby's arms, legs, feet, hands, back, top of head, and, if possible, face and lips with (a) light touch (such as a feathery tickle); (b) medium gentle touch; and (c) gentle firm pressure (a little squeeze or gentle rhythmic massage). Note reactions: no reaction; positive reaction (e.g., pleasure or attentiveness is increased); or negative reaction (e.g., pulling hand away, crying or making sounds suggesting discomfort).

4. *Smell:* If mother wears a cologne or perfume, you can put a little on your finger and put it under baby's nose. Alternatively, use a little lemon juice. Observe calm, pleasurable, focused, or indifferent response versus crying or pulling away.

5. *Movement in space:* While firmly holding baby, gently and slowly move him or her up and down and from side to side,

and then slowly spin around with baby. Gradually increase speed and vigor of each type of movement, but stop and slow down as soon as infant gives any sign of lack of pleasure. Note what types of movement are pleasurable or aversive. Observe if baby craves vigorous movement.

6. *Motor patterns:* As caregiver or clinician holds infant, observe if muscle tone is loose (low) (e.g., infant does not cooperate in the cuddle) or tight (high) so that infant feels overly stiff. See if age-expected motor milestones are being mastered. Make up games in which the infant will be expected to hold up his or her head, turn toward an adult's voice, reach for a toy, and, later on, crawl toward a favorite rattle, to elicit age-appropriate movements. See if baby can plan sequences of movements, such as putting hand in own mouth or systematically examining a new toy. Mom's, Dad's, or the clinician's hair, nose, or hand can be a "toy" as well.

(Note that many of the above capacities can be observed in the free play of the older infant, toddler, or young child.)

*Ability to relate to others*

1. Taking an interest in another person through looking, listening, or moving toward them.

2. Evidencing pleasure in relating to another person through smiles, a joyful look, or just a sense of warm comfort.

3. Seeking out warmth and pleasure with another person through communicating a wish for closeness (e.g., reaching up for a cuddle or jumping into parent's lap, or snuggling warmly).

To elicit these capacities, position yourself near baby (who may be in parent's lap, in infant seat, or on floor). Begin to flirt with and woo baby with interesting facial expressions; warm, inviting sounds; and inviting motor gestures, such as moving face from side to side or back and forth. Be patient and start from eight to ten feet away and move in slowly. If baby seems cautious or concerned, stop moving in and move back and forth, keeping your warm, cooing, funny face, vocalizations, and head movements going. Experiment with the different vocal tones. Also, feel free to put funny toys in your mouth or on your head. Observe if the infant is evidencing signs of relating (e.g., a smile, vocalizations, rhythmic arm and leg movements, reaching out to you and flirting, or just being coy).

For an older child, any type of play may serve as a vehicle for wooing the child with your voice, smiles, touch, or gestural exchanges. Always move in toward the child very slowly, warmly, and sensitively.

*Ability for intentional communication and interaction*

1. Initiating gestures (e.g., smiles, vocalizations, and deliberate motor movements, such as pointing, reaching out to be picked up, covering face).

2. Responding to caregiver's gestures with gestures (e.g., closing or completing a circle of communication by, for example, exchanging one toy for another or searching for the desired toy, or squeezing Dad's nose after it goes "toot").

To elicit these capacities, place yourself in front of baby on the floor with baby up on all fours, lying on stomach, or sitting. Make sure you are three to six feet away at ground level. Create opportunities for interaction. Put a brightly colored squeezable ball in your hand and offer it to baby. If baby takes it and examines it, hold your hand out and see if he or she will give it back. Support your action with words, "Can I have it back?" Use lots of facial gestures (such as nodding) and animated hand gestures which say, "Give it to me." If baby holds on to it, offer another toy in exchange. If baby will not give up the toy, gently take it out of his or her hand, and slowly hide it under your hand and see if baby takes it back. If baby will not take the toy, try putting the toy in your mouth and move close enough so that he or she can reach it. If necessary, try repeatedly with different toys. While interacting, respond to baby's sounds, facial expressions, or motor gestures with sounds and gestures of your own.

You may substitute other activities for the above as long as you create interactive opportunities (e.g., a peekaboo game).

*Ability for complex interaction and communication*

Initiating and responding in a chain of purposeful interactions requires the opening and closing of many circles of communication in a row. Circles of communication, using gestures, are employed to negotiate basic emotional themes such as closeness, anger, curiosity, exploration, and independence.

To elicit this capacity, begin playing with a real or toy telephone and pretend to talk to someone. See if the child comes over and copies what you are doing or tries to babble on the phone in his or her own way. If the child takes the phone, ask for it back saying, "I want to talk," and see if he or she lets you talk for awhile, and so on. If the child will not give it back to you, flirt with the child, offer an exchange, and, if necessary, gently take it and see if he or she vocalizes or gestures to get it back, or just grabs it back. If the child takes the phone, pick up another phone and see if the child will "talk" with you phone-to-phone.

If the phone will not get the child's attention, put on a silly hat and see if he or she will take it off your head and use it. If the child takes the hat, try to get it back using the methods described above to try to get the phone back.

If neither of the above work, walk around on all fours, pretending to be a horsey, and see if the child rides you. If you make noises, does the child also make them?

If none of these ideas work, follow the strategies described under the heading "Ability for intentional communication and interaction." Feel free to improvise and support complex interactions in other ways as well. The goal is to see if the toddler can close a number of circles of communication in a row.

Strategies for assessing young children's symbolic and representational capacities through observation of free play interaction are discussed by Serena Wieder in her chapter in this volume. This section has described only a few semistructured ways of helping a child demonstrate his or her emotional and developmental capacities. These suggestions should only be used if free play is unsuccessful in eliciting the child's capacities. They only start the process. The clinician or caregiver needs to follow the child's lead and keep the action moving. A judgment can then be made about the child's various emotional and developmental capacities. The above play activities may also be useful in helping the infant or young child practice his or her emerging functional capacities. Clinicians, educators, and caregivers should consider these activities to be examples of the types of activities that help an infant or young child explore his or her relationship with them in a way that supports developmental progress.

# A Developmental Approach to Therapy

A careful assessment of an infant's or young child's level of emotional development within the context of his or her important relationships allows the clinician and family to think about the specific types of developmental experience that will be most helpful to this individual child and family. A therapeutic effort may involve paying attention to the infant's unique constitutional and maturational patterns, caregiver-infant patterns of interaction, and/or the family's feelings and past experiences. Whatever therapeutic approach or combination of approaches is decided upon, however, intervention should not only provide general support, but should also provide highly specific types of experiences, which can only be determined through an understanding of the developmental level—and developmental needs—of the individual child and his or her unique world.

The principles of the developmental approach (to therapy) include the following:

1. Opportunities must be created that assist the child in learning basic developmental capacities. The capacities that learning opportunities must foster include (a) the ability to focus and pay attention; (b) the ability to engage warmly and trustingly with others; (c) the ability to communicate intentionally with both simple and more complex gestures. The gestural level must progress to the point where it can be used to negotiate the basic themes of life, such as dependency, aggression, approval or disapproval, and rejection; (d) the ability to represent or symbolize intentions and feelings, as seen in pretend play or in the functional use of language; and (e) the ability to organize and differentiate represented experience in order to distinguish reality from fantasy, the self from nonself, or one feeling from another feeling, and the temporal and spatial characteristics of representations. Creating learning opportunities to support these core developmental capacities is perhaps the single most important goal of a developmental approach to therapy.

2. The capacities must be supported in *a stable and broad-ranging manner.* At each developmental level, and for each capacity, the child may or may not master age-appropriate emotions and themes at that level (such as warmth, dependency, pleasure, excitement, assertiveness, anger, curiosity, self-limit setting, and, for older children, empathy and more stable forms of love). For example, the child may master two-way communication in terms of dependency, but not assertiveness, curiosity, or aggression. Similarly, the child may master a developmental capacity in a stable way so that it tends to survive even under types of stress, such as a mild physical ailment, a brief separation from a parent, or a strong emotional feeling. Alternatively, even a brief period of stress may under-

mine a capacity so that the child loses it. The goal is to create opportunities to learn the key developmental capacities in a stable, wide-ranging manner that encompasses age-appropriate themes and emotions.

3. Developmental capacities depend on the relationships that caregivers (including therapists and educators) have with infants and young children. Developmental approaches to therapy should foster attention and engagement, two-way communication, and the formation of representational or symbolic capacities.

4. In order to create learning opportunities that foster key developmental capacities, it is important to take into account two contributing factors—the constitutional and maturational aspects of the child's development and the interactive and family aspects of the child's experience. Included are (a) the infant or child-caregiver interaction patterns; (b) the family dynamics; (c) the infant's or child's own constitutional and maturational patterns, including hyposensitivity and hypersensitivity, sensory processing, affective patterns, motor tone, and motor planning; and (d) the infant's or child's own way of organizing experiences. This last category includes the child's physiological, behavioral, or gestural level, and, after age 18 months, his or her representational level, as well as the emergence of conflicts between different tendencies, such as conflicts between the child's assertive and aggressive side and the child's interest in safety, security, and dependency.

According to the developmental approach to therapy with children, the main goal, as indicated, is to facilitate the learning of core developmental capacities. When working with the various contributing factors and when preventing and treating developmental defects and constrictions in order to facilitate these capacities, one needs to understand how each infant and child is unique—the individual differences in the child's maturational and constitutional capacities, the family dynamics, and the interaction patterns between the child and his caregivers. Of course, each family member has his or her own personal dynamics that relate to family experiences while growing up. Therefore, as one works with the core developmental capacities, one is also working with the unique physical and interactive characteristics of the infant or child and his or her family. Thus, a key difference between the developmental approach and more traditional approaches to therapy with children is the degree to which one actively promotes the attainment of core developmental capacities and attempts to overcome various delays or disorders in these capacities.

 References

Greenspan, S. I. (1979). Intelligence and adaptation: An integration of psychoanalytic and Piagetian developmental psychology. *Psychological Issues,* Vol. 12, No. 3/4, Monograph 47/48. New York: International Universities Press.

Greenspan, S. I. (1989). *The development of the ego: Implications for personality theory, psychopathology, and the psychotherapeutic process.* Madison, CT: International Universities Press.

Greenspan, S. I. (1992). *Infancy and early childhood: The practice of clinical assessment and intervention with emotional and developmental challenges.* Madison, CT: International Universities Press

# 13. Climbing the "Symbolic Ladder":

## Assessing Young Children's Symbolic and Representational Capacities through Observation of Free Play Interaction

SERENA WIEDER

The most challenging aspect of using observation of free play interaction to assess a child's overall developmental level is keeping track of multiple lines of development simultaneously. The most important, rewarding, and unique part of such an assessment is the comprehensive, integrated view it provides of the child's day-to-day experiences, the ways in which individual differences affect functioning, and the child's ability to organize the emotions, sensations, and ideas coming from his or her interactions. Unstructured interaction reflects how well the child is able, spontaneously and simultaneously, to use developmental capacities to communicate, relate, and share ideas, themes, and feelings with someone. The young child does this first by pretending to perform "real" actions and then by representing feelings, relationships, ideas, and problem-solving in symbolic ways. These symbolic and representational abilities are essential for development.

Stanley Greenspan's chapter on the Functional Emotional Assessment Scale in this volume presents a framework for assessing young children along multiple lines of development and in terms of the essential processes that organize and integrate experience at different developmental levels. The present chapter will complement his discussion of this developmental framework by focusing on the assessment of symbolic and representational capacities as they are observed in free play interaction. It will also show clinicians how to use observation such as this to help parents and other caregivers create "symbolic opportunities" that will encourage young children to reach higher developmental levels.

## The Beginnings of Symbolic Functioning

Beginning at birth, a baby and parent communicate through a variety of sensory pathways. Looking, listening, moving, touching, and reaching all support the development of mutual attention, engagement, and relatedness. As the infant develops new motor and communicative abilities, interactions become more reciprocal. The baby uses more complex gestures to express desires and signal comprehension. By 1 year of age, the symbolic door is usually open, as the child begins to initiate, imitate, and express ideas and feelings through play and language.

Most infants begin to "pretend" long before they can speak. A baby younger than 1 year may pick up a real or toy telephone and hold it up to his or her face, demonstrating recognition of the instrument whose ringing signal is capable of interrupting all household activity. The next steps in the process of symbolizing involve familiar daily experiences. For example, the infant uses a toy bottle to "feed" himself or herself, a doll, or an animal. Similarly, a toddler might actually try to get onto a toy horse or into a small car as he or she learns what is real and what represents reality. These experiments lead the child to use small figures or animals in reality-based roles and purposeful sequential actions. Simultaneously, children, themselves, try to assume different roles, pretending to be the doctor, mommy or daddy, firefighter, or school bus driver. As development unfolds, children are able to enact longer and more complex ideas and feelings in their play with other children.

It is important to remember that even the simplest use of a pretend object requires numerous sensory and motor pathways or functions, combined with gestures or words retrieved from earlier experiences, to convey comprehension. These abilities usually emerge spontaneously and automatically in the course of typical development. But what seems so easy and natural for most children might be an overwhelming challenge for another child, depending on that child's unique organizational ability to self-regulate and to be calm and attentive enough to the world around him to learn from it.

Observing a young child who is pretending to talk on the telephone, in the context of a relationship with a parent or other important caregiver, reveals the child's ability to initiate and carry out a sequence of symbolic functions. Moreover, observing each sensory or motor pathway involved in this activity allows us to assess the level of organization of the child's functioning. For example, the decision to pick up a toy telephone involves, as a first step, perceiving it—discriminating the object in a visual field and recognizing or remembering its use. Moving toward the telephone and picking it up involve motor planning a sequence of actions and coordinating eyes and hands. These actions require comfort with touch and proprioception, and an awareness of the body's position. Exploring or using the toy in a purposeful way involves memory and imitation, as well as motor planning. Responding to a verbal question such as "Do you want to talk to Daddy?" involves receptive and expressive language processing. The child's affect conveys feelings about the relationship—with Daddy as well as with the questioner.

What should we observe next? The next steps are to note the elaboration of the play and to monitor the degree of reciprocity in the interaction between the child and his partner. What is said? How many circles of communication are opened and closed? How is the play ended? For example, will David keep talking on the phone to Daddy, jabbering or speaking in a "conversation"? Or is his use of the phone limited to an initial gesture and hanging up? Similarly, if Ben first sucks on the pretend bottle or tastes the cupcake, will he then feed the cupcake to the doll? Will he also be able to serve the cupcake to you? If you ask for some cookies, will Ben look for a real cookie or a pretend cookie, will he substitute another object which may not even look like a cookie, or will he just use a gesture to hand you an imaginary cookie? Each of these steps reflects the symbolic use of objects.

Affective desire—wanting to feed you or involve you in nurturing activity—internally prompts and organizes the young child's efforts to play with real, pretend, and imaginary cookies, babies, and animals. This desire derives from the many thousands of interactions he or she has already experienced, in which mutual attention, engagement, and interactive reciprocity were practiced. The delight and pleasure the child experiences in symbolic activity are usually self-evident. When such symbolic sequences and pleasurable emotions are not observed, we need to learn more about what is impeding expected symbolic development.

## ▰ Climbing the Symbolic Ladder: The ▰ Development of Representational Abilities

As the young child moves up the symbolic ladder, his or her play is likely to reflect themes and ideas related to expectable developmental characteristics, such as dependency, body integrity, separation, power, fears, and aggression. Abounding in toddlers' play are themes of personal injury, visits to the doctor, car crashes, ambulances and fire trucks rushing to the rescue, repair jobs, playing family or teacher, monsters, power figures, and good-guy/bad-guy battles. Such themes reflect toddlers' awareness of their own separateness and vulnerability as they strive for more autonomy, as well as their emerging assertiveness and ability to solve problems. As children become more competent, they assume that virtually any feat is within their power. They are Superman or a Power Ranger; they can be anyone and do everything. Eventually, between 3 and 4 years of age, a sense of reality begins to impinge on children. As they adapt to reality, they can only pretend to be powerful in play. This adaptation is no easy task. Fortunately, the symbolic world continues to provide a safe place in which children (and adults) can experiment—as the sense of self and personhood develops—with life's major relationships and the central themes of dependency, assertiveness, and aggression.

As children grow, their play will involve longer sequences of action and verbalization, which are organized around affective experiences or motifs and have a beginning, middle, and end. The play expresses feelings and relationships between characters, both animate and inanimate. In some cases, the object a child sees and his or her associations with it will provide a play idea. In other cases, the child's own experiences, thoughts, or wishes will lead to the search for specific props or to the assigning of roles so that an experience can be recreated.

A child on the lowest rungs of the symbolic ladder will just plunge in and begin to act out his or her drama, such as going to a restaurant, being punished for misbehaving, or riding in a car on a highway. Later, the child may be able to abstract, describe, and direct the drama, discussing who everyone should be and what will happen. The child will also eventually reflect upon the play. When a child is not led into the drama or told what to do, and is free to develop his or her own ideas, the child will project his or her subjective experiences, wishes, and concerns in play. Observing this process allows us to understand the child's internal experiences, how much of life the child can embrace, his or her concerns, and how he or she is attempting to cope—in ways both "magical" and realistic—with an expanding sense of reality.

## Symbolic Processes

A child who is operating on the higher rungs of the symbolic ladder is able to integrate pretend play actions that imitate real life experiences with mental understanding, or thinking, a process that is driven or motivated by intense feeling. Some children may be capable of these higher levels of symbolism but do not exhibit them spontaneously. These children require the interest and questions of an adult or another child in order to express themselves. Some children begin to play prompted by a prop, rather than an idea, but they will expand their play if encouraged to do so by even simple responses. For example, "What else do you have to eat? I don't like tea!" "Do you have anything for the baby? She's crying!" "Uh oh, no more left? Oh, you are the best baker in town!" "What did you say the bad guys did? Why?"

Such questions or comments, from the most open-ended to the most specific, challenge the child to think symbolically and to solve the "problem" in the context of any emotional reactions they may feel. To respond to your question, the child might think of another offer of food or drink (categorize), find another reason for the baby's crying (she's hurt, not hungry), react to your rejection of his or her offer (there is only tea, and you must have it), pretend to go to the store to get something else, beam with delight and offer you more, or tell you that robbers stole everything and there is nothing left for you. The child may use other props, substitutions, or just words or gestures to respond. Sometimes a child will tune you out or avoid you because he or she is not pleased or simply does not know what to do next.

The child's elaboration of the play reflects how flexible, organized, and logical his or her ideas can be. As the child develops a more complex sense of self, his or her play will become more complex and elaborate, communicating his or her intentions, recognition of others, and abilities to abstract social rules. Observations of the play and its conversations will reveal which parts of the child's personality have access to these ideational forms, that is, what range of emotions the child can negotiate through symbolic ideas. In assessing the child's emotional thinking, the observer looks for the child's ability to connect one idea with another and to explain cause and effect. Is the child becoming more logical and separating make-believe from reality? Can the child express his or her understanding of the consequences of actions through ideas as well as behavior? Does the child's emotional thinking strengthen his impulse control, help him feel good about himself, and increase his empathy for others? Or does the child repeat the same theme again and again in play, suggesting specific unresolved concerns? For example, the wind and lightning (uncontrollable forces which cannot be blamed) blow the castle down again and again, then the houses, and then the garage, with many getting hurt (body damage fears).

How well does the child express themes and feelings? When observing a child's play, we should not simply identify the theme but should examine the range, complexity, and flexibility of the child's symbolic thinking and feeling. Is the child developing a "story," that is, a sequence of related ideas? Are the ideas logical, demonstrating an understanding of cause and effect? Are there multiple roles or characters involved? Are feelings expressed, and are they related to the actions? Does the child direct the story or elaborate on his or her ideas only upon questioning? Does the child avoid feelings or issues that would ordinarily be related to a story he or she started? Does the child avoid treading on certain areas of experience?

As the child climbs the symbolic ladder, greater elaboration and range are to be expected in play. The representation of normal anxieties in play, for example, is related to the child's increasing understanding of reality and use of logical thinking. As the child moves from level to level, he or she moves from play involving a single schema or the repetition of a schema (e.g., more tea and more cookies, or more cars lined up on the road) to play linking more and more ideas together. Each idea and its elaboration reflect the complexity of the child's thoughts and feelings, as well as the child's ability to cope with the challenge he or she has imagined or that a playmate has presented. In this process, the child moves from magical thinking to logical causes and solutions.

The progression of play ideas below, beginning with simple play involving a toy car and extending to a drama of the ultimate encounter between the forces of good and evil, could be observed as a child and a parent or friend play with toy cars. At first, the child might bridge two ideas, then three, then four or more, including consequences of actions and feelings in the script, as well as reasons or motives for the actions. Since the play is based on the child's projections or inner prompts, it represents the child's concerns, feelings, and ability to organize his or her experience at various representational levels (see Greenspan, this volume). Each time you identify a new stage of elaboration in the play, note the child's affects and verbal expressions as well as how the parent or playmate joins in the play (e.g., facilitates, interrupts, changes, or overwhelms the drama):

- Pushes car back and forth, watching its movement;
- Adds more cars, same or different types;
- Rolls car(s) down ramp again and again; perhaps races cars;
- Crashes cars (again and again);
- Stops cars for red light or stop sign, or to get gas;
- Puts drivers in cars and creates a drama centered on the drivers (policemen, mommies) rather than on the vehicles;
- Has drivers go to a specific destination (to do something); involves others in the story;
- Crashes car and breaks it; deals with effects by saying car is "better" (magical thinking; saying so makes it so!);
- Calls for help after a crash or breakdown; tow truck comes; goes to garage with tow truck; repairs car or needs new car; feels happy, sad, angry;
- Calls ambulance for help because someone is hurt in the crash; goes to hospital; doctor examines hurt people; calls family; hurt people get better or "die"; feels better, scared, sad;
- Crash caused by lion that escaped from the zoo; lion runs all around until captured; scares the children; turns out to be the Lion King;
- Crash caused by monsters hiding in the cars; child scares them away, but they come back;
- Ticket issued to speeding driver, who is sent for driving lessons;

• Crash caused by fleeing robber; Daddy chases and jails robbers; Daddy was scared/was brave/was powerful.

Interactive play provides the best chance to observe a child's highest level of symbolic functioning. In this kind of play, ideas are expressed and a child's responses to the other player's input can be observed as well. Some children control all the roles in a drama when they play; they want the other person to be merely a passive observer, although they may be willing to answer questions or change their stories in response to observer's comments. These children are able to elaborate on their story and enter new territory, as long as they maintain control over the emerging story. Other children are more flexible; they can integrate another person who follows their lead into the play, even enjoying the challenge of the unexpected. These children are able to think on their feet quickly enough to maintain control of the story. Still other children may be much more self-absorbed, uninterested, or unable to share their play with others. When children in play can elaborate on all the roles (the good guys and the bad guys) comfortably and can put themselves in different shoes without feeling too threatened or defensive, they are reaching the highest developmental levels of representational differentiation. They have acquired humanity's most powerful tool for absorbing, understanding, and giving meaning to—and sometimes transforming into art—all the experiences of life.

## ■ Developmental Obstacles to Interaction and ■ Play

Many young children who come to a professional for developmental assessment have difficulties interacting or playing. Indeed, these difficulties may be the source of the family's or caregiver's concern about the child. The developmental problems underlying a child's difficulties with interaction or play may be complex. The following brief descriptions of observations of children between 2-and-a-half and 3 years of age interacting with their parents illustrate the ways in which underlying problems reveal themselves in free play. These descriptions show how observation of free play interaction allows one to form impressions of the child's emotional, social, cognitive, language, sensory, and motor functional capacities. The descriptions also illustrate ways of encouraging interaction between the child and parents to provide opportunities for the child to reveal the highest levels of symbolic functioning of which he or she is capable, and to suggest directions for further assessment and possible intervention.

Steve is lying on his tummy with his face about one inch from the Thomas trains he is moving back and forth. One of the cars uncouples. Steve squeals in frustration as he restores the line of cars he had carefully assembled and again moves them back and forth. The trains go nowhere, but he stares intently at them, only occasionally naming the different cars or muttering something about a tunnel. Steve's parents sit nearby. They appear reluctant to join in the play. If Steve disrupts his own line of trains by mistake or if there is any attempt to touch or move his line, he responds with ferocious rage and crying. Steve ignores any comments about the trains, although he will, from time to time, mutter a phrase from the script of a video of one of the Thomas stories or even echo a word or two from the observer's question. Steve is oblivious to all the other toys in the playroom, having found the trains through his "personal radar." He pays no attention to his parents or the observer. Although he does not answer any questions, when he is told it is time to leave at the end of the session, he begins to screech in protest.

This brief observation reveals the functional level of various developmental capacities and suggests several concerns which should be followed by specific assessments.

### Sensorimotor functioning, muscle tone, and motor planning

Steve has very low muscle tone and seeks the support of the ground because he is unable to maintain upright posture for long periods. On his feet, he will jump constantly, seeking to increase his muscle tone. The fact that Steve lines the trains up and can only move them back and forth in a straight line suggests significant motor-planning difficulties; he cannot sequence other actions to elaborate on his ideas. He is both underreactive and overreactive to sensations and feelings; his regulatory and organizational abilities are quickly stressed.

### Visual processing

Steve's use of vision also appears very constricted as he narrows his visual field and looks so closely at his trains. When more upright, he clearly depends on peripheral vision to negotiate space; he rarely looks directly at objects or people, but he finds what he wants. As he makes his way toward something in the room, Steve steps on everything that is on the floor in his path, appearing oblivious to where his feet are in space. Steve does notice change, reacting vehemently if something he has established is moved or done differently.

### Auditory processing and language

It is evident that Steve has some expressive language, for he names the trains and mutters words he has memorized from a videotape script which he has seen and heard countless times. However, Steve does not respond to what is said to him at any given moment—to words that change and are unpredictable. In other words, his receptive abilities appear to depend upon repeated experiences. The fact that Steve echoes certain words which are meaningful to him suggests that receptive and expressive functions are available, but in very limited ways. Steve appears to learn through music. He is attentive to selective videos and books which provide scripts he can understand, but he cannot process spontaneous language.

### Cognition

It is difficult to assess Steve's cognitive capacity because his range of play behavior is so narrow and his motor-planning and auditory-processing difficulties limit what he can show us. At the same time, several specific observations during the free play suggest no reason to think that Steve may have cognitive limitations. We should remember Steve's interest in the Thomas series of stories and his attempts to replicate some of the scenes from a book and video in his line-up of trains; his good memory for these scenes; his "antennae" or visual discrimination for highly desired objects; and the language capacities noted above.

### Emotional development

Steve requires "total" control over his trains (even though he can do no more than push them back and forth across a small space) because they represent something he both loves and understands. His severe defensiveness is secondary to his auditory-processing difficulties. Because Steve cannot comprehend and express himself consistently, he has turned to a world he can manage, and he guards it, ferociously rejecting any interference by others. Many of Steve's behavioral difficulties are, in turn, secondary to his defensiveness. He becomes overwhelmed by too much sensory input in crowded environments. He is unwilling to give up what he knows (although he is very repetitive and self-absorbed) for what he does not understand and cannot predict. Steve is clearly attached to his parents and very vigilant concerning their whereabouts. He is ready to leap after them if he thinks they will leave and turns to them to help him get what he cannot reach.

## Social development

Steve is only observed with his parents, who must work very hard to interact with him. He would clearly have difficulty communicating or playing symbolically with other children at this time. His parents report that he will sometimes join other children in the playground and take his turn, but he retreats if someone bumps against him.

## Developmental level

Steve has not developed age-expected capacities for mutual attention or engagement. He relies mostly on simple gestures to fiercely communicate his desires and is still unable to organize more complex interactive communication. While his range of affects and ideas is very narrow, the symbolic door is open. Although he is unable to elaborate on it, Steve does use fragments of a script he has memorized.

While these simple observations already suggest further areas for assessment and treatment, it is important to first take the observation to the next level, that is, to challenge Steve to interact and communicate. The parents can be coached to challenge him, or the examiner can do it directly. The approach should be gentle and friendly. The following scenario illustrates possible next steps that you, as the examiner, can take with Steve:

Ask Steve's mother or father to get down on the floor in front of Steve, sit as close as they can to him, and say "Hi" to each of his trains. If the trains uncouple, quickly help Steve fix the line or hand him the dislodged trains to indicate that you are there to help him do what he wants to do. If you dislodge the line somehow, quickly say you are sorry and help him fix it. If Steve accepts these gestures, you might wonder aloud if the last train should go in front, and move it to the head of the line. If he objects, express your sorrow and move it back, "Oh no, was I wrong?" The purpose of expressing these feelings is to convey in a nonthreatening tone your understanding that his arrangement is very important and has meaning to him. While Steve may not comprehend your specific words, the tone of your voice and your slow gestures will register. Even if your initial moves are only to restore his order of the trains (which you may have "accidentally" bumped into), he is beginning to interact with you. If the parent recognizes the fragments of the script Steve is repeating, he or she might try to elaborate on these, perhaps providing a tunnel for the trains.

As Steve becomes more secure with the interaction, you will be able to assess his understanding of any elaborations of the play (which he may not be able to initiate because of motor-planning difficulties). For example, the parent might be encouraged to find the conductor, or add passengers or animals to the train. See if Steve allows this or tries to help. Again, it is important to remember that even if Steve undoes everything you attempt and becomes angry, you are opening and closing circles of communication. The longer these go on, the more mutual attention and engagement develop. While the intention is not to push a child like Steve to total disorganization, if the child does break down in protest over your moves, observe the child's resilience, what it takes to recover (e.g., soothing words, being helped, restoring the previous order, being held and rocked), and whether the child can resume playing.

Several features of Steve's play are frequently seen among children who are referred for developmental assessment, and these features are often misinterpreted. Steve's use of words memorized from a script, for example, is similar to other children's use of alphabet letters and sequences of numbers, which are reassuring because they do not change and look the same in many contexts. Despite his severe auditory-processing difficulties, Steve can enjoy the Thomas video because the visual input, music, and emotional tension in the story "carry" the words. What is most important is that Steve has been able to watch the video repeatedly; he has learned what comes next and can finally recognize certain words in this context. He can use symbolic ideas within the constraints of this script. However, Steve's auditory-processing difficulties prevent him from understanding any changes in the script (he would protest or panic if any alterations were attempted) or from using the same words or phrases meaningfully in any other context.

Since Steve does not move the trains around or pursue the destinations he can express through rote memory of the video script, it is evident that he also has severe motor-planning difficulties. He cannot sequence the movements required to have the trains go anywhere or do anything. Children with motor-planning difficulties often line things up again and again in a horizontal line; they simply do not know how else to move or use the objects. Moreover, these "line-ups" represent children's attempts to understand and control the world the best way they know how. Therefore, any disruption of the lines threatens their security, causes them to become quite upset, and is likely to trigger an emotional storm. If a child has auditory-processing as well as motor-planning difficulties, he will not be able to understand an adult's or playmate's explanation for making a change.

When a child like Steve has a combination of sensory-processing and motor-planning difficulties, it is impossible to predict his future symbolic abilities until he receives treatment for these difficulties. The purpose of challenging him through the interaction is to assess his current responsiveness and test possible intervention approaches. The interactional approach is also a way to insure that the assessment process itself is an intervention since it supports the parents' primary role in treatment, as well as in daily caregiving, by helping them to create symbolic opportunities for their child. Steve is having difficulty climbing the symbolic ladder now, but with appropriate help he may reach the highest rungs.

Jenny's eyes dart about the playroom. She appears to be frantically looking for something familiar. She notices some baskets filled with small toys and rushes over to dump one of the baskets on the floor. She reaches along the shelf for a second basket before her mother can stop her. As her mother says "No!" again and again, Jenny backs away but then wanders over to the table and throws down the tea set, not, however, before glancing at her mother in the mirror behind the table. I ask Jenny's mother to try to turn her random flight into a familiar "I'm going to get you" game, which might help this little girl organize and get comfortable. Jenny responds to the chase game and even begins to play peekaboo behind the curtains of the window.

Jenny moves toward the baskets once again. This time, I give her mother an empty basket and suggest that she encourage Jenny to dump the full basket into the empty one, guiding her hands to do so. At first, Jenny does not appear to be happy with this idea, but when she realizes that she is not being stopped from dumping (one of the few actions she can purposefully accomplish), she begins to go along with it, letting her mother guide the dumping back and forth a few times. Since dumping now has a new meaning—neither expressing the anxiety she felt when she first came in, nor providing a familiar way to provoke (and thus engage) her mother—Jenny looks around for something else to do. She finds some Koosh balls to throw. Again, the basket is employed by her mother to catch the balls, and Jenny's mother gives her back a ball to throw again. As the interaction continues and is given new meanings by her mother's surprising response, Jenny actually seems to smile.

Finally, Jenny seizes upon some silly putty, clutching it secretively so that she can taste it. Instead of asking Jenny's mother to grab it away, I ask her to make the putty into "spaghetti" to eat and to tell Jenny she will help her pull it into strands. Mother and daughter begin to pull long strands of "spaghetti" back and forth, again engaging interactively. When Mom pretends to eat some spaghetti and offers some to Jenny, Jenny imitates eating also and does not actually put the silly putty in her mouth. Next, Mom puts silly putty in a cup and "drinks" it. When she offers a cup of putty to Jenny, Jenny also imitates drinking. Throughout this observation, the only sounds Jenny makes are a few squeals.

Jenny appears bright, quick, and aware. Her provocative behavior reveals her vigilance and desire to pursue interaction with other people. She is also able to respond quickly to new meanings given by others to her behavior. Jenny clearly has severe auditory-processing and motor-planning difficulties. She uses no expressive language, her receptive abilities are unclear, and she has very few purposeful actions in her repertoire, depending primarily on dumping and throwing. The symbolic door does appear open as she imitates drinking from the cup, even though she knows there is only putty in it. On the other hand, her response might just be an automatic gesture in response to seeing a familiar cup. This will have to be explored further. While somewhat excitable and frantic in her movements, Jenny is not primarily aimless or perseverative.

The most important finding from this observation is that Jenny is "tuned in." She can be resourceful, using the gestures she has available. She also appears quite intelligent, testing the environment as a way of understanding it. She is also cognizant of change and flexible enough to respond to change.

Both Jenny and Steve have multiple processing difficulties but different types of regulatory disorders (see ZERO TO THREE's *Diagnostic Classification of Mental Health and Developmental Disorders of Infancy and Early Childhood*, 1994). Steve is locked into his routines and afraid of change, and is therefore quite limited in his adaptability. Jenny can be much more flexible and curious about the world; she can adapt to a new place and situation if given enough space and time to size it up.

Twenty-seven-month-old Max looks around the playroom cautiously. Although he does not speak, he is vigilant and wary. Max's father says, "Max, look at the tow truck!" Max does not look at the tow truck, although he does back away from a basket of jungle animals he has just noticed. His father tries to interest him in a few other toys, but Max shows no interest, not even bothering to reject the toys. He roams the playroom a bit, reaching down to touch some toys. He clearly recognizes the airport with its planes and cars and the basketball net, but he does not initiate play or respond to his father, who mutters, "How can we play if you keep moving away?"

Finally, Max breaks into a smile when his dad pulls two swords from a shelf, says, "Okay, Peter Pan, I'll get you!" and hands Max a sword. The level of engagement "soars" as Max and his dad start a familiar swordfight. Still, Max shows little pleasure in the game and keeps turning away, this time looking into the mirror. Fascinated with his own image, he tries to continue the swordfight without looking away from the mirror. He responds intermittently to his father's calls.

After a few minutes of repetitive play, I suggest that the father put his sword down on the floor, rather than call Max again and again. Within two seconds, Max picks up his father's sword and thrusts it at him. Within less than a minute, however, Max is again swinging the sword aimlessly as he looks in the mirror. This time, Dad hands Max his sword. Max is taken aback, shakes his head "No," and hands the sword back to his father, watching him more carefully now. I encourage the father to keep surprising Max. Dad drops the sword behind the couch, hides it behind the curtain, holds it by the blade, and puts it through a slinky. With each of his dad's actions, Max glowers at his father as if to say, "What are you doing??? How dare you??" Nevertheless, each time the game takes a new turn, Max rushes to find the sword and gives it back to his father, insisting that he play as he usually does! It is quickly apparent that Max has figured out this new "game." The child who appeared so aimless and remote only a few minutes earlier first registers shock, then anger, then insistence, and finally pleasure as he chases his father and they happily communicate. It is important to note that in a formal developmental assessment Max is found to be mentally retarded and autistic.

What does the swordfight tell us about Max's developmental level? Max's father tells us that Max has had some experience with swordplay since he has watched his sisters engaging in this activity, seen Peter Pan on video, and tried the activity at home. However, for Max, the swordfight does not yet represent two opponents fighting over a cause; rather, it is sensorimotor, interactive play which totally engages and pleasurably connects Max and his father. The swordfight also shows us that Max has sufficient motor coordination to actually hit his father's sword (when he is not intrigued with his own image in the mirror or "lost in space"). Max's pursuit of the sword each time his father hides it shows us how smart, quick, purposeful, attentive, and persistent Max can be in a game he understands and feels safe with. Max is at his best when challenged again and again. He responds cleverly, if not verbally.

A second observation reveals additional abilities. Max's earlier wanderings around the playroom suggested that he was interested in toys representing experiences he had already had. The "Peter Pan" swordfight indicated that he was attentive to stories with symbolic content. At this second visit, Max and his dad repeat the swordfighting scene, engaging more quickly and gleefully with each another, but this time the father can also draw Max's attention to related characters and props, getting Max to briefly explore the pirate figures and swords and put them on the pirate ship. Max also finds the planes and cars again. Although he still does not respond to any verbal comments his father makes, Max moves his vehicles purposefully from place to place, avoiding his father's cars when they come toward him on a collision course.

These observations reveal some of Max's very important strengths. He is curious and able to explore. Discriminating objects quickly, he spontaneously manipulates them, both examining and combining them, suggesting adequate motor planning (later also seen in his ability to imitate others' actions) and hand-eye coordination (also seen in his swordfight). Furthermore, Max has clear symbolic interests, related to both realistic toys and symbolic toys, whose meaning he recognizes from the videos he has seen. Max's memory is excellent. On the other hand, Max appears totally dependent on visual experience to cope and adapt. He does not appear to respond at all to verbalizations and does not utter a sound himself. Since he cannot communicate his ideas or wishes verbally, Max seems to have become "dependent on being independent," responding to others through avoidance when he clearly does not comprehend what they say. Only considerable interference with Max's agenda yields a direct response, but even this is always short-lived, as Max goes on to do what he wants to do again—because this is all he can understand. Unfortunately, without interaction and someone to help elaborate on the drama, Max cannot expand much on his play and tends to repeat what he has done before. He does not, however, play in a persevering manner with just one toy, but moves around and incorporates additional objects into his play.

Max's good motor and motor-planning abilities and his symbolic interests provide him with a foundation for developmental progress. His severe auditory-processing difficulties constitute a major challenge and the most critical focus for intervention. Yet Max should be able to thrive in a regular preschool, where typically developing peers will verbalize ideas that Max is able to enjoy. Max, in turn, will readily imitate his peers and interest them.

Ben rushes to the basket of animals, thrilled to find bears, lions, tigers, and elephants. He quickly calls his father over, tells him the bears will protect them from the robbers, and hands him a bunch of animals. Within minutes, Ben has set up his defenses, making sure his father is on his side. He waits for the tigers and lions to attack! Ben and his father quickly go to battle as Ben picks up each enemy separately and tells his dad to "get it," either killing it on the spot or locking it in jail. If his dad picks up an animal without being instructed to do so, Ben screams, "No, put it down! Only one at a time!" Occasionally, Ben, too, goes to bat, using his bear to "get" the tiger, but he is cautious. Ben wants to talk about what the bad animals might do (eat him and his father, steal their food, scare them), and he spontaneously reminds his father of his bad dreams. When his father notices some toy swords and is encouraged to hand one to Ben, Ben tries to spear the "dangerous" animals. However, he will not engage in a swordfight with his dad and insists that they go back to the jungle, just in case some monsters come.

Ben is clearly bright, verbal and imaginative. As a 3-and-a-half-year-old, he is becoming more and more aware of the "dangers" in his world, but he is not quite secure enough to trust his own impulses on how to deal with them. These dangers are experienced very intensely and not yet subject to reality testing, so, feeling very anxious and fearful, Ben tries to find ways to control both the enemy and someone to help him fight. He even tries to understand the enemy's motives, but he is subject to his projections, not quite able to be logical and realistic when he feels frightened. Ben wakes up nightly with bad dreams, will not go to sleep alone, and prefers to play with girls, who are not so "scary." He tends to sit still while he plays and is slow and poorly coordinated in his movements.

Ben often appears self-absorbed and has to be encouraged to go out to play or invite friends over. While he had experienced sleep difficulties as a younger child, he had adapted to sleeping on his own until recent nightmares began to awaken him. Although he has shown some reluctance separating from his family to go to nursery school, he has been able to attend the school. Recently, he has begun to object to baby-sitters in the evening. Ben's play suggests that his fears are more intense than might be expected for a boy his age and that the difficulties he has moving and being more active on his own behalf require further evaluation. Could Ben have low muscle tone or motor-planning difficulties which make it hard for him to mobilize, or is he just extremely anxious? What might have been the reasons for his earlier regulatory difficulties with sleep? Was—or is—he hypersensitive to other input? How did his family respond to his fears and sensitivities?

The questions raised by this observation are quite different from those raised by observation of Steve, Jenny, and Max. Ben's developmental level is much higher. He is already quite representational and perhaps ahead of his expected level. However, Ben's anxiety interferes with his ability to enjoy the full powers of magical thinking expressed through symbolic play, in which he can bravely defeat any imagined enemy on his own.

## ▤ Guidelines for Observing Free Play Interaction and Creating Symbolic Opportunities for Young Children

The brief descriptions of observations of Steve, Jenny, Max, and Ben, along with their parents, indicate how much can be learned from watching young children and parents interact freely in a setting that encourages symbolic play. The vignettes also suggest the value of using guided approaches to discover the highest developmental level that children can reach with appropriate support and to examine the impact of underlying developmental problems on children's ability to interact and play. The guidelines below are designed to help professionals from a range of disciplines to do the following: (a) arrange an appropriate setting for the observation of free play; (b) discuss with parents the reasons for observing their child's free play and how the professional and parents can learn from their joint observation; and (c) coach parents in order to help them elaborate on the interaction they are having with the child and create "symbolic opportunities" both during and beyond the assessment.

### The observation setting

The observation of free play can occur in an office/playroom, home setting, preschool, or child care environment, as long as space is available in which to observe interaction between the child and parent, caregiver, or teacher, or between the child and other children. The room should be equipped with toys suitable for children in the early stages of development, and these toys should be available for the child to choose on his or her own.

The playroom materials might include toys from the categories below (all of these materials can fit in a laundry basket):

- *Sensory toys*: Koosh balls, squeeze animals, a slinky, musical instruments, silly putty, large marbles.
- *Cause-and-effect toys*: Pop-up toys; musical telephones; "magical" toy radios or tape recorders activated by pushing, dialing, or turning knobs; cash registers; pull toys; wind-up toys.
- *Real-life toys*: Doctor kit, tool set, cars and trucks (police cars or tow trucks with sirens, school bus, ambulance, tractor, tank), house or school, playground, garage, play food, kitchen utensils, tea set, large plastic mirror.
- *Figures and props for dramatic play*: Figures representing fam-

ily members, bus drivers, other children, domestic and jungle animals, good-guy/bad-guy characters, and familiar television and movie characters (Barney, Sesame Street and Disney characters); a large baby doll and toddler doll, puppets, dress-up props, including hats and swords.

Materials should be available on shelves the child can reach, or on the floor and table top. A few empty baskets are useful for the "dumpers" and "throwers." While puzzles and games should be available, the use of structured or semistructured materials should be held in reserve until you see what a child will do with open-ended toys. The only rules for children in a free play observation should be not to hurt anyone or break anything on purpose. These rules need not be stated unless a reason to do so occurs during the play session.

## Preparing for the observation of free play interaction

The "new vision for developmental assessment" that forms the core of this volume recommends that the process of assessment begin with establishing an alliance with parents and that it continue with obtaining a picture of the child's development and the family's experience. This is achieved through interviews with the family, observing the child in unstructured interaction with parents or other familiar caregivers, observing interaction between the child and clinician (if appropriate), and conducting specific assessments of the child's individual functions, if needed. Laurence Hirshberg (this volume) and Marilyn Segal and Noreen Webber (this volume) offer wise, detailed guidance concerning how to conduct clinical interviews with families and nonstructured play observations. To complement their chapters, the suggestions that follow include approaches and language that I have found helpful in working with parents who are concerned about their toddler's development.

Before asking parents to play with their young child, I explain the reasons for this kind of observation and what we will be looking for together. As part of the initial interviews with parents, I ask them (depending on the child's developmental stage) about the games they have at home; what the baby or child enjoys; what the parents do to elicit laughter and fun; whether they engage in pretend play; what the child's favorite toys, books, television shows, or videos are; and who else the child plays with. I always acknowledge the importance of the parents' familiarity with and understanding of the child, and I use language similar to the following:

> Your child knows you best. We would like to observe the way you usually play or interact with each other, before we ask him to relate to a new person. There are no right or wrong moves here. Do whatever is familiar and comfortable. This room has a variety of toys, but it does not matter what you do as long as you try to stay engaged and interactive. We will look at what your child notices or chooses to do, how long he or she sticks with it, what feelings are expressed, and what happens next. This unstructured, spontaneous approach will help us learn more about your child's organization, attention, persistence, and range of ideas and feelings.
>
> After a few minutes, we might suggest that you try something to see how your child responds. The purpose of these suggestions will be to challenge your child with a different or surprising response on your part and to see what happens. Why don't one of you [parents] begin playing, and then you can switch. After each parent plays with the child for about ten minutes, I might join you to see if we can play together.

Even if interaction is slow in getting started, it is better not to initiate suggestions or specifically coax the child or parent to play during the first 10 minutes. Allow the child and parent to adapt and demonstrate how they cope with a new challenge. When one parent begins to play, you can quietly check with the other parent to determine whether the play or interaction he sees is characteristic of the child.

## Creating symbolic opportunities

Most children welcome others playing with them and require no preparation for such play. Others, including many children who are brought for assessment, may need to be wooed or supported in this process. The level at which either you, as the examiner, or a parent is able to become involved in the child's drama may indicate the developmental level the child can reach with support, in contrast to what he can do on his own. The principle of following a child's lead remains central. It is crucial to first establish mutual attention and some degree of engagement before trying to create a challenging symbolic opportunity. Follow a child's lead with quiet interest, joining in the activity he or she chooses with comments or gestures that indicate a desire to be helpful in what the child wants to do. Once the child is comfortable with your presence (has not moved away) and begins to open and close circles of communication, you can support the elaboration of play themes and ideas if necessary.

For example, one child might look at a toy tea set or even peek to see if there is tea inside the teapot, but make no further move. You might offer to pour some tea for the child and ask if the child wants sugar or milk, or just pour some for yourself. If the child simply watches, you might blow on your tea, indicating that it is hot, and observe the child's level of understanding. The child might accept the next cup and begin to elaborate on the tea party, or you might have to wait until your tea cools down and follow the child's lead again. To join in, build upon any interest the child shows in materials in the room. The child might eagerly select a favorite toy or wish to explore.

Some children may not spontaneously elaborate on the play and may, instead, pick up different toys and move about. Children may become more focused as you join them and express interest in what they have looked at or as you ask questions about what they like to play. It is important to note the way and the degree of ease with which a child can begin to play and interact with you, for example, letting you in with pleasure; preferring his own self-absorbed, fragmented "islands"; or persisting in aimless wandering despite your overtures.

Let the child direct you by first asking what he or she wants you to do. If this is not productive, wait and observe a bit longer, noting the child's moves. Next, try to reduce the distance between you and the child by "talking through" a familiar character or puppet the child might like. Last, pursue curiosity or pleasure through a "magical" or sensory toy which the child would find hard to resist (e.g., Koosh balls, music boxes, magic wands which light up or play, popular action figures), or follow a clue that the parents have given you.

## Conclusion

A young child may not play for many reasons. Trauma, anxiety, depression, deprivation, and other adjustment or stress reactions can impede a child's ability to play altogether or can constrict his or her level or range of play. In such cases, multiple observations are crucial in order to assess the child's resilience and responsiveness to a supportive situation. They are also crucial to efforts to build a relationship with the child based upon increasingly successful interactions. It is then possible to assess the child's developmental level and identify specific issues which may be impeding the child's functioning.

The children described in this chapter—even those with severe sensory-processing or motor-planning difficulties—had clear attachments to their parents and would turn to them in times of need, using gestures to seek comfort or to signal their wish to leave the assessment room. Even though the levels and range of their play were limited by their difficulties, observation of these children in free play interaction with their parents permitted the assessment of strengths as well as weaknesses, each of which had specific implications for appropriate intervention. Such an approach is especially important for children like Steve, Jenny, and Max, since they do not have the processing capacities needed for meaningful assessment with formal testing protocols.

Determining a child's current levels of interaction and symbolic play provides a baseline assessment for monitoring progress as intervention is provided. How does the child actually function interactively and in play with others? Intervention goals can be defined as achieving the functional abilities of the next developmental level beyond the current baseline. If progress is not observed, it is crucial to reassess the child's needs and the intervention program. It should be certain that the program is not organized around "splinter skills" or narrow curricula. To climb as high as possible on the symbolic ladder, young children need and deserve approaches that not only recognize the importance of both individual differences and functional capacities that enhance intensive interaction, but that are also designed to create sustained, appealing symbolic opportunities.

# References

ZERO TO THREE/National Center for Clinical Infant Programs (1994). *Diagnostic classification of mental health and developmental disorders of infancy and early childhood.* Arlington, VA: Author.

# 14. Toward Earlier Identification of Communication and Language Problems in Infants and Young Children

AMY M. WETHERBY

BARRY M. PRIZANT

Although the word "infant" comes from the Latin word meaning "one who does not speak," infants communicate actively from birth. During the earliest years of life, babies develop impressive repertoires of communicative abilities which become the foundation for emerging language. Babies make deliberate attempts to share experiences with caregivers by sharing attention and affective states (Stern, 1985). When caregivers read babies' signals accurately and respond appropriately, they help to orchestrate the sequence of events during infancy and early childhood that leads to successful development of communication and language (Dunst, Lowe, & Bartholomew, 1990; Tronick, 1989).

Many biological and environmental factors—which affect the child, the caregiver, or the relationship between the child and caregiver—may disrupt this process, however. Communication disorders are among the most prevalent disabilities in early childhood. Eleven percent of all kindergarten children have communication disorders (Beitchman, Nair, Clegg, & Patel, 1986). At least 70 percent of preschool children with identified disabilities have speech, language, and communication impairments (U.S. Department of Education, 1987). Communication and language problems among young children may include a specific impairment of expressive and/or receptive language, a hearing impairment, or a more pervasive impairment in cognitive and/or social development.

A comprehensive assessment is the first step in determining a young child's need for early intervention services to address communication difficulties. Prompt intervention can have a positive impact on many domains of development, since communication and language play such a significant role in a child's ability to develop relationships, to learn from others within the context of social interaction, and to function more independently with increasing age.

Early identification of communication and language problems and appropriate intervention can prevent a number of difficulties that may be closely related to, and may possibly result from, early language and communication disorders. Although many questions remain regarding causal relationships, most investigators agree that infants and toddlers with communication delays or disorders are at high risk for the development of emotional and behavioral disorders (Baker & Cantwell, 1987). We have found a significant relationship among preschool language disorders, emotional and behavioral disorders, and later-appearing academic problems (Prizant et al., 1990). The behavior of many young children with communication difficulties seems to pose significant challenges for parents (Paul, 1991a; Stevenson & Richman, 1976). Furthermore, followup studies of preschool children with speech and language problems have consistently demonstrated long-term persistence of speech and language impairments in a substantial proportion of children, as well as a high incidence of language-learning disabilities (Howlin & Rutter, 1987).

For several reasons, early identification of communication problems in very young children presents a challenge to parents and professionals alike. The primary reason is the fact that children who are developing normally may speak their first words anywhere between 12 and 20 months of age (Bates, O'Connell, & Shore, 1987), and they also vary greatly in the rate at which they acquire language. Families of children with communication problems may experience significant stress and confusion related to difficulties in identifying, acknowledging, and understanding their child's problem (Prizant & Wetherby, 1993). Families and other caregivers may disagree about whether a problem exists and whether they should seek professional guidance (Gottlieb, 1988). Given the absence of definitive criteria, primary health care professionals may delay a referral (Wetherby & Prizant, 1992), nor is it uncommon for professionals to disagree about whether there is cause for concern when a child begins to demonstrate delays in development of communication skills. Since a child's delay in acquiring language or failure to acquire it may be the first symptom that is evident to parents and professionals (in the absence of other significant disabilities), children are typically not referred for assessment of a language delay until they are 3 years old. Significantly delayed referral is more likely to occur when no risk factors (e.g., very low birthweight, perinatal complications) have been identified, or when communication and language delays do not coexist with significant physical, sensory, or cognitive disabilities, any of which may lead to earlier identification and more definitive diagnosis of developmental problems. A better understanding of what communication and language problems may look like in the earliest years of life will, we hope, lead to earlier and more precise identification of children at risk for these problems and will prompt appropriate intervention.

## ■ The Potential for Earlier Identification of ■ Language Impairments

Professionals wishing to evaluate communication and language abilities in very young children face a twofold challenge. First, they must be able to distinguish a child who is late in beginning to talk, but who will catch up spontaneously, from one who will have persisting language problems. Second, in order to identify children who are at risk for delayed language development as early as possible, professionals need sensitive measures capable of detecting the potential for language and communication problems in infants and toddlers.

Commonly used measures of language development are inadequate in meeting these challenges. Determining the number of words and word combinations that a child uses has been the primary measure of language development included on most formal language tests for young children. But measuring vocabulary precludes identifying children at risk for language delays before the expected emergence of words (i.e., before 18 months of age). A checklist that gives parents the opportunity to report their child's vocabulary seems to be a sensitive indicator of delayed vocabularies among 2-year-olds. However, this measure alone does not appear to assist in distinguishing children who will catch up spontaneously from those with persisting language problems (Bates, Bretherton, & Snyder, 1988; Dale, Bates,

Reznick, & Morisset, 1989; Fenson et al., 1991; Rescorla, 1989; 1991).

Is it possible to identify children at risk for persisting language problems before a delay in the onset of expressive language is evident (i.e., earlier than 18 to 24 months)? Patterns that have emerged from recent research suggest that information about specific parameters of a child's early communication and symbolic development has important implications for distinguishing children who will catch up spontaneously from those whose language problems are likely to persist. These patterns of normal communicative and symbolic development are summarized briefly below.

## Social-communicative foundation for words

The development of language involves a complex interplay of emerging abilities in social-affective, communicative, cognitive, and linguistic domains (Bates, 1979). Communication development involves continuity from preverbal communication to the intentional use of language to communicate (Bates, 1979; Harding & Golinkoff, 1979). Infants make deliberate attempts to share experiences with caregivers by sharing attention and affective states before they can communicate specific intentions (Stern, 1985). Babies' early affective expressions and displays help the caregiver read an infant's emotional state and thus help to regulate the interaction between baby and caregiver (Tronick, 1989).

Before they begin to talk, infants and toddlers learn to communicate with gestures and sounds in order to accomplish several important functions:

1. To regulate another's behavior—for example, to request an object or protest an action;

2. To attract or maintain another's attention for social interaction; and

3. To draw joint attention to objects and events (Wetherby, Cain, Yonclas, & Walker, 1988).

Infants and young children learn to coordinate the use of eye gaze, directed toward people and things, and facial expressions to regulate interactions and clarify communicative intentions. They also display persistence in pursuing communicative goals. When a communicative breakdown occurs (i.e., a caregiver does not seem to understand what the child wants, or simply is not paying attention), a young child should be able to repeat or modify the communicative signal (proceeding, for example, from a mild vocalization to a loud demand, accompanied by a strong tug on the caregiver's clothing) to clarify it or repair the communicative breakdown.

## Communicative forms that precede words

Before words emerge, children acquire a large repertoire of gestures and vocalizations to express their intentions (Bates, O'Connell, & Shore, 1987). Children communicate intentionally through proximal and distal gestures, including giving, showing, pushing away, reaching, pointing, and waving. Children later develop the use of head nods and head shakes to indicate affirmation or rejection. These gestures are "conventional," that is, they mean the same thing across cultures. Before they reach the age of two, children become increasingly sophisticated in their vocalizations by using more vocalizations without gestures, by increasing their inventory of consonants, and by using a greater number of consonant and vowel combinations (Kent & Bauer, 1985; Stoel-Gammon, 1991; Wetherby et al., 1988).

## Symbolic bases of verbal communication

As development proceeds, a young child's behavior becomes increasingly more deliberate and goal-directed, shows increased evidence of foresight, and culminates with the ability to plan behavior through symbolic thought. The child shows his or her emerging capacity to symbolize—to make one thing stand for and represent something else—through language and play. In the first two years of life, achievements in language have been found to parallel those in symbolic play (McCune-Nicolich & Carroll, 1981; Shore, O'Connell, & Bates, 1984; Westby, 1988).

Young children first learn to respond to the communicative signals and words of others in highly ritualized contexts (for example, waving "Bye-bye" or playing peekaboo). The transition to using words referentially is gradual. As children begin to understand and produce single words, parallels in play include the use of pretend single action schemes (for example, using the word "baba" for bottle and pretending to drink from a cup). As children move to the comprehension and use of word combinations, they display multiple action schemes in play (for example, using the word combination "baby eat" and pretending to stir food and scoop it up to the baby's mouth).

The interdependence of language and play underscores the importance of considering a child's symbolic capacity across these domains. A child's level of play reflects cognitive abilities that are likely to enhance language acquisition, and participation in play activities provides a social context for cognitive and language development.

## Patterns that predict problems

Studies of children who are late in talking have revealed patterns of communication, summarized in the table below, which predict persistent problems. These findings suggest that a number of different parameters in a child's profile of communicative and symbolic abilities, even prior to the emergence of words, may be a sensitive indicator of the likelihood of subsequent difficulties in communication and language development. Attention to these patterns may lead to earlier identification and treatment of difficulties.

---

### Summary of High Risk Indicators for Persisting Language Problems in Young Children

#### Social-Communicative Foundation for Words
- Deficits in the ability to share attention and affective states with eye gaze and facial expression (Kasari, Sigman, Mundy, & Yirmiya, 1990)
- A low rate of communicating with gestures and/or vocalizations (Paul, 1991b; Thal & Tobias, 1992; Wetherby, Yonclas, & Bryan, 1989)
- A limited range of communicative functions, particularly lacking in the joint attention function (Mundy, Sigman, & Kasari, 1990; Paul, 1991b; Wetherby & Prutting, 1984; Wetherby et al., 1989)

#### Communicative Forms that Precede Words
- A reliance on gestures and a limited use of vocalizations to communicate (Rowan, Leonard, Chapman, & Weiss, 1983; Snyder, 1978; Thal and Tobias, 1992; Wetherby & Prutting, 1984; Wetherby et al., 1989)
- A limited consonant inventory and a less complex syllabic structure in vocal communication (Paul, 1991b; Paul & Jennings, 1992; Wetherby et al., 1989)

#### Symbolic Bases of Verbal Communication
- A delay in both language comprehension and production (Paul, Looney, & Dahm, 1991; Thal, Tobias, & Morrison, 1991)
- A delay in the spontaneous use of action schemes in symbolic play and in the imitation of action schemes (Rescorla & Goosens, 1992; Terrell & Schwartz, 1988; Thal et al., 1991)

---

Research findings on young children who show persistent language impairments indicate that measures of vocabulary alone are insufficient for early identification. Instead, measures of multiple parameters across communicative and symbolic domains appear to be necessary in order to distinguish among three groups of children: (a) children who are late in talking but are likely to outgrow their delay (i.e., late bloomers who show a pattern of slow expressive language development and no other delays); (b) children who are late in talking and are likely to have persistent specific language delay (i.e., a pattern of slow expressive language development combined with delays in other parameters, such as rate of communicating, use of joint attention function, and symbolic play); and (c) children who have more pervasive social and/or cognitive impairments (i.e., slow expressive language development combined with significant delays in many aspects of their social-communicative foundation for words, communicative forms, and symbolic bases, listed in the table above).

The discovery that patterns of strengths and weaknesses in communication and symbolic development can be identified in children younger than 18 months provides important new opportunities for the early identification of communication impairments. Moreover, these findings help us to place a child along a continuum of risk, ranging from more specific language delays to more pervasive social and/or cognitive impairments. Most importantly, these findings suggest greater urgency in initiating intervention that addresses delays, not only in expressive language, but also in other communicative and symbolic domains.

# ■ The Need for New Emphasis in the Direct
# ■ Assessment of Children

Professionals in speech-language pathology have come a long way from the traditional practice of waiting until a child is talking to evaluate that child for a language impairment. We now recognize that early identification and appropriate intervention for language and communication impairments are crucial, due to the far-reaching effects of early communication disorders on family well-being, the child's emotional and behavioral development, and the child's later educational achievement.

Despite a recent proliferation of research in infant communication and socioemotional development, the formal tools that speech-language professionals currently use to directly assess a child's communication and language skills have major limitations, particularly in their capacity to evaluate a child's spontaneous communication during natural interactions. First, most instruments do not allow the family to collaborate in decision-making about the assessment process or to participate to the extent desired by the family, and thus are not family-centered. Second, most instruments involving direct child assessment are primarily clinician-oriented, placing the child in a respondent role, thus limiting observations of spontaneous, child-initiated communication (Wetherby & Prizant, 1992). Third, most formal instruments emphasize language milestones and forms of communication (e.g., number of different gestures, sounds, words, word combinations), rather than the social-communicative and symbolic foundations of language.

Current theories on how children acquire language (Bates, 1976; Bloom & Lahey, 1978; McLean & Snyder-McLean, 1978) suggest the following guidelines for the assessment of language and communication in young children:

1. Communication and language should be assessed within an interactive, meaningful context in which the child is encouraged to initiate communication.

2. The young child's caregiver should be integrally involved in the assessment as an active participant interacting with the child, as an informant about the child's competence and performance, and as a collaborator in decisionmaking.

3. Diagnostic assessment and assessment for program planning should not only identify relative developmental weaknesses, but should also provide information about the child's relative strengths in communication and related areas of development.

4. Assessment should be viewed as an ongoing, dynamic process in which the child's capacity for developing communicative competence is understood over time.

These guidelines are consistent with current trends in assessment strategies for school-age children, which include the use of authentic assessment measures, such as portfolio assessments that evolve dynamically over time (Damico, Secord, & Wiig, 1992). It is now critically important to move toward authentic assessment for infants, toddlers, and developmentally young children as well, in order to assure that assessment practices will yield meaningful measures (Damico et al., 1992). Furthermore, it is important to use dynamic assessment strategies to explore environmental contexts that support or impede the child's acquisition of communicative competence (Olswang, Bain, & Johnson, 1992).

## ▇ A Proposed Framework for Direct Assessment ▇ of Young Children's Communication

In order to formalize a more authentic approach and provide an alternative to currently available formal assessment tools for infants, toddlers, and preschool children, we developed the Communication and Symbolic Behavior Scales (CSBS) (Wetherby & Prizant, 1993). The CSBS is designed to examine communicative, social-affective, and symbolic abilities of children whose functional communication abilities range from prelinguistic intentional communication to early stages of language acquisition (between 8 months and 2 years in communication and language). This assessment instrument is designed to meet the goals of diagnostic assessment and assessment for intervention planning. A developmental screening version of the CSBS is forthcoming.

The CSBS uses a standard but flexible format for gathering data, combining a caregiver questionnaire with behavior sampling procedures. The questionnaire, which can be given to the family before or on the day of the direct child assessment, gathers information from the caregiver about the child's communicative and symbolic competence. Descriptive questions solicit examples of the child's typical behaviors from the caregiver. The direct child assessment involves varying degrees of structured and unstructured behavior sampling procedures. These resemble natural adult-child interactions and provide opportunities for documenting a child's use of a variety of communicative and symbolic behaviors.

The CSBS sampling procedures allow for dynamic assessment of the effects of contextual factors on a child's communicative abilities during a sample. For example:

1. Parameters of the child's communication in the structured communicative opportunities and in the unstructured play within the sample can be compared.

2. The child's ability to persist in repairing communicative break-

downs or misunderstandings can be examined during the opportunities created when the child's communicative attempts are not responded to as he or she intended.

3. If the child does not initiate communication during structured opportunities, a hierarchy of verbal and gestural cues can be offered and the child's responses to these can be examined.

In addition to involving the parent or caregiver in direct interaction with the child during direct assessment and as an informant through the questionnaire, the CSBS procedures enlist the caregiver as a validator after the assessment through a caregiver perception rating of the child's performance. The caregiver is present during the entire assessment and is encouraged to respond naturally to the child's bids for interaction. After the sample is collected, the caregiver validates the representativeness of the child's behavior during direct assessment by rating how typical the child's behavior was along seven different dimensions during the sample: alertness, emotional reaction, level of interest and attention, comfort level, level of activity, overall level of communication, and play behavior. The caregiver's presence and participation during the assessment provide an opportunity for the clinician and caregiver to build consensus on perceptions of the child's communicative strengths and weaknesses displayed during the sample and to compare these patterns to information provided on the caregiver questionnaire.

Behaviors collected in the sample are rated along a number of parameters and are converted to scores on 22 five-point rating scales of communication and symbolic behaviors. Seven cluster scores are derived from the 22 scales, the first six contributing to the child's profile of communication and the last to the child's profile of symbolic behaviors:

1. *Communicative functions*: The use of gestures, sounds, or words for behavior regulation and for joint attention, and the proportion of communication used for social functions;

2. *Gestural communicative means*: The variety of conventional gestures, use of distal gestures, and coordination of gestures and vocalizations;

3. *Vocal communicative means*: The use of vocalizations without gestures, inventory of different consonants, and syllabic structure;

4. *Verbal communicative means:* The number of different words and different word-combinations produced;

5. *Reciprocity:* The use of communication in response to the adult's conventional gestures or speech, rate of communicating, and ability to repair communicative breakdowns by repeating and/or modifying previous communication when a goal is not achieved;

6. *Social/affective signaling:* The use of gaze shifts between person and object, expression of positive affect with directed eye gaze, and episodes of negative affect; and

7. *Symbolic behavior:* Comprehension of contextual cues, single words and multiword utterances, the number of different action schemes and complexity of action schemes in symbolic play, and the level of constructive play.

Normative data on a sample of over 300 normally developing, American, English-speaking children from 8 to 24 months of age and 30 children with developmental disabilities from 18 to 30 months of age have been published (Wetherby & Prizant, 1993). In addition to norms referenced to chronological age, the CSBS presents norms based on the following language stages: prelinguistic, early one-word, late one-word, and multiword stages.

## ■ Assessing the Communication Environment

The assessment of a young child's communicative and symbolic profile provides information about only one-half of the communicative interaction. It is also necessary to assess at least two major dimensions of the communicative environment: (a) opportunities for the child to initiate and respond to communication; and (b) the interactional style of the child's communicative partner(s). Considerations for assessing each of these dimensions of the communicative environment are addressed briefly below.

Both the quality and quantity of a child's opportunities for communication may vary greatly, depending on the caregiving environment. The interventionist needs to consider whether situations and people in the environment provide ample opportunities for the child to initiate and respond to communication for the full range of communicative functions—behavior regulation, social interaction, and joint attention. That is, does the child have the opportunity to communicate in order to get others to do things, to draw attention to himself or herself, and to direct the attention of others to objects or events?

Opportunities to communicate for behavior regulation generally involve situations in which the child requests assistance to get objects out of reach, makes choices about desired objects or activities (e.g., food items, toys, games, or play partners), and indicates undesired objects or activities. Opportunities to regulate behavior should occur throughout the activities selected and not just when materials are first presented or activities are first initiated. Evaluation of behavior regulation opportunities will provide information about the need for arrangement of the environment to increase opportunities for communicating for this purpose (Peck, 1989).

Opportunities to communicate for social interaction and joint attention are more likely to occur within playful, repetitive, turn-taking interactions. Bruner (1978, 1981) suggests that joint action routines provide the optimal opportunity for communication development and provide the foundation for learning to exchange roles in conversation. A joint action routine is a repetitive, turn-taking game or activity in which there is mutual attention and participation by both the child and caregiver, exchangeable roles, and predictable sequences (see Snyder-McLean, Solomonson, McLean, & Sack, 1984). A prototypical example of a joint action routine is the game of peekaboo (Bruner & Sherwood, 1976), which caregivers may play with their child innumerable times during the first year of life. A joint action routine may include activities involving preparation of a specific end product (e.g., preparing food), organization around a central plot (e.g., pretend play), or cooperative turn-taking games (e.g., peekaboo) (Snyder-McLean et al., 1984). Both the quantity and quality of joint action routines provided on a daily basis for a young child should be evaluated.

A young child's communicative behavior will be influenced not only by the opportunities for communication, but also by the interaction style used by communicative partners. The caregiver's ability to respond appropriately to what the child is paying attention to or communicating has been found to be a major influence in the child's developing communicative competence (Dunst, Lowe, & Bartholomew, 1990). Therefore, it is important to determine if the child's partner is using a *facilitative* style that fosters communication or a *directive* style that may inhibit communication.

Developmental literature provides guidelines for assessing caregivers' interaction styles (Girolametto, Greenberg, & Manolson, 1986; MacDonald, 1989) to determine if the following features are present: (a) waiting for the child to initiate communication by pausing and looking expectantly; (b) recognizing the child's behavior as communication by interpreting the communicative function that it serves; and (c) responding contingently to the child's communicative behavior in a manner that is consistent with the communicative intention of the child and that matches the communicative level of the child (MacDonald, 1989). For example, if the child requests an object, does the caregiver offer the desired object immediately? If the child requests comfort, does the caregiver provide the child with social and/or physical attention? If the child is commenting, does the caregiver pay attention to the object or event to which the child is drawing attention?

The interventionist should consider whether the form of the caregiver's communication matches the form of the child's communication. In addition to being able to follow the child's lead, the caregiver should be able to adjust his or her behavior to match the child's developmental level, interest, and style (MacDonald, 1989). MacDonald (1989) uses the image of a caregiver and a child on a staircase to convey the quality of this adjustment: the caregiver who is a "matched partner" has one foot on the child's step and the other foot on the next step above.

The interventionist should also consider the balance between the child and his or her communicative partner. Do the child and caregiver participate equally in communication? Is the interaction reciprocal, that is, does each person influence and respond meaningfully to the other person (MacDonald, 1989)?

In summary, the direct child assessment should provide information that will make it possible to prioritize intervention goals designed to enhance a child's communicative competence. The assessment of the communicative environment should provide information that can be used to increase opportunities for communicating and to enhance the reciprocity of communicative interactions between a child and his or her partners. A rich communication environment, in turn, is likely to have a meaningful impact on the child's overall development.

## Clinical Vignettes

The two vignettes about Casey and Brad below illustrate the use of profiles of a child's communicative and symbolic abilities for diagnostic assessment and intervention planning. In each vignette, identifying details have been changed to protect confidentiality. Each child's CSBS profile is compared to normative data in two ways: (a) by chronological age, to determine the extent of the disability; and (b) by language stage, to provide further information on strengths and weaknesses. Because the CSBS is normed on children up to 24 months of age, children older than 2 years who are at risk for communication impairments and are given the CSBS can be compared to 24-month-olds. The CSBS results for Casey and Brad are presented in the graph below.

## Casey

Casey was referred at 22 months of age by his child care provider, who was concerned that he was not yet talking. His medical and developmental history were unremarkable, other than his delay in talking. Casey, a Caucasian and the younger of two siblings, lived in a suburban setting with his parents and sibling. His mother reported that he used a few protowords (e.g., "baba" for bottle) and communicated primarily with gestures, such as pointing and showing. She reported that he got along well with other children and was generally a happy child.

The CSBS standard scores for Casey in the top half of the graph indicate that, compared to children of his chronological age (the 22-month-old norms), Casey performed more than 1.5 standard deviations below the mean on five clusters—communicative functions, gestural means, vocal means, verbal means, and reciprocity. These results indicate a significant delay for his age. He performed at or above the mean on only one cluster, social-affective signaling. Because Casey did not use any words during the sample, his language stage was "prelinguistic." Compared to other children at this language stage, Casey functioned near or above the mean on all parameters and showed relative strengths in social-affective signaling and symbolic behavior.

Casey's CSBS profile, with depressed scores on many clusters for his chronological age, suggests a high risk for a persisting language and/or speech problem. We recommend early intervention services for Casey rather than waiting to see if he will catch up spontaneously.

## Brad

As an infant, Brad was identified as having a developmental delay and had attended an early intervention center twice a week

**Standard Deviations, Standard Scores, and Percentile Ranks for CSBS Clusters for Casey (Language Delay) and Brad (Social-Communicative Impairment), Compared to Norms Based on Age and Language Stage** (Adapted from Wetherby & Prizant, 1993)

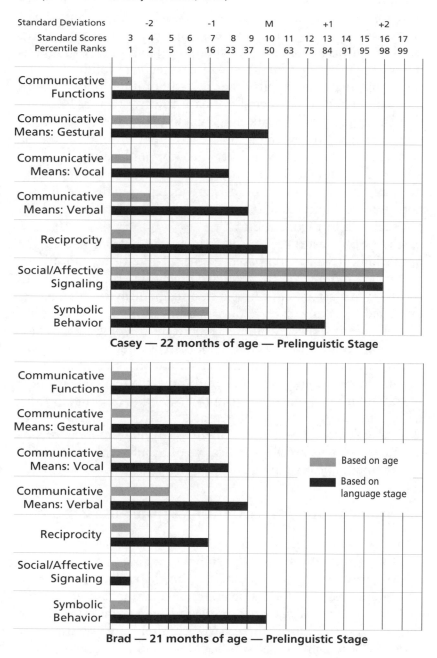

Casey — 22 months of age — Prelinguistic Stage

Brad — 21 months of age — Prelinguistic Stage

for therapy and educational services since the age of 15 months. At 21 months of age, he was referred for a communication and language evaluation by his early intervention center because of concerns about his lack of language and social-communicative development. His medical history was unremarkable, but he was suspected of having pervasive developmental disorder (PDD). Brad, a Caucasian and an only child, lived in a rural setting. His parents reported that he did vocalize, often very loudly, as if he were "playing with sounds," but he did not use sounds to communicate. He rarely directed eye gaze toward people. He communicated primarily by taking people by the hand to an object that he wanted or by giving objects to them to solicit help. He was easily frustrated when he was not understood, and he screamed persistently. At times, Brad slapped himself on the head and chest to protest. Brad's parents reported that he did not appear to be interested in interacting with other children and did not seek comfort from adults.

The CSBS cluster scores for Brad in the bottom half of the graph indicate that, compared to the 21-month-old norms, he performed more than 1.5 standard deviations below the mean on all seven clusters, indicating a significant delay for his age. He exhibited a striking absence of communication for a joint attention function, showed a limited repertoire of conventional gestures and vocalizations, and did not display alternating eye gaze or positive affect during the sample. Compared to children who are also at a prelinguistic stage, Brad showed a relative weakness in communicative functions, reciprocity, and social-affective signaling. In contrast, he performed at or near the mean in verbal skills and symbolic behavior, compared to children in the prelinguistic stage. This profile is indicative of a child with a pervasive social-communicative impairment.

## Implications for Communication Assessment

Profiling a child's relative strengths and weaknesses in communicative, social-affective, and symbolic abilities provides valuable information that can contribute to the early identification of children at risk for language and communication impairments. The clinical vignettes presented here demonstrate how the CSBS profiles of these two children are significantly depressed for many or all CSBS parameters, compared to age norms. Thus, they confirm the existence of high-risk indicators for persisting communication and language problems for these children. We believe that, in order to identify young children at risk for language problems at an earlier age than is now common, interventionists must compare measures of communicative functions, communicative means, reciprocity, and social-affective signaling with measures of symbolic abilities. This is particularly critical if the identification of infants and children under 2 years of age is to be improved.

# Implications for Communication Intervention

Communication intervention with infants and young children should be one dimension of an integrated intervention plan for the child and his or her family (Prizant, Wetherby, & Roberts, 1994). The degree of successful communication and interaction between a child and his or her caregivers, siblings, and peers is likely to have a significant impact not only on the child's social and emotional well-being, but also on parents' sense of competence and the well-being of the family (Theadore, Maher, and Prizant, 1990). Whether services are provided in a home- or center-based program, the child's primary caregivers possess the greatest potential for actuating positive change in the child's communicative abilities (MacDonald, 1989). However, caregivers must be willing and voluntary participants in such endeavors. They must be respected and supported in setting communication priorities and goals that they value.

Prioritizing goals for enhancing a young child's communication should be considered in relation to the child's developmental and chronological age, that is, the child's developmental level of communication. Assessment of communication should provide information to determine a child's language stage (i.e., prelinguistic, first words, first word-combination stage), which provides a frame of reference for understanding the child's relative strengths and weaknesses and for setting developmentally appropriate goals. A child's profile of strengths and weaknesses on the communication and symbolic parameters of the CSBS may be used as a guideline to prioritize intervention goals.

For very young children, the expression of communicative intent emerges gradually as they observe the effects of their behavior on the behavior of adults. Adults' responses reinforce the initiations of children, who develop an awareness of social causality. Thus, intervention activities designed to support the

development of intentional communication must involve responsive communicative partners, who react consistently and pre-
dictably to young children's behavior. Partners should respond
even to very young children as if their behavior is intentionally
communicative. Furthermore, partners' responses need to be
immediate, clear, and naturally reinforcing to the child, and
should eventually involve prompting and modeling, or demonstrating, and more conventional and readable signals once intent
is clearly established.

## Goals for children at the prelinguistic stage

Children at a prelinguistic intentional communication stage are
clearly demonstrating the use of signals to influence the behavior of others. However, signals initially tend to be idiosyncratic
and concrete, and they may be produced inconsistently, or only
in certain routines or contexts. Thus, for children at early prelinguistic intentional levels of communication, high priority communication goals include:

1. Developing more consistent and socially acceptable means for
   expressing intentions;
2. Developing more conventional gestural and vocal means for
   communication;
3. Expanding the range of functions or purposes for communication; and
4. Developing repair strategies (i.e., persistence in communication) (Prizant & Bailey, in press; Wetherby & Prizant, 1993).

The ability to initiate communication within reciprocal social
interactions and the ability to communicate spontaneously with
a variety of partners in a range of situations also continue to be
high-priority goals. (All of these goals are high priority for a
child such as Brad who has social-communicative problems.)

## Goals for children at early language stages

The transition from prelinguistic to linguistic communication is
a gradual process for normally developing children and a challenge for children with developmental disabilities. The challenge
is due, in part, to the greater motor and cognitive demands
inherent in oral language use or the use of other symbol systems.
Due to motor and cognitive limitations, some children with disabilities will communicate more successfully through nonspeech

augmentative communicative means than through speech alone. In light of his strengths in the social-communicative foundation areas, high priority goals for Casey include expanding his repertoire of communicative means, in both gestural and vocal modalities, to enhance the transition to words.

When children begin moving into early language stages, they begin to use words instead of gestures or vocalizations in order to accomplish the same basic functions of behavior regulation, social interaction, and establishing joint attention to objects or events (Lahey, 1988). Children's earliest words refer to the existence or presence of objects, events that recur, objects that reappear or disappear, people acting on objects, actions that change the location of objects, and personal statements of rejection or possession. Children tend to talk more about objects that are moving or changing rather than those that are static. These developmental patterns should be considered in making decisions about initial vocabulary selection. It is important to emphasize that appropriate exposure to and modeling of language and communicative behavior in daily interactions is basic to the successful acquisition of single and multiword utterances. The child's profile of communicative and symbolic abilities can be used to prioritize communication goals that will enhance the child's "readability" by partners and his or her level of sophistication in communicating.

## Enhancing the communication environment

Enhancement of communication in young children involves attention to the communication environment as well as to the child. Intervention should address two primary components of the communication environment: (a) the quality and quantity of opportunities for communicating; and (b) interaction strategies used by communicative partners.

When the child's caregivers are present and are participating in the assessment of his or her communication, as occurs with the CSBS, a natural context occurs for the child's communicative partners and speech-language professionals to collaboratively identify the child's communicative attempts and developmental level. The assessment process may be a first step toward helping the caregiver understand the importance of his or her responsiveness in supporting the child's emerging communicative competence.

## ■ Summary

Language and communication impairments in young children may have a detrimental impact on a child's emotional and behavioral development, his or her later educational achievement, and the family's well-being. The early identification of children at risk for language and communication problems may serve to prevent or mitigate the persistence of speech and language problems and related difficulties for the child, as well as the child's family. Recent research on young children with delayed language suggests that patterns of strengths and weaknesses in communicative and symbolic parameters reveal information that contributes significantly to the early identification of a communication impairment. Assessment of language and communication in young children should occur in authentic, interactive contexts, with the child's caregiver integrally involved as an active participant, informant, and collaborator in decisionmaking. Furthermore, assessment should be viewed as a dynamic process of identifying a child's relative strengths and weaknesses in communication and related areas, as well as understanding the child's capacity for developing communicative competence.

# ■ References

Baker, L., & Cantwell, D. (1987). A prospective psychiatric follow-up of children with speech/language disorders. *Journal of the American Academy of Child and Adolescent Psychiatry, 26,* 546-553.

Bates, E. (1976). *Language and context: The acquisition of pragmatics.* New York: Academic Press.

Bates, E. (1979). *The emergence of symbols: Cognition and communication in infancy.* New York: Academic Press.

Bates, E., Bretherton, I., & Snyder, L. (1988). *From first words to grammar: Individual differences and dissociable mechanisms.* Cambridge, England: Cambridge University Press.

Bates, E., O'Connell, B., & Shore, C. (1987). Language and communication in infancy. In J. Osofsky (Ed.), *Handbook of infant development* (pp. 149-203). New York: Wiley and Sons.

Beitchman, J., Nair, R., Clegg, M., & Patel, P. (1986). Prevalence of speech and language disorders in five-year-old kindergarten children in the Ottawa-Carlton region. *Journal of Speech and Hearing Disorders, 51,* 98-110.

Bloom, L., & Lahey, M. (1978). *Language development and language disorders.* New York: Wiley and Sons.

Bruner, J. (1978). From communication to language: A psychological perspective. In I. Markova (Ed.), *The social context of language.* Chichester, England: John Wiley and Sons.

Bruner, J. (1981). The social context of language acquisition. *Language and Communication, 1,* 155-178.

Bruner, J., & Sherwood, V. (1976). Early rule structure: The case of peekaboo. In J. Bruner, A. Jolly, & K. Sylva (Eds.), *Play: Its role in evolution and development.* Harmondsworth, England: Penguin.

Dale, P., Bates, E., Reznick, J., & Morisset, C. (1989). The validity of a parent report instrument of child language at 20 months. *Journal of Child Language, 16,* 239-249.

Damico, J., Secord, W., & Wiig, E. (1992). Descriptive language assessment at school: Characteristics and design. In W. Secord (Ed.), *Best practices in school speech-language pathology* (pp. 1-8). San Antonio, TX: Psychological Corp.

Dunst, C., Lowe, L. W., & Bartholomew, P. C. (1990). Contingent social responsiveness, family ecology, and infant communicative competence. *National Student Speech Language Hearing Association Journal, 17,* 39-49.

Fenson, L., Dale, P., Reznick, S., Thal, D., Bates, E., Hartung, J., Pethick, S., & Reilly, J. (1991). *Technical manual for the MacArthur Communicative Development Inventories.* San Diego, CA: San Diego State University.

Girolametto, L. E., Greenberg, J., & Manolson, H. A. (1986). Developing dialogue skills: The Hanen early language parent program. *Seminars in Speech and Language, 7,* 367-382.

Gottlieb, M. (1988). The response of families to language disorders in the young child. *Seminars in Speech and Language, 9,* 47-53.

Harding, C., & Golinkoff, R. (1979). The origins of intentional vocalizations in prelinguistic infants. *Child Development, 50,* 33-40.

Howlin, P., & Rutter, M. (1987). The consequences of language delay for other aspects of development. In W. Yule & M. Rutter (Eds.), *Language development and language disorders.* Philadelphia, PA: Lippincott.

Kasari, C., Sigman, M., Mundy, P., & Yirmiya, N. (1990). Affective sharing in the context of joint attention. *Journal of Autism and Developmental Disorders, 20,* 87-100.

Kent, R., & Bauer, H. (1985). Vocalizations of one-year-olds. *Journal of Child Language, 12,* 491-526.

Lahey, M. (1988). *Language disorders and language development.* New York: MacMillan.

MacDonald, J. (1989). *Becoming partners with children.* San Antonio, TX: Special Press.

McCune-Nicolich, L., & Carroll, S. (1981). Development of symbolic play: Implications for the language specialist. *Topics in Language Disorders, 2* (1), 1-15.

McLean, J., & Snyder-McLean, L. (1978). *A transactional approach to early language training.* Columbus, OH: Charles E. Merrill.

Mundy, P., Sigman, M., & Kasari, C. (1990). A longitudinal study of joint attention and language development in autistic children. *Journal of Autism and Developmental Disorders, 20,* 115-128.

Olswang, L., Bain, B., & Johnson, G. (1992). Using dynamic assessment with children with language disorders. In S. Warren & J. Reichle (Eds.), *Causes and effects in communication and language intervention* (pp. 187-215). Baltimore, MD: Paul H. Brookes Publishing Co.

Paul, R. (1991a). Language delay and parental perceptions. *Journal of the American Academy of Childhood and Adolescent Psychiatry, 29,* 669-670.

Paul, R. (1991b). Profiles of toddlers with slow expressive language development. *Topics in Language Disorders, 11,* 1-13.

Paul, R., & Jennings, P. (1992). Phonological behavior in toddlers with slow expressive language development. *Journal of Speech and Hearing Research, 35,* 99-107.

Paul, R., Looney, S., & Dahm, P. (1991). Communication and socialization skills at ages 2 and 3 in "late-talking" young children. *Journal of Speech and Hearing Research, 34,* 858-865.

Peck, C. A. (1989). Assessment of social communicative competence: Evaluating environments. *Seminars in Speech and Language, 10,* 1-15.

Prizant, B., Audet, L., Burke, G., Hummel, L., Maher, S., & Theadore, G. (1990). Communication disorders and emotional/behavioral disorders in children. *Journal of Speech and Hearing Disorders, 55,* 179-192.

Prizant, B., & Bailey, D. (in press). Facilitating acquisition and use of communication skills. In D. Bailey & M. Woolery (Eds.), *Teaching infants and preschoolers with handicaps.* Columbus, OH: Charles E. Merrill.

Prizant, B., & Wetherby, A. (1993). Communication and language assessment for young children. *Infants and Young Children, 5,* 20-34.

Prizant, B., Wetherby, A., & Roberts, J. (1994). Communication disorders in infants and toddlers. In C. Zeanah (Ed.), *Handbook of infant mental health.* New York: Guilford Press.

Prutting, C. (1982). Infans—"(one) unable to speak." In J. Irwin (Ed.), *Pragmatics: The role in language development* (pp. 15-27). LaVerne, CA: Fox Point Publishing.

Rescorla, L. (1989). The language development survey: A screening tool for delayed language in toddlers. *Journal of Speech and Hearing Disorders, 54,* 587-599.

Rescorla, L. (1991). Identifying expressive language delay at age two. *Topics in Language Disorders, 11,* 14-20.

Rescorla, L., & Goosens, M. (1992). Symbolic play development in toddlers with expressive specific language impairment. *Journal of Speech and Hearing Research, 35,* 1290-1302.

Rowan, L., Leonard, L., Chapman, K., & Weiss, A. (1983). Performative and presuppositional skills in language-disordered and normal children. *Journal of Speech and Hearing Research, 26,* 97-106.

Shore, C., O'Connell, B., & Bates, E. (1984). First sentences in language and symbolic play. *Developmental Psychology, 22,* 184-190.

Snyder, L. (1978). Communicative and cognitive abilities and disabilities in the sensorimotor period. *Merrill-Palmer Quarterly, 24,* 161-180.

Snyder-McLean, L., Solomonson, B., McLean, J., & Sack, S. (1984). Structuring joint action routines: A strategy for facilitating communication and language development in the classroom. *Seminars in Speech and Language, 5,* 213-228.

Stern, D. (1985). *The interpersonal world of the infant.* New York: Basic Books.

Stevenson, J., & Richman, N. (1976). The prevalence of language delay in a population of three-year-old children and its association with general retardation. *Developmental Medicine and Child Neurology, 18,* 431-441.

Stoel-Gammon, C. (1991). Normal and disordered phonology in two-year-olds. *Topics in Language Disorders, 11,* 21-32.

Terrell, B. Y., & Schwartz, R. G. (1988). Object transformations in the play of language-impaired children. *Journal of Speech and Hearing Disorders, 53,* 459-466.

Thal, D., & Tobias, S. (1992). Communicative gestures in children with delayed onset of oral expressive vocabulary. *Journal of Speech and Hearing Research, 35,* 1281-1289.

Thal, D., Tobias, S., & Morrison, D. (1991). Language and gesture in late talkers: A 1-year follow-up. *Journal of Speech and Hearing Research, 34,* 604-612.

Theadore, G., Maher, S., & Prizant, B. (1990). Early assessment and intervention with emotional and behavioral disorders and communication disorders. *Topics in Language Disorders, 10,* 42-56.

Tronick, E. (1989). Emotions and emotional communication in infants. *American Psychologist, 44,* 112-119.

U.S. Department of Education (1987). *Ninth annual report to Congress on the implementation of the Education of the Handicapped Act.* Washington, DC: U.S. Dept. of Education.

Westby, C. (1988). Children's play: Reflections of social competence. *Seminars in Speech and Hearing, 9,* 1-14.

Wetherby, A., Cain, D., Yonclas, D., & Walker, V. (1988). Analysis of intentional communication of normal children from the prelinguistic to the multi-word stage. *Journal of Speech and Hearing Research, 31,* 24-252.

Wetherby, A., & Prizant, B. (1992). Profiling young children's communicative competence. In S. Warren & J. Reichle (Eds.), *Perspective on communication and language intervention: Development, assessment, and intervention* (pp. 217-251). Baltimore, MD: Paul H. Brookes Publishing Co.

Wetherby, A., & Prizant, B. (1993). *Communication and Symbolic Behavior Scales—Normed Edition.* Chicago, IL: Applied Symbolix.

Wetherby, A., & Prutting, C. (1984). Profiles of communicative and cognitive-social abilities in autistic children. *Journal of Speech and Hearing Research, 27,* 364-377.

Wetherby, A., Yonclas, D., & Bryan, A. (1989). Communicative profiles of handicapped preschool children: Implications for early identification. *Journal of Speech and Hearing Disorders, 54,* 148-158.

# 15. Strategies for Meaningful Assessment of Infants and Toddlers with Significant Physical and Sensory Disabilities

LUCY JANE MILLER

CORDELIA C. ROBINSON

There are "few injustices deeper than the denial of an opportunity to strive or ever hope, by a limit imposed from without, but falsely identified as lying within" (Gould, 1981, p. 28). This observation by Gould in *The Mismeasure of Man* captures the frustration that almost everyone who works with infants and toddlers with disabilities and their families feels about the assessment of these children's development. The inadequacies of currently available methods and tools burden parents and professionals alike. Parents, fearing a diagnosis that suggests a limited future for their child, are frustrated when they observe professionals basing their assessment on a sampling of behavior that is not representative of what their child does with them outside the assessment context. Professionals are frustrated by the lack of assessment tools developed and normed on children with specific diagnoses, and by the lack of measures capable of reflecting small increments of developmental progress. Professionals are also concerned about the all-too-common practice of using assessment procedures designed for children who are developmentally more advanced with infants and toddlers. The situation is doubly difficult for young children who have multiple and severe disabilities. For them, the limitations of existing assessment measures may result in failure to identify important cognitive and social strengths, leading to potentially tragic denial of opportunities.

This chapter provides a brief view of some important new methodologies for providing meaningful assessment of infants and toddlers with significant physical and sensory disabilities. The strategies fall into two categories:

- Use of naturalistic approaches within the context of daily routines and typical environments; and

- Use of appropriate assessment techniques focusing on the use of scales that include "growth or ability" scores, which are specifically designed to provide more meaningful information about children with significant disabilities than is provided by scales that utilize only traditional standardized scaled scores.

Using appropriate evaluation tools and processes is critical in developing an assessment/intervention continuum for children who have significant disabilities. To illustrate the two categories above and highlight the relationship of these two principles to the assessment/intervention continuum, we begin by looking at Cody, a 2-year-old boy with cerebral palsy.

Cody is an adorable, engaging youngster with bright eyes, a wonderful laugh, and an avid interest in the world around him. He is unable to vocalize, however, and can move only his head and one arm well. His short life has included many medical/surgical interventions, including injections to loosen his muscles and use of a gavage tube to supply nutrients directly to his stomach.

Cody had been receiving traditional feeding and neurodevelopmental therapy from excellent therapists at the local hospital (about an hour from his home) for over a year in twice-weekly, half-hour sessions. However, prior to his referral to Project ENRICH (Enrichment using Natural Resources In the Community and Home), a new community-based intervention program that is designed to integrate therapy for children with significant disabilities into the family's daily routines, no one had tried to play hide-and-seek or peekaboo with Cody. His family was not aware that Cody might be able to use puppets or small play figures to create and communicate dramas of his own invention. Staff at the hospital became concerned because Cody was not gaining weight. He frequently missed scheduled appointments, and, when he did come, he was likely to be accompanied by a different member of his extended family each time. Continuity of care was difficult. The physical therapist at the hospital referred Cody to Project ENRICH.

When Project ENRICH staff visited Cody's home, the gleam in his eye told them he could understand them and wanted to relate to them. His parents' descriptions of Cody's voiceless—but violent—temper tantrums suggested that Cody had strong feelings and desires, but few constructive ways to make choices in his life. Since Cody could use his head to signal "yes" or "no," the therapists and his parents were soon able to discover that Cody could tell (literally at a glance) which complex, three-dimensional shape should go into which hole in a shape-sorting box and could decide whether he wanted the play figure of a baby to be arranged with the mother and father figures near the house or with the animals in the barn. When a Big Bird finger puppet was hidden under a piece of cloth and moved around among other cloths, Cody always knew where Big Bird was.

The next step in learning about Cody involved offering him more choices concerning his daily routines. When his diaper was changed, did he want powder or lotion? He could already nod "yes" or "no." How about learning the signs for powder and lotion? Cody learned to make these signs with his good hand in a single session. Next, visits to the augmentative-communication and powered-mobility clinics were scheduled. Project ENRICH staff thought that an augmentative system with an adapted joystick might allow Cody to create symbolic dramas, of which he was clearly cognitively capable, and to make the classic toddler choices so important to developing autonomy—the red shirt or the blue one? Milk or apple juice? At the powered-mobility clinic, Cody might be able to learn to use a low cart that would let him sit almost at floor level and move a switch to go forward or backward, in order to get to a toy, to pull up to the dining room table, or to leave the room when he was angry.

After Project ENRICH staff become better acquainted with Cody and his family, they will administer assessments designed to document his current cognitive strengths, motor abilities, and functional performance. In addition, information about Cody's environment and the priorities and needs of Cody's family will be obtained. This information will help Cody's family and therapists set appropriate goals and recognize small increments of ability as Cody matures and benefits from intervention.

Cody and his family are beginning to "strive and hope," in Gould's words. But this process could have begun much earlier in Cody's life. This chapter offers a new vision for the developmental assessment of young children like Cody, whose motor and sensory disabilities preclude the valid use of traditional assessment approaches.

The developmental assessment of young children who have multiple disabilities should include four elements:

1. A focus on the child within the context of his or her family's daily routines, paying attention to the skills and supports required to accomplish the tasks involved in daily activities;

2. Assessment within naturalistic environments, to insure contextual validity;

3. Appropriate assessment techniques; and

4. Use of assessment instruments that have been developed specifically for use with this population.

To illustrate the process of putting this vision of developmental assessment into practice, this chapter draws on our experiences in Project ENRICH, a project designed to develop a model of helping families and caregivers integrate therapy for young children with severe sensory and motor problems into daily routines, play, and community activities. We also describe the development of new assessment tools and the need for further efforts in this area.

## ■ Focusing on the Child in the Context of Daily ■ Family Routines

The ability to function includes the ability to carry out essential activities of daily life safely and independently in one's natural environment (Haley, Coster, Ludlow, Haltiwanger, & Andrellos, 1992). For young children, these activities include eating, sleeping, bathing, toileting, moving around in the environment, playing, and communicating and interacting with others.

The assessment of a young child's functional abilities—including an analysis of the supports and services that may be needed to maximize the child's ability to participate fully in the life of his or her family, community, and society—represents a major shift from previous evaluation paradigms. These previous paradigms tend to highlight a child's skills and abilities (or, more frequently, a child's pathophysiological deficits and impairments) in specific domains of development (e.g., cognition, communication, motor ability, and social-emotional development). These paradigms also tend to focus on the attainment of developmental milestones rather than assessing a child's ability to participate in activities of daily life. In contrast, assessment of a child's current functioning in daily activities goes beyond isolated performance domains. Project ENRICH, for example, works with families to observe (and then to enhance) the following dimensions of young children's development:

- Personal independence, including the ability to explore the environment, play alone, and participate in daily routines;
- Daily routines as the basis for development—mealtime, dressing, bathtime, and getting ready for bed or nap;
- Outdoor recreation and journeys—visiting Grandma, the zoo, a park, store, or restaurant; playing outdoors; taking other trips away from home;

- Relationships and social interactions—with family, friends, and other important people in the child's and family's world; and

- Play—using toys and activities as opportunities to integrate cognition, communication, motor, and sensory development.

Assessment of the functional abilities of an infant or young child with significant physical and sensory disabilities should consider the child's current and potential use of assistive technology, including devices for augmentative communication and powered mobility. Augmentative-communication and powered-mobility clinics provide excellent examples of settings that highlight the inseparability of assessment and intervention. For children with profound physical limitations, assistive technology can provide the means to independence. As soon as an infant can make choices, assistive technology can help the infant use whatever motor capacities he or she has to communicate needs and wants, explore and manipulate the environment, and demonstrate his or her capacity for spontaneous play and rich relationships. If a 7-month-old with normal cognition can move any extremity, the child can touch a big red switch to turn an appealing toy on or off. The child is thereby demonstrating an understanding of cause and effect, but more important is the fact that he or she is making a choice. On a trip to the zoo, a 2-year-old can touch a communication board to let his parents know he wants to see the monkeys, not the elephants. After the trip, he can use the board to have a conversation about what he saw. Simple templates will be replaced by more complex ones and, eventually, by a keyboard or icons, controlled by fingers, voice, eye blinks, or breath.

Infants and toddlers with profound physical limitations cannot manipulate their environment or move through it. Consequently, they do not experience their environment as typically developing children do, and their test performances cannot reflect their experiences with movement and space. Powered-mobility devices allow children as young as 15 months to move through their environment if they are able to make reliable responses by activating a switch. Once again, the goal is not only greater "functional" independence in the routines of daily life, but also the opportunity to practice social and emotional autonomy, which are key developmental issues for any toddler.

Assessment to determine candidacy for the use of augmentative communication and powered mobility should begin as soon as it becomes apparent that a child has significant motor involvement. Even if the child eventually becomes independent of such devices, the early access to communication and mobility can provide the motivation and foundation experience necessary for development. An augmentative-communication evaluation is generally a painstaking process, which is accomplished over a number of sessions. Factors to be considered in the selection of a communication device include the choice of the symbol system to be used, the child's most reliable motor responses, and the device that will give the child the best prospects for communicating. Similarly, powered-mobility evaluations need to take a multiplicity of factors into account in order to meet a child's and family's individual needs.

## Assessment Within Naturalistic Environments

Assessing a child's development in the context of a familiar environment reflects the field's growing awareness of and respect for the child's and family's experience and relationships, and the patterns of activity and interaction that occur naturally in the child's daily environment. Neither assessment nor intervention is intrusive. Naturalistic assessment involves observation of the child's daily activities with familiar people in the familiar environment of home, child care, or preschool (Barnett, Carey, & Hall, 1993; Bricker & Cripe, 1992; Linder, 1990; Mahoney & Powell, 1988; Mahoney, Robinson, & Powell, 1992; Robinson & Robinson, 1983; Rosenberg & Robinson, 1988). Naturalistic intervention approaches assume that services should be provided in familiar settings, that familiar caregivers can advance intervention goals, and that preferred interventions are those that accomplish change in the context of children's daily experience.

In Project ENRICH, in which families and professionals are jointly developing a new model of assessment and intervention, therapists first "shadow" families, visiting in the home for an hour or two and following the child and family around through a feeding, bathtime, getting in and out of the car, or play in a backyard wading pool. Eventually, when the family is interested and ready, the therapists may spend half a day with them to see what their life is like and how therapeutic goals can be integrated into existing daily activity routines. If the child is in out-of-home child care, similar observations can occur in the child care setting.

Assessing a child with profound physical limitations within his or her natural environment is not only more comfortable for the child and family, but also allows observation of the interaction between the child and the environment. Therapists can introduce the notion of environmental restructuring early. With a child like Cody, for example, the therapists observe that 2-year-olds need chances to move around and make choices about where they go. How can that happen for a child who is not walking? Powered mobility is part of the answer, but the environment must offer 24-inch-wide paths that Cody can negotiate in his new machine. In addition, picture symbols tailored to Cody's individual environment to indicate "watch video," "swing outside," "swim in plastic pool," and "play with toy animals" must be made available. Observation in the home or child care setting suggests what modifications would be needed to accommodate various devices and determines how easy or difficult these modifications would be. At the powered-mobility clinic, parents and caregivers can see the range of possible options and can choose one that meets the needs of everyone involved. Sometimes we begin with environmental restructuring in a child care setting, which may have more space and flexibility than a family home. Often, however, the home environment is deemed more integral to the child's daily life and is given priority.

A natural environment can be an occasion as well as a place. Very young children with significant physical and sensory disabilities and their families may have few chances to simply enjoy themselves. In lieu of formal parent groups, Project ENRICH offers Community Day-Outs, in which staff handle arrangements for family recreational excursions to restaurants, parks with handicap-adapted nature trails, and story hours at the library. Children develop friendships, and parents have a chance to talk to other parents in a relaxed atmosphere. Parents and other caregivers can also talk to staff informally. Project ENRICH therapists observe that they can frequently learn more about children and families in the home than in the clinic, and more at the zoo than in the home!

## Appropriate Assessment Techniques

When a young child has atypical patterns of motor development, assessing other developmental domains presents considerable challenges. A number of investigators have adapted existing assessment approaches to the needs of young children with motor disabilities. Working with preschool and primary grade children with cerebral palsy, Hauessermann (1958) adapted test materials and their mode of presentation to a child's current response repertoire. She varied materials systematically in order to identify the basis for a child's response. This strategy proved valuable in developing teaching approaches and assessment approaches that are appropriate to a child's developmental level. Uzgiris and Hunt (1975) were interested in observing a child's understanding of causality and means-end relationships, independently of the child's motor skills. Cody's therapists followed the Uzgiris and Hunt approach when they hid a finger puppet under a cloth and moved the cloth among other cloths. As long as a child can signal "yes" or "no," he does not have to make a movement to respond to the questions: "Is Big Bird here? Is he there?" Robinson and colleagues (Robinson & Fieber, 1988; Robinson & Robinson 1983; Robinson & Rosenberg, 1987) provide examples of strategies for children who are operating at the sensorimotor stage of cognitive development and whose motor impairments preclude typical responses. Hauessermann (1958) provides descriptions of such strategies for many of the cognitive tasks which make up typical assessments for children age 2 to 5 years.

## ▤ Use of Scores Derived from Assessment ▰ Techniques

A "score" on any assessment measure is meaningful only if it provides information about a child's current abilities, facilitates the documentation of growth over time, and suggests the skills and processes that should be incorporated into the child's treatment plan. Adapting the presentation of items on a standardized test so that the impact of a child's impairments is minimized may help the assessor gather important information, but this strategy invalidates the final "score" with respect to the standardization sample. Consequently, in addition to adapting the presentation of traditional cognitive assessment items to fit children's motor capacities, researchers are beginning to explore use of Rasch analysis, or "sample-free measurement," to develop unidimensional scales that will document a child's performance at one point in time and then record progress as he or she masters challenges of increasing difficulty in that dimension. For example, using one arm to reach with a circular motion to get close to a rattle, reaching directly up toward the rattle, and finally grasping the rattle are a rank-ordered set of behaviors that can be placed along a numerical scale. Similarly, using a spoon involves a progression from being unable to grasp, to carefully grasping, to grasping but not using the spoon to feed oneself, to getting the spoon close to the mouth, to feeding oneself a mashed banana, to picking up peas with the spoon and getting them into the mouth. Using Rasch methodology, assessors can determine the difficulty of each separate task and place tasks in a progression along a single developmental dimension. A child's increasing total score across multiple dimensions will reflect maturation and the effects of intervention. Changes in scores reflect growth made by individual children; they do not compare a child to any "norm group." In fact, these scores may be referred to as growth- or ability-scaled scores in the literature.

## ▤ Using Assessment Tools Designed for Children ▪ with Significant Disabilities

The fundamental assumption of norm-referenced tests is that they allow diverse children to be numerically ranked and compared in relation to a set of absolute standards (norms) that describe the test performance of a specified group, such as children of a particular age (Meisels, this volume). Using a norm-referenced test with a specific child involves two further assumptions, neither of which is likely to be justified when the child being assessed has significant motor or sensory impairments.

First, using a norm-referenced test assumes that children similar to the child being assessed were included in the sample of children tested when the assessment tool was being standardized. In fact, children with significant motor and sensory impairments are typically excluded when populations are recruited for standardization of developmental assessment instruments. Therefore, a task designed to measure cognitive development (putting shapes in a form board in 30 seconds or retrieving a toy from inside a plastic box) may be physically impossible for a child with a motor impairment to perform. As a result, a child with a physical disability who is tested using a standardized instrument may be judged to lack ability.

Second, using a norm-referenced test assumes that the child being assessed has had life experiences and opportunities for learning that are comparable to those of the children in the standardization sample. In fact, infants and toddlers with significant physical handicaps are unlikely to have had opportunities for experience with the content and tasks of formal assessment instruments that are comparable to the experiences of children in a standardization sample. Again, the competencies of children with disabilities may be underrated. The issue of comparability of opportunities is also important, of course, in considering the validity of standardized assessment tools for children of diverse sociocultural backgrounds (see Barrera, this volume).

Acknowledging the limitations of traditional assessment tools, we nevertheless do not propose abandoning them altogether in the assessment of young children with significant disabilities. However, it is critically important to make sure before using any test with a child with a particular disability that one can answer two questions: (a) What questions about the child's development can this test be expected to answer?; and (b) How do other children with this child's type of disability perform on this test? Answers to the second question come from research studies that include large groups of children with the disability in question.

Several assessment tools designed for use with young children with significant motor or sensory disabilities have recently been developed or are in the final stages of development. These include the Pediatric Evaluation of Disability Inventory (PEDI) (Haley et al., 1992), the Toddler and Infant Motor Evaluation (TIME) (Miller & Roid, 1994), and the Leiter International Performance Scale-Revised (LIPS-R) (Roid & Miller, in press).

The Pediatric Evaluation of Disability Inventory (PEDI) (Haley et al., 1992) examines a child's ability to function independently and documents what a child can do when someone provides assistance. Organizing information this way helps professionals and parents to recognize what the child can already do in his current caregiving environment, to identify limitations, and to plan what to work on next. The PEDI was developed to provide a comprehensive clinical assessment of performance on key functional tasks by children ages 6 months through 7 years. It provides a descriptive measure of the child's current levels of self-care, mobility, and social function, as well as a method for tracking changes over time. Two subtests of the PEDI—the Level of Caregiver Assistance, and Modifications—are particularly useful for assessing children with disabilities. These subtests measure the amount of caregiver assistance a child needs to perform such functional activities as eating, playing, or moving. In addition, they determine which environmental modifications or assistive equipment the child needs to perform routine daily activities. The PEDI has been standardized on a stratified sample of children without developmental delays (n=412) and has also been administered to several cohorts of children with developmental delays (n=102). Using both traditional and newer item response theory (Rasch scaling) methodologies for statistical analysis, the PEDI's authors have developed both standardized scaled scores and Rasch-based scaled scores that can be used to compare an individual child's growth over time to his or her own anticipated development, rather than to the developmental trajectories of typically developing children.

The Toddler and Infant Motor Evaluation (TIME) (Miller & Roid, 1994) assesses eight domains related to the motor and functional abilities of children from 4 months to 3-and-a-half years of age. The TIME evaluates the child's motor abilities and how these abilities affect functional performance. It also determines information which can lead to knowledge about the "next step" in motor development. The scale not only identifies the presence of motoric abilities (i.e., what a child can do), but also focuses on the quality of the movement (i.e., how a child can do it), a construct thought to be essential in differentiating normal from atypical motor development (Bly, 1983). Parents and professionals are partners in the TIME assessment. In as naturalistic an environment as possible, parents (prompted by the examiners) facilitate movement and elicit specific behaviors from the child, and the examiners observe and record the child's responses.

During the standardization of the TIME, a large group of children with disabilities was also assessed so that scores could be determined for children who had specific types of disabilities. Of the 875 children tested, 731 had no motor disabilities and 133 had documented motor disabilities or delays. Data from both groups of children were used to conduct a variety of validity and reliability studies. In addition, data from children with disabilities were aggregated to develop the Atypical Patterns Scaled Score, which provides a standardized rating of the degree of a child's atypicality relative to the group of children in the sample who had developmental delays. Internal reliability (.72 to .97), test-retest reliability (.96 to .99), and inter-relater reliability (.94

to .99) indicate that the TIME scores are stable. Validity studies, including content, construct, and criterion-related studies, provide significant evidence that the scale is measuring what the authors purport.

The TIME's eight subtests (Mobility, Stability, Motor Organization, Atypical Positions, Social-Emotional, Adaptive, Performance Quality Rating, and Component Analysis) are designed specifically to be sensitive to small changes in motor behaviors. For example, a child with a motor delay may initially require assistance to stabilize his or her head when on all fours. If, after intervention, the child can move the head around in all directions without assistance, he or she will be much better able than before to explore the environment and interact with people and objects. Therefore, the quality of the child's experience will be significantly different. Yet most norm-referenced, standardized scales of motor development do not include measurements sensitive enough to detect a change this "small." In contrast, the TIME's Component Analysis subtest looks at all components of normal movement patterns, including position of the head and neck, trunk and pelvis, and upper and lower extremities; weight shifting and weight bearing; and movement into and out of all positions. This level of detail allows parents and interventionists to track (and celebrate) small increments of progress in motor aptitude over time, to continually modify intervention approaches in order to build on the child's emerging abilities, and to keep in mind the overall goal, which is fuller participation in family and community life.

To give children who are motorically impaired, nonverbal, or non-English-speaking an opportunity to demonstrate their cognitive strengths, the Leiter International Performance Scale-Revised (LIPS-R) (Roid & Miller, in press), an updated version of the Leiter International Performance Scale (Leiter, 1979), is being developed. The Leiter scale was originally developed in the 1930s as a nonverbal measure of the understanding of concepts through matching tasks. The LIPS-R, designed for children and young adults who are developmentally between the ages of 2 and 21 years, requires no verbal responses and includes a variety of modifications for children with motor disabilities. For example, a child can direct his or her gaze to the correct response (eye pointing), or an augmentative-communication device can be used as the examiner arranges stimuli on a board and points to possible responses. Children with significant hearing impairments, severe motor disabilities, cognitive disabilities, and communication disabilities, as well as children who speak English as a second language, were sampled in the Research Edition of the LIPS-R and have participated in studies conducted during the national standardization in 1995.

In summary, all three tests, the PEDI, the TIME, and the LIPS-R, have not only drawn upon traditional psychometric techniques, but have also explored uses of Rasch methodology. All three tests provide traditional standard scores but emphasize the availability of growth or ability scores for children who have various disabilities. The inclusion of growth or ability scales that provide the order of items and the relative item difficulty of each task is extremely useful when the goal is to evaluate change over time. When assessing children whose development is atypical, it is almost always appropriate to focus on the abilities of the child, rather than on a score that may seem to be simply a reminder of the child's disability.

# Conclusion

The assessment of young children with significant motor and sensory disabilities requires a highly individualized approach. The issue in assessing such children clearly goes beyond establishing eligibility for intervention programs. We already know that these children and their families will be entitled to specialized assistance. The challenge is, first of all, to make a connection with the child as a person and to understand how the family is living and what its members are hoping and striving for. Next, one must avoid underestimating the capacities of a child with motor or sensory disabilities. Rather, one must use the richest available combination of clinical skills, assistive technology, environmental restructuring, and appropriate assessment scales to reveal the child's current strengths and potential for further development. The final goal of any assessment of a young child with a significant disability is to discover how therapeutic approaches, integrated into daily family routines, can help the child participate in family life, play spontaneously, explore and manipulate the environment, enjoy relationships, and make choices about life.

Let's return to Cody and look at how these methodologies—the use of naturalistic assessment/intervention and the use of appropriate evaluation techniques—affected Cody's life.

Recently Cody's parents and grandparents attended an Individualized Family Service Plan (IFSP) meeting. The meeting was initiated by Project ENRICH staff who had attended Cody's evaluations at the augmentative-communication clinic, the powered-mobility clinic, the special needs pediatric clinic, and the nutrition clinic, and had also attended several of his occupational, physical, and speech therapy sessions. In addition, Project ENRICH staff had made a referral for Part H (IDEA: Individuals with Disabilities Education Act) services, a step which had been overlooked in the past.

In addition to Cody's family, about 20 professionals attended the IFSP meeting. These included Cody's pediatrician, the physician in charge of the nutrition clinic at the hospital, all of Cody's therapists, the clinicians who had been involved in his assistive technology evaluations, community representatives from Part H, and Project ENRICH staff (including the parent of a child like Cody on the team). Prior to the meeting, Project ENRICH staff had carefully discussed with Cody's family what to expect and how the family could be strong advocates for their priorities for Cody and for themselves.

Before the meeting, the various professionals working with Cody had administered a number of scales, including the PEDI, the TIME, and the current edition of the LIPS-R. In previous testing, Cody had received an extremely low standard score on the Bayley Scales of Infant Development (BSID) (PDI (Psychomotor Development Index) < 50; MDI (Mental Development Index) < 50) and on the Receptive Expressive Emergent Scale-2 (RQ=71; EQ=14; LQ=43-49). However, Cody's ability scores on Rasch-based scales were not "low" scores, but rather reflected his abilities on domains assessed. (See examples of Cody's PEDI scores in the figure below.)

Discussion at Cody's IFSP meeting spelled out his strengths clearly and recognized a continuing need for occupational, physical, and augmentative speech therapy. The meeting illustrated the integration of assessment and intervention. Assessments had been administered in natural settings, using approaches designed for children like Cody. Findings stressed Cody's abilities. In addition, time had been spent getting to know Cody and his family in the context of their everyday experiences at home and in the neighborhood. Cody's family and a multidisciplinary team, including a parent of a child like Cody, participated in the assessment process and in the construction of a meaningful intervention plan, which addressed Cody's needs within the context of other family priorities. Cody's Individualized Family Service Plan included several goals: (a) enrolling Cody in an inclusive preschool program; (b) organizing Cody's medical care and therapy so that the family would need to travel to the hospital only one day each week; (c) obtaining health insurance for other members of Cody's family; (d) obtaining respite care; and (e)

## Pediatric Evaluation of Disability Inventory

### Composite Scores

| Domain | Raw Scores | Normative Standard scores | Scaled Scores* |
|---|---|---|---|
| *Functional skills* | | | |
| Self-care | 24 | 25.3 | 44 |
| Mobility | 8 | < 10 | 27 |
| Social function | 21 | 22.4 | 43 |
| *Caregiver assistance* | | | |
| Self-care | 1 | < 10 | 12 |
| Mobility | 1 | < 10 | 12 |
| Social function | 4 | 29.6 | 32 |

### Score Profile

| Domain | Normative Standard Scores | Scaled Scores* |
|---|---|---|
| *Functional skills* | | |
| Self-care | | |
| Mobility | | |
| Social function | | |
| *Caregiver assistance* | | |
| Self-care | | |
| Mobility | | |
| Social function | | |

±2 standard errors
*Rasch-based Ability Scores

Reprinted with permission from Haley, S.M., Coster, W. J., Ludlow L. H., Haltiwanger, J. T., & Andrellos, P. J. *Pediatric Evaluation of Disability Inventory (PEDI)*. Boston: New England Medical Center, 1992.

finding funding for ramps for the front steps of his home.

Assessment must "understand and capture the process of learning and growth, rather than just the 'developmental status' of the child" (Meisels, this volume). When children have significant sensory and motor disabilities, it is especially important to integrate the processes of assessment and intervention. Observing the child within his or her naturalistic environment and using scales specifically designed to highlight a child's abilities are part of a focus on competence and context. This focus will help both families and professionals appreciate the gifts of each child.

# References

Barnett, D., Carey, K., & Hall, J. (1993). Naturalistic intervention design for young children: Foundations, rationales, and strategies. *Topics in Early Childhood Special Education, 13*, 430-444.

Bricker, D., & Cripe, J. (1992). *An activity-based approach to early intervention.* Baltimore, MD: Paul H. Brookes Publishing Co.

Bly, L. (1983). *The components of normal movement during the first year of life and abnormal motor development.* Birmingham, AL: Pittengen and Associates.

Gould, S. J. (1981). *The mismeasure of man.* New York: W. W. Norton.

Haley, S. M., Coster, W. J., Ludlow, L. H., Haltiwanger, J. T., & Andrellos, P. J. (1992). *Pediatric Evaluation of Disability Inventory: Manual.* Boston, MA: PEDI Research Group.

Hauesserman, E. (1958). *Developmental potential of preschool children.* New York: Grune and Stratton.

Leiter, R. G. (1979, 1959) *Leiter International Performance Scale: Instruction manual.* Chicago, IL: Stoelting Co.

Linder, T. W. (1990). *Transdisciplinary play-based assessment: A functional approach to working with young children.* Baltimore, MD: Paul H. Brookes Publishing Co.

Mahoney, G., & Powell, A. (1988). Modifying parent/child interaction: Enhancing the development of handicapped children. *Journal of Special Education, 22,* 82-96.

Mahoney, G. J., Robinson, C., & Powell, A. (1992). Focusing on parent-child interaction: The bridge to developmentally appropriate practices. *Topics in Early Childhood Special Education, 12* (1), 105-120.

Miller, L. J., & Roid, G. H. (1994). *The Toddler and Infant Motor Evaluation: Manual.* Tucson, AZ: Therapy Skill Builders.

Robinson, C., & Fieber, N. (1988). Cognitive assessment of motorically impaired infants and preschoolers. In T. Wachs & R. Sheehan (Eds.), *Assessment of young developmentally disabled children.* New York: Plenum Publishing Co.

Robinson, C., & Robinson, J. (1983). Sensorimotor functions and cognitive development. In M. Snell (Ed.), *Systematic instruction of the moderately and severely handicapped.* (Rev. ed.). Columbus, OH: Charles Merrill.

Robinson, C., and Rosenberg, S. (1987). A strategy for assessing infants with motor impairments. In I. C. Uzgiris & J. M. Hunt (Eds.), *Infant performance and experience: New findings with the ordinal scales* (pp. 311-339). Urbana and Chicago, IL: University of Illinois Press.

Roid, G. H., & Miller, L. J. (in press). *Leiter International Performance Scale-Revised* (Standardization Edition). Wood Dale, IL: Stoelting Co.

Rosenberg, S., & Robinson, C. (1988). Interactions of parents with their young handicapped children. In S. Odom & M. Karnes (Eds.), *Early intervention for infants and young children with handicaps: An empirical base.* Baltimore, MD: Paul H. Brookes Publishing Co.

Uzgiris, I. C., & Hunt, J. M. (1975). *Assessment in infancy: Ordinal scales of psychological development.* Urbana, IL: University of Illinois Press.

# 16.Neuro-developmental Evaluation of Newborns and Infants with Genetic Disorders

CAROLE SAMANGO-SPROUSE

The birth of a baby with a genetic disorder elicits a range of emotional responses, questions, and concerns among parents, other family members, friends, and the family's primary health care providers. Responses to the diagnosis are as different, and as unpredictable, as each person is unique. A growing body of medical research offers answers to families' questions that would not have been available a decade ago. Because genetic disorders are relatively rare, most infants with such disorders benefit from an initial evaluation in a major medical center, where staff are experienced in identifying and helping families address the complex medical and developmental problems that may be associated with a genetic disorder. However, the lack of widely disseminated, accurate information about many genetic disorders means that families may come to an evaluation with misconceptions that could keep them from fully appreciating the baby's current capacities and could lead them to underestimate the child's potential. Consequently, a developmental assessment in a major medical center presents a unique but challenging opportunity for professionals to establish a trusting, mutually rewarding relationship with parents, which will allow them to use all the knowledge available to them to work effectively with parents on their baby's behalf.

At the Division of Infant and Child Studies (ICS) located in the Department of Medical Genetics at Children's National

Medical Center in Washington, D.C., I work with the families of infants with relatively common genetic disorders, such as Down syndrome and neurofibromatosis (NF-1), and with much rarer chromosomal and genetic abnormalities. During the past several decades, advances in genetic technology and increased understanding of newborn behavior and development, along with enlightened social attitudes and more appropriately designed early intervention services, have allowed us to move substantially closer to a new vision of developmental assessment for these children. This chapter describes the technical advances that have marked the diagnosis and assessment of infants with genetic disorders in recent years. It also places these advances in the context of a sustained focus on family strengths and concerns and a commitment to fostering the full developmental potential of every child with a genetic disorder. Our work with newborns who have Down syndrome and their families, also described in this chapter, illustrates the blend of state-of-the-art science and family-centered support that we would like to see available for every baby with a genetic disorder.

## ▤ Issues Concerning the Assessment of Infants ▇ with Genetic Disorders

In the last two decades, neurodevelopmental assessment for all infants has changed dramatically, due to burgeoning research findings, parents' advocacy for their infants' rights, and the enactment and implementation of the Individuals with Disabilities Education Act (IDEA). The assessment of infants with genetic disorders has been changed by the identification of new chromosomal disorders and the advent of neuroimaging of the central nervous system, gene mapping, and DNA linkage studies. In the next 10 years, the study of large groups of children with the same genetic syndrome will help researchers understand more about the functioning of the central nervous system and its impact on behavior. In addition, researchers will learn more about infants' organizational capacities and pathways of learning. As our understanding of the interaction among brain function, genetic syndrome, and behavior increases, we will be able to offer developmental assessments of children with genetic disorders that are both more specific and more individualized. The practitioner's task will be to achieve a balanced awareness of syndrome-specific and individual influences on an infant's behavior, in order to help families appreciate the individuality, strengths, vulnerabilities, and challenges their baby brings to the process of development.

Many factors influence each developmental assessment, such as the baby's age, the diagnosis, and the specific characteristics of the syndrome, including the behavioral, emotional, and developmental profile. Yet one basic dimension of every assessment remains constant: There is always a baby and a family with questions, concerns, anxieties, and fears. The job of the professional in this field is to balance, integrate, and synthesize medical knowledge and developmental findings into practical, sensitive, and sensible information for families. Centuries ago, Hippocrates observed that, in order to practice good medicine, the physician must know the person as well as the disease. The key to a comprehensive and meaningful developmental assessment is the creation of an effective working relationship with both the family and the infant. Within this relationship, the art and science of developmental assessment are blended into an evolving process that responds to the needs of the child and family as they change over time.

The first goal of an assessment of a baby with a genetic disorder is to give parents the information and support they need to feel confident about caring for their child. A successful assessment enhances parents' and professionals' understanding of the baby's evolving capabilities, increases their appreciation of the variations of development that are possible among children with the same genetic syndrome, and facilitates parents' ability to advocate on their child's behalf. At ICS, a variety of mechanisms are designed to support parents. Parents have access to state-of-the-art information about their baby's medical and developmental characteristics. Their own knowledge and expertise, as well as the observations of professionals and the results of medical evaluations, are used to create a plan to optimize the infant's development. Professionals and parents collaboratively construct a family-focused intervention plan that recognizes the baby's unique profile of developmental strengths and vulnerabilities, as well as the family's desired outcomes.

For many families, the medical center provides a "safety net" and serves as a reliable ally in dealing with medical and developmental issues surrounding their child. When medical center professionals are well trained, they recognize that the uniqueness of each family, their expectations, and their agenda for each visit must guide the assessment process. Moreover, expectations and agendas change for each family over time. At ICS, the assessment process continues from the time of diagnosis until the child is 7 years old. The initial evaluation is inevitably stressful, but it offers professionals a unique opportunity to establish a strong working relationship with a family. Later assessments are likely to be more comfortable, with child, family, and developmentalist feeling secure with one another.

An assessment must recognize the interaction between the medical and developmental problems of an infant with a genetic disorder and their combined effect on the family's functioning. If the developmental problems of a baby with a genetic disorder are evaluated and treated in isolation, strategies will be limited and ineffective. For example, if a baby with Down syndrome has a major cardiac deficit, the presence of this problem will affect every aspect of the child's life. The cardiac condition may limit the energy available to the baby for motor development and exploration of the environment. Necessary medical precautions may restrict the whole family's mobility, precluding visits to distant family members, participation in social events, or even trips to the mall. An infant with Williams syndrome, another chromosomal disorder, may be very sensitive to sound, touch, and movement. These behavioral characteristics affect the creation of an appropriate family-centered intervention plan. The syndrome-specific behavior of each infant should serve as a guide to early interventionists as they develop strategies for intervention.

An appropriate assessment of a baby with Down syndrome and a cardiac condition should consider the influence of the cardiac condition on the infant's behavior and the family's life. The assessment should also consider the baby's behavior in relation to the typical profile of an infant with Down syndrome and cardiac disease. The developmentalist can then talk with the family about their baby's unique behaviors, as well as what this baby has in common with other infants with his or her conditions. In practical terms, this discussion might lead to home-based (instead of center-based) early intervention services; clustering of medication doses, when possible, to allow more uninterrupted free time for baby and family; and an effort to identify and train consistently available baby-sitters to allow parents some "adult time" together. At each assessment, the family and the developmentalist go through a five-step process:

1. Observing and discussing the baby's current developmental level and skills;
2. Reviewing the developmental performance that is typical of children with the baby's syndrome;
3. Identifying strengths that can be capitalized on through intervention strategies;
4. Identifying vulnerabilities that need further investigation or specialized services; and
5. Discussing the most appropriate and practical ways to obtain necessary services for the baby and family.

The complexity of each assessment is described through the five-step process. The uniqueness of the infant and the genetic disorder is identified by synthesizing the information obtained from the evaluation process.

## The Impact of a Genetic Diagnosis on the Family

The diagnosis of a genetic disorder in a child will have a unique meaning to each parent, as well as to other family members. A parent who is coping with the same familially inherited disorder as that of the baby will bring the perspective of his or her own experience to the situation. Any family's unique configuration of knowledge, beliefs, and values will affect their view of the child. The developmentalist can use an assessment as an opportunity to help parents appreciate the individuality of their baby, while also learning to recognize behaviors that may be characteristic of the syndrome. It is particularly important to recognize that the timing of the genetic diagnosis—prenatally, soon after birth, or later in infancy or early childhood—is likely to have a powerful impact on the family's experience and, consequently, on the child's development.

In the Department of Medical Genetics at Children's National Medical Center, a genetic diagnosis may be made prenatally, through the Center of Prenatal Evaluation; at birth, through the 24-hour emergency consultative service; or postnatally, through an outpatient visit to the Department of Medical Genetics. The timing of the diagnosis influences the scope of the developmental evaluation, as well as the role and responsibilities of the developmentalist.

## Prenatal diagnosis

If expectant parents have been informed of a genetic diagnosis prenatally, they come to a developmentalist for information about what they can expect, based on that diagnosis. They are likely to have specific questions and concerns: "What is this baby going to be like?" "What can we expect from the baby intellectually?" "What degree of impairment is likely?" In order to present information in a nonjudgmental and nondirective manner, I respond to the parents' questions from several perspectives. First, I discuss the characteristics and typical behavioral and developmental patterns of infants and children with this diagnosis. The developmental information I offer comes from research findings as well as from my own clinical experience with infants who have this syndrome. Since this is a prenatal diagnosis, I encourage parents to talk about the individuality of the fetus within the context of their family's composition, expectations, and values. Parents are offered the opportunity to meet a family that has a child with the same genetic diagnosis, often a family that also confronted the dilemmas of prenatal identification of a genetic disorder.

If the family elects to continue the pregnancy, we plan to meet with the parents and baby within the first month after birth. At this visit, the developmental assessment focuses on the baby as a unique individual. This is an opportunity to demonstrate the infant's strengths to the family, as well as a chance to discuss in detail those behaviors that are typical of all newborns, those that may be related to the genetic diagnosis, and those that represent the baby's individual style. The assessment is usually wonderfully rewarding for both the professional and the family. The professional can help parents identify the baby's capacities, and parents' anxiety is significantly reduced since they made a conscious choice several months earlier and have been long awaiting the baby's birth.

## Neonatal diagnosis

When the diagnosis of a genetic disorder is made just after birth, the first developmental assessment is likely to be an intense, stressful experience. Many parents have barely had time to recover from the stress of delivery before medical and developmental evaluations of the newborn begin. The prognosis for the baby's very survival may be uncertain. Even if the baby is healthy, parents and other family members must adjust to the loss of the "expected child" and prepare for the care of their "real child."

As a developmentalist, in my first encounter with parents of a newly diagnosed newborn, I try to convey clearly that our purpose is to assist them, in whatever ways possible, in caring for their baby. This initial evaluation provides the basis for a beginning understanding of the baby, his or her needs, and the family's desires. It is the beginning of a gradual process of optimizing the baby's developmental potential. I work with the family to demonstrate the baby's individual strengths and style and to identify behaviors that are characteristic of the syndrome. Then, we can determine collaboratively what services are needed immediately and what can wait for a period of time.

### Genetic diagnosis of the older infant or toddler

The family that brings an older infant or toddler to a geneticist for evaluation has had different experiences from those of parents with children who were diagnosed prenatally or in the neonatal period. Families of older infants or toddlers have often been concerned about their children's delayed or atypical development for several months. A child may have been evaluated by many professionals, but without a confirmed diagnosis. Suddenly, with the geneticist's assessment, a diagnosis is determined, and the parents have a specific name and an explanation for their child's developmental problems. For parents who have waited months, if not years, for answers to their questions, a genetic diagnosis may offer relief from uncertainty, combined with frustration at the lengthy process required to make the diagnosis and, perhaps, sadness at the implications of the diagnosis. The developmentalist must be sensitive to and respectful of each family's unique reactions, coping style, and subsequent decisions.

## ▉ Developmental Assessment of Infants with ▉ Down Syndrome

Changes that have occurred in the developmental assessment of children with Down syndrome and in the supports available to these children and their families illustrate the progress we hope to make, over time, in serving all infants with genetic disorders and their families.

Every year, nearly 7,000 babies are born with Down syndrome in the United States (Wishart, 1988). Down syndrome, a medical entity described by Langden Down in 1866, results from the presence of an extra chromosome 21 in all cells of the body. Infants with Down syndrome may have major congenital anomalies, involving the cardiovascular, musculoskeletal, gastrointestinal, ophthalmological, and central nervous systems (Coyle, Oster-Granite, & Gearhart, 1986; Pueschel, 1983; Pueschel & Rynders, 1982; Smith & Berg, 1976). Recent research has focused on the specific developmental challenges that children with Down syndrome may face in motor development, language, cognition, and speech. New findings have dispelled some long-held stereotypic beliefs about the learning, temperament, and personality styles of children with Down syndrome.

In earlier case histories, parents observe that 40 years ago, when a child with Down syndrome was born, the attending obstetrician would go out to the expectant father in the waiting room, announce, "Your baby is Mongoloid," and suggest institutionalization because "these children are better off away from their families." In later years, parents report hearing from professionals, "Take your baby home, love and care for him, but don't expect too much" (Nadel & Rosenthal, 1995). Today, professionals can be much more helpful to families with newborns with Down syndrome, as we use sensitive assessment approaches and knowledge of community supports to help families envision a realistic, unique scenario for themselves and their baby.

In the Department of Medical Genetics, we have incorporated the expertise of both medical and developmental specialists into one department, in order to offer children and their families rapid diagnosis, comprehensive evaluation, and ongoing coordination of appropriate medical and early intervention services. The Department of Medical Genetics provides 24-hour emergency genetic consultation services to families throughout the Washington, D.C., metropolitan area. When an infant with Down syndrome is born, the specialized expertise of a geneticist is available immediately to families and their physicians at the bedside of the infant in the community hospital. Families have the opportunity to discuss their concerns, hopes, and fears with a geneticist who specializes in their baby's conditions and can offer the most current medical knowledge and recommendations for evaluations and procedures designed to optimize the infant's outcome.

As part of this discussion, the physician offers families the opportunity for a neurobehavioral evaluation of their newborn.

Assessment tools such as the Neonatal Behavioral Assessment Scale (NBAS) (Brazelton, 1973) and the Assessment of Preterm Infant Behavior (APIB) (Als, Lester, & Brazelton, 1979) allow professionals to identify and share with parents the individual patterns of their baby and to suggest practical strategies for caregiving that will be responsive to the baby's unique needs and will enhance developmental outcome. Since the neonatal period is a critical period of learning for all newborns, we like to assess a baby with Down syndrome as quickly as possible, usually within the first two to four weeks of life. The assessment gives us a chance to respond to parents' many questions and concerns about the baby's health and behavior, and the potential impact of the diagnosis. Both of the parents, and often the grandparents, are present for the first evaluation.

## ▤ The Neurobehavioral Assessment of an Infant ▤ with Down Syndrome

The neurobehavioral assessment of a newborn with Down syndrome considers the individuality of the infant and family, the neurobehavioral characteristics typical of infants with Down syndrome, and the medical condition of the baby. The assessment evaluates the baby's current capacities and behavioral responses to social interaction and increasingly challenging developmental tasks. Together, the developmentalist and family identify the baby's strengths and challenges, and they develop initial strategies to address both medical and developmental issues in the context of the family's priorities, resources, and concerns.

Parents are astute observers of their babies. During the neurobehavioral evaluation, the developmentalist can often substantiate the parents' perceptions of the baby's behavior and help them think further about the meaning of the behavior. For example, we will review what the baby did easily and what seemed hard for him or her. Conversations often center around whether a newborn's behavior—for example, turning his or her head away—was purposeful, and what it meant. I might say, "Your baby turned her head away because she was tired and could no longer remain engaged with us. As adults, when we feel stressed, overwhelmed, or just bored, we can change the topic of a conversation or offer a polite excuse to leave, but a newborn has fewer options because she cannot talk or walk away."

In the neurobehavioral assessment, we identify and discuss in detail the baby's individual style of social interaction, motoric organization, physiologic regulation, and attentional capacities. We work to insure that the diagnosis of Down syndrome does not keep families from recognizing their baby's capabilities and ways of communicating. For example, by evaluating the baby's preference for visual over auditory stimulation (or vice versa), we can begin a discussion about supportive caregiving that involves the whole family. It is absolutely magical to see parents' pleasure when their newborn with Down syndrome knows their voice, finds their voice, and prefers their voice. This demonstrates clearly the baby's behavioral competence and mobilizes everyone's energy and hope.

We use a similar approach to identify some of the typical challenges confronting a newborn with Down syndrome and to discuss appropriate caregiving strategies. The muscles of infants with Down syndrome tend to be soft (truncal hypotonia and joint laxity), with muscle tone (the ability to hold a position or posture against gravity) frequently better in the legs than in the arms. We can demonstrate this easily to parents during the assessment of reflexes and can then go on to explain that a baby with Down syndrome needs help to bring her hands to her mouth because the muscles in the baby's arms do not provide enough support or stability for the baby to do this on her own. We also explain that being able to bring the hand to the mouth is important since sucking on fingers or the hand increases a baby's ability to be involved in social interaction. We offer parents practical suggestions for developing strength in their baby's arms and demonstrate positions that will facilitate spontaneous hand-to-mouth movement.

## ▤ Implications of Assessment Findings for ▪ Caregiving

In order to talk with parents about using daily caregiving routines to optimize their baby's strengths and to support areas of vulnerability, beginning in the first month of life, we use neurobehavioral observations of the newborn with Down syndrome, taken in the context of principles of neuromotor organization developed by Bobath and Bobath (1964). By both planning and considering the level, location, position, and length of each interaction, family members and other caregivers can help the baby become increasingly organized, differentiated, and modulated, or well controlled. Long-term developmental outcome may also be improved as parents try recommended therapeutic handling procedures, observe the resulting increased motoric organization in the baby, and then adapt and develop their caregiving strategies further.

Although each newborn with Down syndrome has an individual style, as well as strengths and needs, some interactive strategies seem to be helpful for most babies. For example, hand-to-mouth behavior, a challenge for babies with Down syndrome and a key to motor organization and calmer alert states, can be facilitated by the bunting developed by Als and her colleagues. (Use of the bunting with babies with cardiac deficit should be approved by a pediatric cardiologist.) Since newborns with Down syndrome often have difficulty transitioning to sleep and establishing a sleep/wake pattern, parents can use bunting and dim lights to help babies establish sleep/wake patterns. They can wake babies every two to three hours during the day and evening in the first month of life to promote a more predictable feeding pattern. With increasing organization, the infant with Down syndrome becomes more sophisticated in his or her social interactions and more competent in transitioning easily to a variety of states.

Because newborns with Down syndrome avert their gaze, drift into a drowsy state, or increase their motoric activity when overwhelmed, their behavioral cues are often unrecognized. The neurobehavioral evaluation reveals the newborn's individual style and preferences for auditory or visual stimulation, people, and toys. We help parents identify their baby's communication signals and develop strategies for graded stimulation and a selection of toys based on the baby's preferences.

The birth order of the baby with Down syndrome in his or her family also guides our discussion of the neurobehavioral evaluation. With parents of a first-born infant with Down syndrome, we make sure that we identify the behaviors of the baby that are typical of any newborn and discuss basic caregiving questions, such as recognizing hunger cues and thinking about child care settings. We also talk about discussing the diagnosis of Down syndrome with grandparents and friends.

For parents with other children, the neurobehavioral evaluation of the newborn with Down syndrome offers an opportunity to discuss practical concerns, such as options for early intervention and ways siblings can play with the baby. Parents of young children are likely to be balancing many work and family responsibilities already. The evaluation process involves discussing ways that parents can meet their current responsibilities while still feeling confident that the new baby is getting their special attention.

## ■ Anticipating Developmental Issues with ■ Infants and Children with Down Syndrome

As a developmentalist continues to work with families of infants and young children with Down syndrome, it is helpful to continue to use the approach used in the newborn period. The goals are to be aware of features associated with Down syndrome that are likely to influence development, to recognize the impact of other important genetic endowments (for example, height, ethnicity, musical or artistic talent), and to identify caregiving strategies that will support development. Thus, although the mean age for walking among children with Down syndrome is 24 months, I have seen infants with Down syndrome walk independently as early as 13 months (Samango-Sprouse, 1990). African-American infants with Down syndrome and normal cardiac status appear to have better muscle tone in the first several years of life, regardless of gender, than infants with Down syndrome from other racial backgrounds. Caucasian girls with Down syndrome often have better muscle tone than Caucasian boys. As expected, the stronger the muscle tone, the earlier the age of independent walking.

In infants with Down syndrome, for example, the startle (moro) reflex typically persists beyond the neonatal period. Frequent startling leads to motoric disorganization and abrupt changes in state that can be distressing to the baby. The startle reaction can be minimized easily during sleep by swaddling the baby and placing him or her on the side. When moving a baby with Down syndrome from one position to another (such as tummy to back), the startle reflex can be controlled by gently holding arms and legs tucked together, a position that is supportive and helps the infant remain calm, quiet, and alert.

Infants with Down syndrome often prefer to use one side of their body more than the other, a pattern that pediatric physical therapists call "fixing" or stabilizing one side of the body in order to use the opposite side for play. Caregivers may inadvertently encourage this asymmetry by offering a toy to the hand that reaches out first, but, once aware of the importance of play in midline, they can encourage reaching from both sides of the body. Similarly, caregivers can adapt car seats and infant carriers to help babies with Down syndrome overcome muscle weakness and maintain their head in midline. Without such adaptations, newborns with Down syndrome are likely to rest their head on one side of the body (usually the right), resulting in shortened neck muscles and mild flattening of the skull.

As is the case with motor development, parents and professionals need to recognize and build on the interactional styles and social behaviors of infants with Down syndrome. This is not always easy. For example, because many newborns with Down syndrome may have soft or decreased muscle tone of the lips and cheeks, their smiles may not be as broad, active, or bright as those of other newborns. In addition, some infants with Down syndrome react slowly to stimulation (responsivity time is unique to each baby and varies in different situations), leading adults to intervene too quickly with additional stimulation, rather than giving the baby time to complete his or her response to the initial overture by the adult. The neonatal observation of the baby's behavior and "timing" help to identify the infant's interactional style, which can then guide caregiving.

Some older infants and toddlers with Down syndrome are socially adept, communicate clearly with gestures, and, according to their parents, "understand everything" but lack the ability to use their tongues, lips, and other muscles to articulate words. Again, careful observation of these children's social skills and ability to imitate gestures may suggest the introduction of sign language as a form of communication for children for whom spoken language remains a challenge. Young children with Down syndrome may use more complex expressive language in one-on-one conversations with parents and caregivers (Fowler, 1990) than they do in a typical group care environment. Again, awareness of this possibility allows parents and caregivers to make special efforts to support children's use of spoken language in settings outside the home.

# Individual Differences in Temperamental Style, Attentional Capacities, and Motoric Organization

A baby's unique temperamental style, attentional capacities, and motoric organization influence parents' and caregivers' behavior, and, consequently, the developing emotional relationship between the infant and parents. The infant's style of response affects cognitive strategies throughout development. I have observed three interactional patterns among infants with Down syndrome that often persist throughout the preschool years. Recognizing these patterns early helps parents and professionals to take children's challenging behavior in stride and devise appropriate caregiving strategies.

One group of infants with Down syndrome tends to be very easily aroused by sound, smell, light, changes in posture, or movement; they become motorically disorganized rapidly. This type of baby responds quickly to social interaction but lacks the internal organization required to maintain a quiet, alert state. As older infants, these children may be easily distressed by changes in routine or new experiences. Toddlers with this temperamental pattern energetically investigate every inch of their environment once they become mobile, but they may roam from toy to toy rather than engaging in purposeful play and cognitive exploration. Structure and predictability in caregiving routines promote the modulation, organization, and control which help these children develop their social and cognitive capacities.

A second group of infants with Down syndrome is more passive and slow to warm up, and has low muscle tone. As newborns, these infants are easy to care for, tolerate changes in family routines, and are not easily upset. However, if parents and caregivers interpret a baby's passivity as "contentment," they may not initiate social interaction or use specific strategies to enhance motor activity (especially hand-to-mouth behavior) and help babies achieve and maintain an alert state. Older infants in this group may be content to sit quietly in one spot and play with one toy for extended periods of time. Although exploring one toy can be productive, caregivers also need to encourage mobility and active problem-solving. Parents and caregivers may underestimate more passive infants' cognitive strengths and capacities for play. Careful observation will help identify the infant's cues, signaling choices, desires, and needs, and will reveal what types of toys (visual, auditory, tactile) and levels of activity will motivate active exploration and participation in daily family life.

A third group of infants with Down syndrome is robust and well modulated as newborns, actively seeking social interchange and using a diversity of strategies to maintain homeostasis. Although their muscle tone may not be outstanding, they use their motor skills well. They demonstrate good self-regulation and social competency quite early. These babies vary in temperament and personality but, as a group, can control their behavior more actively than other infants with Down syndrome. They may achieve developmental milestones at ages close to those expected for typically developing children. Although interventionists may be tempted to decrease services to these children, given their obvious strengths in many areas, it is important to remember that distinct vulnerabilities in learning and speech will continue to require support in order to promote children's highest possible level of cognitive, social, and emotional development.

Although my observations of behavioral and temperamental patterns among infants with Down syndrome require further investigation, they suggest the importance of continuous careful observation and evaluation of every baby with Down syndrome, beginning immediately after birth and continuing in the context of developmental followup and early care and education. Each child's potential is unique. Ongoing observation and discussion allow parents and professionals to recognize the child's emerging strengths and to devise creative strategies to support development.

# Conclusion

As we gain understanding of genetic syndromes, central nervous functioning, and the many factors that influence development, families and professionals will be better equipped to appreciate a child's individuality, as well as the vulnerabilities and challenges that an infant with a genetic disorder is likely to encounter during the course of development. The enduring task of the professional is to use assessment to identify the myriad factors affecting a child's behavior and developmental potential; to share information with families in a sensitive, supportive manner; and to work together with parents and other caregivers to enhance the development of every child.

**Acknowledgments:** I would like to thank Mirna Amaya and Mary Connelly for typing the manuscript. I am grateful to my husband, Gary Sprouse, and my children, Ryan and Courtney, who have indulged my need to "do it all." Most of all, I thank the parents who have graciously given us the opportunity to learn so much from their special children.

# References

Als, H., Lester, B. M., & Brazelton, T. B. (1979). Dynamics of the behavioral organization of the premature infant. In T. M. Field, A. M. Sostek, S. Goldberg, & H. H. Shuman (Eds.), *Infants Born at Risk* (pp. 173-192). New York: Spectrum Publications.

Als, H., Lester, B. M., Tronick, E. C., & Brazelton, T. B. (1980). Manual for the assessment of preterm infant behavior (APIB). In H. E. Fitzgerald, B. M. Lester, and M. W. Yogman (Eds.), *Theory and research in behavioral pediatrics* (Vol. 1) (pp. 65-132). New York: Plenum Press.

Bobath, K., and Bobath, B. (1964). The facilitation of normal postural reactions and movements in the treatment of cerebral palsy. *Physiotherapy, 50* (8), 256-262.

Brazelton, T. B. (1973). *Neonatal Behavioral Assessment Scale*. Philadelphia, PA: J. B. Lippincott Co.

Coyle, J., Oster-Granite, M., & Gearhart, J. (1986). The urobiologic consequences of Down syndrome. *Brain Research Bulletin, 16*, 773-787.

Fowler, A. E. (1990). Language abilities in children with Down syndrome: Evidence for a specific syntactic delay. In D. Cicchetti & Marjorie Beeghly (Eds.), *Children with Down syndrome: A developmental perspective*. New York: Cambridge University Press.

Nadel, L., & Rosenthal, D. (1995). *Down syndrome: Living and learning in the community*. New York: Wiley and Sons.

Pueschel, S. (1983). The child with Down syndrome. In M. D. Levine, W. B. Carey, A. C. Crocker, & T. T. Gross (Eds.), *Developmental-behavioral pediatrics* (pp. 353-362). Philadelphia, PA: W. B. Saunders.

Pueschel, S., & Rynders, J. (Eds.) (1982). *Down syndrome: Advances in biomedicine and the behavioral sciences*. Cambridge, MA: Ware Press.

Samango-Sprouse, C. (1990). *Average age of ambulation in Down syndrome*. Unpublished data.

Smith, G., & Berg, J. (1976). *Down's anomaly*. New York: Churchill, Livingstone.

Wishart, J. (1988). Early learning in infants and young children with Down syndrome. In L. Nadel (Ed.), *The psychobiology of Down Syndrome*. Cambridge, MA: MIT Press.

# V. Assessment and the Policy Context

# 17. A Values-Based Model of Infant and Toddler Assessment*

LUCY JANE MILLER

BRIAN A. McNULTY

Family-centered care is the compassionate, open, total inclusion of the family in the care and decisionmaking process for their baby. In order to accomplish this, much interaction and education must occur, not only regarding the medical facts, but also about the rights, expectations, and needs of the family. The goal is to *leave the power with the family*, i.e., never take it away in the first place, necessitating "empowering" the family at a later date. (Suzanne Smith-Sharp, 1994)

What is Colorado's vision of a "desirable future" in relation to identifying and assessing children who have a delay or are at risk of developing a delay? In the desirable future envisioned by the state's Interagency Coordinating Council and the Lead Agency for implementing Part H of the Individuals with Disabilities Education Act (IDEA), *all children* will have full access to periodic, community-based screening services on a timely basis. In our desirable future, there will be enough resources so that every child who has a delay or is *at risk* of developing a delay will have access to a comprehensive assessment process and appropriate remediation, utilizing existing natural resources within the "new" services and supports model that we are creating. The Assessment Process Model in our desirable future will include

---

*An earlier version of this chapter appeared in the June/July 1994 issue of *Zero to Three,* the bulletin of ZERO TO THREE: National Center for Infants, Toddlers, and Families.

parents in key evaluative and decisionmaking roles, will assure that each child is evaluated for his or her strengths and competencies, and will result in a service and support plan which highlights utilization of the child's strengths in a compensatory manner, rather than remediating the child's deficits.

Where is Colorado in its journey to a desirable future? In 1993, the state of Colorado adopted guidelines that defined "preferred practices" for the identification and assessment of young children (Colorado Department of Education, 1993). These guidelines are, we believe, remarkable for two reasons. First, they translate the family-centered principles of Part H of IDEA (20 U.S.C. 1400 Et. Seq.) into specific procedural guidelines, within an environment of fiscal austerity, for the day-to-day interactions that affect the lives of young children and their families so profoundly. Second, they are one of the products of our unique approach to the implementation of Part H, a multiyear, statewide endeavor that engages parents, state agency personnel, community representatives, university faculty, and clinical practitioners in values-based decisionmaking, leading to the development of a comprehensive vision of long-term systems change, designed to move Colorado into a desirable future.

The challenge has been the development of administrative rules and regulations, as well as legislative actions, that embody these principles in an environment of fiscal economizing. It is recognized that the implementation of these values-based changes will necessitate a profound systems change, one so significant that many refer to it as a "paradigm shift" (Kuhn, 1970) incorporating many people, including parents, policymakers, researchers, service providers, and existing community resource personnel.

The pivotal issue is: How do we implement the Part H legislation, incorporating its theoretical foundations into day-to-day interactions that affect the lives of young children and their families? How can we actualize the paradigm shift so that not only the theory of what needs to be changed, but also the actual innovative transformations can be implemented (Miller, Lynch, & Campbell, 1990)? And, in particular, how can we *envision a process of child identification and assessment* that embraces the spirit and intent of IDEA?

# The Development of a Values-Oriented Model

Since its initial meeting in 1987, the Colorado Interagency Coordinating Council (CICC) has used a "values-based decisionmaking model" (McNulty, 1989) to implement the legislative intent of Part H: "*to enhance the capacity of families* to meet the special needs of their infants and toddlers with handicaps" (EHA Amendments, 1986). Using this model, the CICC chose to clearly delineate its values and then to fund *only* those local community initiatives which were directed toward actualizing this vision. While the vision and values have been clarified by the CICC over time, they have invariably reflected the primacy of the family, focusing on competencies instead of deficits, and valuing diversity.

The CICC values include the following:

- Children and families are valued for their unique capacities, experiences, and potential.
- Families have the right and responsibility to make decisions on behalf of their children and themselves.
- Communities are enhanced by recognizing and honoring the diversity among all people.
- Families make the best choices when they have comprehensive information about the full range of formal and natural resources in their communities.
- Creative, flexible, and collaborative approaches to services allow for individual child, family, and community differences.

In actualizing these values, the Council has said that it will fund projects which:

- Use natural settings as the primary location for providing services and supports;
- Provide options for families in terms of the types of services and supports to be rendered;
- Develop Individualized Family Service Plans (IFSPs), along with families, which reflect more than just the services and supports available through the providing agency;
- Demonstrate service coordination which occurs across agency lines;
- Demonstrate innovative ways to use current funding to access generic services; and
- Demonstrate linkages with informal supports.

The CICC envisions a *systems change* which, over time, will impact *all agencies* dealing with young children in Colorado, not just agencies related to Part H activities. By expanding both formal and informal systems, our goal is to identify eligible children earlier, while providing families with more natural supports and services that are specifically geared to their individual resources, concerns, and priorities.

In striving toward these goals, Colorado has implemented projects that affect both "formal" and "informal" systems. We are trying to envision a new reality and not settle for just expanding the current service options.

On the "formal" side, the CICC's strategy has been to stretch existing resources and services by focusing on existing service systems. This has included expanding the current "Child Find" system, funding the development of community-based local Interagency Coordinating Councils (ICCs), and increasing the impact of limited Part H funding by qualifying parents and families for SSI funding and linking with Federally Qualified Health Centers. In addition, a focus has been placed on *early implementation* of the Part H mandate by emphasizing family-centered care and Individualized Family Service Plans in Neonatal Intensive Care Units.

On the "informal" side, the CICC has also advocated pursuing nontraditional avenues such as:

- *Parent-to-Parent Support Initiatives*, both state-level and community-based projects, that link families directly with other families;

- *Parents in Leadership*, a project that provides intensive comprehensive training to family members and to adult self-advocates with disabilities so that they are prepared to assume leadership positions; and

- *Utilization of Naturalistic Resources*, a strategy that focuses on the provision of services in existing community settings, such as recreation centers, community infant/tot programs, YMCA/YWCA play groups, and community parks and recreation programs.

## Importance of Community-Based Strategies

In the first phase of Part H planning, Colorado focused on *developing the values* that were to serve as a blueprint for all activities in subsequent years. This was a massive effort, incorporating families, a variety of direct service providers, key representatives of all state agencies which provide services to young children and their families, and individuals representing numerous, diverse communities on an ongoing basis. The focus in the early years was on developing *conceptual models* for each of the required 14 components of Part H, including identification and assessment, which were consistent with CICC values.

In the next phase, Colorado concentrated resources on numerous pilot projects in all parts of the state so that the conceptual models developed in the early years could be implemented and evaluated. In the current phase, Colorado has adopted a "Community-Development Model," funding all communities to develop local ICCs and to engage in thoughtful, change-oriented systems planning. At no point in this process was the provision of direct services to young children and their families the focus of the funding, although children and families have received services along the way. The focus was on creating a system which would be *flexible* enough to deal with individual differences and *creative* enough to stretch existing funding resources so that more children and families could receive supports and services. This strategy of community-based implementation has allowed us to observe and evaluate a variety of models of implementation, as communities are encouraged to have a wide range of approaches which are determined on a local level.

This dual strategy of expanding formal systems and using informal processes to create systems change has evolved slowly and thoughtfully. Communities have provided information that has increased CICC and Lead Agency understanding of the complexities of implementing the vision at the local level and has helped to expand the formal components at the state level.

## ▤ The Child Identification and Assessment ▤ Process

Because the identification and assessment of children eligible for services and supports represent the beginning of a long road for many children and families, it was felt to be crucial that, in the assessment process, the family be supported and validated for their concerns about and perceptions of the child's *abilities*. The child must be viewed within a *competency model*, and the parents must be perceived as *capable and responsible*, thus setting the stage for all future interactions with the system. How, then, can a process of child identification and assessment embrace the spirit and intent of IDEA?

The development of a Child Identification and Assessment Process consistent with CICC values was one of the projects undertaken in the first four years of Part H planning, and it is continuing currently. This was done through an interactive process (including the CICC and a committee called the Screening and Evaluation Process Committee) over a two-year period, using the input of parent members of the committee as a foundation. The committee reviewed current "best practices" literature and consulted with experts in the field in our state, including parents. The committee then developed a conceptual model for implementation of identification and assessment consistent with the spirit of IDEA, with active participation and careful review by parents at each stage of the process.

In 1993, Colorado adopted guidelines that defined "preferred practices" for the identification and assessment of young children (Colorado Department of Education, 1993). The *values base* for the process was developed first, followed by specific procedural guidelines. The values for child identification and assessment are apparent throughout the document in the wording chosen and in the emphasis on parent-driven choices and options. The values embedded in the document are summarized below, and brief examples of the parent-centered emphasis are provided for each value:

- *Focusing on the process of evaluation rather than the final product (i.e., score, delineation of strengths and "weaknesses"):* The process must insure minimal intrusiveness for the child and family, as well as careful consideration of whether the information requested by professionals is actually needed by the child and family. Ultimately, the choice of which information to obtain is made by the family, not the provider of service.

- *Recognizing the value of parent-driven choices:* The importance of family priorities, resources, concerns, and goals must be kept paramount at all times. Families are encouraged to be the primary decisionmakers throughout the screening or assessment process and are supported in this regard. The choice of the families to provide or not to provide information will be respected at all times.

- *Honoring diversity in terms of language, ethnicity, culture, family structure, and preference:* Diverse family values must be thoughtfully considered, particularly typical culture-bound conventions and child-rearing practices. All evaluations are to be conducted in the primary language of the child and family. Prior to deciding to administer a norm-referenced standardized scale, the normative sample must be carefully considered with regard to its representation of the cultural group in which the child is being raised.

- *Recognizing that partnerships encompass families, interdisciplinary teams, and community members from many agencies:* An atmosphere of mutual trust must be created in which respect is generated and rapport developed. This will facilitate informed decisionmaking and joint planning so that families can choose the extent of their involvement.

- *Individualizing the process for the child, family, and community:* The holistic, multifaceted needs of the child, both in developmental domains and in his or her environmental context, will be considered at all times. The team that is making decisions about the processes that are appropriate for the child must include not only the parents, but also professionals from a variety of disciplines which represent the parents' areas of concern. Multiple evaluation strategies must be used, based primarily on an arena-style process.

- *Obtaining family feedback for accountability:* Feedback is elicited from the parents regarding the strengths and needs of the child, as well as the existing naturalistic community services and supports they feel comfortable accessing. In addition, parents are asked to fill out a questionnaire so that feedback can be obtained about their perceptions of the entire process of the screening or assessment. At that time, the parents give reactions to whether the process was family-centered, occurred in a timely manner, met their expectations, was driven by their choices of personnel and procedures, and the like.

Three levels were delineated in the Child Identification and Assessment Process, as represented by the figure below: (a) the Community Screen, (b) the Individualized Screen, and (c) the Assessment Process.* The information presented in *The*

---

*Please note that in the original document developed by the Colorado Department of Education, the third level is referred to as the "Evaluation Process." However, the word

*Colorado Child Identification Process: Birth-Five Years: Screening and Evaluation Process Guidelines* (Colorado Department of Education, 1993) represents our "Vision for a Desirable Future" with regard to each of the levels. The vision has been made available to as many children and families as possible throughout our state through our public awareness efforts, and communities are at various stages of implementation of the vision.

The three levels in *The Colorado Child Identification Process: Birth-Five Years: Screening and Evaluation Process Guidelines* are:

*Level One*

> [The Community Screen] is a child-centered process that encourages family involvement. The process is open and easily accessible to all members of the community and screens children in all areas of development to:
>
> 1. Enhance information-sharing related to child development and parenting practices;
> 2. Enhance child and family linkages with public and private community services and supports;
> 3. Identify children with potential delays/disabilities for whom rescreening or an evaluation is a reasonable next step.
> (Colorado Department of Education, 1993, p. 7)

The Community Screening process is planned and implemented by an interagency group to maximize the utilization of local community resources and to insure nonduplication of screening efforts. The screening process respects the family and the family's cultural background. A variety of screening strategies are used for implementation of the process (i.e., children come to a screening; personnel go to a preschool/child care setting; screenings are done as part of a health fair).

*Level Two*

The Individualized Screening is available when requested by the family or deemed useful by the screening team. It is a family-centered process including both the child and the family, and it is

---

"assessment" is used throughout this chapter instead, in order to maintain consistency with previous literature published by ZERO TO THREE/National Center for Clinical Infant Programs (see, for example, Meisels & Provence, 1989). In this chapter, the context of "assessment" is individual *diagnostic* assessment, not curriculum-based or program assessment.

## Colorado Department of Education Child Identification Process Flow Chart

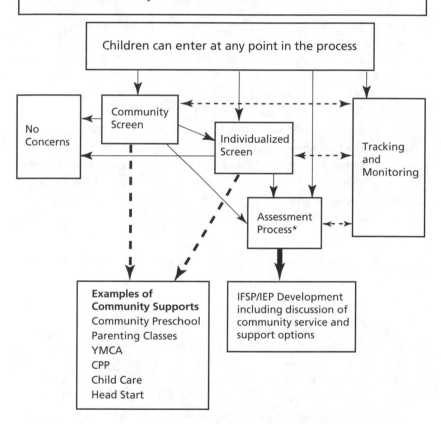

**Referrals**
Child Care Agencies • CCB • DIRS • Public Agencies
• Parents • CRCSN • Public Health • EPSDT • Private Agencies
• Medical Community • Social Services • Other

Children can enter at any point in the process

No Concerns

Community Screen

Individualized Screen

Tracking and Monitoring

Assessment Process*

**Examples of Community Supports**
Community Preschool
Parenting Classes
YMCA
CPP
Child Care
Head Start

IFSP/IEP Development including discussion of community service and support options

———— Children determined eligible/appropriate for service under Colorado's Infant/Preschool definition

– – – Children determined not eligible/appropriate for special services under Colorado's Infant/Preschool definition but may be in need of community services and supports

◄ - - ► Children determined to have no significant needs at the time of screening/evaluation but may be at risk for demonstrating delays at a later date

* See footnote, p. 353.

focused on children who are at higher risk for having a delay/disability, or are believed to have a delay/disability, but have not been previously evaluated. The individual families participate, and children are given a more comprehensive screening than that available during the Community Screening process.

Children are screened in all areas of development to:

1. Obtain a more complete picture of child and *family strengths* and concerns;
2. Enhance information-sharing related to child development and parenting practices;
3. Enhance child and family linkages with public and private community services and supports;
4. Determine the child's need for evaluation.
(Colorado Department of Education, 1993, p. 14)

The Individualized Screening is more comprehensive than the Community Screening, but it is not as detailed or as time-consuming as the Assessment Process in terms of instruments used and numbers of professionals involved. The Individualized Screening process utilizes a team approach and respects the family and the family's cultural background.

*Level Three*

The Assessment Process* is used by the family and the team to:

1. Determine the child's current level of functioning, strengths, and needs in all areas of development;
2. Identify the family's resources, priorities, and concerns;
3. Establish the child's eligibility for services;
4. Identify an array of public and private community service and support options (specialized and non-specialized resources) for the child and family that will enhance the development of the child.
(Colorado Department of Education, 1993, p. 21)

In order to obtain accurate perceptions of the child, multiple sources of information must be incorporated from within the framework of the family, and numerous persons familiar with the child in different settings must be included. Although the administration of scales is not precluded in the Assessment Process, the process focuses on the depth and breadth of knowledge about the child's abilities and competencies in a wide variety of circumstances. In fact, when children have certain conditions associated with a disability or delay (as specified by the

---

* See footnote, page 353.

State Definition for eligibility for Part H services and supports), standardized norm-referenced testing is optional.

In Colorado's desirable future, *all children* will have full access to periodic, community-based screening services on a timely basis. Consequently, the need for Individualized Screening will decrease. Since every child will receive Community Screenings periodically, most children who require a level-three Assessment Process will be identified from Community Screenings. However, when a child is not so identified by the Community Screenings and the parent still has concerns, a comprehensive screening will be available as one option prior to initiating an Assessment Process. In our desirable future, there will be enough resources to provide every child who has a delay, or is at risk of developing a delay, access to a comprehensive Assessment Process, as well as appropriate remediation, using existing natural resources within the new model of services and supports that we are creating. The Assessment Process will include parents in key evaluative and decisionmaking roles; will assure that every child is evaluated for his or her strengths and competencies; and will result in a service and support plan that highlights utilization of the child's strengths in a compensatory manner, rather than remediating the child's deficits.

The three levels of the Child Identification and Assessment Process are not radically different from a traditional model of identification and assessment. What is different is *the role of the family*. The shift from "child-centered" assessment to "family-centered" practices is a major transformation. Parents are seen as key team players who are actively involved in the process and are viewed as informed decisionmakers. The process assumes that the families' concerns, priorities, and resources are critical to developing appropriate outcomes for their children. Beginning with identification, *the process places families in the center of decisionmaking* and finds new ways to provide the services and supports that they decide are important.

# Child Identification in Context

Any time we see systems in apparent chaos, our training urges us to interfere, to stabilize and shore things up. But. . . the dominant shape of our organizations can be maintained if we retain clarity about the purpose and direction of the organizations. If we succeed in maintaining focus, rather than hands-on control, we also

> create the flexibility and responsiveness that every organization craves. What leaders are called upon to do in a chaotic world is to shape their organizations through concepts, not through elaborate rules or structures. (Wheatley, 1992)

Systems change is a complex process. Rather than ignore this complexity, Colorado has chosen to embrace the inconsistencies associated with establishing a new system of services and supports and to find new ways to manage change. In Colorado, there are daily examples of inconsistent, traditional assessment and service delivery models, as well as inadequate services and supports in some areas. Service and support systems are uneven from community to community, depending on the priorities and history of the community and the level at which the community can actualize the CICC vision.

> Chaos breaks symmetries and this is an essential step to the emergence of new order. . . . Systems driven far from equilibrium move through patterns of instability in which previous symmetry or order is broken, thus confronting the system with choices at critical points. . . . A system in this state creates its own environment and its own future. (Stacey, 1992)

Nevertheless, rather than rushing to spend our limited resources helping a few more children get direct services, Colorado has made a commitment to move ahead with its vision of a "values-based" service delivery system which honors and respects the unique needs and talents of each family. The Colorado Interagency Coordinating Council has maintained this leadership vision even amidst obvious statewide inconsistencies in services and supports.

As we face the close of the millennium, we are forced to choose a path. With major health and social welfare policies under scrutiny, Part H in Colorado is seen as a part of the whole debate. In fact, we may find that the Colorado strategy of determinedly pursuing the vision of a radically changed service and support delivery system may be well timed. In fact, a time like the present, when so much is in flux may be an excellent time to ask tough policy questions. When the "new order" emerges from the chaos surrounding health care in general and early intervention in particular, we may find our "desirable future" realized. In Colorado, we are working hard to realize a future that reflects the primacy of the family and focuses on the competencies and potential of all our children.

**Acknowledgments:** This chapter was written in coordination with the Colorado Department of Education, Screening and Evaluation Process Committee, including: Darcy Allen-Young, Jane Amundson, April Block, Carol Chazdon, Dianne Garner, Susan Hall, Linda Iklé, Patsy McAteer, Debbie Medina, Susan Moore, Janis Pottorff, Pat Tesauro-Jackson, Gail Whitman, and Donna Wittmer.

# References

Colorado Department of Education (1993). *The Colorado Child Identification Process: Birth-Five Years: Screening and Evaluation Process Guidelines.* Denver, CO.

Colorado Department of Education (1988). *Creating desirable futures.* Denver, CO.

EHA Amendments (1986). *Part H—Handicapped Infants and Toddlers.* Congressional Record-House. Washington, DC: Superintendent of Documents.

Kuhn, T. S. (1970). *The structure of scientific revolutions* (2nd ed.). Chicago: University of Chicago Press.

McNulty, B. A. (1989). Leadership and policy strategies for interagency planning: Meeting the early childhood mandate. In J. J. Gallagher, P. L. Trohanis, & R. M. Clifford (Eds.), *Policy implementation and P.L. 99-457: Planning for young children with special needs.* Baltimore, MD: Paul H. Brookes Publishing Co.

Meisels, S. J., & Provence, S. (1989). *Screening and Assessment: Guidelines for identifying young disabled and developmentally vulnerable children and their families.* Arlington, VA: ZERO TO THREE/National Center for Clinical Infant Programs.

Miller, L. J., Lynch, E., & Campbell, J. (1990). Parents as Partners: A new paradigm for collaboration. In W. A. Secord & E. H. Wiig (Eds.), *Best practices in school speech-language pathology.* San Antonio, TX: The Psychological Corporation.

Stacey, R. D. (1992). *Managing the unknowable: Strategic boundaries between order and chaos in organizations.* San Francisco, CA: Jossey-Bass Publishers.

Wheatley, M. J. (1992). *Leadership and the new science: Learning about organization from an orderly universe.* San Francisco, CA: Bennett-Koehier Publishers.

ZERO TO THREE/National Center for Clinical Infant Programs (1989). *The intent and spirit of P.L. 99-457.* Arlington, VA: Author.

# 18. Family-Directed Child Evaluation and Assessment under the Individuals with Disabilities Education Act (IDEA)

CAROL BERMAN

EVELYN SHAW

This chapter discusses practices which families and program staff of projects conducted by the U.S. Department of Education's Early Education Program for Children with Disabilities (EEPCD) believe contribute to quality family-directed child evaluations and assessments. These practices take into account the primacy of families with respect to their children, cultural and linguistic diversity, the use of technological advances, and information about a child's health status and needs.

A team of NEC*TAS staff* developed this chapter to help state and EEPCD project personnel learn about family-directed evaluations and assessments from one another. Several EEPCD outreach projects were selected to be interviewed for the chapter because of their proven models and responsibility for disseminating what they had learned. Questions were reviewed by the team, who then paired off to interview project personnel and

---

*NEC*TAS, National Early Childhood Technical Assistance System, in
Chapel Hill, North Carolina, is a collaborative system, coordinated by the Frank
Porter Graham Child Development Center of the University of North Carolina at
Chapel Hill with the Federation for Children with Special Needs; Georgetown
University Child Development Center; Hawai'i University Affiliated Program,
University of Hawai'i at Manoa; National Association of State Directors of Special
Education (NASDSE); and ZERO TO THREE: National Center for Infants, Toddlers,
and Families.

parents known to these projects. The principal authors prepared the chapter, which was then reviewed by the team and by those who had been interviewed.

# Introduction

The first experience of a family with a child who may need early intervention services typically involves a process of identification, evaluation, and assessment, in which the need for services is established and defined. Ongoing evaluation and assessment are opportunities to reveal the child's strengths and developmental needs, as well as the family's resources and priorities, and to help guide the direction of intervention. These opportunities are highly significant to the family and service providers. Depending on the program and the degree of a child's disability, the initial evaluation to determine whether the child qualifies for services and subsequent re-evaluations for that purpose may be seen as rites of passage into early intervention or as threats to eligibility. The degree to which the family is active in the evaluation and assessment processes is likely to influence the child's performance, the extent of followup, and the relevance of the evaluation or assessment in guiding the child's developmental program.

This chapter discusses policies and practices for family-directed child evaluation and assessment under the Individuals with Disabilities Education Act (IDEA). Because many family-directed practices originated in programs for infants and toddlers and because language emphasizing family roles and supports appears throughout Part H (the Infants and Toddlers Program) of IDEA, the chapter may appear to emphasize Part H policies and practices over those for the population of Section 619 (the Preschool Program) of IDEA. However, the scope of the chapter includes practices across the early childhood age spectrum, birth through five years. The chapter defines commonly used terminology and identifies issues and recommended approaches for evaluation and assessment processes. Following a summary of characteristics of successful child evaluation and assessment and brief recommendations for policymakers, the chapter concludes with lists of project resources and other resources.

# Definitions

## "Family-directed"

As the NEC*TAS team began interviewing parents and professionals for this chapter, it quickly became aware that many terms are used to describe the family's involvement in the evaluation or assessment process. The terms "family-focused," "family-friendly," "family-driven," "family-directed," and "family-guided" tend to be used interchangeably by some people, and used with specific meaning by others. All of these terms convey to some degree the general philosophy of family-centered care, which recognizes the family's constant, central role in the child's life and places family priorities and values over those of the professional or the agency. Although the differences in terminology may appear to be minor, each term does suggest a difference in emphasis and in the family's role.

The NEC*TAS team elected to use the term "family-directed" because it suggests an active role for the family throughout the evaluation and assessment processes. Parents and project staff whom we interviewed emphasized that, if professionals relate to the family in a way that is friendly and supportive but fail to allow the family to determine the outcomes it desires, then evaluations and assessments will fall far short of meeting the needs of the child, of the family, and, ultimately, of the service providers. Although it is important that evaluations and assessments be conducted as early as possible in the child's life by personnel who are knowledgeable about appropriate resources, effective evaluation and assessment practices also are respectful of parents and the primacy of their role in their child's care and education. The term "family-directed" offers a suitable emphasis on appropriate parent participation in the process.

## "Evaluation" and "assessment"

The term "evaluation" under Part H of IDEA generally means the determination of eligibility, whereas "assessment" refers to the ongoing process of determining the child's and family's strengths and needs. Regulations for Part H (Department of Education, 1993; 34 CFR §303) define evaluation and assessment as follows:

> §303.322(b)(1) *Evaluation* means the procedures used by appropriate qualified personnel to determine a child's initial and contin-

uing eligibility under this part, consistent with the definition of "infants and toddlers with disabilities" in §303.16, including determining the status of the child in each of the developmental areas in paragraph (c)(3)(ii) of this section.

(2) *Assessment* means the ongoing procedures used by appropriate qualified personnel throughout the period of a child's eligibility to identify:

(i) the child's unique strengths and needs and the services appropriate to meet those needs; and

(ii) the resources, priorities, and concerns of the family and the supports and services necessary to enhance the family's capacity to meet the developmental needs of their infant or toddler with a disability. (p. 40971)

An easy way to remember the distinction made within the Part H regulations is that the terms "evaluation" and "eligibility" both start with the letter "e." Despite their distinct meanings under Part H, the terms evaluation and assessment tend to be used interchangeably by parents and practitioners in the field.

The term "assessment" does not appear in the regulations for Part B of IDEA (Department of Education, 1992); "evaluation" is used instead. Under Part B, which includes Section 619, evaluation focuses on the educational needs of the child and requires that "no single procedure is used as the sole criterion for determining an appropriate educational program for a child" and "the evaluation is made by a multidisciplinary team or group of persons" (see 34 CFR §§300.532(d) and (e)). When interpreting evaluation data in making placement decisions, each public agency shall "draw upon information from a variety of sources, including aptitude and achievement tests, teacher recommendations, physical condition, social or cultural background, and adaptive behavior" and "ensure that information obtained from all of these sources is documented and carefully considered" (see 34 CFR §§300.533(a)(1) and (2)).

State Part H and Part B-Section 619 programs address family involvement in evaluation and assessment processes, but with different emphases. Under Part H regulations, child assessment includes identification of the "resources, priorities, and concerns of the family" (see 34 CFR §303.322 (b)(2)(ii)). Although parents are not specifically mentioned in the Part B regulations, many states have recognized the important contributions and primary decisionmaking role of parents throughout the process. Many state guidelines for evaluating preschool children—such as those in Arizona, Colorado, Ohio, Pennsylvania, Rhode Island, and Vermont—do encourage multidisciplinary evaluation teams to involve parents as contributing members.

### "Family assessment"

"Family assessment" is a term that often is misunderstood and that does not convey the collaborative working relationships between families and professionals that are at the heart of family-directed services. Family assessment is defined as "family-directed and designed to determine the resources, priorities, and concerns of the family related to enhancing the development of the child." Family assessment is voluntary and, if carried out, must be "based on information provided by the family through a personal interview" (see 34 CFR §303.322(d)). Families need to be able to define themselves; a family often extends beyond parents and siblings and may include elders, spiritual leaders, and extended family members. Linda Kjerland of Project Dakota, in Eagan, Minnesota, who prefers the term "family information-gathering" to "family assessment," emphasized that early intervention professionals are not being asked to intrude upon the privacy of families, but are charged with providing opportunities for families to choose to share the challenges for which they want help and support.

In attempting to respect the individuality of families and the differences among them, a system should not be set up which meets the requirement for family-directed assessments by simply adding a form for families to complete. Linda Kjerland put it this way: "The worst mistake we can make is to think we have met the intent of the law by having families fill out a form instead of shaping the whole process." Project Dakota has developed questionnaires and other reminders to practitioners to be responsive to the family at every step.

## ■ Characteristics of Family-Directed Child ■ Evaluations and Assessments

Throughout the interviews with EEPCD project personnel and parents, a number of key concepts emerged relating to assessment and evaluation practices, many of which have policy and practice implications. These are presented below, grouped in four issue areas: (a) family issues; (b) process issues; (c) personnel preparation issues; and (d) service system issues.

## Family issues

### *Value parents as experts.*

Programs with family-directed assessments insure that parents have input at every step. An environment is created in which parents are made to feel comfortable about contributing as important team members. At Child Development Resources (CDR), Norge, Virginia, assessment reports are stamped "draft" and mailed to parents for their review and comment. In this way, the program emphasizes that input still is being sought, especially when a report has been typed for readability and may appear to be more final than intended. Roger and Lisa Bailey, parents from Eugene, Oregon, told us why they were satisfied with services at the AEPS Linked System of Assessment, Intervention, and Evaluation for Early Intervention Project (AEPS) headed by Diane Bricker: "Testers tell us how they are going to test, what they will be looking for, information about the test, what to expect. They did their own testing, made their own observations, and asked us what [our child] did at home. There is no way one individual can figure out a child. We feel it's very important to take information from parents." Ken Gillies, a parent from Eagan, Minnesota, whose child was seen at Project Dakota, said: "The professionals in any family's case need to be the *listeners*. It's hard for people in our structure of society to take on that role. Unless you have gleaned significant information from the family, you aren't in a position to offer any opinion."

Angela Deal, of the Family, Infant, and Preschool Program (FIPP), Morganton, North Carolina, acknowledged that the purpose of evaluation for preschool children and the people involved in it may be different than they are for infants and toddlers, but the process still can be driven by the families' perspectives and priorities. Families want their children to be successful in preschool. John Guthman, a parent from St. Paul, Minnesota, emphasized that if important skills are needed for success in the preschool setting, then the assessment team should draw on parents' experience and knowledge of their child at home to find out what the child's abilities are in relation to those skills.

### *Respect individual differences and values as well as families' styles of involvement.*

Families vary considerably as to the role and amount of control they want to assume in evaluation and assessment, and throughout early intervention and preschool. Some parents may want to be more active than others in making decisions and in coordinating services. John Guthman told us: "We asked questions. Not all families do, especially for the initial assessment when they don't know what to expect. They are not in a comfortable place, or they may [expect to] hear bad news."

Even if parents choose to do no more than observe, the process of engaging them as "active" observers still is a step in articulating the *family's* desired outcome for the child. Glenda Witt, a parent from Williamsburg, Virginia, who experienced family-directed assessments at CDR, put it this way: "If the family doesn't feel involved, nothing will change." Angela Deal, of the FIPP project, concurred: "What happens must be dictated by the comfort level of the family and how and what they choose. Even as an observer, what is being done is based on the family's outcomes."

Diane Bricker, of the AEPS project, emphasized that an active family role does not mean abdication by professionals of their responsibilities. It is imperative that professionals help families shape a reasonable course of action by suggesting and describing appropriate options.

As in any partnership, parents have a responsibility to work in partnership with practitioners during the evaluation and assessment processes. For example, parents can help practitioners by communicating their expectations for their child, by observing and commenting on their child's performance during assessment, and by asking questions about aspects of the evaluation and assessment that are unclear to them. A publication by the ERIC Clearinghouse on Disabilities and Gifted Education (1994), *Rights and Responsibilities of Parents of Children with Disabilities*, although primarily directed at parents of children enrolled in a program, offers guidance to parents about their rights and responsibilities in the special education process, including evaluations.

By and large, the professionals and parents we interviewed strongly favored a very active role for families, one in which they participated in every aspect of evaluation and assessment.

### Encourage the presence and participation of parents and other family members.

It is inappropriate to evaluate a young child without the presence of someone who knows the child very well, particularly if eligibility for services is being considered. The person who knows the child best may be a parent or a grandmother, aunt, uncle, or neighbor. Most parents want and need to be present during evaluation and assessment, particularly when the child is an infant. Denise Booth, a Pittsfield, Illinois, parent, liked having a sibling included in her child's assessment and appreciated the benefits of using a videotape to capture the interaction between the children.

The need to include families has implications for assessments performed at child care program locations and other community settings. For example, assessments should be arranged at times and in settings which are convenient for families and for professionals. Renee Dulin, a parent from Troutman, North Carolina, whose child receives services from the FIPP project, spoke of the need for a parent presence and for preliminary home visits: "A family with a special needs child spends a lot of time with [personnel who are] strangers. It is so important for the parents as well as for the child to have a familiar face present on assessment day. Personally, I can't imagine having to endure an assessment for a child younger than school age without being allowed to be present. I would not allow my child to be put into a room with strangers and be expected to perform [optimally]. An assessment of this type is unfair to the child and to the team members."

## Process issues

### Appreciate the process leading to a plan.

Families have the right to be part of planning an assessment process that culminates in a report that is honest, that presents what the team knows, and that steers them toward solutions and resources. Ken Gillies thought the term "discover" might better describe what the process should be. He said: "When I hear the word 'discover,' sunshine pops into my mind. But 'assessment' and 'evaluation'—you think of piles of paper and raised eyebrows. That's not the purpose. It's to get good things for our child." John and Teresa Guthman described assessment as "part of an ongoing process of setting goals."

The assessment that recognizes a linked continuum of services helps define needed services that will benefit the child and family. Diane Bricker, of the AEPS project, offered this description of the linked continuum:

*Screening*, as a first level, is an economical strategy for determining which children need further evaluation. Not all children are screened; some are evaluated or assessed as a first step in the process of early intervention. Screening is one entry route into the early intervention program.

The *evaluation*, as a second level, leads to a possible diagnosis, to a determination of eligibility, to a description of the nature of any problem, and to an interim placement, if necessary.

*Assessment*, as the third level, determines therapeutically appropriate intervention. If a child is enrolled in early intervention services, assessment should be continuous. It can be carried out at varying levels of formality; sometimes, it is a structured interview or observation, or it may occur during the intervention process.

An important aspect of the linked continuum of services is that it is far more than a label, a quotient, or a score. The emphasis should be on child and family priorities and should lead to reasonable educational and therapeutic plans and outcomes.

### Value the importance and impact of every interaction.

Every interaction that occurs between parents and professionals is an important event. The NEC*TAS team affirmed in our interviews that those contacts can be warm, exhilarating, fearsome, or devastating. Parents often dread an experience in which they feel that their child and, for that matter, they are being judged. Evaluations and assessments by professionals or teams who fail to express any positive findings can be demoralizing and can undermine relationships between parents, between parent and child, and between parent and professional.

Attention should be paid to nonverbal and situational cues. The behavior of professionals—gestures, smiles, the way they hold a child, openness, their preparedness for the child and family, even the way the appointment is made—can be as illuminating as what is said. Barbie Perry, of Toano, Virginia, whose child had been followed by CDR, described a family-directed experience: "[My child's] name was on the paperwork when I got there. I knew this was where she was supposed to be."

Lynn Gillies emphasized that "information shared with families after an assessment should start with the positives and then move to areas of concern." Glenda Witt said that "the report should make you feel good about your child and always leave you on an up note. Their [CDR's] report was very positive and highlighted skills. [We] felt that the professionals were on our side. Reports should emphasize what the child knows, not just what he does not do."

### Provide necessary information at the most opportune time.

The goals and purposes of assessment should be articulated from the beginning, before the actual assessment, so parents know what to expect. This pre-assessment communication also can help allay fears.

Nelda Thompson, a parent from Mooresville, North Carolina, who was satisfied with family-directed assessments at FIPP, talked about the benefit of periodically checking with parents to see what they need in terms of materials or information. Neither written materials without followup, nor discussion without written materials, is sufficient. To the extent possible, materials should be individually tailored for a particular family. Language differences and literacy levels always should be considered.

Parents want access to the same information that is available to the professionals on the team. Information about test scores or a diagnosis should be provided with explanations. Families should be encouraged to obtain, keep, and organize copies of their child's records for their own reference and to facilitate care. In order for parents to be able to fully participate in team decisions, fact and opinion should be clearly distinguished and all available options presented. Roger and Lisa Bailey said: "Parents may not know what questions to ask. It helped us when someone said, 'These are the options' and 'Here's what I think I see' and fed us questions. . . . It's important to have a multidisciplinary team assess the child. You get an amazingly complete and accurate picture, and it helps you to come up with appropriate goals."

Parent-to-parent support was particularly helpful to some of the parents we interviewed, including Ken and Lynn Gillies, who suggested that programs may need to overcome the attitude of "we know what's best" to connect parents to someone who has "been there."

### Allow for flexibility in location, timing, and personnel.

Virtually every family member who talked about good evaluation and assessment experiences had been contacted before the assessment, perhaps through a home visit. Because they had been prepared beforehand, they knew what to expect. Parents of infants, toddlers, and preschool children felt that home visits were important and should precede a formal assessment. In contrast, parents who were dissatisfied with evaluation and assessment procedures felt that they had little say in the arrangements. The system needs to allow for an evaluation or assessment to be conducted in a setting and at a time that works best for a family and child. Although some families are comfortable with professionals coming to their homes, other parents may prefer to meet at the program site or other neutral setting.

Renee Dulin said: "Trust is very important. You can't do that 'til you are comfortable. . . . If it was nap time, nursing time, whatever, [my child's] needs were, they came first." In contrast to her family-directed evaluation at the AEPS program, Oregon parent Kelly Perron characterized a less positive experience elsewhere: "We were there from 8:30 a.m. until 12:15 p.m. We had no preparation. I didn't bring a snack. As a result, I had a cranky, tired, and hungry baby."

"Let families have a choice," said Ken Gillies. "A difficult piece of the assessment puzzle is assigning individuals to an assessment team. Perhaps one individual does not 'click' with the family; the family needs to express to the professional team member that they are not comfortable and should be able to ask for a change in a team member. Flexibility in scheduling is important. Early mornings or evenings are usually best for families."

Corinne Garland, of the Trans/Team Outreach Project housed at CDR, emphasized flexibility as a cornerstone of family-directed assessments. She noted that families differ widely and that every assessment team may require a different level of preparation, composition, and level of support to engage parents as active participants. Her program often uses transdisciplinary arena assessments. A transdisciplinary arena assessment is a planned observation process which typically involves a facilitator, who serves as the primary interactor/contact with the child and family during the assessment process; a coach, who supports the facilitator, provides cues for missed items, or reflects on what could be done to enhance the assessment; observers, who serve as multidisciplinary "eyes and ears" and contribute expertise from a variety of backgrounds and training; and, parent(s), who serve as additional evaluators, observers, and contributors.

***Recognize the limitations of current instruments and encourage the use of informal measures.***

Whether we use standardized or informal measures or both, we should acknowledge the shortcomings of current instruments. When we use formal measures, we need to be fully familiar with them and choose only those that are appropriate for the language and culture of the child and family. Further guidance on these concepts is available in other NEC*TAS reports (see Biro, Daulton, & Szanton, 1991; Meisels & Provence, 1989; Shackelford, 1994).

Corinne Garland emphasized that we may be asking the wrong questions when we restrict ourselves to the parameters of standardized instruments. Important questions that should be asked include: What is the child capable of doing? What does the family tell us about this child? Would assistive technology help in drawing out optimal performance? What kinds of help might this child need? Diane Bricker, of the AEPS Project, commented: "One of the problems with assessments in general is the diagnostic label. We have conveyed to a lot of families that a label, a score, a diagnostic quotient is a 'something.' What is important are the child's needs, reasonable educational and therapeutic goals, and family outcomes."

Common themes expressed in our interviews were the need to recognize and respect the accuracy of parent reporting, the importance of verifying with families the information gleaned from observation of play, and the difficulty in eliciting a representative sample of a young child's behavior. We need to check with parents to know whether or not we saw a representative sample of the child's abilities. Consideration of the child's health, medication, level of fatigue, and other factors is important, and family members are likely to be the best informants about the caliber of a child's performance.

One method of assuring that staff and family perceptions are blended is the use of a collaborative description of the child. Project Dakota adapted transdisciplinary post-assessment discussion methodology and integrated elements of the McGill Action Planning System (MAPS) (Pearpoint & Forest, 1992) into a functional team activity. In this collaborative description, families and staff cite child abilities, interests, and motivators, which are things to celebrate, as well as concerns, frustrations, worries, and desired next steps. Through this partnership, families and professionals can clarify what parents expect to gain and whether the plans that are developed are consistent with family priorities and goals. In the original MAPS process—which was designed to plan for the inclusion of children with disabilities in regular classrooms and activities—the child, family members, friends, and professionals meet as a group with a facilitator and generate ideas around key questions, such as "What would the child's ideal day at school look like?" and "What must be done to make it happen?" Lynn Gillies spoke with affection of an Individualized Family Service Plan (IFSP) meeting convened in her living room, in which neighbors were involved in helping to design her child's program.

### Integrate health evaluations into the total evaluation.

Information about a child's medical diagnosis and health status are of vital interest to early intervention and preschool programs, including how health status influences the child's development and what, if any, restrictions health status places on the child. Information from a health evaluation can enable staff to design more appropriate programming for a child and may uncover a physical basis for learning difficulties or lack of progress. Such information also may be necessary to insure the child's safety. Likewise, health professionals can benefit from the information from developmental assessments.

Our interviews with Barbara Jackson and Joan Dinsmore, of Project Continuity, and with Pat Haley and Jan Valluzzi, of the M-FIRST Project, emphasized the importance of integrating health assessments into the evaluation process for children with special health care needs, as well as for children who do not have medical complications. Child assessment must include an assessment of health needs. Information from health evaluations should be interpreted and integrated into the planning of a child's daily program.

Project Continuity staff members emphasized the importance of communicating information from health care professionals to other professionals. Similarly, Rodd Hedlund, of the NICU Follow-Through Project, stressed the importance of making developmental assessment information available to medical and health personnel in hospital settings. Staff from all three projects emphasized the importance of regular communication between health care providers and early intervention and preschool programs, and suggested the following strategies:

• Providing information in a written format, free of jargon;

- Incorporating health status information in the IFSP and the Individualized Education Program (IEP);
- Encouraging health care providers' participation in the evaluation and IFSP process;
- Pursuing mechanisms to reimburse medical and health personnel for their participation in these processes; and
- Planning to implement and integrate health interventions in the educational setting.

### Benefit from technology in evaluation and assessment.

Technology can make things easier for many people, and, for people with disabilities, it often makes things possible. Patti Hutinger, Carol Schneider, and Linda Robinson, from Project ACTT (ACTT Outreach), emphasized that assistive technology (AT) should be an inseparable part of the assessment and evaluation processes, both in terms of obtaining optimal information about the child and in planning appropriate interventions. In the same way that the concerns and priorities of family members cannot be an "add-on," assistive technology should be a standard consideration for young children with moderate to severe disabilities in developing their IFSP or IEP. Indeed, for some children with severe disabilities, technology may be the only means by which their abilities can be accurately assessed and by which they can reach their potential.

The range of assistive technology is wide. Although factors related to its use are complex (such as a child's mobility and the length of time it takes to learn to use a device or system), many AT needs are met with simple adaptations and often low-cost solutions. Attitudinal, personnel, and finance issues associated with advances in technology affect evaluation and assessment processes. These issues include overcoming "tech-phobia"; system-wide awareness of resources; and monetary allocations for specific devices, repairs, adaptations, on-going technical assistance, and training for children, families, and personnel. Early intervention and preschool personnel who work in settings that lack the technology necessary for evaluations and assessments need to learn how to access AT, how to ensure timeliness while doing so, and how to advocate for acquiring the appropriate technology in their setting.

Families most often are the initiators of and advocates for technology assessment and intervention. Project ACTT staff confirm that the majority of referrals for AT assessment come from families. Denise Booth said: "Technology will open the door for my child."

*Anticipate and plan for transition.*

Home visits conducted prior to a child's first assessment constitute a transition process that helps allay parents' concerns and fears and helps them understand what to expect. This can occur at any age in the process of service delivery.

An eligibility determination process is particularly significant for families of children whose eligibility is borderline, especially at age 3 years, when making the transition from Part H services to preschool services. Although it is desirable to offer a "seamless system" of services for children to move from one program to another, in practice this is not always the case. The transition from Part H to Part B services, or from Part H to some other community-based service system, can be especially difficult if there are different eligibility criteria, or if there is a conflict between what professionals see as the needed services and what the parents believe to be necessary and desirable for their child.

Lynn Gillies, who has worked with other Minnesota families, pointed out that all transitions are difficult. However, the experience at transition is not always unfavorable, and families are best served by evaluation and assessment experiences that aid the transfer of records (with the parents' knowledge and approval), incorporate visits from personnel, and result in an uncomplicated entry into new services.

Our interviews highlighted some of the problems associated with evaluation and assessment at the time of transition. Glenda Witt related that "parents don't get as much attention in public school" settings as they do at CDR. She did appreciate, however, that the preschool accepted the last evaluation from CDR so that the evaluation process did not have to be repeated. Barbie Perry's experience with transition to a preschool program also contrasted unfavorably with her experience at CDR. She said: "The preschool program did not let me know what to expect. . . . We did not understand the process for the transition placement. No one explained what would happen. We did not know how long it would take—paperwork was not at the school, the teacher was not present for the evaluation, and we were not welcomed to the program."

Transition planning conferences, in which families are actively involved in decisionmaking, are an appropriate and necessary course of action in order to ease such transitions.

## Personnel preparation issues

### *Recognize the importance of personnel qualifications.*

The person who conducts the assessment should be the one who knows the child best, and should be well trained and experienced. Professionals' skills need to be fine-tuned so that they can change with the evolution of the team and adapt to the nature of families. Personnel preparation for early intervention work requires myriad experiences. Training should equip professionals to:

- Work with young children and their families;
- Work with teams that include many discipline and agency perspectives;
- Understand and appreciate family-centered, culturally appropriate approaches;
- Be knowledgeable and skilled in the use of instruments and to know when to apply clinical judgment; and
- Understand how to access community resources, including services for children and families, technology, and technology training.

The parents we interviewed were attuned to the level of experience of personnel, and it was important to them. In one instance reported to us, a preschool professional was so inexperienced in assessment practices that the parent, Barbie Perry, took matters into her own hands and showed the professional which toys to use and what to do with them. "She didn't know how to pick up babies. . . . I bared my child's soul to a total stranger. We wanted to learn from this. We wanted someone with experience." In contrast, she described a better experience: "In the hands of trained professionals at CDR—they were prepared and knew what they were doing . . . I knew the assessment would be fine."

A family's earliest contact with professionals tends to be with health professionals, including nurses, physicians (particularly general practitioners and pediatricians), and local health department personnel. Those who have early contact with a child with disabling conditions need to be aware of the resources available to families. This is particularly critical in remote areas where there are likely to be few, if any, community providers. Denise Booth stated that staff, who provided an assessment far from her home, directed her to services in her own community which she had not known were available.

Ongoing developments in technology that can aid evaluation and assessment have amplified the need for personnel training. Family members also play a key role in increasing awareness of these training needs. Training models and strategies should be designed to take advantage of the expertise of parents and of professionals in the areas of allied health, technology, and early childhood development. An all too common story is that of a child's communication board sitting in the corner of the closet because personnel were not trained to use it. Program administrators should be aware of the benefits of technology and should support training for direct service providers. Even small increases in awareness can be enlightening. Denise Booth quoted a school system administrator who said, "This assessment gave me a whole new picture of what your daughter can do!"

### Respect individual differences, values, and preferences.

Enlightened preservice and inservice training program staff recognize the significance of understanding and respecting cultural differences when working with families. According to Helen Hammond and Lawrence Ingalls, of Project Vision, unless professionals understand and acknowledge their own values and biases, judgmental attitudes and prejudices can interfere with family-directed assessment and evaluation processes. Thus, providers of preservice and inservice training in evaluation and assessment should address this important aspect of interactions between parents and professionals.

Not everyone shares the same values about what constitutes appropriate child development. Some of the milestones that professionals have come to regard as universal, based on standardized instruments and child development literature, may conflict with what some families expect and want for their child.

If a family does not speak English well or at all, the program needs to acquire the services of an interpreter who understands both language and cultural cues. This individual needs to understand the level of information that is being transmitted. For example, if health or medical information is being discussed, some familiarity with the terminology is needed in order to translate appropriately. An understanding of the appropriate and desired level of confidentiality of information also is important. Although it may be convenient to involve a client's neighbor as an interpreter, this may be inappropriate if the family wants to maintain their privacy in the subject area. Each program should consider adopting guidelines for working with interpreters in evaluation and assessment.

Materials about the program, evaluation and assessment procedures, and, particularly, informed consent notices should be available in the native language of the program's client population. Programs that are responsive to cultural differences focus on conducting thorough assessments and evaluations, rather than on developing a list of traits for a given population. Doing so acknowledges the dynamic nature of culture and its influences on our lives.

## Service system issues

### *Consider cost in relation to benefit.*

Angela Deal, of the FIPP project, pointed out that it is penny-wise and pound-foolish to try to economize by not taking time to understand the family's questions and their hopes for their child through assessment and early intervention. Without family buy-in, teams of professionals may spend time and dollars working toward outcomes that are less likely to be attained or less meaningful to the family. This problem was illustrated by Michael and Nelda Thompson's contrasting a greatly valued experience at FIPP with one that had been frustrating: "In [one] evaluation, we had no idea what was in store for us. . . . They told us what we already knew. . . . The reason for the evaluation needs to be understood. . . . FIPP was a godsend to us. . . . Linda came to our house and established rapport. She was there at the center. Everyone was tuned in. The team watched him play, eat lunch, and be himself, instead of making him perform."

There may be increased costs to assessment when processes are family-directed. These costs are associated with the need for flexibility on the part of professionals in conducting evaluations and assessments that will elicit the child's optimal performance and the family's questions, expectations, and hopes for their child. In order to make evaluation and assessment convenient, informative, and supportive of the family-child relationship, such costs may involve staff travel, altered hours of operation, and other means of adapting to family needs. Such expenditures are relatively modest, yet immensely important (Barnett & Escobar, 1990).

Lynn Gillies (1990) wrote about the importance and economy of considering the family's priorities and needs. She likened parents' involvement in the development of an IFSP to being involved in the design of a blueprint for a family home. Just as floor-plan changes are costly when a builder constructs a house "on spec," in her experience it is even more important to build early intervention plans around each family's goals, priorities, and resources, so that efforts are likely to have maximum payoff.

### Have realistic expectations for policies and monitor their implementation.

Just because those who write laws and regulations want something to happen in practice does not mean that it will actually occur. It is not always possible to control the experience at the grassroots level through written policy. Parents provide a reality check for which there can be no substitute. Hence, a forum, perhaps through state and local interagency coordinating councils, should be available for parents to provide information about their experiences at the federal, state, and local levels.

It was obvious from our interviews with parents that evaluations and assessments are not always family-directed. Nelda Thompson, who contrasted her evaluation at FIPP with an experience she characterized as "at the bottom," was aware that family-directed practices are not yet universal. In contrast to what she believed she could expect on the basis of laws and policies she had seen, the evaluation's purpose, in her view, was not for the family, but rather to satisfy the program's own need to fill in some numbers. She needed encouragement and received none. She needed emotional support and got none. Professionals in the program did not believe her personal reports. They did not respect her knowledge. She felt defensive about her child. She saw no purpose in the evaluation and assessment.

Our interviews confirmed that there is wide variation in practice, even within a community. This variation serves as a goal for parents, practitioners, and policymakers to encourage family-directed evaluation and assessment in all programs.

### Negotiate conflicting opinions.

The outcomes of an evaluation and assessment should be a common definition of any problems and common expectations of the course of assessment and treatment. However, team members may disagree about recommended services or some other aspect of the assessment or plan. Whether the difference of opinion is among staff, or between staff and parents, it is important to come to agreement quickly, in order to avoid delaying needed intervention. This may require negotiation among the team. Policymakers should develop a system that values the needs of parents, respects the knowledge of the entire team (including parents), and recognizes that resources are finite.

The professionals and parents we interviewed indicated that families do not want to "drive" themselves through a process or receive services that are unnecessary. They do not want to spend more time in evaluation, assessment, or programs than their child needs. It is important that teams strive for consensus about service needs. This consensus is most likely to occur when families have participated in each step of the process.

Denise Booth emphasized that she wanted her views valued but that she also respected those of the professionals. She said, "Consider my opinion, and, if we see things differently, we can discuss it." Parents emphasized the importance of listening and valuing parents' knowledge, expertise, concerns, and goals for their child.

In acknowledging resource limitations, state policymakers may find it useful to develop guidelines that offer direction concerning the nature of appropriate treatment, such as the process required for reaching decisions about an IFSP. If such guidelines are developed, flexibility to accommodate the priorities of each child and family and to accommodate diversity across neighborhoods and cultures should be incorporated into them. It is clear that no formula for frequency and duration of services will apply to all young children and families, just as no universal interventions exist that are appropriate for all.

# Recommendations for Policymakers

Through interviews, selected EEPCD project directors and parents of young children with disabilities shared their thoughts about the characteristics of successful, family-directed child evaluations and assessments. These are summarized in the table below.

---

### Characteristics of Family-Directed Child Evaluation and Assessment

*Family Issues*

Value parents as experts.

Respect individual differences and values, and families' styles of involvement.

Encourage the presence and participation of parents and other family members.

*Process Issues*

Appreciate the process leading to a plan.

Value the importance and impact of every interaction.

Provide necessary information at the most opportune time.

Allow for flexibility in location, timing, and personnel.

Recognize the limitations of current instruments and encourage the use of informal measures.

Integrate health evaluations into the total evaluation.

Benefit from technology in evaluation and assessment.

Anticipate and plan for transition.

*Personnel Preparation Issues*

Recognize the importance of personnel qualifications.

Respect individual differences, values, and preferences.

*Service System Issues*

Consider cost in relation to benefit.

Have realistic expectations for policies and monitor their implementation.

Negotiate conflicting opinions.

---

Throughout the interviews, the following overarching recommendations for those who legislate and administer policy were articulated:

1. Be realistic about what happens once a law is written. Policymakers need to remain vigilant about a law as it is applied. The leap from policy to practice is made more difficult when interpretations and nuances are added to legislation or regulation, which then take on a life of their own. By providing clear guidelines and holding forums recurrently about the intent of the law, policymakers will provide the direction that administrators, service providers, advocates, and families need.

2. Seek the advice of leaders of the various cultural communities on how to increase and sustain family involvement.

3. Listen to parents. Parents and other family members provide a reality check for which there can be no substitute.

4. Appreciate the significance of family-directed approaches and support the costs associated with enacting the spirit as well as the letter of IDEA and other legislation. If, in listening to families, it is determined that evaluations and assessments are not family-directed, it is well worth the effort and resources to insure that they are.

The authors hope that the lessons learned from this report will be taken into consideration by those who plan policies and provide services to young children with disabilities and their families. Families have taught us that the principles articulated throughout this chapter make a very important difference in the success of early intervention services.

The references and resources listed in the following sections represent a fragment of the materials that are available concerning processes related to family-directed child evaluation and assessment. They illustrate the wealth of resources available from the projects that participated in the development of this chapter, as well as the rich array of projects supported by the Early Education Program for Children with Disabilities.

**Acknowledgments:** This chapter was also published as a monograph which was produced and distributed by the National Early Childhood Technical Assistance System (NEC*TAS), pursuant to contract number HS-91-01-1001 from the Office of Special Education Programs, U.S. Department of Education. Contractors undertaking projects under government sponsorship are encouraged to express their judgment in professional and technical matters. Opinions expressed do not necessarily represent the Department of Education's position or policy.

This chapter and a related article, which appeared in the June/July 1994 issue of *Zero to Three* (Berman, 1994), were developed from the contributions of NEC\*TAS staff members, the staff of selected projects supported under the Early Education Program for Children with Disabilities (EEPCD) sponsored by the U.S. Office of Special Education Programs (OSEP), and parents of young children with disabilities.

Carol Berman and Evelyn Shaw, NEC\*TAS staff members who planned, conducted, and summarized telephone interviews, were the authors. Betsy Ayankoya, contributed content on culture and diversity; Joan Melner contributed content on culture and diversity and developed the resource sections at the end of the chapter; Jo Shackelford contributed content on integrating health care information; and Mary Shields and Janie Ward-Newton contributed content on assistive technology. The authors also thank other NEC\*TAS staff members who were involved in planning this chapter or in reviewing drafts, or both: Joan Danaher, Nancy Guadagno, Evelyn Hausslein, Joicey Hurth, Trish Isbell, and Pascal Trohanis. Peggy Cvach, Project Officer at OSEP, and Melodie Friedebach, Director of Early Childhood Special Education in Missouri, provided valuable insights through their review of the chapter.

The EEPCD project staff interviewed for this paper were:

Diane Bricker of AEPS Linked System of Assessment, Intervention, and Evaluation for Early Intervention, Eugene, Oregon;

Angela G. Deal of Family, Infant, and Preschool Program (FIPP), Morganton, North Carolina;

Corinne Garland of Trans/Team Outreach at Child Development Resources (CDR), Norge, Virginia;

Pat Haley and Janet Valluzzi of Medically Fragile Inservice for Related Services Team (M-FIRST), Portland, Oregon, and Seattle, Washington;

Rodd Hedlund of NICU Follow-Through Project, Seattle, Washington;

Patricia Hutinger, Carol Schneider, and Linda Robinson of ACTT Outreach: Activating Children Through Technology, Macomb, Illinois;

Lawrence Ingalls and Helen Hammond of Project Vision, Moscow, Idaho;

Barbara Jackson and Joanie Dinsmore of Project Continuity Outreach, Omaha, Nebraska; and

Linda Kjerland of Project Dakota, Eagan, Minnesota.

(Contact information and product listings for each project are included in the resource section at the end of this chapter.)

The following parents contributed to this study:

Lisa and Roger Bailey, of Eugene, Oregon;

Denise Booth, of Pittsfield, Illinois;

Renee Dulin, of Troutman, North Carolina;

Ken and Lynn Gillies, of Eagan, Minnesota;

John and Teresa Guthman, of St. Paul, Minnesota;

Kelly Perron, of Springfield, Oregon;

Barbie Perry, of Toano, Virginia;

Michael and Nelda Thompson, of Mooresville, North Carolina; and

Glenda Witt, of Williamsburg, Virginia.

All were knowledgeable, generous of their time, and immensely interested in sharing their insights. Their contributions greatly enriched our thinking and understanding by providing tangible experiences and recommendations.

The Individuals with Disabilities Education Act (IDEA) provides grants to states and jurisdictions to support the planning of service systems and the delivery of services, including evaluation and assessment, for young children who have disabling conditions or are at risk for developing them. Funds are provided through the Infants and Toddlers Program (known as Part H of IDEA) for services to children from birth through 2 years of age, and through the Preschool Program (known as Section 619 of IDEA) for services to children 3 through 5 years of age.

To assist states and jurisdictions in meeting the challenges of implementing IDEA, the U.S. Department of Education's Early Education Program for Children with Disabilities (EEPCD) sponsors a wide variety of research institutes as well as model demonstration, inservice training, data systems, and outreach projects. Outreach projects specifically are funded to assist states in identifying and implementing system and service delivery models, model components, and personnel training approaches.

The National Early Childhood Technical Assistance System (NEC*TAS) supports the implementation of IDEA in its role as a national technical assistance provider to state, jurisdictional, and EEPCD project personnel. Part of its mission is to facilitate linkages between states and jurisdictions and EEPCD projects. NEC*TAS publications are one vehicle for bringing information from EEPCD projects—in this case, outreach projects—to state policymakers and program coordinators.

# References and Resources

## References

Barnett, W. S., & Escobar, C. M. (1990). Economic costs and benefits of early intervention. In S. J. Meisels & J. P. Shonkoff (Eds.), *Handbook of early childhood intervention* (pp. 560-582). Cambridge, MA: Cambridge University Press.

Berman, C. (June/July 1994). Family-directed evaluation and assessment under the Individuals with Disabilities Education Act (IDEA): Lessons learned from experiences of programs and parents. *Zero to Three, 14* (6), 16-22.

Biro, P., Daulton, D., & Szanton, E. (1991). *Informed clinical opinion.* NEC*TAS Notes No. 4. Chapel Hill, NC: NEC*TAS.

ERIC Clearinghouse on Disabilities and Gifted Education. (1994). *Rights and responsibilities of parents of children with disabilities.* Reston, VA: Author.

Gillies, L. (October 1990). IFSP: A new way of building. *ARC Light,* pp. 1-2. (Apple Valley, MN: ARC Suburban).

*The Individuals with Disabilities Education Act, P.L. 101-476, 104 Stat. 1103* (1990) (codified as amended at 20 U.S.C. Secs. 1400-1485).

Meisels, S. J., & Provence, S., with the Task Force on Screening and Assessment of the National Early Childhood Technical Assistance System. (1989). *Screening and assessment: Guidelines for identifying young disabled and developmentally vulnerable children and their families.* Arlington, VA: ZERO TO THREE/National Center for Clinical Infant Programs.

Pearpoint, J., & Forest, M. (1992). MAPS: Action planning. In J. Pearpoint, M. Forest, & J. Snow (Eds.), *The inclusion papers: Strategies to make inclusion work. A collection of articles from the Centre for Integrated Education and Community.* Toronto: Inclusion Press.

Shackelford, J. (1995). *State/jurisdiction eligibility definitions for Part H* (NEC*TAS Notes No. 5) (Rev. ed.). Chapel Hill, NC: NEC*TAS.

U.S. Department of Education. (September 29, 1992). 34 CFR Parts 300 and 301. Assistance to States for the Education of Children with Disabilities Program and Preschool Grants for Children with Disabilities; Final rule. *Federal Register, 57* (189), 44794-44852.

U.S. Department of Education. (July 30, 1993). 34 CFR Part 303. Early

Intervention Program for Infants and Toddlers With Disabilities; Final rule. *Federal Register, 58* (145), 40958-40989.

## Resources from Participating EEPCD Projects

ACTT Outreach: Activating Children Through Technology
Patricia Hutinger, Carol Schneider, and Linda Robinson
Macomb Projects
Western Illinois University
27 Horrabin Hall
Macomb, IL 61455
(309) 298-1634
Fax: (309) 298-2305

*Products:*
Technology Team Assessment Process ($69.95)
Other resources on the use of technology.
Product list available on request.

The AEPS Linked System of Assessment, Intervention, and Evaluation for Early Intervention
Diane Bricker
Center on Human Development
University of Oregon
901 E. 18th Street
Eugene, OR 97403
(503) 346-0807
Fax: (503) 346-5639

*Products:*
*AEPS for Infants and Children* (2-volume set; $88)
  Volume 1: *AEPS Measurement for Birth to Three Years* (1992; $39)
  Volume 2: *AEPS Curriculum for Birth to Three Years* (1992; $59)
AEPS Data Recording Forms, Birth to Three Years (Package of 10; $21)
AEPS Family Report, Birth to Three Years (Package of 10; $15)
AEPS Family Interest Survey, Birth to Three Years (Package of 30; $10)
AEPS Test Three to Six Years (Experimental Edition 2) ($40)
AEPS Family Report Three to Six Years ($10)
Product list available on request.

Family Enablement Project at the Family, Infant, and Preschool Program (FIPP)
Angela G. Deal
Family, Infant, and Preschool Program
Western Carolina Center
300 Enola Road
Morganton, NC 28655
(704) 433-2611
Fax: (704) 438-6457

*Products:*
Product list available on request.

Medically Fragile Inservice for Related Services Team (M-FIRST)
Pat Haley (Coordinator)
CDRC-Oregon Health Sciences University
P.O. Box 574
Portland, OR 97207-0574
(503) 494-8095, 494-2794,
494-6868; and
Janet Valluzzi (Coordinator)
CDMRC-University of Washington
CTU, WJ-10
Seattle, WA 98195
(206) 543-7403, 685-1350
Fax: (206) 543-5771
Internet: valluzzi@u.washington.edu
*Products:*
Product list available on request.

NICU Follow-Through Project
Rodd Hedlund
Experimental Education Unit, WJ-10
University of Washington
Seattle, WA 98195
(206) 543-0925
Fax: (206) 543-8480
*Products:*
*Infant Behavioral Assessment (IBA).* Hedlund and Tatarka (1988)
*IBA Training Manual* (1991)
IBA Slide and Video Presentation
The Synactive Model Slide and Video Presentation
The Interactional Protocol
Goal Attainment Scale
Product list is available only to current or prior project trainees.

Project Continuity Outreach
Barbara Jackson and Joanie Dinsmore
Meyer Rehabilitation Institute
University of Nebraska Medical Center
600 South 42nd Street
Omaha, NE 68198-5450
(402) 559-5765
Fax: (402) 559-5737
*Products:*
A Case Management System for Infants with Chronic Illnesses and
Developmental Disabilities. (1992). *Children's Health Care,* 21 (4), 224-232
Product list available on request.

Project Dakota
Linda Kjerland
Dakota, Inc.

680 O'Neill Drive
Eagan, MN 55121
(612) 455-2335
Fax: (612) 455-8972

*Products:*
Product list available on request.

Project Vision
Lawrence Ingalls and Helen Hammond
Center on Developmental Disabilities
University of Idaho
129 West 3rd Street
Moscow, ID 83843
(208) 885-6605
Fax: (208) 885-9056

*Products:*
*Delivering Sensitive Information* (a manual)
*Planning Family Goals: A Systems Approach to the IFSP* (1992; $35.00)
Product list available on request.

Trans/Team Outreach
Corinne Garland
Child Development
Resources
P.O. Box 280
Norge, VA 23127-0280
(804) 566-3300
Fax: (804) 566-8977

*Products:*
"Transdisciplinary Arena Assessment Process: A Resource for Teams" (43-minute videotape and accompanying Viewing Guide; $149.95)
"A Family-Centered Team Process for Assessment" (15-minute videotape; $59.95)
"A Family-Centered Team Process for IFSP Development" (15-minute video-tape; $59.95)
*Understanding the Individualized Family Service Plan (IFSP): A Resource for Families* ($15.00; 26 or more copies, $9.95 each)
Product list available on request.

## Resources Related To Technology

The consumer- and advocacy-oriented Alliance for Technology Access Projects and projects funded under the Technology Related Assistance for Individuals with Disabilities Act of 1988 (Tech Act) are valuable resources for early intervention programs. They are administered by the National Institute of Disabilities and Rehabilitation Research (NIDRR) of the U.S. Department of Education. Most states have access to one or both of these kinds of projects. The national offices for these projects can provide a directory of projects and additional information about resources in each state. Their addresses are listed below.

Alliance for Technology Access Projects
2173 E. Francisco Boulevard, Suite L
San Rafael, CA 94901
(415) 455-4575; and
1531 Dawn Drive
Louisville, KY 40216-1617
(502) 449-0654

Tech Act Projects
RESNA Technical Assistance Project
1101 Connecticut Avenue, NW, Suite 700
Washington, DC 20036
(202) 857-1140 (voice/TDD)

## Additional Readings

The following are selected resource materials that may be of interest to those who develop policy. We include them because they either were suggested by those we interviewed or came to our attention serendipitously. This is by no means an exhaustive list.

Bailey, D. B., Jr., Simeonsson, R. J., Winton, P. J., Huntington, G. S., Comfort, M., Isbell, P., O'Donnell, K. J., & Helm, J. M. (1986). Family-focused intervention: A functional model for planning, implementing, and evaluating individualized family services in early intervention. *Journal of the Division for Early Childhood, 10* (2), 156-171.

Barnett, D. W., Macmann, G. M., & Carey, K. T. (1992). Early intervention and the assessment of developmental skills: Challenges and directions. *Topics in Early Childhood Special Education, 12* (1), 1-20.

Bristol, M. M., & Gallagher, J. J. (1982). A family focus for intervention. In C. Ramey & P. Trohanis (Eds.), *Finding and educating high-risk and handicapped infants* (pp. 137-161). Baltimore: University Park Press.

Colorado Department of Education. (January 1993). *Colorado child identification process, birth-five years: Screening and evaluation process guidelines.* Denver, CO: Author.

DEC Task Force on Recommended Practices. (1993). *DEC recommended practices: Indicators of quality in programs for infants and young children with special needs and their families.* Reston, VA: Council for Exceptional Children, DEC.

Gathering family information: Procedures, products, and precautions [Special issue]. (Spring 1990). *Topics in Early Childhood Special Education, 10* (1).

Graham, M. A. (September 1992). *Evaluation and assessment of infants and toddlers: Creating family-centered, developmentally appropriate evaluations. Instructor's guidebook.* Tallahassee, FL: Center for Prevention and Early Intervention Policy, the FSU Institute of Science and Public Affairs.

Haynie, M., Porter, S., & Palfrey, J. (1989). *Children assisted by medical technology in educational settings: Guidelines for care.* Boston: Project School Care.

Neisworth, J. T., & Bagnato, S. J. (1992). The case against intelligence testing in early intervention. *Topics in Early Childhood Special Education, 12* (1), 1-20.

Peters, D. F., & Ponder, H. (December 1985). *Symbolic interaction: A useful tool for working with special families.* Paper presented at the Fourth Biennial National Training Institute of ZERO TO THREE/National Center for Clinical Infant Programs, Arlington, VA.

Stein, R. E. K., Bauman, L. J., Westbrook, L., Coupey, S. M., & Ireys, H. T. (March, 1993). Framework for identifying children who have chronic conditions: The case for a new definition. *Journal of Pediatrics, 122* (3), 342-347.

Stevens-Dominguez, M. (1991). Developing individual education programs (IEPs): A quality of life approach. In *Project resource information packet #6 for assessment and programming teams.* Albuquerque, NM: Training and Technical Assistance Unit at the New Mexico University Affiliated Program, UNM, School of Medicine.

Taner-Leff, P., & Walizer, E. H. (1992). *Building the healing partnership— Parents, professionals, and children with chronic illnesses and disabilities.* Cambridge, MA: Brookline Books.

Thomas, D. D., & Simeonsson, R. J. (November 1992). *Early childhood eligibility: The value of parental report—Vehicle for understanding cultural differences* (participant's manual). Minneapolis, MN: The Council for Exceptional Children Topical Conference on Culturally and Linguistically Diverse Exceptional Children.

# Index

P

# Contributors

**Isaura Barrera,** Ph.D., is the coordinator of the Multicultural Early Childhood Special Education Graduate Program at the University of New Mexico. A native of South Texas, Dr. Barrera has worked with young children since 1969. She developed programs in Texas and New York prior to going to New Mexico, where she conducts preservice and inservice training in a variety of settings.

**Carol Berman,** Ph.D., is Associate Director of ZERO TO THREE: National Center for Infants, Toddlers, and Families, where she has worked since 1983. She serves as the subcontract manager for the National Early Childhood Technical Assistance System (NEC*TAS), which assists states and jurisdictions in implementing services for young children and families under the Individuals with Disabilities Education Act (IDEA). Her special interests include early identification and assessment of infants and toddlers with special needs, and the system of services for helping their families to meet those needs.

**T. Berry Brazelton,** M.D., is Emeritus Professor of Pediatrics, Harvard Medical School, and Founder, Child Development Unit and Brazelton Center for Infants and Parents, Children's Hospital, Boston, Massachusetts. Dr. Brazelton is the author of numerous publications for professional and general audiences, including the *Neonatal Behavioral Assessment Scale* and *Touchpoints: Your Child's Emotional and Behavioral Development*. Dr. Brazelton is a founding member and former president of ZERO TO THREE: National Center for Infants, Toddlers, and Families.

**Diane Bricker**, Ph.D., is a professor and Associate Dean for Academic Programs, College of Education, University of Oregon. She also directs the Early Intervention Program at the university. Her professional career has focused on the development of screening, assessment, and intervention procedures for infants, toddlers, and young children who are at risk or disabled.

**Joanna Erikson**, M.P.H., has administered programs for young children with special needs for more than 20 years and has been a faculty member at the Child Study Center, Yale University, since 1975. She has consulted on interagency and early childhood policy and program development to the Connecticut Department of Health Services and the Connecticut Department of Education. As Program Director of the Infant-Toddler Developmental Assessment (IDA), she coordinated the planning, field-testing, evaluation, and dissemination of the program.

**Emily Fenichel**, M.S.W., is Associate Director of ZERO TO THREE: National Center for Infants, Toddlers, and Families, where she has worked since 1979, and is editor of the bimonthly bulletin, *Zero to Three*. Her special interests include infant mental health, infant/toddler child care, and the training and professional development of infant/family practitioners.

**Stanley I. Greenspan**, M.D., is Clinical Professor of Psychiatry, Behavioral Sciences, and Pediatrics at the George Washington University Medical School and a practicing child psychiatrist. He was previously Chief of the Mental Health Study Center and Director of the Clinical Infant Development Program, National Institute of Mental Health. A founding member and former president of ZERO TO THREE: National Center for Infants, Toddlers, and Families, Dr. Greenspan is the author of numerous books for professional and general audiences, including *Infancy and Early Childhood: The Practice of Clinical Assessment and Intervention with Emotional and Developmental Challenges*.

**Laurence M. Hirshberg**, Ph.D., is Clinical Assistant Professor in the Department of Psychiatry and Human Behavior, Brown University School of Medicine. He is in private practice in Providence, Rhode Island, specializing in infancy and early childhood, and consults to early intervention, visiting nurse, and preschool special education programs in southeastern New England.

**Brian A. McNulty**, Ph.D., is Assistant Commissioner of Education in Colorado. He previously served for seven years as State Director of Special Education. He has published extensively in the area of early childhood and special education and has presented testimony to the U.S. House of Representatives and the U.S. Senate on Early Childhood Part H Technology and the re-authorization of the Individuals with Disabilities Education Act (IDEA).

**Samuel J. Meisels**, Ed.D., is a professor in the School of Education and is a Research Scientist at the Center for Human Growth and Development at the University of Michigan. A member of the Board of Directors of ZERO TO THREE: National Center for Infants, Toddlers, and Families, Dr. Meisels has conducted research and published widely in the fields of early childhood assessment, early intervention, and developmental consequences of high-risk birth. He is the co-author of the Early Screening Inventory and the Work Sampling System.

**Lucy Jane Miller**, Ph.D., O.T.R, is an assistant professor in the Department of Pediatrics, University of Colorado Health Sciences Center, and Executive Director of the KID Foundation, a nonprofit public charity. Since 1972, she has been involved in the development and validation of standardized scales to screen and assess children who are at risk for or who have been diagnosed with delays or disabilities. Nationally standardized scales include Screening Test for Evaluating Preschoolers (FirstSTEP), Miller Assessment for Preschoolers (MAP), Toddler and Infant Motor Evaluation (TIME), and Leiter International Performance Scale-Revised (LIPS-R). Dr. Miller served for three terms (eight years) on the Colorado Interagency Coordinating Council (CICC).

**Barbara K. Popper**, M.Ed., IBCLC, has participated in consumer advocacy activities for more than 20 years, with particular concern for pediatric and perinatal hospital policies and state regulation of hospitals relative to family-centered care. She has written and spoken on topics related to parent involvement in policy issues, hospital planning, breast-feeding management, and support for the hospitalized nursing mother/baby. She has served as a hospital assessor for UNICEF's Baby Friendly Initiative in Pakistan and is currently working with the National Early Childhood Technical Assistance System (NEC*TAS) and with Family Voices at the Federation for Children with Special Needs in Boston, Massachusetts.

**Barry M. Prizant**, Ph.D., CCC-SLP, is a professor in the Division of Communication Disorders, Emerson College, Boston, Massachusetts, and a Fellow of the American Speech-Language-Hearing Association. He is an editorial consultant for seven professional journals in the areas of communication and language development, and autism and other social-communicative disorders in young children. He is co-author with Amy M. Wetherby of the Communication and Symbolic Behavior Scales (CSBS), a nationally standardized instrument that assesses communication, symbolic, and social-affective abilities in young children.

**Cordelia C. Robinson**, R.N., Ph.D., is Associate Professor in Pediatrics and Psychiatry at the University of Colorado Health Sciences Center and Director of the Colorado University Affiliated Program, John F.

Kennedy Center for Developmental Disabilities. Over the past 20 years, she has directed a number of federally- and state-funded training, demonstration, and research projects serving young children with disabilities and their families.

**Susan Rocco** is the mother of Jason, a charmingly eccentric teenager, and the coordinator of the Special Parent Information Network in Honolulu, Hawaii. Her passions lie in supporting families' visions for their children and in making the community a more welcoming place for people with disabilities.

**Carole Samango-Sprouse**, Ed.D., has served since 1987 as Director of Infant and Child Studies in the Department of Medical Genetics, Children's National Medical Center, Washington, D.C. Her special interests include assessment of infants with complex medical needs, congenital malformations, and neuromotor dysfunction; brain imaging of infants with developmental diagnoses; and the professional development of practitioners who evaluate and treat infants and their families.

**Marilyn Segal**, Ph.D., is Dean of the Family and School Center of Nova Southeastern University in Fort Lauderdale, Florida, where she has worked for 25 years. She is a member of the Board of Directors of ZERO TO THREE: National Center for Infants, Toddlers, and Families and Chair of its Publications Committee. Her special interests include parent-child interactions, pretend play, and social-emotional development in the early years.

**Evelyn Shaw**, M.Ed., works as a technical assistance coordinator for the National Early Childhood Technical Assistance System (NEC*TAS), Frank Porter Graham Child Development Center, University of North Carolina, Chapel Hill. Her special interests are early childhood policy and best practice in the areas of early identification and assessment and the implementation of comprehensive, coordinated service systems for infants, toddlers, and preschoolers with special needs.

**Noreen T. Webber**, Ph.D., has been Program Professor of Education in Programs in Education and Technology at Nova Southeastern University in Fort Lauderdale, Florida, since 1991. She teaches courses in child development. Her interests include infant assessment and service coordination for families with young children.

**Amy M. Wetherby**, Ph.D., CCC-SLP, is a professor and Chair of the Department of Communication Disorders at Florida State University (FSU), where she has worked since 1983. She is Executive Director of the FSU Center for Autism and Related Disabilities and is co-author (with Barry M. Prizant) of the Communication and Symbolic Behavior Scales (CSBS). Her clinical and research interests include autism, developmental language disorders, and the early identification of children with communicative impairments.

**Serena Wieder**, Ph.D., is a clinical psychologist in private practice in Silver Spring, Maryland. She lectures frequently and is a consultant to research and clinical centers in the United States and Israel. She was formerly Clinical Director of the Clinical Infant Development Program, National Institute of Mental Health, and Founding Director of the Reginald Lourie Center for Infants and Young Children. A member of the Board of Directors of ZERO TO THREE: National Center for Infants, Toddlers, and Families, Dr. Wieder has served as Co-Chair (with Stanley I. Greenspan) and Clinical Director of the organization's Diagnostic Classification Task Force, editor of ZERO TO THREE's *Diagnostic Classification of Mental Health and Developmental Disorders of Infancy and Early Childhood (DC: 0-3)*, and clinical supervisor in the Developmental Specialists in Pediatric Practice project.

**G. Gordon Williamson**, Ph.D., O.T.R., is the director of several research and training projects in pediatric rehabilitation at the John F. Kennedy Medical Center, Edison, New Jersey, and is Associate Clinical Professor in the Rehabilitation Medicine Department at Columbia University. He has a long-term interest in fostering the adaptive and social development of young children and in supporting their families. This commitment is reflected in his most recent book, *Adaptive Behavior and Resilience*.